The National versus the Foreigner in South America

Since the turn of the century, South American governments and regional organisations have adopted the world's most open discourse on migration and citizenship. At a time when restrictive choices were becoming increasingly pre-dominant around the world, South American policy makers presented their discourse as being both an innovative and exceptional 'new paradigm' and part of a morally superior, avant-garde path in policy making. This book provides a critical examination of the South American legal framework through a histor-ical and comparative analysis. Diego Acosta uses this analysis to assess whether the laws are truly innovative and exceptional, as well as evaluating their feasi-bility, strengths and weaknesses. By analysing the legal construction of the national and the foreigner, he demonstrates how this relates to the history of the continent. An invaluable insight for anyone interested in global migration and citizenship discussions.

Diego Acosta is a Reader in European and Migration Law at the University of Bristol.

The Law in Context Series

Editors: William Twining (University College London),
Christopher McCrudden (Queen's University Belfast) and
Bronwen Morgan (University of Bristol).

Since 1970 the Law in Context series has been at the forefront of the movement to broaden the study of law. It has been a vehicle for the publication of innovative scholarly books that treat law and legal phenomena critically in their social, political and economic contexts from a variety of perspectives. The series particularly aims to publish scholarly legal writing that brings fresh perspectives to bear on new and existing areas of law taught in universities. A contextual approach involves treating legal subjects broadly, using materials from other social sciences, and from any other discipline that helps to explain the operation in practice of the subject under discussion. It is hoped that this orientation is at once more stimulating and more realistic than the bare exposition of legal rules. The series includes original books that have a different emphasis from traditional legal textbooks, while maintaining the same high standards of scholarship. They are written primarily for undergraduate and graduate students of law and of other disciplines, but will also appeal to a wider readership. In the past, most books in the series have focused on English law, but recent publications include books on European law, globalisation, transnational legal processes, and comparative law.

Books in the Series

Ali: *Modern Challenges to Islamic Law*
Anderson, Schum & Twining: *Analysis of Evidence*
Ashworth: *Sentencing and Criminal Justice*
Barton & Douglas: *Law and Parenthood*
Beecher-Monas: *Evaluating Scientific Evidence: An Interdisciplinary Framework for Intellectual Due Process*
Bell: *French Legal Cultures*
Bercusson: *European Labour Law*
Birkinshaw: *European Public Law*
Birkinshaw: *Freedom of Information: The Law, the Practice and the Ideal*
Brownsword & Goodwin: *Law and the Technologies of the Twenty-First Century: Text and Materials*
Cane: *Atiyah's Accidents, Compensation and the Law*
Clarke & Kohler: *Property Law: Commentary and Materials*
Collins: *The Law of Contract*
Collins, Ewing & McColgan: *Labour Law*
Cowan: *Housing Law and Policy*
Cranston: *Legal Foundations of the Welfare State*
Darian-Smith: *Laws and Societies in Global Contexts: Contemporary Approaches*
Dauvergne: *Making People Illegal: What Globalisation Means for Immigration and Law*
Davies: *Perspectives on Labour Law*

Seneviratne: *Ombudsmen: Public Services and Administrative Justice*
Seppänen: *Ideological Conflict and the Rule of Law in Contemporary China*
Siems: *Comparative Law*
Stapleton: *Product Liability*
Stewart: *Gender, Law and Justice in a Global Market*
Tamanaha: *Law as a Means to an End: Threat to the Rule of Law*
Turpin & Tomkins: *British Government and the Constitution: Text and Materials*
Twining: *Globalisation and Legal Theory*
Twining: *Rethinking Evidence: Exploratory Essays*
Twining: *General Jurisprudence: Understanding Law from a Global Perspective*
Twining: *Human Rights, Southern Voices: Francis Deng, Abdullahi An-Na'im, Yash Ghai and Upendra Baxi*
Twining & Miers: *How to Do Things with Rules*
Ward: *A Critical Introduction to European Law*
Ward: *Law, Text, Terror*
Ward: *Shakespeare and Legal Imagination*
Wells & Quick: *Lacey, Wells and Quick: Reconstructing Criminal Law*
Zander: *Cases and Materials on the English Legal System*
Zander: *The Law-Making Process*

International Journal of Law in Context: A Global Forum for Interdisciplinary Legal Studies

The *International Journal of Law in Context* is the companion journal to the Law in Context book series and provides a forum for interdisciplinary legal studies and offers intellectual space for ground-breaking critical research. It publishes contextual work about law and its relationship with other disciplines including but not limited to science, literature, humanities, philosophy, sociology, psychology, ethics, history and geography. More information about the journal and how to submit an article can be found at http://journals.cambridge.org/ijc

The National versus the Foreigner in South America

200 Years of Migration and Citizenship Law

DIEGO ACOSTA
University of Bristol

CAMBRIDGE
UNIVERSITY PRESS

University Printing House, Cambridge CB2 8BS, United Kingdom

One Liberty Plaza, 20th Floor, New York, NY 10006, USA

477 Williamstown Road, Port Melbourne, VIC 3207, Australia

314–321, 3rd Floor, Plot 3, Splendor Forum, Jasola District Centre, New Delhi – 110025, India

79 Anson Road, #06-04/06, Singapore 079906

Cambridge University Press is part of the University of Cambridge.

It furthers the University's mission by disseminating knowledge in the pursuit of education, learning, and research at the highest international levels of excellence.

www.cambridge.org
Information on this title: www.cambridge.org/9781108425568
DOI: 10.1017/9781108594110

© Diego Acosta 2018

First published 2018

Printed in the United Kingdom by Clays, St Ives plc

A catalogue record for this publication is available from the British Library.

Library of Congress Cataloging-in-Publication Data
Names: Acosta, Diego, author.
Title: The national versus the foreigner in South America :
200 years of migration and citizenship law / Diego Acosta.
Description: Cambridge [UK]; New York, NY: Cambridge University Press, 2018. |
Series: Law in context | Includes bibliographical references and index.
Identifiers: LCCN 2018002418 | ISBN 9781108425568 (hardback)
Subjects: LCSH: Citizenship – South America. |
Emigration and immigration law – South America – History.
Classification: LCC KH561.A92 2018 | DDC 342.808/3–dc23
LC record available at https://lccn.loc.gov/2018002418

ISBN 978-1-108-42556-8 Hardback

Contents

Preface

In the summer of 2009 I presented my work on the European Union (EU) Returns Directive in Santiago de Chile (IPSA Conference), Rio de Janeiro (ISA-ABRI Conference) and in Bogotá (Universidad de los Andes and Universidad Libre). The EU Returns Directive establishes the procedure for returning migrants in an irregular situation to their countries of origin. While preparing my presentation, I thought it would be a good idea to include one slide on how all South American governments, as well as Latin American ones more generally, had vigorously criticised the adoption of this Directive. That slide, I thought, would be a good way to connect with my audiences (large or small) as well as to highlight the outcry that this piece of law had caused throughout the region. While presenting in Rio de Janeiro, my PhD supervisor at the time, Professor Elspeth Guild, found the slide intriguing. It was, she said, worth exploring how the Returns Directive was a terrible exercise in public relations, given the EU has a special partnership with the whole region, which fiercely opposed a law that affected their emigrants' rights. In November 2009, I published a policy brief on the topic with the Centre for European Policy Studies (CEPS), a think tank based in Brussels.[1] A few months later, I received a request from that same think tank to produce a small report on how Argentina, Brazil and Chile regulated irregular migration. This would have been part of a larger project that the EU Fundamental Rights Agency was developing in order to better understand how other regions were dealing with undocumented migration. Whilst I had already lived, worked and studied in Brazil and Colombia, this was to be my first navigation through South American migration law – what I found truly captured my attention. Having read all the critiques of the EU, I expected to find much more open legal regimes and a much more generous approach towards irregular migrants and their rights. If you criticise something, I thought, surely it means you are doing things much better. As always, reality proved to be much more complex. Whilst with great interest I examined the 2004 Argentinean migration law, the 2002 MERCOSUR Residence Agreement and some regularisation procedures that had taken place in the three countries, I could not be but shocked to find that the Brazilian and Chilean migration laws were still the

---

[1] D. Acosta, *Latin American Reactions to the Adoption of the Returns Directive*, Brussels: CEPS, 2009.

same ones that had been adopted in 1980 and 1975, respectively, during their last military dictatorships. These laws included numerous examples of legally sanctioned restriction, exclusion and discrimination towards non-nationals. It was at this point that I realised the importance of starting to thoroughly analyse the region's legal regime. The book you hold in your hands is the result of that journey from 2009 to 2018.

There are numerous institutions to which I would like to extend my gratitude for having supported me throughout this research. I have conducted one-month research visits to Fundação Getulio Vargas in Rio de Janeiro, Universidad di Tella in Buenos Aires and Universidad Javeriana in Bogotá. I am especially thankful for the hospitable environment in all three institutions, in particular to Paula Wojcikiewicz Almeida, Alejandro Chehtman and Roberto Vidal, respectively, for their warm welcome. Preliminary results of this work have been presented at numerous universities and other institutions in Bogotá, Buenos Aires, Brasilia, Lima, Montevideo, Quito, Rio de Janeiro and Santiago de Chile. The list of colleagues to mention in each of these places is enormous but I would like to especially mention the following. In Argentina: Pablo Ceriani, Ana Paula Penchaszadeh, Diego Beltrand, Lelio Mármora, Leiza Brumat, Adriana Alfonso, and Fr. Mario Miguel Santillo and Juan Artola, who unfortunately passed away in 2016 and 2018 respectively. In Brazil: Paulo Sergio de Almeida, Duval Fernandes, Lieselot Vanduynslager, Helion Póvoa Neto and José Sacchetta. In Chile: Tomás Pascual, Jorge Leyton, Delfina Lawson, Miguel Yaksic, Cristián Doña Reveco, Patricia Roa and Rodrigo Sandoval. In Colombia: William Mejia, Marco Velásquez, René Urueña and Beatriz Sánchez Mójica. In Ecuador: Michel Levi, Gioconda Herrera and Marco Navas. In Peru: Guido Mendoza, Luis Tello, Esther Anaya Vera and Ana Neyra. In Uruguay: Ana Santestevan, Victoria Prieto and Martín Koolhaas.

I must also recognise the generous support from the University of Bristol Law School, which offered me a one-year research period during the academic year 2015–2016 in order to initiate this book. I would like to thank several colleagues at the University, in particular, Matthew Brown, Jon Fox, Chris Bertram, Phil Syrpis, Tonia Novitz, Clair Gammage, Malcolm Evans, Steven Greer, Achilles Skordas, Chris Willmore, Janine Sargoni, Matias Rodríguez Burr and Florian Scheding, who have all provided comments on various drafts or helped me in other ways.

During my research year, I had the honour to be a Fernand Braudel Fellow at the EUI in Florence (September–December 2015) and an Emile Nöel Fellow at NYU in New York (January–June 2016). At the EUI, I would like to thank Bruno de Witte, Philippe Fargues, Philippe de Bruycker, Anna Triandafyllidou and Ruth Rubio Marín. At NYU, a special thanks go to Gráinne de Búrca, Wojciech Sadurski, Adam Cox and Samuel Issacharoff.

Many others have commented on or discussed my work in the numerous places where I have presented it around the world, or supported my research for this project in various other ways. They include José Moya, Alex Aleinikoff, François Crépeau, Damian Chalmers, David Abraham, Ana Margheritis, Juliet

Stumpf, Catherine Tinker, Iris Goldner, Peter Spiro, Jaya Ramji-Nogales, David FitzGerald, Elspeth Guild, Kees Groenendijk, Violeta Moreno Lax, Jennifer Gordon, María Lorena Cook, and especially Dimitry Kochenov.

This project has benefited from the research support from Laura Sánchez Carboneras and Claudia Gimeno Fernández, as well as from excellent copy editing and comments by Victoria Finn. Part of the research leading to these results received funding from the European Research Council under the European Union's Seventh Framework Programme (FP/2007–2013) / ERC Grant Agreement no. 340430 for the project Prospects for International Migration Governance (MIGPROSP) awarded to Professor Andrew Geddes, in which I participate as co-investigator. I would like to thank Andrew for his continuous support of my work, as well as all of my colleagues in the project, particularly Marcia Vera Espinoza and Jason Freeman. Special thanks go also to all the excellent team at CUP, which has made the editing process of the book a very easy task.

Finally, and perhaps most importantly, there are four colleagues with whom I have discussed at length numerous aspects of this research and whose comments have been key in shaping some of the ideas in my work. They are Rainer Bauböck, Jacopo Martire, Feline Freier and Jacques Ramírez. I extend my greatest appreciation to the four of you.

The research for this book has been conducted in numerous places throughout South America, Europe and the USA. It has been a most enjoyable journey for me and I have been fortunate to have visited numerous research institutions and libraries, among which I would like to especially mention the Biblioteca Hispánica in Madrid, which seems to have always miraculously had any manuscript that I could not find elsewhere. The resulting present volume would not have been possible without the support of my wife, mother and sister. This book is dedicated to the memory of my father, el Profesor Rafael Acosta, born in Sativa Sur, Boyacá, Colombia, in 1943.

Diego Acosta Arcarazo
January 2018, Bristol

Acronyms

ACHPR	African Charter on Human and People's Rights
ACHR	American Convention on Human Rights
AMF	Andean Migration Forum
CAN	Andean Community
CAT	Committee Against Torture
CEDAW	Convention on the Elimination of All Forms of Discrimination against Women
CELAC	Community of Latin American and Caribbean States
CEPAL	Economic Commission for Latin America
CJEU	Court of Justice of the European Union
CMW	Committee on the Protection of the Rights of All Migrant Workers and Members of their Families
CRC	Convention on the Rights of the Child
CRPD	Convention on the Rights of Persons with Disabilities
ECtHR	European Court of Human Rights
EU	European Union
HR Comittee	United Nations Human Rights Committee
IACHR	Inter-American Commission on Human Rights
IACtHR	Inter-American Court of Human Rights
ICCPR	International Covenant on Civil and Political Rights
ICERD	International Convention on the Elimination of All Forms of Racial Discrimination
ICESCR	International Covenant on Economic, Social and Cultural Rights
ICJ	International Court of Justice
ICMW	International Convention on the Protection of the Rights of All Migrant Workers and Members of Their Families
ICPPED	International Convention for the Protection of All Persons from Enforced Disappearance
ILO	International Labour Organization
IOM	International Organization for Migration
IPPDH	Instituto de Políticas Públicas y Derechos Humanos del MERCOSUR (MERCOSUR Institute for Public Policies and Human Rights)

LAFTA	Latin American Free Trade Association (ALALC Treaty in its Spanish acronym)
LAIA	Latin-American Integration Association (ALADI in its Spanish acronym)
MEP	Member of the European Parliament
MERCOSUR	Common Market of the South
MIGPROSP	Prospects for International Migration Governance
NAFTA	North American Free Trade Agreement
NGO	Non-Governmental Organisation
OAS	Organization of American States
SACM	South American Conference on Migration
TCN	Third-Country National
TFEU	Treaty on the Functioning of the European Union
UDHR	Universal Declaration of Human Rights
UNASUR	Union of South American Nations
UN	United Nations

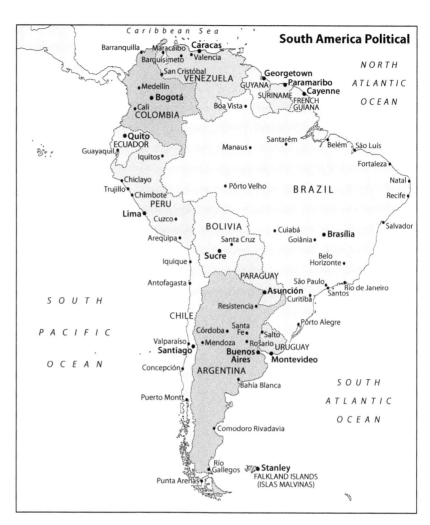

Political Map of South America

1

South America's Central Role in Migration and Citizenship Law

The human right to migration and the recognition of migrants as Subjects of Law must be at the centre of States' migration policies. In line with this, the South American Conference on Migration claims the unconditional respect of the Human Rights of migrants and their families and we condemn all xenophobic, discriminatory and racist acts, as well as the utilitarian treatment of migrants, regardless of their migratory status, and reject any attempt to criminalise irregular migration.[1]

Introduction

Migration and citizenship or nationality laws define who does, and who does not, legally belong in any given society; who is entitled to particular rights and public goods; and who can be discriminated against in certain contexts. Migration and citizenship laws transform political membership and the linkage between borders, territory and population.[2] 'Citizens and noncitizens are not beings found in nature; they are made and unmade by way of law and politics, and their making and unmaking can have momentous consequences.'[3] This is precisely the interest of this book in a region – South America – with two centuries of experience in regulating migration and citizenship.[4]

---

[1] The South American Conference on Migration (SACM; note that the Spanish acronym for the conference is CSM) Buenos Aires Declaration. Positioning before the II UN High Level Dialogue on International Migration and Development, Buenos Aires, 28 August 2013, signed by all twelve governments in the region (author's translation). 'El derecho humano a la migración y el reconocimiento de las personas migrantes como Sujetos de Derecho, debe estar en el centro de las políticas migratorias de los países. En ese sentido, la CSM reivindica el respeto irrestricto de los Derechos Humanos de las personas migrantes y sus familiares y condena todo acto de xenofobia, discriminación y racismo, así como el tratamiento utilitarista de los migrantes, independientemente de su condición migratoria, y rechaza todo intento de criminalización de la migración irregular.'

[2] S. Castles and A. Davidson, *Citizenship and Migration: Globalization and the Politics of Belonging* (New York: Routledge, 2000).

[3] L. Bosniak, 'Persons and Citizens in Constitutional Thought', *International Journal of Constitutional Law*, 8 (2010), 9–29, on 11.

[4] This book refers to South America as the geographical area located between Colombia and Venezuela in the north and stretching to Argentina and Chile in the south. For reasons explained in footnote 10, this book does not study Guyana or Suriname. At times, there will be references to Latin America, which includes Central America, Mexico and the former Spanish colonies in

Migration has become one of the world's most debated and politically contested issues. Reactions are seen daily in the form of Brexit; the response to refugees from Syria; discussions on reintroducing border controls in the EU's Schengen area; critiques of the treatment of migrant workers building football stadiums for the 2022 World Cup in Qatar; or proposals for a wall between the USA and Mexico. Current international migration and citizenship debates can be framed within the context of transformations brought by globalisation. States have lost control of various global aspects, notably financial matters, affecting their decision-making capacity as sovereign entities.[5] Migration and citizenship law has been defined by Dauvergne as 'the last bastion of sovereignty'[6] through which governments try to offer 'an appearance of control'.[7] With legislative frameworks in constant flux everywhere, it is challenging to assess whether the overall picture is becoming either more open or restrictive. Yet, there is a general perception that the tendency is towards a harder line – especially since the terrorist attacks on 11 September 2001 – both in the global North and South, with migration being perceived as a security issue and, at times, being coupled with growing anti-Islamic ideology.[8] The opening up of certain categories, such as highly skilled workers or students, is balanced everywhere with a closing down of others, such as family members or undocumented migrants. That is, everywhere except in South America.[9]

This book analyses the legal construction of the national and the foreigner in ten countries in South America over a period of two hundred years and

the Caribbean – namely Cuba and Dominican Republic. Some scholars also incorporate Haiti in this enumeration. References to Hispano-America include all the former Spanish colonies in the Americas, and thus exclude Brazil and Haiti. For a critical analysis on conceptualising Latin America and its boundaries, see: W. D. Mignolo, *The Idea of Latin America* (Oxford: Blackwell Publishing, 2005).

[5] S. Sassen, *Losing Control? Sovereignty in an Age of Globalization* (New York: Columbia University Press, 1996).

[6] C. Dauvergne, *Making People Illegal. What Globalization Means for Migration and Law* (Cambridge University Press, 2008), p. 2.

[7] D. S. Massey, J. Arango, G. Hugo, A. Kouaouci, A. Pellegrino and J. E. Taylor, *Worlds in Motion: Understanding International Migration at the End of the Millennium* (Oxford University Press, 1998), p. 288.

[8] C. Dauvergne, *The New Politics of Immigration and the End of Settler Societies* (Cambridge University Press, 2016); S. W. Goodman and M. M. Howard, 'Evaluating and Explaining the Restrictive Backlash in Citizenship Policy in Europe', *Studies in Law, Politics and Society*, 60 (2013), 111–139; R. Rubio-Marín, 'Human Rights and the Citizen/Non-Citizen Distinction Revisited' in R. Rubio-Marín (ed.), *Human Rights and Immigration* (Oxford University Press, 2014), pp. 1–18, on p. 2.

[9] De Haas *et al.* have pointed out how migration policies have become less restrictive since 1945, although they show important divergences across migrant categories and policy types. They conclude that South America presents a historical exception by having opened up their migration regimes since the 1990s. In their analysis, Latin America (South America plus Mexico) is measured as the least restrictive region globally. H. de Haas, K. Natter and S. Vezzoli, 'Growing Restrictiveness or Changing Selection? The Nature and Evolution of Migration Policies', *International Migration Review*, Fall (2016) online early view version DOI: 10.1111/imre.12288, 1–44.

attempts to put the region on the agenda of migration and citizenship scholars.[10] Since the turn of the century, South American governments and regional organisations have adopted the world's most open discourse on migration and citizenship.[11] This discursive openness has made its way into numerous laws and policies at both the national and regional level, representing a unique phenomenon worldwide. In contrast to the USA, Europe and other countries and regions, South American politicians and civil servants stress the universality of migrants' rights and the inefficacy of restrictive responses.[12] Three principles guide this approach: the non-criminalisation of undocumented migration; considering migration as a human right; and, finally, open borders. These three principles form part of a more wide-ranging promotion of equal treatment between nationals and foreigners in a process striving towards some sort of universal citizenship. While some principles overlap with what is offered to certain migrant categories in other legal systems (e.g. the EU), what distinguishes South America is its aspirational universal application.

At a time when restrictive choices seem to be increasingly predominant around the world, South American policy makers and scholars alike have presented this attitude towards universality as both an innovative and exceptional 'new paradigm' and part of a morally superior, avant-garde path in policy making.[13] The aim of this book is to provide a critical examination of the South American migration and citizenship legal framework through a historical and comparative analysis. This allows us to then assess whether it is truly innovative

[10] In alphabetical order: Argentina, Bolivia, Brazil, Chile, Colombia, Ecuador, Paraguay, Peru, Uruguay and Venezuela. Suriname and Guyana have been excluded due to their distinct colonial history. These states did not gain independence until 1966 and 1975 respectively, which strongly affects their legislative choices on this matter, as well as their weaker association with regional integration processes. They are not full members of the Common Market of the South (MERCOSUR), nor the Andean Community (CAN). It is for the same reason that this book also omits Mexico, Central America and the former Spanish possessions in the Caribbean, namely Cuba and Dominican Republic. None of these countries – except for Mexico's membership in the Pacific Alliance – is a member of any of the regional processes taking place in South America: Union of South American Nations (UNASUR), MERCOSUR and CAN. Consequently, whilst some of these countries have a similar colonial history, recent developments distinguish them from South America, notably when it comes to the ongoing process towards the free movement of people and eventual establishment of a regional citizenship. Nonetheless, the book will make references to these and other countries when needed.

[11] 'Open' in this context refers to policies aiming at securing migrants' rights and striving towards free mobility for all, without discrimination. In turn, 'openness' refers to any policy change towards less control over or fewer restrictions on migration.

[12] See references and discussion on the dichotomy between discourse and outcomes in South America in D. Acosta and L. F. Freier, 'Turning the Immigration Policy Paradox Up-side Down? Populist Liberalism and Discursive Gaps in South America', *International Migration Review*, 49 (2015), 659–697, on 662–664.

[13] There are, of course, examples of critical approaches to this alleged 'new paradigm'. See, among others: E. Domenech, '"Las Migraciones son como el Agua": Hacia la Instauración de Políticas de "Control con Rostro Humano." La Gobernabilidad Migratoria en Argentina', *Polis Revista Latinoamericana*, 35 (2013), 1–20; P. Ceriani, 'Luces y Sombras en la Legislación Migratoria Latinoamericana', *Nueva Sociedad*, 233 (2011), 68–86.

and exceptional, as well as permitting us to evaluate its feasibility, strengths and weaknesses. The following chapters interpret the history of migration and citizenship regulation in ten South American states through a descriptive and explanatory investigation. I show not only how citizenship and migration laws have functioned during the last two centuries but also why states have opted for certain regulation choices. The legal construction of the national and the foreigner as categories is a political choice. Considering South America's central historical role as both a destination and source of migration flows – combined with its two hundred years of legal and political discussions on the matter – it is crucial for all those interested in migration and citizenship debates at the global level to better understand this region.

In the nineteenth century, South American countries became the precursor of open borders for individuals: their Constitutions enshrined clauses guaranteeing the right of any foreigner to enter and settle in their territories as well as receive equal rights with nationals. Today, the right to migrate understood as a human right emerges again in the South American discourse and law. Open borders was originally a civilisation project in an effort to create nations out of weak nascent states which had recently gained independence. The agents of the civilisation effort were to be white, male, industrious Europeans. The ideal migrant was to populate regions presented as deserted, bring industries needed to participate in global markets, and contribute to the whitening of mixed-race populations. Unlike what we may imagine today, the motive behind these open borders and recruitment was absolutely not a humanistic project, but a utilitarian one.

South America distinguished itself early on from other settler societies, namely the USA.[14] For example, South Americans largely abolished slavery much faster. They also granted nationality to those born within the territory through *ius soli* – this included *all* those born there, not only free white persons. Although comprising numerous contradictions, this approach permitted building 'formally inclusionary nations, but on deeply hierarchical grounds'.[15] Membership was, however, not necessarily structured around nationality. For example, Hispano-Americans – a category that included those from the former Spanish colonies in South America, Central America, Mexico and the Caribbean – enjoyed privileged legal treatment. Thus, South America became a fascinating hub of state- and nation-building processes related to government, territory and population.

Initially, South America was not completely successful in attracting migrants. However, between the 1870s and 1930s, the region became the second-largest global recipient of migrants, following the USA. Millions arrived spontaneously,

[14] H. Motomura, *Americans in Waiting: The Lost History of Immigration and Citizenship in the United States* (Oxford University Press, 2006).

[15] M. Loveman, *National Colors: Racial Classification and the State in Latin America* (Oxford University Press, 2014), p. 5.

mainly from Europe, although a few thousand migrants travelled with subsidised passages to Argentina or Brazil.[16] Within this period, doubts also progressively arose regarding the previous openness towards foreigners. The same states that had been precursors of open borders were then among the first to eagerly experiment with restrictions against foreigners on ethnic, racial, political and moral grounds. Later, during the Cold War, migration and citizenship exclusions peaked during the 1970s military dictatorships: the foreigner was portrayed as a dangerous threat to national security.

Following re-democratisation in the 1980s, South America transformed from a region of immigration to one of emigration. This process, which had begun during the military regimes in the 1970s, accelerated as economic instability dominated throughout the following two decades. Democracy sealed constitutional reforms that put more of a spotlight on international human rights law, mainly the American Convention on Human Rights (ACHR) and its interpretation by the Inter-American Court (IACtHR).[17] The resulting legal architecture on migration, mobility and citizenship, which continues to affect us in the twenty-first century, is striking.

First, practices of 'external citizenship'[18] have become widespread, notably through states accepting dual citizenship as well as extending the franchise to nationals residing abroad. This also impacts immigrants living in South America, who can now enjoy dual citizenship as well as political rights, particularly at the local level. Three out of the five countries in the world that extend the franchise to foreigners in national elections without discriminating by citizenship are located in the region: Chile, Ecuador and Uruguay.[19]

Second, new migration laws in various countries enshrine the non-criminalisation of undocumented migrants and position the right to migrate as a human right. In various forms, this holds true in Argentina (2004), Uruguay (2008), Bolivia (2013), Brazil (2017), Ecuador (2017) and Peru (2017), and it is present in law proposals in Chile (2017) and Paraguay (2016).[20] Globally, this approach is unique since no international instrument has recognised these principles as universal nor as an individual right.

Third, there is a strong push towards open borders at the regional level. The 2002 MERCOSUR Residence Agreement, which is in force in nine out of

---

[16] In the case of Argentina, immigration agents granted 133,428 free passages to Buenos Aires amongst various European countries between 1888 and 1890. However, this represented only 2 per cent of the total number of migrants who arrived to Argentina. J. C. Moya, *Cousins and Strangers: Spanish Immigrants in Buenos Aires, 1850–1930* (Berkeley, CA: University of California Press, 1998), p. 52. In the case of Brazil, see J. Sacchetta, *Laços de Sangue: Privilégios e Intolerância à Imigração Portuguesa no Brasil (1822–1945)* (São Paulo: Edusp/Fapesp, 2011), p. 179.

[17] See Part II, Consolidation, pp. 113–117.

[18] R. Bauböck, 'Introduction' in R. Bauböck (ed.), *Transnational Citizenship and Migration* (London and New York: Routledge, 2017), pp. 1–18, on p. 3.

[19] See Chapter 6, pp. 161–162.

[20] The laws referred to throughout this book are valid as of 1 October 2017.

the twelve South American countries, has transformed the mobility regime. It grants South American nationals a right to reside and work in any other state that is part of the agreement. It also offers migrants various rights, such as equal treatment in working conditions, social and economic rights, and family reunion. Proposals have also advanced the possible adoption of a South American supranational citizenship, which would incorporate not only South American nationals but also foreigners permanently residing in the region. An extensive regional citizenship as such would establish a new international 'gold standard' and place South America as a leading innovative force in migration law.

Finally, South American citizenship laws are peculiar in a comparative perspective. *Ius soli* represents the general rule and residence periods before naturalisation are short, allegedly resulting in possibly the least restrictive regimes worldwide.[21]

The aim of this book is to see whether this framework through which the national and the foreigner are legally constructed confirms the claims of innovation and exceptionalism. A comparative and historical analysis of ten cases across two centuries uncovers wider transnational trends and legal mechanisms that are hidden while merely juxtaposing national studies. The book contains two parts: the first (Chapters 2–4) analyses the construction of the 'national' and the 'foreigner' since the early nineteenth century until the end of the twentieth century, and assesses to what extent these concepts are actually novel and innovative. Many of the regulatory choices these countries made immediately following independence are, perhaps surprisingly, still in force today. The second part of the book (Chapters 5–7) thoroughly dissects the three potentially ground-breaking principles emerging in the region during the twenty-first century: non-criminalisation; migration as a human right; and open borders. These three combined aspirations are a unique phenomenon at the global level: rather than the deprivation of rights when crossing a border, it points towards equal treatment as a general rule throughout the region in an effort to make migration and citizenship law more enlightened and humane. A careful analysis of these three principles – including their actual scope when materialised into rights – allows us to evaluate the true reach of the exceptionalism claim, as well as its contradictions and flaws.

My main focus is on legal texts, both domestic and international, as well as academic sources. When necessary, administrative regulations, case law and reports by national and international actors serve as supplementary material. One of the greatest challenges of analysing ten countries over two centuries is that for each generalisation or common legal historical regional pattern I reveal, there are partial exceptions, opposing examples or national oddities. While the book shows a strong convergence of migration and citizenship regulation over two hundred years, it also unearths country-specific peculiarities.

---

[21] See Chapter 6, pp. 165–169.

Administrative practices are of course also central in understanding how law works in practice since – regardless of what the law states – they sometimes serve as tools for selecting certain migrants.[22] Motomura has distinguished between immigration law on the books versus immigration law in action. He argues that 'immigration law itself can operate outside the rule of law' since immigration law in action depends on 'countless government decisions that reflect the exercise of discretion, which responds to political and economic pressures that fluctuate'.[23] At times, discretion depends on normative preferences. For instance, for years Argentina did not detain undocumented migrants, despite it legally being possible. This changed in 2016 with a new government, which had a more restrictive discourse and opened a new detention centre.[24] Consequently, readers who are interested in the challenges surrounding implementation will find numerous examples and bibliographic pointers throughout the chapters. When needed, I highlight the gaps requiring further research. However, this does not deviate the book from its main focus, which is not to offer country case studies of implementing migration and citizenship law in practice but rather to elucidate general trends at the regional level through a panoramic, historical and comparative vision.

This book's substance stems from my understanding of migration and citizenship law in South America. I have gained this knowledge through my comparative and historical legal analysis, from participating in more than twenty research and conference visits to the region since 2009, as well as from conducting over 100 interviews with government officials, legal practitioners, academics, and individuals within international organisations, NGOs and migrants' associations.[25]

Contribution to Academic Debates

This book fills a central gap in the existing literature, as well as contributing to various debates. First, and most obviously, it fits into the vast literature on domestic and comparative migration and citizenship law.[26] This represents an opportunity to study a major aspect of a region in the Global South, whose countries emerged two hundred years ago. The analysis of South America

---

[22] D. S. FitzGerald and D. Cook-Martin, *Culling the Masses. The Democratic Origins of Racist Immigration Policy in the Americas* (Cambridge, MA: Harvard University Press, 2014), pp. 331–332.

[23] H. Motomura, *Immigration Outside the Law* (Oxford University Press, 2014), p. 4.

[24] See Chapter 5, pp. 130–131.

[25] Around sixty of these interviews were conducted within the framework of the five-year Prospects for International Migration Governance (MIGPROSP) project. The research leading to these results has received funding from the European Research Council under the European Union's Seventh Framework Programme (FP/2007–2013) / ERC Grant Agreement n. 340430.

[26] The number of works within this area is too extensive to make reference to here, but the countries most often analysed are Australia, Canada, the USA and a few states in Western Europe – mainly France, Germany, the Netherlands and the UK.

expands our understanding of alternative ways to regulate migration and citizenship. It also provides tools for challenging taken-for-granted assumptions currently embedded into legal concepts and practices in Europe, North America, Australia and beyond. This work generates regional knowledge regarding South America but moreover on the individual ten countries under analysis as well. Given the fact that more than 40 per cent of all international migration comprises South–South flows,[27] it is a grave concern that analysing immigration and citizenship law beyond Western liberal democracies has overall been neglected.[28] This book is a challenge to those who generalise Western models into universal social facts and a boost to others to look outside the usual suspects for paradigms.

Second, this book also advances the literature on international migration law and human rights.[29] There is basic intrinsic importance in understanding the relationships between the international, regional and domestic levels in South America. Moreover, at the outset it must be highlighted that many ideas that historically first appeared as part of a Latin or South American regional consensus – such as peaceful solution of controversies or non-intervention – were later converted into general international law.[30] For example, the 1984 Cartagena Declaration expanded the 1951 Convention's definition of 'refugee' and has since been praised as pushing the boundaries of asylum law.[31] Whilst refugee law is not the core subject of this book,[32] the region plays a central

---

[27] United Nations (UN), Department of Economic and Social Affairs, Population Division (2015). International Migration 2015 Wallchart (United Nations publication, Sales No. E.16.XIII.12).

[28] There are an increasing number of academic works investigating South–South migration. See, for example, P. de Lombaerde, F. Guo and H. Póvoa Neto, 'Introduction to the Special Collection. South–South Migrations: What is (Still) on the Research Agenda?', *International Migration Review*, 48 (2014), 103–112.

[29] See, among others: M.-B. Dembour, *When Humans Become Migrants: Study of the European Court of Human Rights with an Inter-American Counterpoint* (Oxford University Press, 2015); V. Chetail and C. Bauloz (eds), *Research Handbook on International Law and Migration* (Cheltenham: Edward Elgar, 2014); B. Opeskin, R. Perruchoud and J. Redpath-Cross (eds), *Foundations of International Migration Law* (Cambridge University Press, 2012); P. de Guchteneire, A. Pécoud and R. Cholewinski (eds), *Migration and Human Rights: The United Nations Convention on Migrant Workers' Rights* (Cambridge University Press, 2009).

[30] A. Becker Lorca, *Mestizo International Law: A Global Intellectual History 1842–1933* (Cambridge University Press, 2014).

[31] E. Arboleda, 'Refugee Definition in Africa and Latin America: The Lessons of Pragmatism', *International Journal of Refugee Law*, 3 (1991), 185–207.

[32] The legal regulation of refugees and asylum seekers is not the subject of this book since it deals with individuals leaving their country of origin due to persecution. The distinction between forced and other modalities of migration is not an easy or definitely settled one, but it is generally accepted by most scholars for methodological purposes. With this in mind, the current volume engages in an investigation of non-asylum-related mobility in South America, leaving aside refugee law questions, which do not form the focus of this research. The tradition of asylum has, however, been historically important in Latin America, with its roots in the nineteenth-century practice of extending asylum to politically persecuted individuals. Nonetheless, in 1950 the International Court of Justice held that diplomatic asylum was not part of customary international law: instead, the Court established that it depended on reciprocal action between states through bilateral or multilateral treaties. See the Colombian-Peruvian Asylum Case, Judgment, 20 November 1950: I.C.J. Reports 1950. For a historical investigation,

role, notably through the jurisprudence of the IACtHR, in developing human rights and international law on migration and citizenship in numerous other aspects.[33]

Third, the book adds to the discussion on the evolving relationship between nationality and alienage. Beginning in the 1990s, a large body of literature has questioned the traditional definitions of the legal categories of the foreigner and the national, arguing that they do not correspond with reality. Scholars have coined terms such as denizens or postnational, flexible or transnational citizens to label those who, even if residing in a territory for a long time without citizenship, nonetheless enjoy a number of civil, social and, to a lesser extent, political rights.[34] Central to the discussion has been the allegedly declining role of the state, alongside new emerging modalities of membership.[35] These theories have been utilised while analysing a limited number of cases in Western liberal democracies, as well as on European citizenship as a new legal status. Identifying applications outside this sample has substantial value for theory building – especially when aspects such as the extension of rights to foreigners has taken place in South America for two centuries.

Fourth, the book is relevant for those interested in state- and nation-building processes.[36] In the early nineteenth century, ten new states emerged from the previous Spanish and Portuguese possessions in South America, and thus are among the oldest in the world. With their newly gained independence, South Americans turned their attention to asserting their statehood through the delineation of three constitutive elements: government, territory and population. This was a state- and nation-building exercise in a transitional period from colonial societies into republics, where collective identities were forming and where the relationship with foreigners was vital in both determining the polity's boundaries and in constructing the nation.[37]

---

see: N. Ronning, *Diplomatic Asylum. Legal Norms and Political Reality in Latin American Relations* (The Hague: Martinus Nijhoff, 1965). For a more current analysis of refugee law in South America, see: D. Cantor, L. F. Freier, and J. P. Gauci (eds), *A Liberal Tide? Immigration and Asylum Law and Policy in Latin America* (London: Institute of Latin American Studies, 2015).

[33] See Chapters 5 and 6.

[34] T. Hammar, *Democracy and the Nation State* (Aldershot: Avebury, 1990); Y. N. Soysal, *Limits of Citizenship: Migrants and Postnational Membership in Europe* (University of Chicago Press, 1994); A. Ong, *Flexible Citizenship: The Cultural Logics of Transnationality* (Durham, NC: Duke University Press, 1999); R. Bauböck, *Transnational Citizenship: Membership and Rights in International Migration* (Cheltenham: Edward Elgar, 1994).

[35] Sassen, *Losing Control?*; S. Benhabib, *The Rights of Others: Aliens, Residents and Citizens* (Cambridge University Press, 2004); L. Bosniak, *The Citizen and the Alien: Dilemmas of Contemporary Membership* (Princeton University Press, 2006).

[36] The literature on state- and nation-building processes is very extensive. For a solid and comprehensive collection, see: J. Breuilly (ed.), *The Oxford Handbook of the History of Nationalism* (Oxford University Press, 2013).

[37] M. A. Centeno and A. E. Ferraro, 'Republics of the Possible: State Building in Latin America and Spain' in M. A. Centeno and A. E. Ferraro (eds), *State and Nation Making in Latin America and Spain. Republics of the Possible* (Cambridge University Press, 2013), pp. 3–24; B. Anderson, *Imagined Communities: Reflections on the Origin and Spread of Nationalism* (London: Verso, 1983).

Finally, advances in migration and citizenship law will interest constitutional researchers and are properly considered part of a new Latin American Constitutionalism.[38] This new approach grants international law instruments, notably the ACHR and its interpretation by the IACtHR, a central place in the domestic legal order. The Inter-American Court developed a legal doctrine of conventionality control, which obliges all national authorities to measure their actions' validity against the ACHR and the Court's interpretation. Some of the new constitutions and the IACtHR's jurisprudence extend numerous civil, social and political rights to foreigners, including to undocumented migrants, and thus conflict with the traditional understandings of which rights are associated with citizenship.

South America offers a truly captivating and rich history of legal regulation on the status of the national and the foreigner. The following pages will help the reader gain a better understanding of South America's idiosyncrasies through insights into migration flows, actors and regional debates, before concluding with a final section in this chapter where I summarise each of the remaining seven chapters.

Migration Flows in South America

Immigration in South America

During the late nineteenth and early twentieth centuries, South America was the second-largest recipient of migrants in the world, after only the USA. Argentina, Brazil and Uruguay were the true champions in a race to attract European settlers, a race in which all ten countries participated. Between 1856 and 1932, an estimated 6.4 million people arrived in Argentina, 4.4 million in Brazil and 700,000 in Uruguay.[39] Foreigners represented an impressive percentage of the total population in the three main destinations: one-third of the Argentinean population was foreign-born by 1914.[40]

Moya has identified five global revolutions of demographic, agricultural, industrial, transportation and liberal change to account for Argentina's prominent place in attracting migrants based on its incorporation into the world capitalist system. Argentina had fertile lands but lacked farmers. The

---

[38] See the references in Part II, Consolidation, pp. 113–117.

[39] H. Oddone and J. Guidini, 'Políticas Públicas sobre Migraciones y Participación de la Sociedad Civil en Paraguay' in L. M. Chiarello (ed.), *Las Políticas Públicas sobre Migraciones y la Sociedad Civil en América Latina: Los Casos de Bolivia, Chile, Paraguay y Perú* (New York: Scalabrini International Migration Network, 2013), pp. 243–390, on p. 251.

[40] IOM, *Perfil Migratorio de Argentina* (Buenos Aires: IOM, 2012), p. 17. In Uruguay, 17 per cent of its population was foreign-born by 1908, with more than 30 per cent of Montevideo's residents being foreigners. See IOM, *Perfil Migratorio de Uruguay* (Buenos Aires: IOM, 2011), pp. 43–44. In Brazil, 7.3 per cent of the total 17.3 million inhabitants and more than 20 per cent in the states of São Paulo and the former Guanabara (now part of the Rio de Janeiro state) were foreigners by 1900. See M. S. Ferreira Levy, 'O Papel da Migração Internacional na Evolução da População Brasileira (1872 a 1972)', *Revista Saúde Pública*, 8 (1974), 49–90.

concentration of factories in industrial centres resulted in the Old World's pro-liferating urban population, which also had a high demand for food. Argentina became a crucial supplier of wheat and meat, thus requiring manpower to take this leading economic role. New technologies such as refrigeration facilitated exports. Easier and faster transportation, and opening the gates for immigrants in Argentina as well as for emigrants in Europe, resulted in large movements of people.[41] Uruguay went through a similar, but scaled-down process, particu-larly due to the large difference in geographic size between the two countries. In Brazil, the production of coffee – and to a lesser extent rubber – was the main driver behind its insertion into global markets. Brazil's most important immi-gration decade was 1888–1898 when more than 1.3 million people arrived, which coincided with the abolition of slavery in 1888.[42] Following the massive slump in coffee prices after the 1929 crash, immigration then almost com-pletely halted.[43]

Chile, Peru and Venezuela also attracted a notable number of migrants. In the case of Peru, it was mostly Asians,[44] whereas Chile drew foreigners from a multitude of origins throughout Europe, the Middle East and its South American neighbours. At its peak in 1907, Chile's foreign-born population was almost 140,000 or 4 per cent of the total population.[45] Venezuela tirelessly, but largely unsuccessfully, designed projects to attract migrants. Then with the dis-covery of oil in the early twentieth century – coupled with American and British companies' ensuing investment in the sector – migrants began to arrive, then even more so from the 1950s onwards. Between 1950 and 1958, new residents moving to Venezuela numbered 332,000 and then by 1961, the foreign-born comprised 7 per cent of its population. Arrivals from Europe disappeared by the 1970s but were replaced by Colombians and nationals from the Southern Cone.[46]

Finally, few foreigners settled into Colombia or Ecuador, but those who did largely chose the coastal cities of Barranquilla and Guayaquil, respectively.[47]

---

[41] Moya, *Cousins and Strangers*, pp. 45–59.

[42] Sacchetta, *Laços de Sangue*, p. 180.

[43] *Ibid.*, pp. 198–201.

[44] Between 1849 and 1875, 100,000 Chinese and circa 20,000 Europeans settled in Peru. By 1857, almost a third of the 90,000 inhabitants of Lima were foreign-born. A second period (1875–1930) saw the arrival of 25,000 Japanese and around 12,000 Europeans. G. Bonfiglio, 'Introducción al Estudio de la Inmigración Europea en el Perú', *Apuntes*, 18 (1986), 93–127, on 95 and 99.

[45] J. Martínez Pizarro, M. Soffia, J. D. Cubides Franco and I. Bortolotto, 'Políticas Públicas sobre Migraciones y Participación de la Sociedad Civil en Chile' in Chiarello (ed.), *Las Políticas Públicas sobre Migraciones*, pp. 117–242, on p. 125.

[46] C.-Y. Chen and M. Picouet, *Dinámica de la población: Caso de Venezuela* (Caracas: UCAB-Orston, 1979), pp. 29–30. Also see A. Pellegrino, *Historia de la Inmigración en Venezuela Siglos XIX y XX* (Caracas: Academia Nacional de Ciencias Económicas, 1989).

[47] For example, in Colombia in 1938, there were only 55,000 foreigners, which was about 0.63 per cent of the population. R. Vidal, R. M. Martín, B. E. Sánchez and M. Velásquez, 'Políticas Públicas sobre Migración en Colombia' in Chiarello (ed.), *Las Políticas Públicas sobre Migraciones*, pp. 277–446, on p. 287. In Ecuador, there were around 10,000 foreigners in Guayaquil in 1899, or around 15 per cent of its population, but then by 1906, there were fewer than 1,500 in Quito,

Bolivia and Paraguay, despite having also received some immigrants, can be historically categorised as origin countries, displaying negative net migration.[48] Notwithstanding these variations, immigration made its mark at demographic, economic, political, social and cultural levels in all ten countries. *Ius soli* meant migrants' descendants born in the territory became nationals in all respects, including statistically. Migrants originated from an incredible plethora of countries: primarily from Italy, Portugal and Spain, but also from Belgium, Britain, Croatia, France, Germany, the Netherlands, Poland and Switzerland. This diversity was further enriched through flows from Asia, notably China and Japan,[49] as well as from the Middle East, comprised mainly of Christians from Lebanon, Palestine and Syria – then part of the former Ottoman Empire.[50]

Regional mobility

Regional mobility, even if less prominent than European immigration, was always notable in some countries. By the end of the nineteenth century, Argentineans, Peruvians and Bolivians represented 67 per cent of all non-nationals in Chile;[51] whilst 7 per cent of Uruguay's total population resided in Argentina by 1914.[52] Argentineans and Brazilians emigrated to Uruguay[53] and Paraguay.[54] Paraguayans moved in the reverse direction to both Argentina and Brazil[55] whereas Peruvians and Colombians went to Ecuador.[56]

representing only 2.6 per cent of the population. J. Ramírez, 'Del Aperturismo Segmentado al Control Migratorio' in J. Ramírez (ed.), *Ciudad-Estado, Inmigrantes y Políticas. Ecuador, 1890–1950* (Quito: IAEN, 2012), pp. 15–52, on p. 23.

[48] IOM, *Perfil Migratorio de Paraguay* (Buenos Aires: IOM, 2011), on p. 11; IOM, *Perfil Migratorio de Bolivia* (Buenos Aires: IOM, 2011), on p. 7.

[49] W. Look Lai and T. Chee-Beng (eds), *The Chinese in Latin America and the Caribbean* (Leiden: Brill, 2010); D. M. Masterson with S. Funada-Classen, *The Japanese in Latin America* (Champaign, IL: University of Illinois Press, 2004).

[50] I. Klich and J. Lesser (eds), *Arab and Jewish Immigrants in Latin America: Images and Realities* (Abingdon: Routledge, 1998).

[51] Martínez Pizarro *et al.*, 'Políticas Públicas sobre Migraciones', on 127.

[52] IOM, *Perfil Migratorio de Uruguay*, p. 15. Uruguayans were part of the approximately 200,000 migrants from neighbouring countries inhabiting Argentina by that date. In fact, migrants from adjacent states have always represented between 2 and 3 per cent of its total population after 1869. See L. Mármora, M. G. Altilio, M. L. Gianelli Dublanc and Y. Vega, 'Políticas Públicas y Programas sobre Migraciones en Argentina: La Participación de la Sociedad Civil' in L. M. Chiarello (ed.), *Las Políticas Públicas sobre Migraciones y la Sociedad Civil en América Latina. Los Casos de Argentina, Brasil, Colombia y México* (New York: Scalabrini International Migration Network, 2011) pp. 1–150, on p. 6.

[53] M. Koolhaas, A. Pellegrino, B. Diconca and A. Santestevan, 'Las Políticas Públicas sobre Migraciones y la Sociedad Civil en América Latina: El caso de Uruguay', unpublished report, 2016, p. 6.

[54] S. Fischer, T. Palau, N. Pérez, 'Inmigración y Emigración en el Paraguay 1870–1960', Documento de Trabajo no. 90, Base Investigaciones Sociales IPGH, Instituto Panamericano de Geografía e Historia, 1997.

[55] It is estimated that there were almost 30,000 Paraguayans in Argentina and more than 17,000 in Brazil by 1914 and 1920, respectively. See IOM, *Perfil Migratorio de Paraguay*, p. 11.

[56] J. Ramírez (ed.), *Ciudad-Estado, Inmigrantes y Políticas. Ecuador, 1890–1950* (Quito: IAEN, 2012).

What drove mobility in South America? In the frontier regions, trade was an important factor. Agriculture and stockbreeding also played their role too, for example, between Bolivia and Argentina.[57] Mining explained the movement of Chileans to Peru and Bolivia in the nineteenth century, before the Pacific War.[58] Political instability and civil wars resulted in higher mobility, as did soldier recruitment, as exemplified by Colombians in Ecuador.[59]

With the almost complete demise of European flows in the 1960s, coupled with a reduction in arrivals from Asia and the Middle East, regional migration gradually became proportionally larger. From the 1970s until the turn of the century, at least two million South Americans emigrated to countries within the region, with Argentina and Venezuela serving as the main destinations.[60] Since 2000, all ten states are both senders and recipients at the regional level (see Table 1).[61] By 2015, there were an estimated 5.6 million immigrants in South America, 63 per cent of whom were regional migrants.[62]

Emigration from South America

Emigration beyond the region was historically rare in South America. There was largely no movement outside the continent in the nineteenth century, with the exception of diplomats and wealthy individuals travelling to Europe or the USA. The 5,000 Chileans who departed from Valparaiso to San Francisco during the gold rush represent a colourful exception.[63] Excluding Bolivia and Paraguay, South American states were overall net migrant recipients, not senders, and remained so until the end of the 1950s.

Economic and political instability reversed this trend. Three periods can be singled out. First, during the 1960s and 1970s, eight out of the ten countries suffered from non-democratic military regimes.[64] An unprecedented number of political exiles and refugees was a shared trait: for example, an estimated 200,000 Argentineans and between 300,000 to 500,000 Chileans left their countries.[65] Second, the 'lost decade' of the 1980s forced large numbers to leave

[57] IOM, *Perfil Migratorio de Bolivia*, p. 36.
[58] IOM, *Perfil Migratorio de Chile* (Buenos Aires: IOM, 2011), p. 42.
[59] C. Escobar, *Report on Citizenship Law: Colombia* (Florence: European University Institute, EUDO Citizenship), p. 8.
[60] IOM, *La Situación Migratoria en América del Sur* (Buenos Aires: IOM, 2001), p. 4; Massey *et al.*, *Worlds in Motion*, ch. 7.
[61] E. Texidó and J. Gurrieri, *Panorama Migratorio de América del Sur 2012* (Buenos Aires: IOM, 2012), pp. 18–20; R. Cordova Alcaraz (ed.), *Dinámicas Migratorias en América Latina y el Caribe (ALC) y entre ALC y la Unión Europea* (Geneva: IOM, 2015).
[62] OECD and OAS, *International Migration in the Americas: Third Report of the Continuous Reporting System on International Migration in the Americas (SICREMI)* (Washington, DC: Organization of American States, 2015), on p. 153.
[63] D. M. Wright, 'The Making of Cosmopolitan California: An Analysis of Immigration, 1848–1870', *California Historical Society Quarterly*, 19 (1940), 323–343.
[64] Chapter 4, pp. 101–104.
[65] Mármora *et al.*, 'Políticas Públicas y Programas sobre Migraciones en Argentina', p. 15; IOM, *Perfil Migratorio de Chile*, p. 43.

Table 1 Estimated Immigration and Emigration Stocks by Country, South America, 2015

Country	Foreign-born (Regional Migrants)	% Country's Population (Regional)	Estimated Emigrants (in the Region)	% Country's Population (in the Region)	Total Population
Argentina	2,086,302 (1,698,907)	4.8% (3.9%)	940,273 (257,278)	2.2% (0.6%)	43,417,000
Bolivia	142,989 (93,924)	1.3% (0.9%)	799,605 (513,982)	7.4% (4.8%)	10,725,000
Brazil	713,568 (206,622)	0.3% (0.1%)	1,544,024* (192,810)	0.7% (0.09%)	207,848,000
Chile	469,436 (359,187)	2.7% (2.0%)	612,409 (275,574)	3.4% (1.5%)	17,948,000
Colombia	133,134 (74,919)	0.3% (0.15%)	2,638,852** (1,217,239)	5.3% (2.5%)	48,229,000
Ecuador	387,513 (239,461)	2.4% (1.5%)	1,101,923 (82,688)	6.7% (0.5%)	16,144,000
Paraguay	156,462 (136,814)	2.4% (2.1%)	845,373 (734,212)	12.0% (11.5%)	6,339,000
Peru	90,881 (43,438)	0,3% (0.13%)	1,409,676*** (470,207)	4.5% (1.5%)	31,377,000
Uruguay	71,799 (37,980)	2.1% (1.1%)	346,976 (173,979)	10.1% (5.0%)	3,432,000
Venezuela	1,404,448 (1,095,504)	4.5% (3.5%)	606,344**** (68,787)	1.9% (0.2%)	31,108,000
Total	5,656,532 (3,986,756)	1.3% (0.95%)	10,845,455 (3,986,756)	2.6% (0.95%)	416,567,000

   * According to Brazil's government, the number of Brazilians abroad in 2013 was 3,091,274. See: www.brasileirosnomundo.itamaraty.gov.br/a-comunidade/estimativas-populacionais-das-comunidades/estimativas-populacionais-brasileiras-mundo-2014/Estimativas-RCN2014.pdf

  ** According to some estimates from the Colombian Ministry of Foreign Affairs, the real number of Colombians residing abroad in 2014 was 4.7 million: see B. E. Sánchez Mójica, 'In Transit: Migration Policy in Colombia' in Cantor et al., *A Liberal Tide?*, pp. 81–103, on p. 87.

 *** According to some sources, the number of Peruvians abroad in 2015 was between 2.4 and 3.5 million: see IOM, *Perfil Migratorio del Perú*, p. 81.

**** The number of Venezuelans abroad is possibly much larger, with some estimates numbering as high as 2 million, which would have been 7 per cent of the total population in 2016: T. Páez, 'Amid Economic Crisis and Political Turmoil, Venezuelans Form a New Exodus', 14 June 2017, Migration Policy Institute, Washington, DC.

Source: Own elaboration with data from *Trends in International Migrant Stock: Migrants by Destination and Origin* (United Nations database, POP/DB/MIG/Stock/Rev.2015).

behind countries that were experiencing increased inequality, hyper-inflation, unemployment and precariousness.[66] The 1980s witnessed the consolidation

[66] L. Bértola and J. A. Ocampo, *The Economic Development of Latin America since Independence* (Oxford University Press, 2012), ch. 5.

of an important extra-regional diaspora, notably in the USA. For instance, an estimated 1.8 million Brazilians emigrated during this decade.[67] In the case of Colombia and Peru, increasing levels of internal violence added to the number of people fleeing.[68] Finally, after a period of neoliberal policies in the 1990s, complete with privatisations, a diminishing role for the state and labour market flexibility, the economic crisis at the turn of the century resulted in what has been defined as a 'migratory stampede'.[69] The main destinations were the USA and Europe, chiefly Spain. The magnitude of the exodus was enormous. Almost 400,000 Argentineans,[70] over 250,000 Bolivians,[71] one million Brazilians,[72] 1.9 million Colombians,[73] around half a million Ecuadorians,[74] 100,000 Paraguayans,[75] 1.4 million Peruvians,[76] and 120,000 Uruguayans[77] left their countries. Many of these migrants ended up in an irregular situation in the destination countries.[78] Across the region there were just two exceptions to this trend. In Venezuela, high oil prices meant that originally, emigration remained low. But with the political and economic instability since 2014, the country has seen an increasing number of Venezuelans setting out for countries either within the region or the USA: specifically, at least 200,000 departed Venezuela in 2016 alone.[79] Conversely, in Chile, economic growth and political stability since the return to democracy in 1990 have meant fewer Chileans leaving the country while migrants have been attracted to arrive – with the increased immigration being mainly regional.[80]

[67] IOM, *Perfil Migratório do Brasil 2009* (Geneva: IOM, 2010), p. 35.
[68] IOM, *Perfil Migratorio del Perú 2012* (Lima: IOM, 2012), p. 78; Vidal *et al.*, 'Políticas Públicas sobre Migración en Colombia', p. 293.
[69] F. Ramírez and J. Ramírez, *La Estampida Migratoria Ecuatoriana. Crisis, Redes Transnacionales y Repertorios de Acción Migratoria* (Quito: Centro de Investigaciones CIUDAD-UNESCO-ABYA YALA-ALISEI, 2005).
[70] Between 2000 and 2010: IOM, *Perfil Migratorio de Argentina*, p. 43.
[71] To Spain and the USA between 2000 and 2010: Texidó and Gurrieri, *Panorama Migratorio de América del Sur 2012*, p. 27.
[72] Between 2002 and 2008: IOM, *Perfil Migratorio Brasil*, p. 40.
[73] Between 1996 and 2005: M. Cárdenas and C. Mejía, 'Migraciones internacionales en Colombia: ¿Qué sabemos?', Working Paper no. 30, September 2006, CEPAL, p. 7.
[74] To Spain and the USA between 1999 and 2005. S. Bertoli, J. Fernández-Huertas and F. Ortega. 'Immigration Policies and the Ecuadorian Exodus', *The World Bank Economic Review*, 25 (2011), 57–76.
[75] To Spain: IOM, *Perfil Migratorio de Paraguay*, p. 35.
[76] Between 2000 and 2007: IOM, *Perú: Estadísticas de la Migración Internacional de Peruanos, 1990–2007* (Lima: IOM, 2008), p. 21.
[77] Koolhaas *et al.*, 'El Caso de Uruguay', p. 29.
[78] For example, 277,165 South Americans in an irregular situation in Spain were able to regularise their status in 2005. The regularisation most affected, in order, the following nationalities: Ecuadorians, Colombians, Bolivians and Argentineans: see Secretaría de Estado de Inmigración y Emigración, Observatorio Permanente de la Inmigración, *Anuario Estadístico de Inmigración: Año 2005* (Madrid: Ministerio de Trabajo y Asuntos Sociales, 2007), p. 802.
[79] J. Martínez Pizarro and C. Orrego Rivera, *Nuevas Tendencias y Dinámicas Migratorias en América Latina y el Caribe* (Santiago de Chile: CEPAL, 2016), pp. 19–22; Páez, 'Amid Economic Crisis'.
[80] IOM, *Perfil Migratorio de Chile*.

Returnees and New Immigrants, 2005–2015

Following two decades of economic stagnation, South America's growth regenerated in the mid-2000s, mostly due to foreign investment and an export commodities boom.[81] By the end of 2010, at the height of the global economic crisis, the UN praised the region as one of the most dynamic in the world.[82] GDP growth was impressive.[83] Economic performance – coupled with soaring unemployment in destination countries, such as Spain – resulted in unfulfilled expectations for increasing numbers of both returnees and immigrants. Emigration decreased after 2008 but returns were far from massive.[84] For example in Peru, around 30,000 Peruvians returned each year from 2011 to 2013, contrasted with the estimated 2.7 million who emigrated between 1990 and 2013.[85]

The media and some policy makers helped convey an inflated image of what was to be expected. For example, fresh migration flows from Africa, Asia, the Caribbean and Europe – despite being small – were presented as evidence showing that South America was a new global immigration hub. Brazil's position as the sixth-largest economy in the world in 2012, together with its hosting of the World Cup (2014) and Olympic Games (2016), as well as the discovery of important oil reservoirs, led some to conclude that thousands would arrive in search of opportunities in sectors such as engineering.[86] Although some Europeans indeed arrived, it is difficult to define a specific number. At the same time, almost one million nationals originally from Latin America and the Caribbean – mainly from South America – naturalised in a European country between 1998 and 2013, primarily in Spain. Statistics on the return of these new dual nationals have been a major headache for investigators.[87]

Taking advantage of hindsight, statistics offer a more nuanced picture. For instance, whilst in the 1990s the number of immigrants in the region decreased,[88]

---

[81] Bértola and Ocampo, *The Economic Development of Latin America since Independence*, ch. 5.

[82] CEPAL, *Economic Survey of Latin America and the Caribbean 2009–2010: The Distributive Impact of Public Policies* (Santiago de Chile: UN, 2010).

[83] In the best year for each of these countries, their growth was: 14 per cent in Paraguay (2013), 9.4 per cent in Argentina (2010), 8.4 per cent in Peru (2010), 7.8 per cent in Uruguay (2010), 7.8 per cent in Ecuador (2011), 7.5 per cent in Brazil (2010), 6.8 per cent in Bolivia (2013) 6.5 per cent in Colombia (2011), 5.6 per cent in Venezuela (2012) and 5.8 per cent in Chile (2011). World Bank Data, available at http://data.worldbank.org/indicator/NY.GDP.MKTP.KD.ZG

[84] Córdova Alcaraz (ed.), *Dinámicas Migratorias en América Latina*, pp. 71–74; OECD and OAS, *International Migration in the Americas*, pp. 24–30; F. Lozano Ascencio and J. Martínez Pizarro (eds), *Retorno en los Procesos Migratorios de América Latina: Conceptos, Debates, Evidencias* (Rio de Janeiro: ALAP Editor, 2015).

[85] Instituto Nacional de Estadística e Informática, 'Estadísticas de la Migración Internacional en el Perú 1990–2013', December 2014.

[86] The Economist, 'The New New World: Long an Exporter of Talent, Latin America is now Importing it', 6 April 2013.

[87] Córdova Alcaraz (ed.), *Dinámicas Migratorias en América Latina*, pp. 74–75 and 112–122.

[88] They decreased by almost 100,000 from 4,196,669 in 1990 to 4,101,372 in 2000: see UN, *Trends in International Migrant Stock 2015*.

the period 2000–2015 brought an increment of more than 1.5 million.[89] However, in the case of extra-regional immigration, no country received truly significant inflows, with the exception of the considerable number of Haitians who moved to Brazil following the 2010 earthquake in Haiti.[90]

The future of migration flows in South America is uncertain. GDP growth has slowed down over the period 2014–2017, notably with Argentina, Brazil and Venezuela having experienced recessions. Volatile commodity prices have caused economic stress in most countries. It is hard to predict to what extent this will influence migration flows. Nonetheless, we can expect that South American countries will continue to have negative net migration – meaning they have more emigrants abroad than immigrants at home (see Table 1) – with Venezuela becoming an important emigration country.

Actors in South America

A detailed scrutiny of actors in South America reveals a tapestry demonstrating how a rights-based approach and securitisation is laid out in parallel.[91] The former is what Mármora has labelled a 'human development approach to migration'.[92] This entails a certain fatigue with restrictive responses since they are considered to have been largely ineffective in meeting any of their stated objectives. By contrast, securitisation perspectives approach migration as a potential security threat.[93] The human rights-based approach has advanced at a staggering speed, but does not show a clear rupture with the past since it is mixed in with the current 'migration management perspective'. In managing migration, 'human rights would play a central but ambivalent' role given that rights coexist alongside security and control tools. Restrictions include, for instance, visa mechanisms, rejection at the border or possible expulsion on many grounds,[94] what Domenech has labelled a 'policy of control with a human face' in the Argentinean case.[95]

---

[89] The increase was of 1,555,160 from 4,101,372 in 2000 to 5,656,532 by 2015. This jump was valid in all countries except Paraguay and Uruguay. Argentina and Chile received the largest numbers of migrants. In Argentina, the migrant numbers expanded from 1,540,219 in 2000 to 2,086,302 in 2015. In Chile, immigrants numbered 177,332 in 2000, then 469,436 in 2015. See *ibid.*

[90] See Chapter 5, pp. 133–134.

[91] Acosta and Freier, 'Turning the Immigration Policy Paradox Up-side Down?'; A. Margheritis, 'Piecemeal Regional Integration in the Post-Neoliberal Era: Negotiating Migration Policies within Mercosur', *Review of International Political Economy*, 20 (2012), 541–575.

[92] L. Mármora, 'Modelos de Gobernabilidad Migratoria. La Perspectiva Política en América del Sur', *Revista Interdisciplinar da Mobilidade Humana*, 35 (2010), 71–92.

[93] See Chapter 4.

[94] E. Domenech, 'Crónica de una Amenaza Anunciada. Inmigración e "Ilegalidad": Visiones de Estado en la Argentina Contemporánea' in B. Feldman-Bianco *et al.* (eds), *La Construcción Social del Sujeto Migrante en América Latina. Prácticas, Representaciones y Categorías* (Quito: FLACSO, 2011), pp. 31–77, on pp. 66–68.

[95] Domenech, ' "Las Migraciones son como el Agua" ', p. 2.

The International Level

International law renewed its importance in South America with the return to democracy in the 1980s. Newly elected governments hastened to ratify international instruments. Today, South America is the world region with the best ratification record of the nine core international instruments.[96] These include the 1990 UN Convention on the Rights of Migrant Workers (ICMW), ratified by all ten countries except for Brazil, where they have debated whether to sign it, and Venezuela – a signatory that has yet to ratify the instrument. The Committee on Migrant Workers (CMW) thus emerges as an important regional actor.[97] All eight countries have produced one or two reports. Although the Committee's concluding observations show that there is often a considerable gap between the convention's formal ratification and its implementation, the Committee's observations have played a central role in states adopting new legislation such as Peru.[98]

The CMW has recurrently called on South American states to ratify the International Labour Organization's (ILO) migration instruments. However, a mere four countries have ratified Convention 97[99] and only Venezuela has also done so with Convention 143.[100] The ILO has also been an important, but subtle, actor. For example, some of the migration agreements adopted in the

---

[96] We refer to the 1965 International Convention on the Elimination of All Forms of Racial Discrimination (ICERD) (which entered into force in 1969 and was ratified by all ten countries out of the 177 countries in total); the 1966 International Covenant on Civil and Political Rights (ICCPR) (entered into force in 1976, ratified by all, out of 168 in total); the 1966 International Covenant on Economic, Social and Cultural Rights (ICESCR) (entered into force in 1976, ratified by all, out of 164); the 1979 Convention on the Elimination of all Forms of Discrimination against Women (CEDAW) (entered into force in 1981, ratified by all, out of 189); the 1984 Convention against Torture and Other Cruel, Inhuman or Degrading Treatment or Punishment (entered into force in 1987, ratified by all, out of 159); the 1989 Convention on the Rights of the Child (CRC) (entered into force in 1990, ratified by all, out of 196); the 2006 International Convention for the Protection of all Persons from Enforced Disappearance (ICPPED) (entered into force in 2010, ratified by all except Venezuela, which has only signed it, out of 52 state parties); and the 2006 Convention on the Rights of Persons with Disabilities (CRPD) (entered into force in 2008, ratified by all, out of 166 countries).

[97] Participating countries are required to submit reports to the CMW one year after acceding and every five years thereafter. The Committee then proposes recommendations and observations regarding the correct implementation of the convention at the national level, which then feeds into the national legislative frameworks and, in theory, leads to their amendment.

[98] L. Izaguirre, E. Busse, and T. Vásquez, 'Discursos en Tensión y Oportunidades de Cambio: la Nueva Ley de Migraciones en Perú' in J. Ramírez (ed.), *Migración, Estado y Políticas. Cambios y Continuidades en América del Sur* (La Paz: Vicepresidencia del Estado Plurinacional de Bolivia-CELAG, 2017), pp. 153–178.

[99] ILO Migration for Employment Convention, 1949 (no. 97): Brazil, Ecuador, Uruguay and Venezuela.

[100] ILO Migrant Workers (Supplementary Provisions) Convention, 1975 (no. 143): even if not directly addressed to migrants, it is notable that, as of 1 June 2017, seven out of the twenty-four state parties within the Domestic Workers Convention are in our sample. All ten except for Brazil, Peru and Venezuela have ratified the convention (Brazil ratified it in early 2018 but it will only enter force on 31 January 2019). ILO Domestic Workers Convention, 2011 (no. 189).

1990s, such as the ones between Argentina and Bolivia or Peru, were inspired by its template used for bilateral treaties.[101] When it comes to labour mobility, the ILO's technical assistance has also been important at both the MERCOSUR and CAN levels.[102]

The Organisation of American States (OAS) must of course be included as an actor in the region. Beyond the multilateral dialogue in various commissions,[103] the OAS's importance centres around the Inter-American Commission on Human Rights (IACHR) and the IACtHR. Both institutions promote and protect the inter-American human rights system: this includes the American Declaration of the Rights and Duties of Man (American Declaration)[104] and the ACHR.[105] The IACHR was created in 1959 and is composed of seven independent members. Its work rests on an individual petition system, monitoring individual countries and paying attention to priority thematic areas. Since 1996, a special rapporteurship exists regarding the rights of migrants. This mandate was extended in 2012 to cover all situations involving human mobility at both the domestic and international level. In turn, the IACtHR had its first hearing in 1979 and comprises seven judges.[106] The Commission itself or a state party may refer cases to the Court. Individual citizens can only address a petition to the Commission. A case can reach the Court only after the friendly settlement procedure before the Commission fails. The Court also has advisory jurisdiction and has produced notable opinions on migration. Both the Court and the Commission have advanced migrant rights within the region.[107]

The Regional Level

Since the turn of the century, the number of institutions dealing with migration and mobility has proliferated. The South American Conference on Migration (SACM) has been central in setting the agenda. This is a regional consultative process, serving as a space for the exchange of ideas and information, where governments can reach common positions in a non-binding forum.[108] Its work has put regional

---

[101] ILO Migration for Employment Recommendation (Revised), 1949 (No. 86): see E. Geronimi, *Acuerdos Bilaterales de Migración de Mano de Obra: Modo de Empleo* (Geneva: ILO, 2004), p. 21.

[102] A. Alfonso, *Integración y Migraciones: El Tratamiento de la Variable Migratoria en el MERCOSUR y su Incidencia en la Política Argentina* (Buenos Aires: IOM, 2012), p. 35.

[103] Since 2012 there has been a permanent Commission on migration. Other important institutions include the General Secretariat, the Rapporteurship on the Rights of Migrants, and the Continuous Reporting System on International Migration in the Americas (SICREMI, in its acronym in Spanish). For a complete list, see: www.oas.org/en/topics/migration.asp

[104] Also known as the Bogotá Declaration, or Charter of the OAE, 30 April 1948.

[105] Adopted in 1969 but entered into force in 1978. All ten countries have ratified it but Venezuela denounced it in 2012.

[106] All ten states have acknowledged the Court's contentious jurisdiction. However, Venezuela denounced the American Convention on Human Rights on 10 September 2013.

[107] See Chapters 5 and 6.

[108] V. Finn, C. Doña Reveco and M. Feddersen, 'The South American Conference on Migration: A Regional Approach to Migration Governance', unpublished paper, 2017.

migration on the agenda and led to building consensus around common interests, as seen through all Member States signing the SACM's final declarations.[109] The International Organization for Migration (IOM) serves as the SACM's secretariat, and constitutes a vital source of knowledge and expertise informing policies and laws in all ten countries.

At the MERCOSUR level,[110] since 2003 the Migration Forum has reunited the Interior Ministers of all MERCOSUR and associate states. The Forum's resolutions are adopted by consensus and can then potentially become binding instruments for ratification. With regard to CAN,[111] the Andean Migration Forum (AMF) was established in 2008 and aims to strengthen discussions between government representatives, civil society and academics. In turn, unlike the AMF, the Andean Committee of Migration Authorities is part of the Andean system of integration. Its recommendations then feed up to the two institutions with legislative capacity: the Commission and the Andean Council of Ministers of Foreign Affairs. The Andean Committee of Migration Authorities has had the Forum's proposal for a new Andean Migration Statute under discussion since 2013.[112]

Three newer organisations must be briefly mentioned. UNASUR, created in 2008, positioned migration at the core of its *raison d'être*, through its founding treaty promising to aim to establish a regional citizenship.[113] Under this motivated framework, a South American citizenship working group adopted a conceptual report, which UNASUR's Council of Foreign Ministers approved in 2014, but later developments then lost momentum.[114] Second, the Pacific Alliance aims to progressively establish an area with free circulation of goods, services, capital and people.[115] With that purpose, it has facilitated short-term

---

[109] A precedent to the first SACM is the South American meeting on migration, integration and development that took place in Lima in 1999.

[110] MERCOSUR is a regional organisation that was established with the 1991 Asunción Treaty. Its original goal was to constitute a common market by the end of 1994, which would have implied the free circulations of goods, services and factors of production. This was never achieved. Its current Member States are Argentina, Bolivia, Brazil, Paraguay and Uruguay. Venezuela has been suspended since 2016 and Bolivia is still, at the time of writing in October 2017, in the process of fully joining the organisation. The remaining six South American countries are all Associate States and may ratify international treaties adopted under the MERCOSUR framework.

[111] The Andean Community is a regional organisation, established by the Treaty of Cartagena in 1969. Its main objective has been to promote development, better standards of living for residents and accelerate growth through economic integration, with the final aim of establishing a common market. This last goal has not yet been reached. Its current members are Bolivia, Colombia, Ecuador and Peru. Chile and Venezuela left the organisation in 1976 and 2006, respectively.

[112] See Chapter 7, pp. 178–179.

[113] UNASUR is a regional organisation comprising all twelve countries in South America. It aims to construct a cultural, economic, social and political space in the region. Its founding 2008 Brasilia Treaty entered into force on 11 March 2011.

[114] UNASUR Resolution 14/2014, Council of Foreign Ministers, Conceptual Report on South American Citizenship.

[115] The Pacific Alliance (*Alianza del Pacífico*) is a trade bloc, created by the Declaration of Lima on 28 April 2011. See also Framework Agreement on the Pacific Alliance, Paranal, Antofagasta

business visits through visa exemption agreements[116] and has also worked on certain aspects of reciprocal consular protection and the free movement of labour.[117] Finally, the Community of Latin American and Caribbean States (CELAC) was established in December 2011 as a mechanism of dialogue between the thirty-three Latin American and Caribbean countries.[118] The final declaration from its 2016 meeting of Heads of State and Government included the need to decriminalise migration and adopt a human rights approach – an idea that has advanced in its several migration summits, which have taken place since its inception.[119]

The Domestic Level in South America

Migration politics in South America are multilevel and multi-actor. The fact that adopting legislation at the regional level requires unanimity provides a stronger role for states.[120] To the triad of government, parliament and courts at each domestic level, we must also add non-governmental organisations (NGOs), the Ombudsman, the office of public defence, unions, business groups, migrant organisations and scholars, as well as, more loosely, public opinion. These additions call for some clarifications.

To begin with, there is great variation within most countries between the views of the main ministries involved – mainly those of Foreign Affairs, the Interior and Labour.[121] The fact that Foreign Affairs representatives attend the SACM explains in part its progressive final declarations, compared with the more cautious institutional approach of, for instance, MERCOSUR's Migration Forum in which Ministers of the Interior participate. Labour Ministries have a less significant importance, as exemplified by the fact that all national immigration councils depend on the Ministry of the Interior, with the exception of Brazil.[122] The courts – although not the most central actors – have played an

(Chile), 6 June 2012. Its current members are Chile, Colombia, Mexico and Peru. Both Costa Rica and Panama have expressed interest in joining.

[116] A sub-group of migratory security has been established for this purpose under the Pacific Alliance.

[117] The first meeting of the respective Ministers of Labour took place in 2016. Agencia EFE, 'Analizan Movilidad Laboral en la Alianza del Pacífico', 8 April 2016.

[118] Caracas Declaration establishing CELAC, Caracas, 3 December 2011.

[119] See the Quito Political Declaration, CELAC IV Summit, 27 January 2016.

[120] Unanimity is required in the three most important institutions: MERCOSUR (Art. 37, 1994 Ouro Preto Protocol), CAN (Art. 17, 1969 Cartagena Treaty) and UNASUR (Art. 12, 2008 Brasilia Treaty).

[121] On Brazil, see: C. M. Sbalqueiro Lopes, *Direito de Imigração: o Estatuto do Estrangeiro em uma Perspectiva de Direitos Humanos* (Porto Alegre: Nuria Fabris, 2009); on Chile, R. Faúndez García, 'The Liberal Dilemma and Immigration Policy in Chile' in D. Rivera Salazar (ed.), *Chile: Environmental and Social Issues* (New York: Nova Science Publishers, 2012), pp. 195–234; on Ecuador, J. Ramírez, 'Lo Crudo, lo Cocido y lo Quemado: Etnografía del Proyecto de Ley Orgánica de Movilidad Humana en Ecuador' in Ramírez (ed.),*Migración, Estado y Políticas*, pp. 93–127; on Peru, Izaguirre *et al.*, 'La Nueva Ley de Migraciones en Perú'.

[122] ILO, *La Migración Laboral en América Latina y el Caribe: Diagnóstico, Estrategia y Líneas de Trabajo de la OIT en la Región* (Lima: ILO, 2016), pp. 80–81.

important role in countries such as Argentina, Chile and Colombia.[123] The significance of the Ombudsman, as well as the office of public defence, must also be underlined in certain countries, such as Ecuador and Peru.[124] In turn, civil society has had a varied role: in Argentina, it was an important actor since it took part in the legislative process.[125] This is not reflected at the regional level, where the top-down structure of the policy-making process in MERCOSUR, CAN and UNASUR leave little space to incorporate the views of civil society or other actors.[126]

Furthermore, the proliferation of forums in which migration is debated has led to a dialogue between communities of experts, including civil society representatives and academics. This has resulted in 'the emergence of different ideational constructions of the migration issue' and a greater willingness by some actors 'to embrace rights-based approaches'.[127] This development has been facilitated by the lack of a strong negative counter-narrative from either political parties or public opinion. Regarding the former, there are certainly divergent visions regarding migration, as exemplified by more restrictive approaches during the mandate of conservative leaders Sebastián Piñera in Chile (2010–2014) and Mauricio Macri in Argentina (in power since 2015). Nonetheless, political parties have largely avoided politicising migration or, at least, such politicisation has been less intense than in other regions. Regarding public opinion, it seems to be more receptive towards migration than in other parts of the world. According to a 2015 report, a majority of residents in all South American countries – except Ecuador and Bolivia – approved of immigration levels remaining the same or increasing.[128]

[123] L. García, 'Nueva Política Migratoria Argentina y Derechos de la Movilidad: Implementación y Desafíos de una Política Basada en Derechos Humanos a través de las Acciones ante el Poder Judicial (2004–2010)', PhD Thesis, University of Buenos Aires, 2013.

[124] Ramírez, 'Etnografía del Proyecto de Ley Orgánica de Movilidad Humana en Ecuador'; Izaguirre et al., 'La nueva Ley de Migraciones en Perú'. IOM, El Papel de las Instituciones Nacionales de Derechos Humanos en la Protección de los Derechos de los Migrantes (Buenos Aires: IOM, 2012).

[125] L. Brumat and R. A. Torres, 'La Ley de Migraciones 25.871: Un Caso de Democracia Participativa en Argentina', Estudios Políticos, 46 (2015), 55–77. Civil society has also contributed to advancing migrants' rights in other South American countries: see L. M. Chiarello (ed.), Las Políticas Públicas sobre Migraciones y la Sociedad Civil en América Latina: Los Casos de Argentina, Brasil, Colombia y México (New York: Scalabrini International Migration Network, 2011); L. M. Chiarello (ed.), Las Políticas Públicas sobre Migraciones y la Sociedad Civil en América Latina. Los Casos de Bolivia, Chile, Paraguay y Perú (New York: Scalabrini International Migration Network, 2013).

[126] Margheritis, 'Piecemeal Regional Integration'.

[127] D. Acosta and A. Geddes, 'Transnational Diffusion or Different Models? Regional Approaches to Migration Governance in the European Union and Mercosur', European Journal of Migration and Law, 16 (2014), 19–44, on 37.

[128] In Ecuador and Bolivia, 62 per cent and 51 per cent, respectively, favour decreasing immigration levels: N. Esipova, J. Ray, A. Pugliese, D. Tsabutashvili, F. Laczko and M. Rango, How the World Views Migration (Geneva: IOM, 2015), p. 10. Europe, with great variations between countries, has the most negative view in the world towards immigration, whereas views in the USA are similar to those in Argentina and Brazil.

Debates in South America

As epitomised by the opening quotation that began this chapter, South America has become the world region containing the most open discourse on migration. Examples are abundant.[129] When states united in 2000 at the first SACM, they merely recognised a general concern with human rights protection and the importance of promoting well managed and orderly migration.[130] Afterwards, things evolved rather quickly since the main elements of a human rights-based approach had already formed by 2004.[131] The three main principles under analysis in this book – non-criminalisation, a human right to migrate and open borders – have been progressively defined under the wider umbrella of equal treatment. Reminders of migrants' contributions, the centrality of family reunion and the importance of regularisation have been a consistent part of this discourse. This represents a remarkable shift from the 1990s when, even after the demise of military dictatorships, official discourse remained securitised, restrictive and often openly racist.

The open discourse has not been confined to the regional perspective. Domestically, many governmental actors, including presidents, have referred to migration in a positive light and as part of broader human rights concerns in countries such as Argentina, Brazil, Chile, Ecuador and Uruguay.[132] However, since 2016 the Argentinean government has shifted the discourse towards framing migration in restrictive terms, which has led to an amendment to its migration law.[133] As seen in Chapter 4, the way in which the Macri administration in Argentina equates foreignness with criminality does not require comparison with parallel discourses in Europe or the USA since its roots lie in a long-standing South American tradition.[134]

What has also been repositioned is the figure of the South American emigrant. During the 1990s, 'emigrant communities came to be viewed as economic footholds in developed economies ... [they] were reconceived as a kind of natural resource'.[135] Remittances became a major source of income,

[129] For numerous examples since the early 2000s, see Acosta and Freier, 'Turning the Immigration Policy Paradox Up-side Down?'; L. F. Freier and D. Acosta, 'Beyond Smoke and Mirrors? Discursive Gaps in the Liberalisation of South American Immigration Laws' in Cantor, Freier and Gauci (eds), A Liberal Tide?, pp. 33–56.

[130] Final Declaration, I South American Conference on Migration, Buenos Aires, 18–19 May 2000.

[131] Final Declaration, V South American Conference on Migration, La Paz, Bolivia, 25–26 November 2004. Also see the MERCOSUR Declaration on Migration Principles, Santiago de Chile, 17 May 2004.

[132] Acosta and Freier, 'Turning the Immigration Policy Paradox Up-side Down?'; Freier and Acosta, 'Beyond Smoke and Mirrors?'.

[133] Since 2016, the Chilean opposition has also started a more restrictive discourse, preceding their 2017 presidential elections: see M. V. Espinoza, L. Brumat and A. Geddes, 'Migration Governance in South America: Where is the Region Heading?', blog entry, MIGPROSP, 4 August 2017.

[134] Mauricio Macri has been the Argentinean President since 2015. During his mandate, discourse on immigration has toughened in comparison to his predecessors Nestor and Cristina Kirchner.

[135] P. J. Spiro, At Home in Two Countries: The Past and Future of Dual Citizenship (New York University Press, 2016), p. 89.

whilst emigrants also reduced unemployment rates at home. With faster and cheaper communications, it was now easier to participate from afar in the origin country's economic and political life. Emigrants' rights turned into a type of political capital, or currency, which was reflected in the regional political discourses. South American states developed institutions to court their diaspora in order to assist and protect it, as well as to capture its resources.[136] Numerous laws on dual citizenship and enfranchising nationals abroad testify to this trend, as do stronger reintegration programmes for returnees in all ten countries.[137]

South American governments have been eager to oppose the restrictive immigration policies present in the USA and Europe.[138] South American governments have even committed to reforming their own laws in order to set an example for the kind of treatment they expect for their emigrant nationals abroad. For example, in 2009, all states clearly expressed the need to adopt measures honouring international commitments for migrants' rights: 'guaranteeing migrants inside our region, the same rights that we seek for our nationals in transit and destination countries ... in order to ensure the principles of coherence, equality and non-discrimination'.[139]

Finally, it must be underlined that the regional agenda – which had grown stagnant in its original, purely economic aims – began to introduce social items such as labour rights.[140] These factors played out under a context of South American presidents historically holding rather strong positions regarding integration processes, particularly regional migration management.[141] The constant interaction between government officials and external actors facilitated an elite consensus that then prompted policy transfer and emulation; in some cases, it has even provoked legal transplants. Put differently, the migration narratives that inform policy makers in the region are more positive than compared to Europe, for example.[142] The driving force behind South American integration in the twenty-first century has not simply been the traditional material interests – such as security, economic growth and trade considerations. It has also been ideational factors, for instance, a common history, mutual values and a shared vision for the future.

---

[136] A. Margheritis, *Migration Governance across Regions: State-Diaspora Relations in Latin America-Southern Europe Corridor* (Abingdon: Routledge, 2016).

[137] See Chapter 6, pp. 155–158 and 161–162. Texidó and Gurrieri, *Panorama Migratorio de América del Sur 2012*, pp. 46–47.

[138] Acosta and Freier, 'Turning the Immigration Policy Paradox Up-side Down?'; Acosta, 'Latin American Reactions to the Adoption of the Returns Directive'.

[139] Declaration of the IX South American Conference on Migration, Quito, 2009, para. 5.

[140] See Chapter 7.

[141] Margheritis, 'Piecemeal Regional Integration'.

[142] A. Geddes and M. V. Espinoza, 'Framing Understandings of International Migration: How Governance Actors Make Sense of Migration in Europe and South America' in A. Margheritis (ed.), *Shaping Migration between Europe and Latin America: New Perspectives and Challenges* (London: Institute of Latin American Studies, 2018).

Whilst governmental discourse on migration matters, 'rhetoric is also often highly symbolic, designed to appease different constituents or signal commitment to a particular course of action', and policy practice 'may end up being effectively "decoupled" from such rhetoric'.[143] Discourse is also often a tool that countries use to appear modern, enlightened and advanced. For more than a decade, Argentina was presented as the paradigmatic example of how open law could follow open discourse. Yet in January 2017, the Macri government adopted an Executive Decree amending the law. They replaced it with a much tougher approach towards irregular migration, regularisation and family reunification, as well as limiting numerous guarantees on access to justice.[144] At the time of writing, the Executive Decree had been the subject of an appeal in front of the Argentinian justice on the grounds of unconstitutionality, as well as exhortations to its derogation by the UN Committee Against Torture (CAT) and the IACHR.[145] In contrast, in 2017, Brazil, Ecuador and Peru adopted new, more progressive migrations laws. These constitute excellent examples of the rapidity with which migration and citizenship law evolves, as well as the need to study regional dynamics through a comparative and historical lens.

Both policy makers and a large part of the regional academic community have portrayed South America's approach towards migration and citizenship law as being simultaneously innovative and exceptional. Is this truly the case? This book allows each reader to answer this question by laying out the evidence through a critical, historical and comparative analysis of two hundred years of migration and citizenship laws, focusing on their strengths, weaknesses and contradictions.

Organisation of the Book

Part I of this book, in Chapters 2–4, dives into a rich history to assess the claim of novelty in migration and citizenship laws. We will see how South America's general approach and key legal principles originated in the early nineteenth century, and are linked with the particular circumstances surrounding independence (1810–1826). Part II, in Chapters 5–7, offers a precise and critical account, given through a comparative scrutiny, of the emergent principles of non-criminalisation, the right to migrate as a human right, and open borders. These chapters seek to clarify whether a coherent system truly exists and aim to identify these underpinning principles' shortcomings and opportunities. The book suggests that the South American approach, notwithstanding its inconsistencies, emerges as a distinctive migration and citizenship model. It offers

---

[143] A. Geddes and C. Boswell, *Migration and Mobility in the European Union* (Basingstoke: Palgrave Macmillan, 2011), p. 45.

[144] See Chapters 5–7.

[145] Committee Against Torture, CAT/C/ARG/CO/5–6, 24 May 2017; Buenos Aires Herald, 'IACHR Criticises Government's "Regressive" Immigration Policy', 24 March 2017.

us alternative solutions to common global challenges, but also requires further refinement.

Chapter 2 describes the historical origins of the division between the national and the foreigner in South America. In the early nineteenth century, all the former Spanish possessions in South America as well as Brazil achieved independence. With this freedom, the new countries turned their attention to asserting their statehood by delineating three constitutive elements: government, territory and population. The new governments had to define who would be considered as nationals, citizens and foreigners, and which rights pertained to each category. All the newly established countries were concerned with attracting settlers; from very early on, they introduced constitutional provisions regarding open borders and equal treatment for foreigners. White, male Europeans were the targeted audience of open borders provisions, meant to entice them to settle in territories that were presented as 'empty', of course disregarding the presence of indigenous groups. It was also believed that these migrants could introduce new industries, sciences and arts, as well as contribute to 'whitening' the mixed race populations. Whilst weak statehood came with independence, forming nations was a much longer process, one in which states used migration and citizenship policies as tools to shape the definition of nationhood.

Chapter 3 shifts gears to focus on the legal regulation of the Hispano-American subject. From the early stages after independence, a third figure complicated the national–foreigner divide: the Hispano-American, who was a former Spaniard from the Americas. It was something of a halfway presence: not quite a national, yet never a foreigner. The term 'Hispano-American' was far from a simple discursive artefact. Rather, it represented a legal status enshrined in multilateral conventions, bilateral treaties, national laws and constitutions. Automatic naturalisation, freedom of movement and residence, equal rights, dual nationality and diplomatic protection abroad were all part of an emerging common legal jargon in the nineteenth century. The rationale was to provide Hispano-Americans – arguably those who could be identified as Creoles – with a new common fatherland and the right to freely choose their residence. The nineteenth-century Hispano-American legal figure represents a different form of membership: a level of polity located not at the national level, but at the supranational.

Chapter 4 takes the historical analysis into the twentieth century. From the 1880s onwards, large numbers of migrants finally arrived in South America, mostly in Argentina, Brazil and Uruguay. Faster transatlantic and railway transportation contributed to massive movements of people, as did increasing European demand for both food and other goods, such as rubber during the industrialisation period. Up until 1930, South America was the second-largest recipient of migrants in the world after the USA. Coinciding with the arrival of more foreigners, the 1880s also manifested the early signs of border closures and migration control. Previous free movement and equal treatment provisions gradually deteriorated in favour of restrictions on various ethnic, racial, ideological, moral, physical and economic grounds, ushering in a new era of control. As if constructing a wall, individual bricks representing despised categories of foreigners were slowly but surely stacked up throughout an entire century of legislative and administrative provisions, up until the 1980s. This chapter offers a periodisation to explain how South America legally constructed the foreigner as undesirable. The chapter concludes by explaining how restrictive laws, practices and administrative approaches continue to exert their influence today, paving the way for Part II of the book, which contains analysis of present-day legislation.

Part II begins with a short introduction that serves as a transition from the historical analysis section into present-day legislation. Since the return to democracy, a process known as the new Latin American Constitutionalism has been under way. Procedurally, the new Latin American Constitutionalism is defined by a more democratic constitution-making method open to various actors. At a material level, it involves incorporating extensive catalogues of rights protecting vulnerable groups, such as afro-descendants and indigenous populations, as well as migrants. Regulating foreigners' rights constitutes a component of this new constitutionalism. The emphasis on international and human rights law partly explains the three emergent principles that the following chapters consider.

Chapters 5, 6 and 7 focus on investigating the non-criminalisation of irregular migration, the right to migrate as a human right and open borders. The three principles can be broadly categorised as part of a continuum; in turn, each affects the rights of undocumented migrants, foreigners with a residence permit, and nationals of South American states. The chapters analyse how regional migration and citizenship law legally constructs these three different categories. In comparison, on a global level, South America is pursuing pioneering legislative efforts regarding regularisation, the right to family reunification, as well as regional mobility and citizenship. In particular, the right to migrate as a human right would signify a radical departure from traditional understandings of territorial sovereignty, generally favoured and considered valid since the late nineteenth century. Does the right to migrate challenge the alleged state right to control entry, residence and expulsion of non-nationals? Is it a purely ornamental, or aspirational, provision that actually has few legal implications? Part II is intended to reveal the extent to which the three emerging legal principles hold true in South America, as well as to highlight their strengths, inconsistencies and flaws.

The conclusion in Chapter 8 summarises the main findings of the book and highlights which select findings South America enriches – through confirming, expanding or simply contradicting – in the migration and citizenship literature. This is intended to stimulate further queries to define future research, as well as to spark interest in continued exploration of South America, and other regions around the globe, which the literature has largely ignored. The chapter concludes with final thoughts bridging historical and modern law.

South America is a region that has regulated massive migratory inflows and outflows throughout two centuries. Thus this experience comprises vital lessons for those working with migration at a global level, whether from a historical, sociological, political or legal perspective.

Part I
The Nineteenth and Twentieth Centuries

2

Open Borders in the Nineteenth Century: Constructing the National, the Citizen and the Foreigner

Of what benefit are the extensiveness, the richness, and geographical disposition of America, to us; enslaved as we are? We have numerous and immense regions, unoccupied but by the inhabitants of the forest; but, you prevent man from entering them. If we cultivate the ground, you seize the principal part of the productions of our labour; and by shutting up our ports, you render the finest harbours, and the most extensive rivers in the world, nugatory or useless to us.[1]

Introduction

In the nineteenth century, open borders for people became a reality in South America, but this process was fraught with demographic, economic and racial implications. Open borders was primarily a civilising project in which the agents were to be white, male, productive Europeans. For the early legislators, the ideal migrant populated regions conceived of as empty, brought industries that were needed to participate in global markets and contributed to the whitening of mixed race populations. Similar to the USA, loosening restrictions on human mobility was not a humanistic project but rather a utilitarian one. Nonetheless, there were striking differences to the USA.[2] For instance, South Americans abolished slavery much faster. They granted nationality to all those born – not only to free white persons – within the territory through *ius soli*. Equal civil rights were offered to foreigners, albeit with no political entitlements. And whilst they facilitated naturalisation without any racial discrimination, the offices accessible to naturalised individuals were more restricted. Contrarily, the USA prohibited only the positions of President and Vice-President.

Population was only one aspect of state formation and consolidation. With South American independence in the early nineteenth century from Spain, and in the case of Brazil from Portugal, the map of the region changed dramatically. This shift occurred with staggering speed from 1810 to 1826.[3] Newly

---

[1] W. Burke, *South American Independence: Or, the Emancipation of South America, the Glory and Interest of England* (London: J. Ridgway, 1807), p. 12.

[2] On the USA case, see: Motomura, *Americans in Waiting*.

[3] The remaining Dutch and British territories – present-day Suriname and Guyana – only became independent in the twentieth century. French Guiana continues to be part of French territory.

freed, these ten countries began to assert their statehood and seek nationhood through delineating three constitutive elements: government, territory and population. Whilst independence came with weak statehood, forming nations was a much longer process and an arduous struggle. States used migration and citizenship policies as tools to define nationhood. In parallel, elites asserted and attempted to strengthen statehood in the name of their nascent nations.[4]

A state was first required to possess a public authority in charge of ordering and directing internal and external affairs.[5] This public or political authority was what Vattel labelled as 'sovereignty'. Sovereignty was crucial in his view since only states that were independent and sovereign had rights and were subject to the law of nations.[6] At the time of Vattel's writings in the mid-eighteenth century, sovereignty resided with the monarch or prince.[7] Thereafter sovereignty transferred to the nation due to the French Revolution, the 1789 Declaration of the Rights of Man and the 1791 French Constitution. This model was also adopted in the 1812 Cádiz Constitution, which greatly influenced South American constitutional thought. To enact their sovereignty, the newly liberated countries rapidly embarked on signing various international bilateral agreements, thereby reaffirming their independence while attempting to achieve international recognition.[8]

Second, in regards to territory, it was Simón Bolívar who enunciated the principle of *uti possidetis juris 1810*. The principle established that the new republics should adopt the colonial administrative units that were in place in 1810. This year was presented as the last one of validity of the Spanish decrees. Therefore, this year was used as the departing point to temporarily delimit territorial lines.[9] Even though this principle found its way into many constitutions and treaties, territorial disputes sometimes ended in conflict.[10] Brazil independently rejected the principle; instead, in its bilateral delimitation agreements Brazil favoured *uti possidetis de facto*, by which territorial ownership was grounded on effective possession rather than colonial title.[11]

---

[4] Centeno and Ferraro, 'Republics of the Possible: State Building in Latin America and Spain'.

[5] E. de Vattel, *The Law of Nations or the Principles of Natural Law* (1758), Book 1, Chapter 1, § 1.

[6] *Ibid.*, § 4.

[7] *Ibid.*, Book 1, Chapter 4.

[8] As an example, see the various Peace, Friendship, Navigation and Commerce Conventions signed between Colombia and respectively the USA (Bogotá, 3 October 1824), Netherlands (London, 10 May 1829) and his Majesty the King of the French (Bogotá, 14 November 1832). See also the United Province of the Río de la Plata–Great Britain Treaty of 2 February 1825.

[9] C. A. Parodi, *Politics of South American Boundaries* (Greenwood, Westport, CT: Praeger, 2002), p. 5.

[10] *Ibid.*, pp. 1 and 5. As Parodi explains, of the twenty-five existent territorial borders in South America, eight were marked by major wars, eight by lesser ones and five by some level of violence. Some of these conflicts still affect regional politics, such as the dispute between Bolivia and Chile in the International Court of Justice.

[11] B. García, *The Amazon from an International Law Perspective* (Cambridge University Press, 2011), pp. 53–54.

Finally, there was the matter of population. The fledgling states had to define who they would consider as nationals, citizens and foreigners, as well as the rights that pertained to each category. In each territory, the classifications would have consequences for the particular conception and construction of the nation, national sentiment and national identity. In other words, they needed to settle who was going to be admitted into the body of the polity, who would be entitled to rights and who would be subject to obligations. At least four central elements were at stake: original acquisition of nationality; the conditions under which nationals could become citizens in the sense of exercising full rights, including political ones; the requirements that foreigners needed to fulfil to obtain nationality, and their status once naturalised; and the rights of foreigners. A fifth concern, to which Chapter 3 is devoted, related to the legal status of nationals of countries from the former Spanish territories in the Americas. In this chapter, our attention focuses on the first four elements of this conundrum. This examination is important since there is robust historical continuity in the region in the relationship between citizenship, migration and the legal construction of the national and the foreigner, with recent debates often being nothing more than a modern expression of historical discussions.

Birthright Citizenship in South America

After independence and without exception, all the constitutions of the new republics adopted *ius soli* as the automatic route to nationality upon birth in the territory. This choice has proven resilient: all ten countries still automatically award citizenship to persons born in their territory.[12]

When the new constitutions were drafted, it was far from clear that *ius soli* would prove an obvious choice. At that time, *ius sanguinis* was much more prevalent in theory and practice. For example, Vattel argued that 'natives, or natural-born citizens,' were 'those born in the country, of parents who are citizens'. This was understood as a matter of self-preservation and perpetuation for society and the expected order of things, where 'children naturally follow the condition of their fathers, and succeed to all their rights'. Vattel indeed mentioned England as one of the few states where 'the single circumstance of being born in the country naturalizes the children of a foreigner'.[13] In contrast, France had included a form of *ius soli* in its 1791 constitution[14] but established *ius sanguinis* with its 1804 civil code.[15] Meanwhile in the USA, *ius soli* was only

---

[12] This general rule is only partially breached in Colombia, where *ius domicilii* functions as an additional condition by which one of the parents must be domiciled in the country at the moment of birth. See Chapter 6, pp. 165–166.

[13] De Vattel, *The Law of Nations*, Book 1, Chapter 19, §§ 212 and 214.

[14] France, Art. 2, The Constitution of the 1791 National Assembly, 3 September 1791.

[15] France, 1804 French Civil Code, Book I, Title I, Chapter I, Of the Enjoyment and Privation of Civil Rights, § 9.

available to free white men until after the Civil War when the 1868 Fourteenth Amendment extended it to African Americans.[16]

Why did the new South American states opt for *ius soli*? Some authors argue that it was the result of an emphasis on 'national territory rather than natural belonging or ethnicity'.[17] Others cite the need to populate large territories, as reflected in the countries' subsequent immigration traditions.[18] Whilst such explanations help us understand why *ius soli* continues to apply after two centuries,[19] they miss the point as to why the South American states originally enshrined this principle in their earlier constitutions.

The Influence of the 1812 Cádiz Constitution

The Spanish 1812 constitution played a crucial role in the legal construction of the national and the foreigner, serving as a model that the new republics and Brazil followed almost verbatim in various aspects. The Cádiz Constitution, as the 1812 text is known, was one of the first national constitutions to achieve global influence and an advanced articulation of the traits a modern state should possess.[20] The particular circumstances in which it was drafted, with most Spanish territory occupied by Napoleonic troops, contributed to a liberal product whose prestige soon extended to Europe and the Americas.[21] The constitution was in force in large parts, although not all, of the pre-independent American territories.[22] Importantly, the constitution had been drafted by elected representatives from both European Spain and the Americas, since sixty-three 'Americans' participated in the *Cortes* (representative body) legislative term between 1810 and 1813.[23] The text was thus the most prominent document readily available when the new independent countries drafted their own constitutions.[24]

The Cádiz text clearly set out that the Spanish nation comprised Spaniards from both hemispheres and was free, independent and sovereign. A clear

---

[16] The recognition of Asians and Native Americans as citizens took even longer; see Motomura, *Americans in Waiting*, pp. 72–73.

[17] O. Vonk, *Nationality Law in the Western Hemisphere: A Study of Grounds for Acquisition and Loss of Citizenship in the Americas and the Caribbean* (Leiden: Martinus Nijhoff, 2014), p. 19.

[18] *Ibid.*, p. 9; R. Brubaker, *Citizenship and Nationhood in France and Germany* (Cambridge: Harvard University Press, 1992), p. 33.

[19] For instance, in the case of Colombia, where *ius soli* has no longer been automatic since its 1886 Constitution, Escobar presents low immigration levels as a possible explanation for this unique regulation in South America. Escobar, *Report on Citizenship Law: Colombia*, p. 16.

[20] M. C. Mirow, *Latin American Constitutions. The Constitution of Cádiz and its Legacy in Spanish America* (Cambridge University Press, 2015).

[21] J. A. Escudero López (ed.), *Cortes y Constitución de Cádiz. 200 años* (Madrid: Espasa Calpe, 2011).

[22] R. Gargarella, *Latin American Constitutionalism, 1810–2010: The Engine Room of the Constitution* (Oxford University Press, 2013), p. 17.

[23] M. T. Berruezo, *La Participación Americana en las Cortes de Cádiz. 1810–1814* (Madrid: Centro de Estudios Constitucionales, 1986), p. 3.

[24] Mirow, *Latin American Constitutions. The Constitution of Cádiz*.

political project lay behind this ground-breaking and plural vision of the nation. Beyond equality between the residents of both continents, the central idea was to reconfigure the whole system by transforming the previous colonial society into a homogeneous one, 'united by common political and economic interests' and therefore capable of 'facing a collective national destiny'.[25]

This inclusive understanding of the nation incorporating as equals Spaniards from both hemispheres – from the motherland and its colonies – opened crucial membership questions. To begin with, who would actually be considered a Spaniard? It must be remembered that this was a constitution for a large empire, the future of which was far from secure since the French occupation of the peninsula in 1808 spurred the hopes of several emancipatory movements. Creole elites despised centralism and the preeminence of *peninsulares*[26] in official positions and were eager to liberalise economic trade.[27] In this context, the American members of the Cádiz parliament advocated equality with those born in the peninsula. Any other prospect would have been unthinkable and rejected.[28] Those born in both hemispheres – including American Spaniards, who were *peninsulares*' descendants, also called Creoles – had to have equal status.

The discussions rather turned around the position of indigenous and African origin populations. This was not an ethical debate but rather was based on the political power of numbers. Each member of the *Cortes* was elected by 70,000 naturals[29] and American representatives were all too aware of it.[30] To maintain their preeminence in Congress, the European Spanish representatives pleaded against the inclusion of indigenous and *mestizo* communities in the electoral census,[31] arguing that they were backward and easily manipulated by Creole ruling classes.[32] This exclusion was rejected following opposition by the American group. However, when discussing the status of African descendants, the American block was split. Some Americans, such as the representative from Havana, disapproved of their inclusion, reflecting the prejudices of white oligarchies. Europeans also resisted their incorporation not only because of the aforementioned representation issues, but also because of the fear aroused by

---

[25] M. L. Rieu-Millan, *Los Diputados Americanos en las Cortes de Cádiz* (Madrid: Consejo Superior de Investigaciones Científicas, 1990), p. 173.

[26] The term *peninsulares* refers to Spaniards born in the European part of the Empire in the Iberian Peninsula.

[27] Berruezo, *La Participación Americana en las Cortes de Cádiz*, p. 12.

[28] This equality was already established in the Decree of 15 October 1810 on the Equality of Rights between Europeans and overseas Spaniards.

[29] Naturals, or natural-born individuals, included women and children in Europe, although they were not entitled to vote. In the Spanish America, it did not include *castas* (any individual of African descent on either maternal or paternal side). Mirow, *Latin American Constitutions*, pp. 97–99.

[30] See Arts 29 and 31, 1812 Cádiz Constitution.

[31] Mestizos were those individuals of mixed race, especially the offspring of a Spaniard and an American Indian.

[32] Rieu-Millan, *Los Diputados Americanos en las Cortes de Cádiz*, p. 173; also see pp. 111–117.

the Saint-Domingue black slaves revolution and Haiti's subsequent 1804 declaration of independence.[33] The final compromise was an *ad hoc* status by which African descendants were considered part of the nation, but generally not as citizens. This compromise – being inclusive of indigenous and *mestizos* but excluding all those with any African ancestry[34] – meant the populations, and thus the number of representatives, from the peninsula and the American provinces remained almost equivalent.[35] Finally, the constitution did not truly address the position of slaves although those who obtained their freedom were to be included as part of the nation, and therefore as Spaniards.[36] Political pragmatism meant that even those opposing slavery accepted leaving the issue untouched in order 'to maintain union within the Spanish monarchy',[37] in line with the interests of American deputies representing regions highly dependent on slave labour, particularly Cuba.

In conclusion, discussions regarding both indigenous peoples and African descendants related primarily to representational concerns rather than to ethical questions of inclusion or exclusion in the polity. At stake was an ongoing process of collective homogenisation, by which these groups were valued to the extent that they could serve the interests of both a new society and the reconfigured colonial system.[38] The preference for *ius soli* and the distinction between nationals and citizens is best understood considering this background. Civil rights and obligations were granted to all male nationals, to the full body of the nation comprising Spaniards from both hemispheres. Per contra, the status of citizen, understood as the holder of political rights, remained confined to a smaller category of nationals, thus allowing for a gradual transformation of society rather than a radical rupture to the established order.[39]

Ius Soli in the Constitutions of the New Republics and Brazil

With independence, *ius soli* became enshrined in all the South American constitutions. It was granted to all freemen born in the territory, including both indigenous and African descendant populations, but excluding slaves.[40]

---

[33] *Ibid.*, pp. 146–168. On the Haitian Revolution and Toussaint L'Ouverture see C. L. R. James, *The Black Jacobins* (London: Penguin Books, 2001).

[34] At the time the term that was used to refer to individuals of mixed white and black ancestry was 'mulattos'.

[35] Rieu-Millan, *Los Diputados Americanos en las Cortes de Cádiz*, p. 278.

[36] *Ibid.*, pp. 168–172.

[37] M. C. Mirow, 'Visions of Cádiz: The Constitution of 1812 in Historical and Constitutional Thought', *Law, Politics and Society*, 53 (2010), pp. 59–88, on pp. 75–76.

[38] Rieu-Millan, *Los Diputados Americanos en las Cortes de Cádiz*, p. 173.

[39] H. Sabato, 'On Political Citizenship in Nineteenth-Century Latin America', *American Historical Review*, 106 (2001), pp. 1290–1315.

[40] This was different in the USA case since neither indigenous nor African-descent populations obtained nationality. See E. Román, *Citizenship and its Exclusions. A Classical, Constitutional, and Critical Race Critique* (New York University Press, 2010).

Following what had occurred in Haiti,[41] slavery was also soon abolished in most states as a result of the new constitutional order.[42] *Ius soli* was not simply consequential with equality advocated by American representatives in Cádiz. Rather, it was the best means to create 'citizens out of colonial subjects' and to forge 'national communities from colonial societies marked by stark social divisions'.[43] Following the Cádiz model, sovereignty now resided in the nation.[44] Elites eagerly proclaimed the end of racial discrimination and the integration of Indians and blacks as nationals.[45] As San Martín, liberator of Peru, decreed in 1821: 'in the future the aborigines shall not be called Indians or natives; they are children and *citizens* of Peru and they shall be known as Peruvians'.[46] *Ius soli* was thus a principle well suited for new, still politically fragile, states that were in a process of national construction and assertion over their territories and populations, although blacks and Indians were discriminated against in various ways, as will be seen below. Moreover, *ius soli* was not only an inclusive enterprise but also served the purpose of rejecting those born in the peninsula, and who could be expected to oppose independence.[47] Thus in chronological

---

[41] On this, see A. Ferrer, 'Haiti, Free Soil, and Antislavery in the Revolutionary Atlantic', *American Historical Review*, 117 (2012), pp. 40–66.

[42] See Peru, Art. 11, 1823 Constitution; Bolivia, Art. 11(5), 1826 Constitution; Argentina, Art. 181, 1826 Constitution; Uruguay, Art. 131, 1830 Constitution; Chile, Art. 132, 1833 Constitution; Paraguay, Art. 25, 1870 Constitution. In the case of Colombia this only took place with its third Constitution, that of Nueva Granada in 1832, Art. 5(6). In Ecuador, abolition occurred in 1851 by means of a Decree of 25 July. In Venezuela, slavery was abolished with the adoption of a Decree on 24 March 1854. In Brazil, slavery was abolished only with the adoption of the *Lei Áurea* on 13 May 1888.

[43] N. P. Appelbaum, A. S. Macpherson and K. A. Rosemblatt, 'Introduction. Racial Nations' in N. P. Appelbaum, A. S. Macpherson and K. Alejandra Rosemblatt (eds), *Race and Nation in Modern Latin America* (Chapel Hill, NC: University of North Carolina Press, 2003) pp. 1–31, on p. 4.

[44] 1819 Venezuelan Constitution, Preamble, Art. 3 and Title III, Section I, Art. 2; 1821 Colombian Constitution, Arts 1–2; 1822 Chilean Constitution, Arts 1–2; 1823 Peruvian Constitution, Arts 1–3; 1824 Brazilian Constitution, Arts 1 and 12; 1826 Bolivian Constitution, Arts 1–2 and 8; 1826 Argentinian Constitution, Arts 1–2 and 8; 1830 Uruguayan Constitution, Arts 1–4; 1830 Ecuadorian Constitution, Art. 2. This is even clearer in the 1835 Ecuadorian Constitution, Arts 1–2; 1870 Paraguayan Constitution, Arts 1–2. Some consider the 1844 Paraguayan Political Administration law (Asunción, 16 March 1844) as the first country's constitution. In this chapter, we mostly refer to the 1870 Constitution since it is this second text which included all the provisions on access to citizenship, nationality and the rights of foreigners, which had been absent in the 1844 document. In the Chilean case, there were provisional documents adopted in 1812, 1814 and 1818. The first that can be considered a fully fledged Constitution is the 1822 document that also had the adjective 'provisional' deleted from its title.

[45] Loveman, *National Colors*, pp. 79–80.

[46] Peru, Decree of August 27, 1821, cited in Anderson, *Imagined Communities*, pp. 49–50.

[47] T. Schwarz, 'Políticas de Inmigración en América Latina: El Extranjero Indeseable en las Normas Nacionales, de la Independencia hasta los Años de 1930', *Procesos Revista Ecuatoriana de Historia*, 36 (2012), pp. 39–72, on p. 41. Certainly, reality during the wars of independence was much more complex since Indians, as well as slaves, sometimes 'became allies of the Iberian forces simply because they were directly exploited by the criollos and they feared that independence would exacerbate their servitude'. J. Larrain, *Identity and Modernity in Latin America* (Cambridge: Polity, 2000), p. 71.

order, Venezuela, Colombia, Chile, Peru, Bolivia, Argentina, Uruguay, Ecuador and Paraguay adopted *ius soli*.[48]

Finally, and perhaps surprisingly, Brazil's first 1824 Constitution was also similar to those of the former Spanish territories. It too adopted *ius soli*[49] even though the 1822 Portuguese Constitution, which had been in force in Brazil, only recognised *ius sanguinis*.[50] The Cádiz Constitution was well known in Brazil and had been sworn in and published by decree by D. João VI in Rio de Janeiro – the then capital of the Kingdom – on 21 April 1821, although he decided to revoke it the day after.[51] The 1812 Constitution had also served as one of the models for the Portuguese text of 1822.[52] Thus *ius soli* was favoured, although it excluded slaves, who represented a quarter of Brazil's population at the time of independence.[53]

A peculiarity of the Brazilian case was that it included as part of the nation those who resided in Brazil when it became independent but who had been born in Portugal or in Portuguese possessions.[54] This was a product of Brazil's friendlier independence settlement with Portugal, compared to the Spanish case.[55] Some of the new republics also considered both those who were loyal to the Creoles' cause and resident in their territory as nationals.[56] Unlike in Brazil, this was worded in a general manner and not addressed to Spaniards in particular, although it was obvious that they would benefit the most.

One final issue is worth mentioning. Whereas *ius soli* prevailed, *ius sanguinis*, in a legislative forward-looking process, was not neglected. Access to nationality for those born outside the territory was included in all the initial constitutions of the ten new countries.[57] In most cases, nationality was

---

[48] Venezuela, Title III, Arts 1–4, 1819 Constitution. This is even clearer in Art. 10(1) of the 1830 Venezuelan Constitution promulgated after the separation from Gran Colombia; Colombia, Art. 4, 1821 Constitution; Chile, Art. 4, 1822 Constitution; Peru, Art. 10, 1823 Constitution; Bolivia, Art. 11, 1826 Constitution; Argentina, Art. 4, 1826 Constitution. This last constitution was short-lived and access to citizenship was not regulated in the 1853 Constitution but rather by the 1857 citizenship law, which enshrined territorial birthright citizenship (Argentina, Citizenship Law 145, Buenos Aires, 7 October 1857); Uruguay, Art. 7, 1830 Constitution; Ecuador, Art. 9, 1830 Constitution; Paraguay, Art. 35, 1870 Constitution.

[49] Brazil, Art. 6, 1824 Constitution.

[50] Portugal, Art. 21, 1822 Constitution. This was possibly the result of the influence of the 1804 French Civil Code.

[51] On this, see V. de Paulo Barreto and V. Pimentel Pereira, '¡Viva la Pepa!: A História não Contada da Constitución Española de 1812 em Terras Brasileiras', *Revista do Instituto Histórico e Geográfico do Brasil*, 452 (2011), pp. 201–223.

[52] M. H. Saboia Bezerra, 'A Constituição de Cádiz de 1812', *Revista de Informação Legislativa*, 198 (2013), pp. 89–112.

[53] Sacchetta, *Laços de Sangue*, p. 60.

[54] Brazil, Art. 6, 1824 Constitution.

[55] On this, see Sacchetta, *Laços de Sangue*, especially the Introduction and Chapter 1.

[56] Colombia, Art. 4(2), 1821 Constitution; Argentina, Art. 4, 1826 Constitution; Uruguay, Art. 8, 1830 Constitution, which added a further criteria: to have a child born in the territory; Venezuela, Art. 11, 1830 Constitution.

[57] Colombia, Art. 4, 1821 Constitution; Chile, Art. 4(2), 1822 Constitution; Peru, Art. 10(2), 1823 Constitution; Brazil, Art. 6(2), 1824 Constitution; Bolivia, Art. 11(2), 1826 Constitution;

passed on by either parent. This is a remarkable early form of gender neutrality at a time when many nationality laws, including the Cádiz Constitution, only applied *ius sanguinis ex patre*.[58] It preceded by more than a century a provision in the 1979 UN CEDAW.[59]

Nationals and Citizens in the New Order

Nationality and citizenship are sometimes used as synonyms. However, the word citizenship may have different meanings depending on whether it is formal, understood as membership of the state or nation, or substantive, interpreted as the possession of rights and duties.[60] This conceptualisation of multiple forms of citizenship is apparent in the changing forms of electoral franchise with, for example, women having been denied equal voting rights for decades.[61]

The French Revolution, and its 1791 Constitution, introduced a crucial distinction between *citoyens français* and *citoyens actifs*. As explained by Brubaker, '[t]hrough this distinction, the Constituent Assembly aimed to combine a universalist, egalitarian civil citizenship with a graded scheme of political citizenship'.[62] This later developed into the orthodox distinction between nationality and citizenship, the former indicating a legal bond between the state and the individual, the latter adding political rights to that bond.[63] Thus, under the classical definition of the components of citizenship as membership of a political community, rights and benefits deriving from that membership and, finally, political participation in the development of the community;[64] the first two pertained to nationals, or *citoyens*, whereas the third was only available to citizens or *citoyens actifs*. This division made its way into the Cádiz Constitution and the question of who should enjoy political rights was fiercely battled over, later affecting the new states in South America.

Argentina, Art. 4, 1826 Constitution; Uruguay, Art. 8, 1830 Constitution; Ecuador, Art. 9, 1830 Constitution; Paraguay, Art. 35, 1870 Constitution. The only exception is Venezuela, which included this possibility in Art. 10 of its 1830 Supreme norm rather than in the first one of 1819.

[58] This was the case for all the countries' first constitutions, except in the cases of Colombia and Venezuela. For these two countries, the principle of *ius sanguinis* as deriving also from the mother's line came only in their second constitutions in 1830. Argentina included this provision in its first 1857 Citizenship Law.

[59] Art. 9(2) of the CEDAW reads: 'States Parties shall grant women equal rights with men with respect to the nationality of their children.'

[60] Hammar, *Democracy and the Nation State*, p. 3.

[61] W. Maas, 'Equality and the Free Movement of People: Citizenship and Internal Migration' in W. Maas (ed.), *Democratic Citizenship and the Free Movement of People* (Leiden: Martinus Nijhoff, 2013), pp. 9–30, on p. 14.

[62] Brubaker, *Citizenship and Nationhood in France and Germany*, p. 87.

[63] Vonk, *Nationality Law in the Western Hemisphere*, p. 25.

[64] R. Bauböck, 'Recombinant Citizenship' in M. Kohli and A. Woodward (eds), *Inclusions and Exclusions in European Societies* (London: Routledge, 2001), pp. 38–58.

The Influence of the 1812 Cádiz Constitution

The Cádiz Constitution followed the then French tradition and distinguished between 'Spaniards' and 'Spanish citizens'. Spaniards were all those freemen born and settled in the *dominios de las Españas* (literally the dominions of the various 'Spains', thus comprising the Americas and the Philippines), as well as their offspring, thereby also including *ius sanguinis ex patre* for the first generation living abroad. This encompassed indigenous communities, mestizos, Spaniards with African ancestry but excluded women and slaves.[65] Being a Spaniard, a national, carried the obligations of loyalty to the Constitution and the law, love for the homeland, payment of taxes and, most importantly, conscription.[66] As a counterbalance, it also brought the enjoyment of civil rights.[67]

However, only citizens had access to municipal employment and to the political rights of representation and voting.[68] Citizens were those who, being Spaniards, and residing in Spanish territory, were descendants (on both sides) from individuals from the Spanish dominions in either hemisphere.[69] In other words, while nationality was mainly obtained through *ius soli*, citizenship involved *ius sanguinis*. The first people immediately excluded by this definition were those with 'African blood', even if African ascendancy was found several generations earlier. In the minds of colonial officials, 'the "stain" of African origins (was) indelible'.[70] They were barred from exercising political rights, as well as excluded from the calculation of population that formed the basis for proportional representation in a territory. The concept of African origin excluded all those who had any 'mixed' element in their ascending lines, whether *peninsulares*, Creoles or indigenous. Indeed, the representational base only included Spaniards originally from the Spanish territories in both ascending lines, as well as foreigners who had become citizens.[71] As previously argued, debates on membership, here understood as enjoying full political rights, were spurred by both ideological concerns and more immediate representational anxieties. European Spanish deputies feared that the addition of African descendants to the representational base would lead to American Creoles becoming the masters of the monarchy's destiny, the Americas being slightly more populous than the European part.[72]

---

[65] The term freemen could lead to discussion as to whether it was a way to refer to humans. Scholars analysing Art. 5, the parliamentary debates and the general structure of the 1812 Constitution have denied that. Therefore, women were neither citizens nor nationals. See: I. Castells Oliván and E. Fernández García, 'Las Mujeres y el Primer Constitucionalismo Español (1810–1823)', *Historia Constitucional*, 9 (2008), 163–180.

[66] Spain, Arts 6–9, 339 and 361, 1812 Cádiz Constitution.

[67] See for example Arts 247, 280, 287 regarding access to justice, 306 on security of property and 371 on freedom of expression, 1812 Cádiz Constitution.

[68] See, among others, Arts 23, 27, 29, 35, 45, 313, 317 and 330, 1812 Cádiz Constitution.

[69] Art. 18, 1812 Cádiz Constitution.

[70] Loveman, *National Colors*, p. 62.

[71] Art. 29, 1812 Cádiz Constitution.

[72] Rieu-Millan, *Los Diputados Americanos*, p. 278.

The distinction between civil rights, available to all male freeborn Spaniards regardless of their race or social origin, and political rights, enjoyed only by those who were 'recognized as being intellectually capable of participating in the *res publica*',[73] made the enumeration of the circumstances under which the latter could be lost or suspended even more relevant. Citizenship was lost if one naturalised in another country or accepted employment from another government.[74] Citizenship rights could be suspended if an individual was a bankrupt debtor, a domestic servant, had an unknown employment status or when there was a judicial interdiction due to moral or physical incapacity. A literacy requirement was supposed to be introduced in 1830 but never was.[75] The minimum age to exercise citizenship was set at twenty-one years old for voting and twenty-five for being elected.[76] Women were always disqualified from being considered citizens.

Thus citizenship, in contrast to nationality, was a much more limited privilege from which several groups based on origin, gender, social background or wealth were debarred. It was also discriminatory on grounds of race. Freedmen, who would have been mostly former black slaves, could become Spaniards if they had obtained freedom within the territory. Thus, any free African descendant was immediately considered as a Spaniard upon birth in the territory and capable of enjoying the same civil rights and carrying out the same duties as the rest of the nation. They could also become citizens if Parliament granted them a citizenship charter under certain conditions, namely that they had performed services for the homeland, were distinguished by their talent, application and conduct, were born from legitimate wedlock, were married, resided in the territory and performed a profession, trade or useful industry with their own capital.[77] In brief, to become a citizen, the African Spaniard needed to be a paragon of virtue. The ideal citizen was a prosperous independent active worker, was literate, free from 'African blood' and male. This representation also made its way into the Americas.

Nationals and Citizens in the Constitutions of the New Republics and Brazil

The same distinction between passive citizens, usually called nationals, and full citizens, labelled with terms such as *sufragante*, *elector* or *ciudadano activo*, was enshrined in all of the first South American constitutions, along with the various exclusions limiting access to full citizenship.[78] The same held true regarding the

---

[73] J. Varela Suanzes-Carpegna, 'Propiedad, Ciudadanía y Sufragio en el Constitucionalismo Español (1810–1845)', *Historia Constitucional*, 6 (2005), 105–123, on 106.

[74] Art. 24, 1812 Cádiz Constitution. It could also be lost by judicial sentence and by residing for five years outside Spanish territory without a government licence.

[75] Arts 24 and 25, 1812 Cádiz Constitution.

[76] See Arts 21, 45, 75, 91, 251, 317 and 330, 1812 Cádiz Constitution.

[77] Art. 22, 1812 Cádiz Constitution.

[78] Some countries did not make such a distinction and labelled both as citizens. However, they included several conditions that needed to be satisfied in order to access political rights and

duties and civil rights coupled with nationality, the political rights for citizens and, lastly, the suspension and loss of citizenship. This was the case, in chronological order, in Venezuela, Colombia, Chile, Peru, Brazil, Bolivia, Argentina, Uruguay, Ecuador and Paraguay.[79]

The image of the ideal citizen closely followed what had been established in Cádiz. The qualities of the citizen were described in 'racialized and gendered terms'.[80] The holder of political rights had to be male, literate, married and individually autonomous either through property, trade, capital or independent profession. Only these men were 'deemed to have "civic virtue"; only they were capable of self-government; and only they accrued equal rights'.[81] This clearly excluded large segments of the population, most immediately women, unmarried people and those younger than the age of majority (usually twenty-one or twenty-five years old). Criminals, the insane and debtors were also rejected. Finally, domestic servants or farm workers were not encompassed either. Thus, whereas the nation was inclusively defined through *ius soli*, the political sphere remained reserved for a minority. Discrimination certainly did not end with independence.[82] Whilst both indigenous communities and African-descent populations were incorporated into the nation, their rights were often violated. When it came to political voice, Creole elites continued to hold sway.[83] This understanding of the nation, with white elites of European origin holding a dominant role, greatly influenced immigration and naturalisation policies.

Naturalisation of Foreigners

With naturalisation, the rite of passage from foreigner to national citizen is, in principle, complete. The new citizen should in theory enjoy full political rights and equal treatment to those who acquired citizenship by birth. Today, naturalisation is mainly understood as a process by which the individual accesses further rights. Historically, military service or obligatory conscription worked

---

thus full citizenship. These countries were Argentina, Brazil, Paraguay and Uruguay. In the case of Uruguay, foreigners can never become nationals but only legal citizens since there is no legal route to naturalise. See A. Margheritis, 'Report on Citizenship Law: Uruguay', European University Institute, EUDO Citizenship, Florence, 2015.

[79] Venezuela, Title I Arts 13 and 16, Title III, Arts 1–9, Title IV, Art. 2, Title VI, Sections 2 and 3, 1819 Constitution. Venezuela differentiated between active and passive citizens; Colombia, Arts 4–5, 15–17, 21–22, 156, 178, 1821 Constitution; Chile, Arts 6–9, 14–16, 37, 199, 219, 243, 1822 Constitution; Peru, Arts 10, 15–25, 30, 193–194, 1823 Constitution; Brazil, Arts 6–8, 90–96, 136, 173–179, 1824 Constitution; Bolivia, Arts 11–19, 20, 24, 79, 98, 109, 112, 116, 132, 149, 155, 157, 1826 Constitution; Argentina, Arts 4–6, 13, 15, 24, 69, 152, 166, 1826 Constitution; Uruguay, Arts 6–12, 116, 122, 140, 146, 1830 Constitution; Ecuador, Arts 9–13, 24, 58–59, 64–66, 1830 Constitution; Paraguay, Arts 35–41, 1870 Constitution.

[80] Appelbaum, Macpherson and Rosemblatt, 'Introduction. Racial Nations', p. 4.

[81] *Ibid.*

[82] Loveman, *National Colors*, pp. 80–81.

[83] For example, as late as 1870, out of one million inhabitants in Bolivia, only 20,000 could vote. Mirow, *Latin American Constitutions*, p. 170; See also Larrain, *Identity and Modernity in Latin America*, pp. 70–74.

as a powerful deterrent for foreigners to acquire citizenship. Indeed, Napoleon himself preferred *ius soli*, rather than *ius sanguinis*, as was finally adopted in the 1804 French Civil Code, since 'he was more concerned with the military obligations that could be imposed on citizens than with the civil rights they would enjoy'.[84]

Naturalisation in Spain has been regulated since at least the sixteenth century. Foreigners were forbidden from accessing and trading with the Americas, known as *Las Indias*.[85] Foreigners had only two legal routes to join a hefty business taking place between both continents: obtain a royal licence or naturalise.[86] A third possible route was a sort of regularisation procedure for migrants who had clandestinely settled in the Americas. This was known as *composición* and entailed paying a sum which allowed the individual to naturalise and rightfully remain in *Las Indias*. The Crown's scarcity of funds played a crucial role in its regulation. An early regularisation mechanism was the 1596 Royal Decree, which was applied several times in the following decades.[87] A few years later, in 1608, the requirements for naturalisation were set out in a royal decree, although other informal arrangements had already been in place.[88] The number of naturalisations granted was always extremely low and reflected the zeal with which the Spanish Crown protected its monopoly on trading with the Americas.[89] The Cádiz Constitution echoed these concerns.

The Influence of the 1812 Cádiz Constitution

There were four different categories of people in the Spanish Constitution of 1812: nationals, citizens, African descendants and foreigners who could become Spaniards either by obtaining a naturalisation certificate from the Cortes or by residing in any town for ten years.[90] Once naturalised, the new nationals could become citizens by obtaining a citizenship special charter from Parliament,

---

[84] Brubaker, *Citizenship and Nationhood*, p. 88.

[85] This was forbidden since the beginning of the colonial expansion after the first voyages of Cristobal Colón, and continued in the centuries after through several royal decrees. See, for example, Felipe II Decree, 6 June 1556, establishing the death penalty for those having traded with foreigners: cited in R. H. Zorrilla, *Cambio Social y Población en el Pensamiento de Mayo (1810–1830)* (Buenos Aires: Belgrano, 1978), pp. 26–27. See for an in-depth analysis T. Herzog, *Defining Nations. Immigrants and Citizens in Early Modern Spain and Spanish America* (New Haven, CT: Yale University Press, 2003).

[86] Others preferred to trade through intermediaries or to resort to piracy: see A. Domínguez Ortiz, 'La Concesión de "Naturalezas para Comerciar en Indias" durante el Siglo XVII', *Revista de Indias*, 19 (1959), 227–239.

[87] R. Konetzke, 'Legislación sobre Inmigración de Extranjeros en América durante la Época Colonial', *Revista Internacional de Sociología*, 3 (1945), 269–299.

[88] The requirements can be summarised as having resided for twenty years, ten in some cases, in Spain, being married and possessing a particular amount of wealth in property. Domínguez Ortiz, 'La Concesión de Naturalezas', p. 228.

[89] See *ibid.* for the number of naturalisations in the different periods. For example, during the last quarter of the sixteenth century, only twenty-five foreigners were naturalised.

[90] Art. 5, 1812 Cádiz Constitution.

thereafter enjoying political rights and access to municipal jobs. To qualify for citizenship, marriage to a Spanish woman was required, as well as having completed one of the following: brought a significant invention or industry to the territory of the *Españas*; acquired real estate for which direct taxes had been paid; established a commerce with his own capital; or performed noteworthy services in the defence of the nation.[91] These four routes – industry, property, commerce and important services – deeply influenced South America.

Two paradoxes were remarkable. First, foreigners who had naturalised could more easily access citizenship than African Spaniards. Second, naturalised foreigners were disqualified from performing the highest offices in the three branches of government: executive, legislative and judicial. Naturalised citizens could not serve as members of Parliament, Secretaries of Office (ministers), judges or magistrates, or be part of the State Council.[92] Therefore, the status of naturalised foreigner lay somewhere between the Spaniard and the Spanish citizen, but was always ahead of the African Spaniard. Indeed, they not only had an easier route towards full political rights, but were also included, unlike the African Spaniard, in the population counts used to determine political representation in both hemispheres.[93]

Naturalisation of Foreigners in the Constitutions of the New Republics and Brazil

As previously mentioned, South American elites resented several aspects of their relationship with the colonial authorities: centralism, the preeminence of *peninsulares* in official positions and the impossibility of liberalising economic trade. A fourth one can be added. Many decades before the Argentinian Alberdi wrote his famous sentence 'to govern is to populate',[94] other thinkers, deeply influenced by English liberalism, had already clarified the need to open borders for the migration and settlement of Europeans to populate large extensions of territory. Considering the Spanish position on the matter, this was conceivable only if independence was achieved. William Burke was possibly the first to clearly verbalise this. This obscure character, whose existence is questioned by some observers,[95] wrote his works in England in 1807–1808 before moving to

---

[91] Arts 19–20, 1812 Cádiz Constitution. According to Art. 21, those born in Spain to foreign parents, and therefore already Spaniards by virtue of the *ius soli* provision of Art. 5, could become citizens upon the age of twenty-one if they performed a useful profession, trade or industry and had never left the territory without government licence.

[92] Arts 96, 193, 223, 231, 251, 1812 Cádiz Constitution.

[93] Arts 28–29, 1812 Cádiz Constitution.

[94] Juan Bautista Alberdi was an Argentinian political theorist and diplomat (1810–1884): J. B. Alberdi, *Bases y Puntos de Partida para la Organización Política de la República Argentina, derivados de la Ley que Preside al Desarrollo de la Civilización en América del Sud* (Buenos Aires: Imprenta Argentina, 1852).

[95] Some authors are of the opinion that William Burke was a pseudonym used by Francisco de Miranda and his friend the British economist and utilitarian philosopher James Mill. See

Caracas in 1810. Later, from 1810 to 1811, several articles were published under his name in the *Gazeta de Caracas* and subsequently compiled in two volumes with the title *Derechos de la América del Sur y México*. In these writings, a plea was made in favour of the arrival in South America of foreigners with capital, entrepreneurship, industry and useful knowledge in the sciences or arts. Luring such migrants required South American countries to provide them with as many advantages as possible, including immediate equal rights and naturalisation after a residence of just three years.[96]

Whether Burke really existed, or whether he was in reality a pseudonym for Francisco de Miranda,[97] is irrelevant for our purposes. What matters here is the fervent plea in favour of open borders, which would lead to new towns becoming 'the habitation of civilized men', as well as increased production, which would greatly alleviate 'the wants and distresses of other countries' and, most importantly from the English point of view, 'new and numerous markets for the sale of European manufactures'.[98] Burke expressed a clear chain of events, which was mirrored in the minds of other early thinkers and independence leaders: migration by Europeans would lead to advancing civilisation, which would lead to increased manufacturing and production through intensive farming and exploitation of vast territories, which would lead to economic growth through freely trading with Europe. At the time, population was considered the 'beginning of the industry and the foundation of States' happiness'.[99] By today's standards, the continent was scarcely populated,[100] with an estimated nine million residing in the whole of Spanish South America.[101] Many independence leaders, including not only Miranda but Bolívar, Andrés

M. Rodríguez, *'William Burke' and Francisco de Miranda: The Word and the Deed in Spanish America's Emancipation* (Lanham, MD: University Press of America, 1994). Racine, however, briefly refers to him as a journalist: K. Racine, *Francisco de Miranda: A Transatlantic Life in the Age of Revolution* (Lanham, MD: Rowman & Littlefield Publishers, 2002), pp. 183–184.

[96] W. Burke, *Derechos de la América del Sur y de México* (Caracas: Academia Nacional de la Historia, 1959 edn), pp. 144–147.

[97] Francisco de Miranda has been considered as one of the fathers of South American independence. He resided in London for several years in the late seventeenth and early eighteenth centuries before returning to what is now Venezuela to unsuccessfully attempt its independence. See Racine, *Francisco de Miranda*.

[98] Burke, *South American Independence*, p. 15. See also W. Burke, *Additional Reasons for our Immediately Emancipating Spanish America: Deduced from the New and Extraordinary Circumstances, of the Present Crisis and Containing Valuable Information, Respecting the Late Important Events both at Buenos Ayres and in the Caraccas: as well as with Respect to the Present Disposition and Views of the Spanish Americans: Being Intended as a Supplement to "South American Independence"* (London: J. Ridgway, 1808).

[99] Preamble, Argentina, Decree on Promotion of Immigration and Colonisation of Public Land, 4 September 1812.

[100] For example, in Argentina there were less than half a million residents by 1810: see Moya, *Cousins and Strangers*, p. 45.

[101] Burke, *South American Independence*, p. 47. Of these, Burke – or Miranda – mentioned that only two million were Spaniards, Creoles or persons of mixed races; of the two million, around half were Spaniards (*peninsulares*) and of these, around one-fifth were ecclesiastics, monks and nuns.

Bello and Bernardino Rivadavia, the first Argentinian President, spent time in London. There these leaders befriended Jeremy Bentham and James Mill, who were fervent advocates of utilitarian, laissez-faire and free trade liberal doctrines. These connections decisively influenced the thinking of early legislators, which was in stark opposition to the previous Spanish Crown's monopoly on trading routes.[102]

Free movement and open border provisions rapidly made their way into the early laws and constitutions adopted by South American governments. The 1811 Venezuelan Constitution introduced a novel clause, which all countries in the region sooner or later replicated: 'All foreigners of any nation will be admitted into the State.'[103] The same article provided for equal treatment regarding personal property and security. Naturalisation was possible after seven years of residence.[104] Also in 1811, the Act of Federation of the United Provinces of Nueva Granada[105] provided that asylum would be granted to all foreigners seeking peaceful domicile, as long as they respected the laws, brought healthy intentions and some useful industry and would for that purpose obtain a naturalisation charter. Argentina followed suit by adopting a decree in 1812 offering its immediate protection to members of any nation and their families willing to fix their domicile in its territory.[106] Finally, in 1813 Simón Bolívar invited all foreigners of any nation and profession to settle in Nueva Granada.[107] These models exerted a profound influence on South American constitutionalism in the nineteenth century. In country after country, open border provisions and clauses announcing admittance for all foreigners with freedom, security and

[102] See K. Racine ' "This England and This Now": British Cultural and Intellectual Influence in the Spanish American Independence Era', *Hispanic American Historical Review*, 90 (2010), 423–454. However, for some cautionary remarks on the influence of Bentham on South America's independence leaders, see J. Harris, 'Bernardino Rivadavia and Benthamite "Discipleship"', *Latin American Research Review*, 33 (1998), 129–149.

[103] Art. 169, 1811 Venezuelan Constitution, Valencia 21 December 1811. This was the first constitution of the region and was repealed on 21 July 1812 when Francisco de Miranda capitulated against the Spanish army. This clause had already been introduced in 1811 by the 1st of July Law, which declared individuals' rights (*Derechos del Pueblo*). Art. 25 declared that all foreigners of any nation would be welcomed in the province of Caracas.

[104] Venezuela, Art. 222, 1811 Constitution. The same wording was used in Art. 320 of the 1812 Caracas Constitution. A similar clause had been introduced earlier in the 1811 Merida's Province Constitution, which in its third article established that all foreigners, provided they were Catholic, would be admitted to live and become domiciled in the province. See Art. 3, Constitution of the Merida Province, 31 July 1811.

[105] Art. 38, Act on the Federation of the United Provinces of Nueva Granada, 27 November 1811. Also see Art. 9, Title XIII, of the Cartagena de Indias Constitution, 14 June 1812. Similar provisions were included in the Constitution of Barcelona Colombiana, 12 January 1812.

[106] Argentina, Decree 4 September 1812. Even earlier before independence, the provisional junta adopted another Decree in 1810 allowing English, Portuguese and other foreigners from countries not at war with Argentina to freely settle in its territory: cited in Zorrilla, *Cambio Social y Población*, p. 44.

[107] G. Parra Aranguren, *La Nacionalidad Venezolana de los Inmigrados en el Siglo XIX* (Caracas: Editorial Sucre, 1969), p. 32. Decree 16 August 1813.

equal rights for themselves and their properties were enshrined among their supreme norms.[108]

Open borders were coupled with equal treatment and naturalisation after short residence periods. These enticements targeted European migrants. Let us not forget that when Alberdi argued that to govern was to populate, he saw such settlement as a means of civilisation. As such, it was only to be performed by those he considered to be civilised: that is, Europeans. Immigration by others deemed less virtuous – such as Ottomans, Indians, Chinese or Africans – was to be avoided.[109] Even with that caveat in mind, the free movement of people represented a radical split with the previous colonial system and its restrictions.

Early on, South America entered a race to attract European permanent settlers by adopting numerous laws and policies. These included the dispatch of immigration propaganda agents to Europe,[110] and the legally ratified provision of land, tax exemptions, free accommodation, assistance to find jobs and internal transport to final destinations.[111] The laws and decrees were addressed to Europeans at large or to particular countries in the old continent.[112] However, numerically speaking, these programmes were a failure since arrivals never met

---

[108] Colombia, Art. 183, 1821 Constitution; Venezuela, Art. 218, 1830 Constitution; Uruguay, Art. 147, 1830 Constitution; Ecuador, Art. 107, 1835 Constitution; Bolivia, Art. 162, 1839 Constitution, and an earlier Law 24 May 1826 promulgated by Mariscal Sucre; Argentina, Art. 25, 1853 Constitution; Paraguay, Art. 33, 1870 Constitution; Brazil, Arts 10 and 72, 1891 Constitution and its 1926 Amendment. In Chile, the preamble to the 1822 Constitution discusses the need to attract foreigners by offering them all the freedom they enjoy in other regions. In Peru, the right of entry was explicitly recognised only in Art. 29 of its 1920 Constitution, although it was implicit in previous ones. Earlier, a Decree from 14 March 1835 by General Salaverry had introduced a right of entry and automatic citizenship for any foreigner settling in Peru and registering in its civil registry. This was opposed by conservative sectors, leading to an annulment of the provision. For Peru, see M. E. del Rio, *La Inmigración y su Desarrollo en el Perú* (Lima: Sanmarti y Cia, 1929).

[109] It is true that Alberdi cautioned against the naivety of seeing all European migrants as worthy. In his view, whereas everything civilised was European, not everything European was civilised and there were more savages in European territories than in all of South America. Alberdi, *Bases y Puntos de Partida para la Organización Política de la República Argentina*.

[110] See Moya, *Cousins and Strangers*, p. 50.

[111] See for example Argentina, Law 2 August 1821 offering transport to European families to settle in the country. See also Decree 22 September 1822 offering transport and land to those European families going to Patagonia beyond the Indian frontier. See the later Argentina Law 817, 19 October 1876, known as 'Ley Avellaneda'; Chile, Colonisation Law 18 November 1845 offering lands and other benefits to foreign settlers; Colombia, Decree to Promote the Immigration of Foreigners and the Colonisation of Land, Bogotá, 7 June 1823, authorising the executive power to promote the immigration of Europeans and North Americans and provisions offering lands for such purpose; Ecuador Law No. 47, Quito, 17 July 1861 promoting the arrival of US nationals and Europeans; Peru, Arts 4–5 Decree, Lima, 19 April 1822 (offering citizenship and facilitating the arrival of those bringing industry, arts or science, or coming to work the land) and Decree 25 January 1845 granting lands and tax exemptions for twenty years; Uruguay, Law 320 on colonisation, 4 June 1853 and Law 2096 to promote migration, 10 June 1890; Venezuela, Law 24 May 1845 providing land to immigrants.

[112] Brazil, Immigration Law, 14 January 1823 addressed to Portuguese; Venezuela Decree 13 June 1831 addressed to inhabitants of the Canary Islands in Spain. On the latter, see: Parra Aranguren, *La Nacionalidad Venezolana*, pp. 37–42.

expectations, which was a major headache for national parliaments debating how to increase their numbers. Whilst *ius soli* ensured that migrants' children would automatically become nationals, easier access to naturalisation was considered one way to promote the entrance of more industrious and white settlers.[113] Sometimes this was automatic upon arrival[114] or after only one year.[115] In some countries, foreign residents were spontaneously declared nationals if they had resided in the territory since before independence or the adoption of the constitution,[116] and had registered as citizens.[117] However, it was only in the late nineteenth century that foreigners, mainly Southern Europeans, arrived in large numbers, and mostly to Argentina, Brazil and Uruguay.[118]

The requirements to naturalise remained similar throughout the nineteenth century and followed the model adopted in the 1812 Cádiz Constitution. South American countries looked for the virtuous foreigner. In the elite's narrative, 'virtuous' essentially meant of independent means. Only four paths, corresponding to the ones in the 1812 Cádiz Constitution, could be followed to become a national: property; capital invested in trade or commerce; performance of an industry, science or art; or outstanding services to the state.[119] Literacy was also necessary. Marriage was always understood as an element which, when not a *sine qua non* condition,[120] reduced the required period of residence for accessing nationality.[121] Marriage contracted with a national was further rewarded with shorter residence requirements.[122] As Brown has argued, foreigners 'who married Creole women became linked to the national family through affection and love and through their children who were *naturales* of the *patria*'.[123] This gendered narrative presented the perfect citizen as protecting

---

[113] Argentina, with its 1853 Constitution, its 1869 Citizenship Law (Law 346 Buenos Aires 1 October 1869) still in force, and its 1876 Immigration Law, represents the clearest example of this vision. See F. J. Devoto, *Historia de la Inmigración en la Argentina* (Buenos Aires: Editorial Sudamericana, 2003).

[114] Peru, Art. 19, 1823 Constitution; Colombia, Law 14, 11 April 1843; Brazil, Decree 808-A, 23 June 1855.

[115] Venezuela, Art. 6, 1819 Constitution.

[116] Colombia, Art. 4, 1821 Constitution; Ecuador, Art. 9(4), 1830 Constitution; Uruguay, Art. 8, 1830 Constitution.

[117] Argentina, Art. 4, 1826 Constitution.

[118] See Chapter 1, pp. 10–12.

[119] Chile, Arts 4–5, 1822 Constitution; Brazil, Art. 5, Naturalisation Law, 23 October 1832; Ecuador, Art. 6, 1835 Constitution. Sometimes these requirements were relaxed when the country was unsuccessful in attracting enough migrants. For example, in 1843 Colombia adopted a Decree by which the executive could naturalise foreigners even if they did not have property or capital and with no required residence period. See Colombia, Law 14, 11 April 1843 and Decree 5 June 1843.

[120] Chile, Art. 6, 1823 Chilean Constitution; Venezuela, Art. 6, 1819 Constitution.

[121] Peru, Art. 20, 1823 Constitution.

[122] Chile, Art. 6, 1828 Constitution; Uruguay, Art. 8, 1830 Constitution; Ecuador, Art. 6(3), 1835 Constitution; Paraguay, Art. 36, 1870 Constitution.

[123] M. Brown, *Adventuring through Spanish Colonies. Simón Bolívar, Foreign Mercenaries and the Birth of New Nations* (Liverpool University Press, 2006), pp. 195–196.

'the sexual virtue of their women dependents'.[124] The importance attached to marriage also reflected the Catholic Church's exclusive power in this domain since civil marriages only became a reality – and a strongly contested one – in the 1880s in countries such as Chile, Argentina and Uruguay.[125]

Thus, the South American elites expected the same qualities for an ideal citizen as for an ideal immigrant. From the very beginning, the vision was that of a white European male, married and with independent means. The endurance of some of these requirements is striking.[126] However, unlike in the USA, where only free white persons could naturalise up until 1870,[127] race did not play such a central role in South American naturalisation laws. For example, even if Asians were not the main targets of immigration policies, they were explicitly invited to naturalise in Colombia in 1847 and in Venezuela in 1855.[128]

In stark contrast, and in line with the Cádiz model, newly naturalised individuals were not considered worthy of exercising the highest mandates in the three branches of government. In other words, full legal equality was not extended to new nationals. This was the result of the dichotomy between open door policies and concerns over the loyalty of new subjects during a period when there was a looming threat of invasion by European powers.[129] The ruling elites also wanted to avoid direct competition for representative positions.[130] Indeed, it was not uncommon during legislative debates for them to refer to the new nationals as 'naturalised foreigners', a contradictory term in itself.[131] Furthermore, prohibitions on migration during colonial times meant that local populations, as well as the Catholic Church, were not accustomed to foreigners in general,

---

[124] Appelbaum *et. al.*, 'Introduction. Racial Nations', pp. 16–17.

[125] M. C. Mirow, *Latin American Law. A History of Private Law and Institutions in Spanish America* (Austin, TX: University of Texas Press, 2004), pp. 147–148.

[126] See Chapter 6, pp. 165–169.

[127] Motomura, *Americans in Waiting*, pp. 73–75.

[128] Colombia, Law 2 June 1847 and Decree 10 September 1847; Venezuela, Executive Decree 2 July 1855.

[129] R. Zahler, 'Heretics, Cadavers, and Capitalists. European Foreigners in Venezuela during the 1820s' in M. Brown and G. Paquette (eds), *Connections after Colonialism. Europe and Latin America in the 1820s* (Tuscaloosa, AL: University of Alabama Press, 2013) pp. 191–206.

[130] Herzog has proven how the distinction between natives and foreigners who naturalised was already prevalent in the Spanish America in the eighteenth century. This was a construction used by merchant associations to maintain their monopoly on various commercial interests and to exclude individuals who had naturalised from such trade. Herzog, *Defining Nations*, pp. 94–118.

[131] See debates in Venezuela in 1843 on who could hold a position as Senator in F. Vetancourt Aristeguieta, *Nacionalidad, Naturalización y Ciudadanía en Hispano-América* (Caracas: El Cojo, 1957), p. 64. See also the debates in Peru denying naturalised citizens access to employment in J. Basadre, *La Iniciación de la República. Tomo Primero* (Lima: Fondo Editorial de la Universidad Nacional Mayor de San Marcos, 2002). In Brazil, Art. 136 in the 1824 Constitution provided that foreigners, even if naturalised, could not be Ministers. Still today this continues to be used in legal texts. Interestingly, in its Spanish wording the term foreigner comes before naturalised ('extranjero naturalizado') thus reinforcing the continuing foreignness of the individual even after having naturalised. For example, see Colombia, Law 6 of 1991 on the medical anaesthesiology specialisation.

let alone to those who were Protestants or Jews, who had previously kept a low profile or converted to Catholicism. Besides mercenaries who had fought in the independence wars, these early newcomers were mainly merchants. They often had their own established networks and were thus in a better position to take advantage of the transatlantic trade. This created resentment among local artisans who suffered from the abundance of cheap imported foreign goods now available after the Spanish trade monopoly ended.[132]

Traditionally, the highest positions in the executive, legislative and judicial powers were reserved for citizens by birth.[133] In other cases, newly naturalised individuals had to wait for a number of years before they could perform any of these functions.[134] This still applies today in all ten countries: to different degrees of restriction, they all limit access to the executive, legislative and judiciary, which can be considered peculiar through a comparative perspective.[135]

The Rights of Foreigners

According to Brubaker, the French Revolution coined the concept of the foreigner, as a consequence of having invented the national citizen.[136] Their status had, however, been the subject of much earlier regulation. For example, Vattel argued in the mid-eighteenth century that they enjoyed 'only the advantages which the law or custom gives them'.[137] In some respects, foreigners were clearly underprivileged, notably when it came to the *droit d'aubaine* and the *droit de détraction*, both of which were widespread practices in Europe until the nineteenth century.[138]

---

[132] Zahler, 'Heretics, Cadavers, and Capitalists', pp. 195–198; D. Rock, 'Porteño Liberals and Imperialist Emissaries in the Rio de la Plata. Rivadavia and the British' in Brown and Paquette (eds), *Connections after Colonialism*, 2013, pp. 207–222.

[133] This was the case to become President in Venezuela (Title VII, Section I, Art. 2, 1819 Constitution), Colombia (Art. 106, 1821 Constitution), Peru (Art. 75, 1823 Constitution), Argentina (Art. 69, 1826 Constitution), Chile (Art. 82, 1822 Constitution), Bolivia (Art. 79, 1826 Constitution), Ecuador (Art. 33, 1830 Constitution), Uruguay (Art. 74, 1830 Constitution) and Paraguay (Art. 35, 1870 Constitution). Exclusions for other positions such as Minister or Member of Parliament were also present in Paraguay and in many of the countries' succeeding constitutions. In Brazil, newly naturalised individuals could not be Deputies or Ministers (Arts 95 and 135, 1824 Brazilian Constitution).

[134] For example 12 years in Colombia to become Senator (Art. 96, 1821 Constitution); 9 years in Argentina to become Senator, Governor or Magistrate of the Supreme Court (Arts 24, 112 and 131, 1826 Constitution); 10 years in Uruguay to become Minister and 14 years for Senator (Arts 30 and 87, 1830 Constitution); 6 years in Bolivia for Senator (Art. 46, 1826 Constitution).

[135] See Chapter 6, pp. 168–169.

[136] Brubaker, *Citizenship and Nationhood*, pp. 67–72.

[137] De Vattel, *The Law of Nations*, Book 1, Chapter 19, § 213.

[138] The *droit d'aubaine* meant the appropriation by the sovereign of a deceased foreigner's property coupled with the inability to inherit; the *droit de détraction*, replacing the former, referred to the tax imposed on the right of a foreigner to inherit such property. L. Lütz, *Essai Historique sur le Droit d'Aubaine en France* (Geneva: Imprimerie Ramboz et Schuchardt, 1866). This was, for example, abolished in France by the Loi du 14 juillet 1819 relative à l'abolition du droit d'aubaine et de détraction.

The legal status of foreigners improved in Europe during the nineteenth century. They had, both in theory and often in practice, the right to equal enjoyment of certain civil rights. For example, in 1874 the first session of the Institute of International Law in Geneva acknowledged that international law required the recognition of foreigners' civil rights and the legal capacity to realise those rights. This was a duty of international justice, rather than being derived from bilateral treaties, and thus was independent of their existence.[139] Foreigners were granted certain civil rights, such as protection of the freedom to contract, to own or transfer property, to access to tribunals, to engage in trade and to acquire land.[140] However, despite the theoretical extension of civil rights, even in the period before the First World War when passport controls became pervasive,[141] individual foreign citizens could be deported for various reasons, including being 'poor, sick, or perhaps because of a criminal offense, but also for direct political reasons, "in the public or national interest"'.[142]

The Influence of the 1812 Cádiz Constitution

On the particular question of the rights of foreigners, the Cádiz Constitution remained by and large silent. The provisions on the right to property and individual liberty included all residents, nationals or not.[143] Most rights, however, were exclusively available to Spaniards.[144] Except in the context of routes towards nationality and, eventually, citizenship, there were few articles in which the word 'foreigner' appeared. As previously explained, even foreigners who had naturalised were excluded from holding certain elective positions. Foreigners were also forbidden from travelling to and trading with *Las Indias*. In the case of the peninsula, where several foreign merchants had settled – most notably in Seville and Cádiz – there was always the possibility to naturalise after a period of ten years, or earlier if the individual obtained a naturalisation charter. The particular legal status of those who remained foreigners was the subject of a number of royal decrees, and was part of the bilateral practice with other European powers.[145]

---

[139] Institut de Droit International, Session de Genève – 1874 Utilité d'un accord commun des règles uniformes de droit international privé.

[140] See, for example, the Spanish case in Art. 25, 1869 Constitution; for France, Art. 11, 1804 Civil Code granting civil rights to foreigners on the basis of reciprocal agreements with other states; for Germany see Brubaker, *Citizenship and Nationhood*, pp. 67–72.

[141] J. Torpey, *The Invention of the Passport: Surveillance, Citizenship and the State* (Cambridge University Press, 2000).

[142] Hammar, *Democracy and the Nation State*, p. 42.

[143] Art. 172, 1812 Cádiz Constitution.

[144] See for example Arts 247, 280, 287 and 373, 1812 Cádiz Constitution.

[145] J. M. González Beltrán, 'Legislación sobre Extranjeros a finales del Siglo XVIII', *Revista de Historia Moderna y Contemporánea*, 8–9 (1997), 103–118.

The Rights of Foreigners in the Constitutions of the New Republics and Brazil

Foreigners were lured into migrating to the new territories with open border provisions, short residence requirements for naturalisation and the other benefits mentioned above. Their rights were also specifically integrated into many of the early constitutions, which often conferred equal civil rights; exercise of any industry, trade or profession; possession, purchase and selling of property; and, in some cases, freedom of religion.[146] The rights of particular nationalities were also the subject of bilateral navigation and commerce agreements between the new countries and various European powers.[147] Similar provisions on access to justice, personal property, freedom to trade or freedom of religion were incorporated into these treaties.

Foreigners who did not naturalise also enjoyed two rights not available to nationals, namely the exemption from military service and diplomatic protection by their respective countries. While the first prerogative created resentment among national populations, the second had more far-reaching and significant consequences. During the nineteenth century, both the USA and European powers frequently resorted to what has been labelled 'arrogant diplomatic protection' in their relations with Latin America.[148] This meant the practice of employing diplomatic means – or even using force – rather than normal procedural mechanisms before local tribunals when the foreigner was a US or European national residing in the region. These practices often interfered in the internal affairs of the newly established sovereign republics and Brazil.[149]

According to the contemporary Argentinian scholar Carlos Calvo, these sorts of diplomatic claim were rejected when they were put forward between European powers since otherwise nationals would have had fewer rights than foreigners originating from dominant states.[150] Thus, the 1868 Calvo Doctrine proposed two standards. On the one hand, it set out the need to exhaust local remedies and the impossibility of diplomatic claims, unless justice had been denied at the national level. On the other hand, and as a corollary to the first principle, it established the equal treatment of both nationals and foreigners with regards to civil rights, including the protection of property and access to

---

[146] Argentina, Art. 20, 1853 Constitution; Brazil, Art. 72, 1891 Constitution; Bolivia, Art. 162, 1839 Constitution; Chile, Art. 12, 1833 Constitution; Colombia, Art. 183, 1821 Constitution; Ecuador, Art. 107, 1835 Constitution; Paraguay, Art. 33, 1870 Constitution; Peru, Art. 178, 1839 Constitution; Venezuela, Art. 218, 1830 Constitution.

[147] See, for example, Colombia–USA, 3 October 1824; Argentina–Great Britain, 2 February 1825; Brazil–Great Britain, 17 August 1827; Gran Colombia–Netherlands, 10 May 1829; Colombia (Nueva Granada)–France, 28 October 1844; Peru–Belgium, 16 May 1850; Argentina–Prussia, 19 September 1857; or Venezuela–Italy, 19 June 1861.

[148] R. Gómez Arnau, *México y la Protección de sus Nacionales en Estados Unidos* (México D.F.: Universidad Nacional Autónoma de México, 1990), p. 35.

[149] See examples of this in M. Offut, *The Protection of Citizens Abroad by the Armed Forces of the United States* (Baltimore, MD: The Johns Hopkins Press, 1928).

[150] C. Calvo, *Derecho Internacional Teórico y Práctico de Europa y América* (Paris: D'Amijot: [Caminos de Hierro], 1868), p. 393.

tribunals. These principles influenced several constitutions in the region and the adoption of various covenants at regional congresses.[151]

Naturalisation rates were always extremely low. For example, by 1914 only 1.4 percent of all foreigners had naturalised in Argentina compared to 52 per cent in the USA. Moya argues that this resulted from the lack of incentives to naturalise.[152] Foreigners enjoyed most citizenship rights except for voting – and the value of the latter was dubious considering the largely oligarchical political systems that prevailed. In turn, they were exempted from the military and continued to enjoy diplomatic protection. The situation was rather different in the USA. For a start, the military draft included foreigners. Moreover, acquiring the right to vote could offer benefits that were more tangible in particular cities: many municipal jobs, for example, required citizenship.[153] Faced with similar low naturalisation rates, Brazil and Venezuela opted to naturalise their foreigners without their consent. These 'great naturalisations' led to serious condemnation and protests by the governments of the European countries of origin.[154]

A final point must be re-emphasised. The desire to attract Europeans to settle in territories that were presented as being as empty as deserts[155] was part of a demographic, economic, political and racial project. Whereas *ius soli* in principle considered those born in the territory as members of the nation, some have seen this as an ideological device to flatten the cultural indigenous reality and to 'negate the Indian as a space of difference' in, for example, Peru or Bolivia.[156] Certainly, at the same time that indigenous peoples were being incorporated into the new national body, processes of internal 'othering' portrayed them as enemies and savages, such as in the case of the Mapuches in Chile.[157] In Rouquié's words, 'the elimination of the guarantees granted to

---

[151] Convention on the rights of alienage (Second American International Conference, 1901–1902), Mexico City, 29 January 1902; Convention on the Conditions of Foreigners (Sixth International American Conference, La Habana – 1928), Habana, 20 February 1928. The Convention was signed by all South American States as well as Costa Rica, Cuba, El Salvador, Guatemala, Haiti, Honduras, Mexico, Nicaragua, Panama, the Dominican Republic and the USA.

[152] Moya, *Cousins and Strangers*, p. 489.

[153] *Ibid.*

[154] Brazil, Decree 58A, 14 December 1889 and Art. 69, 1891 Constitution; see Saccheta, *Laços de Sangue*, pp. 125–131. Venezuela, Resolution 1 December 1865; see Parra Aranguren, *La Nacionalidad Venezolana*, p. 88 and for similar proposals in Argentina, see L. A. Bertoni, 'La naturalización de los extranjeros, 1887–1893: ¿Derechos políticos o nacionalidad?', *Desarrollo Económico*, 32 (1992), pp. 57–77.

[155] For example, Alberdi considered South America to be 'deserted': Alberdi, *Bases y Puntos de Partida*, p. 90.

[156] J. L. Martínez, V. Gallardo and N. Martínez, 'Construyendo Identidades desde el Poder: los Indios en los Discursos Republicanos de Inicios del siglo XIX' in G. Boccara (ed.), *Colonización, resistencia y mestizaje en las Américas, siglos XVI-XX* (Quito: ifea/Ediciones Abya Yala, 2002), pp. 27–46.

[157] V. Romero, 'Legislación y Políticas en Nueva Granada y Chile para atraer la Inmigración Extranjera a mediados del Siglo XIX', *Amérique Latine Histoire et Mémoire. Les Cahiers ALHIM*, online version 24 (2012), published online 8 February 2013.

Indians by the Spanish crown and the formally egalitarian spirit of liberalism that dominated the new republics opened the way to the breakup of Indian communities'.[158] Through the expansion of the frontier, native groups were either exterminated or forcefully assimilated in Argentina, Chile and Uruguay. In Brazil and Colombia, the prevailing understanding was that the only way to *civilise* their countries was through the gradual replacement of natives with Europeans.[159] As Rouquié eloquently puts it, 'the mechanisms for the exclusion of those who are dominated are ambivalent and involve both together and separately the methods of obligatory cooptation and marginalization'.[160] Open borders for Europeans always represented a civilisation and utilitarian project, not a humanistic one.

Discussion

In a comparative perspective, South American countries have both more restrictive and more liberal aspects than those in the USA, Europe and other regions. In one sense, they appear to be more liberal as they all have, similarly to the USA, territorial birthright citizenship and short residence periods to access nationality. Moreover, the recent legislative practice on migration has included more generous provisions with regards to extending equal rights to foreigners, including voting rights, enunciations of non-criminalisation, the right to migrate and open borders.[161] Nonetheless, naturalised citizens face limitations in serving in the highest state offices. Furthermore naturalisation requirements, beyond the length of residence, are often difficult to fulfil in practice and procedures are cumbersome, and thus naturalisation rates remain strikingly low.[162]

All these characteristics can be traced back to the particular circumstances involving independence from Spain and Portugal. Indeed, the 1812 Cádiz Constitution was used as a model to introduce many elements still present today, such as *ius soli* and limitations for naturalised nationals. By contrast, the context of post-colonial societies resulted in open borders, short-term residence periods before naturalisation and equal treatment of foreigners. Previous migration prohibitions applicable to non-Spaniards led to open borders and

---

[158] Rouquié, *The Military and the State in Latin America* (Berkeley, CA: University of California Press, 1987), p. 21.

[159] Larrain, *Identity and Modernity*; R. J. Cottrol, *The Long, Lingering Shadow: Slavery, Race, and Law in the American Hemisphere* (Athens, GA: University of Georgia Press, 2013), specially ch. 4; T. Katerí Hernández, *Racial Subordination in Latin America The Role of the State, Customary Law, and the New Civil Rights Response* (Cambridge University Press, 2012), especially ch. 2; R. Gaune and M. Lara (eds), *Historias de Racismo y Discriminación en Chile* (Santiago de Chile: Uqbar, 2009).

[160] Rouquié, *The Military and the State in Latin America*, p. 29.

[161] See Chapters 5–7.

[162] See Chapter 6, pp. 167–168.

the promise of equal treatment for residents and foreigners alike. To clarify, this was not an invitation to the entire world to immigrate to South America. Through constitutional law, the ruling Creole elites clearly delineated the image of the perfect citizen, matching that of the perfect migrant. This was portrayed as a white, male, married, autonomous and industrious European, or a European descendant. These gendered and racialised views were preserved for several decades. Opening borders did not derive from a humanist or cosmopolitan approach, but rather from a demographic and racial project with the clear aim of populating large territories with white European settlers and, often in the process, eradicating indigenous communities. This was a state- and nation-building exercise in a period of transition from colonial societies into republics, where collective identities were far from settled and where the relationship with foreigners was vital in determining the boundaries of the polity.[163] Two questions are pertinent here. First, how is it possible that so many new countries followed the same pattern? Second, and perhaps more importantly, how can we explain the persistence of both liberal and conservative elements through almost 200 years of constitutional practice?

Diffusion in South America's Construction of the Foreigner and the National

Many of the legislative choices on citizenship and migration that were adopted in South America originated from the influence of the Cádiz Constitution. Three reasons can be proposed for this. First, the Cádiz Constitution had been in place over large parts of the territories that later became independent countries.[164] Second, numerous American deputies had participated in its drafting. Third, this constitution carried an enormous prestige among liberal circles and was influential not only in the Americas but also in Europe.[165] This explains the adoption of *ius soli*, the distinction between nationals and citizens, the limited possible routes to naturalisation and the restrictions on political rights of representation for those who naturalised. These four elements perfectly suited the needs of the ruling elites in the new republics, as well as in Brazil. These legislative choices cannot be considered as legal transplants since in many respects this was a continuation of the previous framework and practices. In other words, concepts and institutions that had already been in place were replicated and adapted to the postcolonial reality in which new countries faced similar challenges. It is important to stress in any case that other constitutional models (mainly from the USA, England and France) were also important in the

---

[163] M. Brown, 'Not Forging Nations but Foraging for Them: Uncertain Collective Identities in Gran Colombia', *Nations and Nationalism*, 12 (2006), 223–240.

[164] This was, for example, the case in Ecuador and Peru and during certain periods in Chile, Colombia and Venezuela, although it was not in Argentina, for instance.

[165] Escudero López (ed.), *Cortes y Constitución de Cádiz*, especially the chapters in Volume III.

early South American constitutionalism.[166] However, it was the Cádiz example that most affected our present subject of study.

By contrast, the closed borders, long residence periods before naturalisation and limited rights for foreigners worked against the hope of luring European settlers to populate large territories. They were also self-defeating to open trade in global markets, something that had not been possible under the Spanish Crown's monopoly. The race to attract migrants resulted in clauses granting equal treatment and short-term residence periods before naturalisation. Any other strategy would have been counterproductive. Here we can refer to legal transplants as playing a crucial role in South America through a process of emulation.[167] The legislators were, of course, aware of how other countries in the region were dealing with the matter. At least from the 1830s onwards, national representatives often met in regional congresses and were also in contact through links forged in, for instance, London, Paris or New York, and through transnational networks of newspapers. Knowledge of foreign rule is of central importance for successful transplantation.[168] Open borders is the best example of this. The phrase 'any foreigner of any nation will be welcomed to the territory', first used in the 1811 Venezuelan Constitution, was then copied verbatim by various other countries.

More interestingly, the countries that first adopted more restrictive conditions were forced to liberalise their immigration laws in a process of strategic adjustment,[169] so as not to be left behind in this race for migrants. For example, Peru and Ecuador – which in their first constitutions did not grant extensive rights to foreigners and stipulated long residence periods before naturalisation[170] – shifted their laws to become more appealing. Consequently, diffusion and legal transplants were normal at the regional level. The 1821 Colombian Constitution exercised an important role. This constitution covered the territory of what was then known as Gran Colombia, which also included present day Ecuador, Panama and Venezuela. Moreover, Simón Bolívar and other important independence heroes participated in the Congress of Cúcuta at which the final text was drafted. Earlier failed constitutions, such as the 1811 Venezuelan one, also had a clear influence. This aligns with the findings of other authors who have pointed out that '[c]ountries with similar levels of power often model their policies after each other reciprocally, in a process of iterative emulation'.[171]

166   J. Simon, *The Ideology of Creole Revolution: Imperialism and Independence in American and Latin American Political Thought* (Cambridge University Press, 2017), pp. 38–39.
167   A. Watson, *Legal Transplants. An Approach to Comparative Law* (Athens, GA: University of Georgia Press, 1993, second edn).
168   A. Watson, 'Comparative Law and Legal Change', *Cambridge Law Journal*, 37 (1978), 313–336, on 315.
169   FitzGerald and Cook-Martin, *Culling the Masses*, p. 26.
170   These residence periods were as long as five years. See, for example, Ecuador, Art. 6, 1835 Constitution; Peru, Art. 10, 1823 Constitution.
171   FitzGerald and Cook-Martin, *Culling the Masses*, p. 23.

Path Dependency in South America's Legal Construction of the Foreigner and the National

Persistent central elements in the relationship between the national and the foreigner through 200 years of constitutional practice merit our attention. Once again, the work of Alan Watson is illuminating here. Watson argues not only that most legal change takes place through transplantation but, most decisively, that longevity of the law is the general rule and that 'to a large extent law possesses a life and vitality of its own' despite 'changes in societal structure'.[172] In his view, several countervailing forces determine whether legal change takes place or not. There are forces arguing in favour of change ('pressure forces'), and those resisting any alteration. However, since order and stability are essentially society's stake in the law,[173] and since 'the ruling elite have a generalised interest in no change', the pressure forces must be much stronger than the opposition ones for transformation to take place.[174] In the political science literature, this has been analysed under the framework of path dependency theories designed to explain how history matters.[175] This is a framework that we can apply to some of the elements in the case at hand.

In Gargarella's opinion, the two foundational ideas of Latin America's constitutionalism were 'individual autonomy' and 'collective self-government'.[176] Both notions lie at the core of the division between nationals, citizens and foreigners and of the rights that pertain to each category, including political ones. Gargarella points out that three different approaches have been prevalent since independence: conservative, republican and liberal.[177] In his view, the dominant force has been the alliance between the liberal and the conservative project, as reflected in two centuries of constitutional practice.[178] The conservative paradigm 'implied a commitment with two theoretical positions of enormous importance in America, namely political elitism and moral perfectionism'.[179] The liberal approach had a 'double commitment to the equilibrium of powers and State's moral neutrality', which was based on the value of 'individual autonomy'.[180] This opposed the 'moral perfectionism' of conservatives, notably their 'vocation to organize society around the demands of a particular religion', and also contrasted with them in proposing a 'list of individual, inviolable, and unconditional rights' since conservatives 'made rights dependent on

---

[172] Watson, 'Comparative Law and Legal Change', pp. 314–315.
[173] A. Watson, *The Nature of Law* (Edinburgh University Press, 1977).
[174] Watson, 'Comparative Law and Legal Change', p. 331.
[175] See, among others, P. Pierson, *Politics in Time. History, Institutions, and Social Analysis* (Princeton University Press, 2004); J. Mahoney, and K. Thelen (eds), *Explaining Institutional Change. Ambiguity, Agency, and Power* (Cambridge University Press, 2010).
[176] Gargarella, *Latin American Constitutionalism*, p. 5.
[177] *Ibid.*, p. 6.
[178] *Ibid.*, Chapter 2.
[179] *Ibid.*, p. 11.
[180] *Ibid.*, p. 14.

the needs of religion'.[181] According to Gargarella, both sides – being elitists –
were mostly concerned with, and agreed upon, preventing property expropri-
ation and the rise of more radical governments based on an extended franchise.
Consequently, both tendencies combined in a liberal–conservative alliance.
This led to the 'formula of limited political liberties and ample civic (economic)
liberties'. This architecture was diffused, gained stability and remained 'basic-
ally the same' for 150 years.[182]

This explains why both projects fundamentally agreed on the construction
of the national, the citizen and the foreigner. For example, both liberals and
conservatives shared views on limiting the extension of citizenship, and its cor-
respondent political rights, through legal devices such as property, literacy or
economic requirements.[183] So too was the idea of limiting access to political
positions for newly naturalised individuals. At the same time, economic development was then understood as a consequence of migration, larger populations
and entrance into world trade markets. Both liberals and conservatives agreed
on this and shared the image of the ideal migrant as a white, European male
with property, capital or knowledge.

As a result, significant digressions from this approach were by and large
absent during the nineteenth century. One exception was the adoption of the
1886 Colombian Constitution. This document, considered to be very conservative, was approved in a highly specific context of economic struggles and
internal and external conflicts. This ended a very liberal period, epitomised
by the 1863 Constitution.[184] The conservative character of the 1886 text is evident due to its limitations on access to citizenship, its reduction of rights for
naturalised citizens and of foreigners' rights in general. Most importantly,
the 1886 Colombian Constitution ended the absolute *ius soli* tradition in the
country, which makes Colombia an anomaly in the region.

Importantly, however, whereas central aspects such as *ius soli* have continued
until today, the figure of the foreigner was later deconstructed during the twentieth century so that particular categories became excluded on the grounds of
race, ethnicity, political affiliation and moral or economic factors. This will be
the subject of discussion in Chapter 4.

Conclusion

During the nineteenth century, the construction of the national, the citizen
and the foreigner was a complex social and legal process. The 1812 Cádiz
Constitution profoundly influenced such construction, as did the early constitutional texts in Colombia and Venezuela, which emphasised open borders,

[181] *Ibid.*, p. 15.
[182] *Ibid.*, p. 198.
[183] *Ibid.*, pp. 47–49.
[184] *Ibid.*, p. 40.

equal treatment and short residence periods before naturalising. The immigration project was intended to address not only concerns regarding the size and distribution of the population, but also contribute to the whitening of local populations and the segregation of indigenous groups. In the nineteenth century, the Creole elites used migration and citizenship policies tools to define nationhood. As López Alves has argued, 'weak states in formation struggled to link institutions of government with heterogeneous populations that were lumped together under the label of a "one and unifying nation" in the context of strong international pressures'.[185] The commonality of interests between the liberal and the conservative elites was thus crucial in providing continuity and stability to the legal regulation of the national, the citizen and the foreigner. This was necessary to preserve the colonial social order that privileged a miniscule minority of the population. The elite's vision was one of a gradual transformation of society, rather than a radical rupture with the previous colonial order, with the exclusion of the indigenous and black populations, mainly from political rights. This created new boundaries in the slow process of creating national communities.

As shown in Chapters 5–7, it is fair to say that much of the current legislative practice is heir to discussions and legislation dating back to the nineteenth century, as well as to the restrictions later introduced in the twentieth century. The same holds true regarding current debates on the construction of a South American citizenship. The next chapter shows how, from the early nineteenth century, a third figure was added to the traditional dichotomy between foreigner and national: the Hispano-American subject.

---

[185] F. López-Alves, 'Visions of the National: Natural Endowments, Futures and the Evils of Men' in Centeno and Ferraro (eds), *State and Nation Making in Latin America and Spain. Republics of the Possible* (Cambridge University Press, 2013), pp. 282–306, on p. 288.

3

The Construction of the Hispano-American Legal Figure in the Nineteenth Century

Una sola debe ser la Patria de los americanos, ya que en todo hemos tenido una perfecta unidad.[1]

Introduction

From the early stages of independence in the nineteenth century, a third figure complicated the national–foreigner divide: the Hispano-American, who was a former Spaniard from the Americas. This was something of a halfway presence: not quite a national, yet never a foreigner. The term Hispano-American was far from a simple discursive artefact. Rather, it represented a legal status enshrined in multilateral conventions, bilateral treaties, national laws and constitutions. Automatic naturalisation, freedom of movement and residence, equal rights, dual nationality or diplomatic protection abroad, were all part of an emerging common legal jargon. The rationale was to provide Hispano-Americans, arguably those who could be identified as Creoles, with a new common fatherland and the right to choose their residence freely.

The regional location of that fatherland was often understood as Hispano-America rather than South America. Thus, this included Mexico and the former Spanish colonies in Central America and the Caribbean, and excluded the French, Dutch and British possessions in South America.[2] Three other countries must be mentioned. The relationship with Brazil was unstable during the nineteenth century. Whilst on some occasions Brazil was invited to participate in debates and join select agreements, it was also seen as an odd element. This was due to its different colonial past, non-republican character, territorial ambitions and possible association with the Holy Alliance,[3] which promoted

---

[1] Simón Bolívar, letter to Juan Martín de Pueyrredón, Supreme Director of the United Provinces of the Río de la Plata. Angostura, 12 June 1818. 'Only one must be the fatherland for Americans, since we have already had perfect unity in everything' (author's translation).

[2] These possessions later became the independent Republic of Suriname and the Co-operative Republic of Guyana. French Guiana continues to be a region of France as an overseas department.

[3] The Holy Alliance is the name given to the treaty signed in 1815 by Austria, Prussia and Russia after the fall of Napoleon.

Spanish intervention to recover control of the former colonies.[4] Second, Haiti was simply left out of the negotiations. Initially this had to do with Colombia's, and Bolívar's, unwillingness to disrupt relations with France.[5] Moreover, the revolution of Haiti's black slaves had caused apprehension among the ruling elites. Finally, the USA was first censured by Bolívar following the indifference with which its government treated the struggle against Spain.[6] The 1823 Monroe Doctrine also stirred mixed feelings.[7] Various later interventions in the new republics, including the annexation of parts of Mexico, were hardly conducive to US inclusion.[8] As such, it was not until the first Pan-American Conference in 1889 that all three countries – Brazil, Haiti and the USA – participated in the regional dialogue.

The legal construction of the Hispano-American in the nineteenth century has been largely neglected in the academic literature on migration, citizenship and constitutional development. This chapter fills that gap through investigating this important aspect of state and nation formation. As argued in Chapter 2, states came before nations, thus thereafter struggled to create nations from populations divided by race, class and caste. Nonetheless, there was a small group of elites with a sense of 'American-ness'.[9] According to Centeno, Creoles did not see themselves as 'separate from their creole neighbours' and indeed 'identified themselves as Americans – as opposed to Spaniards – but not as a specific subnationality'.[10] However, as Herzog has elucidated, Creolism was problematic since it lacked properly 'defined borders' for the 'new, natural community it instituted'.[11] At times the 'new community seemed to embody the entire American continent', whilst at others it only referred to 'a vice-royalty, a province, or even a single city'.[12]

In that regard, the nineteenth-century Hispano-American legal figure represents a different form of membership: a level of polity located not at the national level, but rather at the supranational. This partly explains the difficulties in constructing nations in a region where the gap 'between white, black

---

[4] R. A. Martínez, *El Panamericanismo. Doctrina y Práctica Imperialista. Las Relaciones Interamericanas desde Bolívar hasta Eisenhower* (Buenos Aires: Aluminé, 1957), pp. 33–35.

[5] A. del Castillo Martínez, *El Congreso de Panamá de 1826 Convocado por el Libertador: Iniciación del Panamericanismo (Sus Actas y Tratados)* (Bogotá: Universidad Jorge Tadeo Lozano, 1982), p. 32. See also J. Gaffield, *Haitian Connections in the Atlantic World: Recognition after Revolution* (Chapel Hill, NC: University of North Carolina Press, 2015).

[6] Martínez, *El Panamericanismo*, pp. 26–32.

[7] The Monroe Doctrine refers to a US policy under President James Monroe by which any effort by European powers to colonise either North America or South America would be considered an act of aggression demanding US intervention. Martínez, *El Panamericanismo*, pp. 52–59.

[8] Gómez Arnau, *México y la Protección de sus Nacionales en Estados Unidos*, pp. 39–43; del Castillo Martínez, *El Congreso de Panamá de 1826*, p. 35.

[9] M. A. Centeno, *Blood and Debt. War and the Nation-State in Latin America* (Pennsylvania University Press, 2002), on p. 24.

[10] *Ibid.*, p. 172.

[11] Herzog, *Defining Nations*, p. 151.

[12] *Ibid.*

and Indian within countries was always greater than the differences between any of these groups across borders'.[13] In other words, in the Hispano-American context there was never a simple dichotomy between national or citizen and foreigner. Thus, even when states attempted to construct and 'imagined'[14] the nation in opposition to neighbours depicted as the *Other*, the analysis of legal sources provides a clear picture of parallel inclusion. The essence of this inclusion was understanding equality as the central component in the treatment of those coming from elsewhere in the region, arguably understood as members of a small Creole elite. Certain rights associated with nationality or citizenship – including consular protection abroad, mobility and residence and even political rights – were granted to Hispano-Americans. Moreover, many legal instruments enshrined automatic naturalisation for those who were willing to pursue that route. As will be seen in Chapter 8, this comparative and historical work temporally and geographically expands what had been notoriously European-centric analysis of forms of membership beyond traditional citizenship.

Nineteenth-century Hispano-America does indeed represent a region where rights often associated with citizenship were available to non-nationals. States in the Americas granted rights to all residents, regardless of their nationality, in what could be considered as a postnational approach, when postnationality is simply 'understood as the enjoyment of rights'.[15] As seen in Chapter 2, foreigners – namely Europeans – enjoyed certain rights not by virtue of supranational agreements but rather through domestic constitutional provisions. Indeed, European immigrants had many more entitlements than most local populations. In the case of Hispano-Americans, arguably a small Creole elite, the picture became more complex. To begin with, they enjoyed access to the rights available to foreigners in general, and often more. They also had privileged and faster routes to naturalisation and more political rights. Both before and after naturalisation, they were categorically closer to national citizens than to other foreigners, either from Europe or elsewhere. To complicate the picture even further, other rights – e.g. consular protection abroad and recognition of qualifications – were extended to Hispano-Americans through supranational instruments in the form of multilateral and bilateral treaties. Nineteenth-century Hispano-America enriches debates on postnational and supranational forms of membership not only geographically and temporally, but also in the sense of offering much more complex categorisations of membership based on nationality, class and race. Whilst it might be argued that the norms analysed in the following sections were mostly applicable or intended

---

[13] Centeno, *Blood and Debt*, p. 175.

[14] Anderson, *Imagined Communities*.

[15] L. Bosniak, 'Denationalizing Citizenship' in T. A. Aleinikoff and D. Klusmeyer (eds), *Citizenship Today. Global Perspectives and Practices* (Washington, DC: Carnegie Endowment for International Peace, 2001) pp. 237–252, on p. 242.

only for a small Creole elite, they represent a fascinating ensemble affecting membership, state-building and the construction of the nation.

Examining the early construction of the Hispano-American is vital also because it provides historical context for current debates on a South American regional citizenship.[16] These discussions are exclusively focused on developments in the twenty-first century, thus excluding a rich legal history of both accommodating and negotiating the status of regional citizens.

This chapter is structured as follows: the first three sections investigate the legal construction of the Hispano-American figure through multilateral, bilateral and domestic treaties and laws over a period spanning several decades. The final section explains the emergence of the Hispano-American as a legal status and the implementation of the various instruments in practice. The chapter closes with thoughts on how this narrative potentially influences today's legislative debates, both at the national and regional levels, regarding the creation of a South American citizenship.

The Regional Hispano-American as a Multilateral Concern

After independence, confederation remained an official aspiration of some governments in Hispano-America for more than fifty years, from 1811 until at least 1865.[17] The first antecedent may be found in the 1811 Venezuelan Constitution, which welcomed anyone from the provinces of the previous Spanish Americas to join the union.[18] Moreover, executive power was to reside with three individuals born on the Colombian continent, a proxy used by Miranda to refer to Hispano-America.[19] This inclusive ethos continued in other early constitutional texts. In Colombia, for instance, the 1815 revision of the 1812 Cundinamarca (Colombia) Constitution established that naturals (natives) from other states in Free America were not to be considered as foreigners.[20] Similarly, in Argentina the 1819 Constitution of the Santa Fe region declared all Americans to be citizens.[21]

Five confederation congresses took place between 1826 and 1865. External events threatening the new republics' sovereignty provided the momentum for these assemblies: European powers, including Spain, and the USA continued to hold military interests in the region, which served as a central factor in driving

---

[16] See Chapter 7.

[17] G. A. de la Reza, 'La Asamblea Hispanoamericana de 1864–65, Último Eslabón de la Anfictionía', *Estudios de Historia Moderna y Contemporánea de México*, 39 (2010), 71–91.

[18] Art. 128, 1811 Venezuelan Constitution.

[19] Art. 73, 1811 Venezuelan Constitution.

[20] Art. 128, Reform plan or revision of the 1812 Cundinamarca Constitution (Colombia), 13 July 1815.

[21] Argentina, Art. 3, Provisional Statute of the Santa Fé Province, 26 August 1819. Also, in 1812 the Argentinean assembly granted the right to vote to all Americans, Spaniards, mestizos, Indians and freemen. See Vetancourt Aristeguieta, *Nacionalidad, Naturalización y Ciudadanía en Hispano-América*, p. 39.

convergence. Yet the agreements that resulted from these five congresses were not limited solely to mutual military assistance in the case of invasion. They included provisions for free movement, equal treatment and consular protection abroad. These clauses – together with those on arbitration and preferential trade – reveal a willingness to establish a supranational alliance under which an incipient regional legal status, understood as the enjoyment of rights regardless of current residence, was already a crucial component. The Hispano-American thus emerged as a third legal construction who was located between the national/citizen and the foreigner. The essence behind this inclusion was understanding that equality was the central component in the treatment of those coming from the regional space.

The Construction of a Regional Hispano-American in the First Bilateral Agreements (1822–1826)

The idea of confederation was championed not only by Simón Bolívar but also by other distinguished revolutionaries and thinkers from the independence period, including Juan Egaña, Juan Martínez de Rozas and Bernardo O'Higgins in Chile, Francisco de Miranda in Venezuela, José Cecilio Díaz del Valle in Central America, and Bernardo Monteagudo and José San Martín in Peru and Argentina.[22] The independence struggle took place between 1808 and 1826. Between 1822 and 1825 the first steps to establish a confederation between the new republics had already been taken through military means as well as constitutional methods.[23] As part of this effort, under Bolívar's instructions and leadership, Colombia signed five bilateral treaties with Peru,[24] Chile,[25] Buenos Aires,[26] Mexico[27] and Central America.[28] The 1822 Peru–Colombia agreement included far-reaching provisions. Article 4 is worth reproducing in full:

> In order to ensure and perpetuate in the best possible manner the good friendship and relations between both States, the citizens of Peru and Colombia will enjoy

[22] E. Lagos Valenzuela, 'El Arbitraje Internacional de América', *Anales de la Facultad de Derecho*, IV (1938), available at: https://revistas.uchile.cl/index.php/ACJYS/article/view/4117

[23] G. A. de la Reza, *El Congreso de Panamá de 1826 y Otros Ensayos de Integración Latinoamericana en el Siglo XIX* (México D.F.: Universidad Autónoma Metropolitana, 2006), p. 17.

[24] Union, League and Perpetual Confederation Treaty between the Republic of Colombia and the Peruvian State, 6 July 1822. Both Colombia and Peru ratified this agreement.

[25] Union, League and Perpetual Confederation Treaty between the Republic of Colombia and Chile, Santiago, 21 October 1822. The Chilean Senate did not authorise the ratification of this agreement.

[26] Friendship and Alliance Treaty between Colombia and Buenos Aires, Buenos Aires, 8 March 1823. Ratified by Colombia in 1824.

[27] Friendship, Union, League and Perpetual Confederation between Colombia and Mexico, Mexico City, 3 October 1823. Both parties ratified this agreement.

[28] Union, League and Perpetual Confederation between the Republic of Colombia and the United Provinces of Central America, Bogotá, 15 March 1825. This agreement was not ratified. The

all rights and privileges which the citizens born in both territories possess. In other words, Colombians in Peru will be considered as Peruvians and the latter in the Republic of Colombia as Colombians. This does not affect the extension or restriction that the legislative power of both States would have done or could do in the future with regard to the [individual's] characteristics needed in order to be able to exercise the first magistracies. However, in order to enjoy any of the other citizens' active and passive rights, it is sufficient for an individual to establish his residence in the State to which he would like to belong (author's translation).[29]

This was a ground-breaking agreement. Not only did it provide for almost absolute equal treatment, but it went as far as to automatically consider foreign residents as nationals. In turn, Article 5 established the right to free entry and exit not only for citizens of both states but also for the subjects, as well as equal civil rights. The extension of rights and free entry to both citizens and subjects is also present in other early agreements.[30]

The Peru–Colombian agreement served as a blueprint that others later adopted. Future treaties varied their titles: confederation, league, union, friendship or alliance, but, regardless, they were composed of the same core principles. From 1826 onwards the words 'commerce' and 'navigation' were incorporated into most of them. To exemplify the decisive role that the 1822 agreement played as a treaty prototype, we can assess the 1826 treaty between Chile and Argentina. Following Colombia's five signed agreements, this was the first bilateral agreement that other states proactively created. It provides that citizens, but not other subjects, of the contracting parties (the two states) will enjoy the same rights and privileges in both territories as those granted by law to naturals of the country in which they reside.[31] Thus the principle of equal treatment for regional nationals/citizens was established immediately after independence in an enormously diverse number of legal documents, including multilaterally, as discussed below.

Republic of Central America consisted of the present-day states of Guatemala, El Salvador, Honduras, Nicaragua and Costa Rica.

[29] Art. 4: 'Para asegurar y perpetuar del mejor modo posible la buena amistad y correspondencia entre ambos Estados, los ciudadanos del Perú y de Colombia gozarán de los derechos y prerrogativas que corresponden a los ciudadanos nacidos en ambos territorios, es decir, que los colombianos serán tenidos en el Perú por peruanos y estos en la República de Colombia por colombianos; sin perjuicio de las ampliaciones o restricciones que el Poder Legislativo de ambos Estados haya hecho o tuviere a bien hacer con respecto a las calidades que se requieren para ejercer las primeras magistraturas. Mas para entrar en el goce de los demás derechos activos y pasivos de ciudadanos, bastará que hayan establecido su domicilio en el Estado a que quieran pertenecer.'

[30] Art. 6, 1822 Agreement between Colombia and Chile. The agreement with Central America is almost identical but uses the word *habitantes* (inhabitants) rather than *sujetos* (subjects). See Art. 10 of the Treaty between Colombia and Central America.

[31] Art. 7, Treaty on Friendship, Alliance, Commerce and Navigation between the Republics of Chile and the United Provinces of the Río de la Plata, Santiago de Chile, 20 November 1826.

The Construction of the Hispano-American in Multilateral Agreements (1826–1865)

At the five regional congresses that took place between 1826 and 1865, states also adopted far-reaching multilateral agreements. The agreements demonstrated a clear progression in the number of topics addressed and their personal scope also evolved. Whereas the first Panama Congress only mentioned citizens as holders of rights of mobility and equality – and thus included a minority of individuals in each country[32] – the congresses in 1848 and thereafter referred to 'nationals' and thus enormously broadened their character.[33]

The first congress, under the auspices of Simón Bolívar, took place in Panama in 1826. Representatives from Colombia (which at that time included present-day Colombia, Ecuador, Panama and Venezuela), Central America (which included present-day Costa Rica, El Salvador, Guatemala, Honduras and Nicaragua), Peru and Mexico attended and signed several agreements, which later were not ratified.[34] For our purposes, the most relevant is the Union, League and Perpetual Confederation Treaty.[35] This was essentially a mutual defence pact which also included provisions on the friendly settlement of disputes through conciliation, mediation and the arbitration of a General Assembly established in the agreement. Articles 23 and 24 become relevant. Article 23 provided for an automatic naturalisation process for nationals residing in the territory of another state who wanted to acquire citizenship. After swearing allegiance to the constitution, these new nationals could access all employment positions except for those reserved for natural citizens. As discussed in Chapter 2, these positions were usually in the highest executive, legislative and judiciary offices. In this regard, naturalised Hispano-American citizens did not have a superior status to other naturalised foreigners. However, unlike the latter, they had a preferential automatic path to naturalisation.

---

[32] See Chapter 2, pp. 41–42.

[33] The only deviation from this trend of expansion is the 1856 Washington Agreement, in which only citizens are included. This possibly manifests the difficulty in reaching agreement on issues of such import, as well as the divergent regulation at the national level where some countries, such as Costa Rica, still maintained property requirements to access citizenship, while others, such as Peru, had eliminated such stipulations. See the 1856 Peruvian Constitution and the 1848 Costa Rican Constitution.

[34] Chile was not able to participate due to internal strife in the country. The Bolivian representative arrived late to the Congress. Argentina did not send any plenipotentiaries even though the Parliament had agreed to it. Brazil was invited but did not participate. The two US representatives could not join the debate since one died on his way and the other arrived late. Delegates from the UK and the Netherlands, countries which had territorial interests and possessions in the region, also attended as observers. Haiti, for reasons explained above, was not invited. See Lagos Valenzuela, 'El Arbitraje Internacional de América'; G. A. de la Reza, 'The Formative Platform of the Congress of Panama (1810–1826): the Pan-American Conjecture Revisited', *Revista Brasileira Política Internacional*, 56 (2013), 5–21.

[35] Union, League and Perpetual Confederation Treaty between the Republics Colombia, Central America, Peru and the United States of Mexico, Panamá, 15 July 1826. Only Colombia ratified this treaty.

Naturalisation also brought political rights. Article 24 set out that those not wishing to naturalise nonetheless had certain rights, including residence and all civil rights regarding the administration of justice, the protection of person and property, as well as the freedom to exercise any profession or occupation, but no political rights.

After the Panama Congress, despite Mexico taking the lead to replicate the experience, a new meeting did not take place until 1847, this time in Lima.[36] Several agreements were signed at the conclusion of the Lima Congress in 1848, two of which need to be highlighted. The Commerce and Navigation Treaty provided that nationals of the signing states enjoyed free movement to reside in any of the other states' territories, as well as enjoy the same liberty, freedoms and civil rights as nationals, including the freedom to exercise any type of profession.[37] Those who resided in the territory for two years while also exercising a profession, or while keeping an agricultural, commercial or industrial establishment, were considered as domiciled and subject to the same taxes as nationals. In turn, the Consular Convention included the provision of services in favour of any national residing in the territory of one of the signing state parties in cases where their country of origin did not have a Consul.[38] This new entitlement appeared 150 years before the European Union (EU) and contradicts those who have considered it a European innovation in public international law.[39] Consular protection was introduced with caution, remaining a possibility rather than an obligation. Later, consular protection was one of the central elements in many of the bilateral and multilateral accords adopted in the following decades.

The next attempt at confederation took place in 1856 in Santiago, Chile, where representatives from Chile, Ecuador and Peru signed the Continental Treaty.[40] According to Article 23, the treaty was open to other Hispano-American states, and also Brazil, should they wish to accede. Article 1 is of interest here. As had already become the norm, it established that naturals or citizens of any of the contracting parties were to enjoy the same treatment as nationals in the

---

[36] Peru and Bolivia had a short-lived experience as a confederate state between 1836 and 1839: see N. Sobrevilla Perea, *The Caudillo of the Andes: Andrés de Santa Cruz* (Cambridge University Press, 2011).

[37] Arts 1 and 2, Commerce and Navigation Treaty between Peru, Bolivia, Chile, Ecuador and Nueva Granada, Lima, 8 February 1848. Only Nueva Granada ratified this treaty.

[38] Art. 4, Consular Convention between Peru, Chile, Ecuador and Nueva Granada, Lima, 8 February 1848. All these countries ratified this agreement.

[39] The Treaty of Maastricht in 1993 established the right for EU citizens to enjoy consular protection in the territory of a third country where the Member State, of which they are nationals, is not present; some have wrongly considered this a European invention. See J. Weyland, 'La Protection Diplomatique et Consulaire des Citoyens de l'Union Européenne' in Epaminondas A. Marias (ed.), *European Citizenship* (Maastricht: European Institute of Public Administration, 1994) pp. 63–68, on p. 64.

[40] Continental Treaty between Chile, Ecuador and Peru. Continental Congress, Santiago de Chile, 15 September 1856. Ecuador ratified this treaty, as did Costa Rica, Guatemala, Nicaragua and El Salvador.

territory of the others. It also incorporated a first attempt at mutual recognition of professional qualifications, and equal access to consular protection in the territory of a third party.[41] Here we can observe a clear progression with new items entering the agenda and others consolidating and developing their status. For the first time, it established consular protection as an obligation – rather than a possibility as in the 1848 accord – and extended it to cover the territory of third parties. Mutual recognition of professional qualifications makes a circumspect debut, accompanied by two caveats: the need to adopt a common system of academic studies, and the remission to the formalities and tests to be followed in the host countries, as established by professional colleges for their own nationals. Mutual recognition of professional qualifications remained one of the central elements in the discussions to come.

Also in 1856, two months later, another congress took place in Washington: Costa Rica, El Salvador, Guatemala, Mexico, Nueva Granada, Peru and Venezuela participated, although the USA was not involved. The resulting final Confederation and Alliance Treaty included two interrelated provisions.[42] Article 8 set out that citizens from allied republics will be considered as citizens throughout the republics, enjoying all rights within the limitations established by each national constitution. In turn, Article 12 established the obligation for diplomatic ministries, consuls and vice-consuls to protect citizens from other republics, when their own consular agents did not offer such protection. The transition from prerogative to obligation is noteworthy.

New international events threatening the independence of Hispano-American states – such as the Spanish Crown re-annexing Santo Domingo in 1861 – precipitated a final Congress in Lima in 1864–65.[43] Several signed agreements resulted, with the Treaty on Commerce and Navigation of 12 March 1865 being the most relevant to our discussion. This agreement provided for the freedom of movement without a passport for both naturals and neighbours, thus included foreigners residing in each other's territory.[44] Those covered under the agreement were also guaranteed equal treatment with nationals, with the exception of positions reserved for nationals under each country's constitution.[45] Finally, Article 11 included consular protection abroad for all naturals or naturalised individuals from the contracting parties.

As was often the case, the treaties were not ratified. There are multiple reasons for this: for one thing, a dichotomy existed between, on the one hand, internal processes of state building and consolidation and, on the other

---

[41] Ibid., Arts 8 and 11.

[42] Confederation and Alliance Treaty between the Republics of Venezuela, Nueva Granada, Guatemala, El Salvador, Costa Rica, Mexico and Peru, Washington, 8 November 1856. The Treaty did not take effect.

[43] De la Reza, 'La Asamblea Hispanoamericana de 1864–65'.

[44] Art. 9, Commerce and Navigation Treaty between the Governments of Peru, Bolivia, Colombia, Ecuador, Guatemala, El Salvador and Venezuela, Lima, 12 March 1865.

[45] Ibid., Art. 10.

hand, the search for a supranational union. This was aggravated by domestic instability and changing governments, constitutions and even territories.[46] Additionally, when the dangers that had once existed – such as the invasion of Nicaragua by the filibuster Walker in 1855, or the French invasion of Mexico in the 1860s – disappeared, momentum for a meeting was lost.[47] In these negotiations, short-termism was the rule. Anderson has also argued that 'the "failure" of the Spanish-American experience to generate a permanent Spanish-America wide nationalism reflects both the general level of development of capitalism and technology in the late eighteenth century and the "local" backwardness of Spanish capitalism and technology in relation to the administrative stretch of the empire'.[48] He parallels this to the comparative advantage that the original thirteen colonies in North America had in being 'bunched geographically together' in an area much smaller than Argentina or Venezuela.[49] In that regard, it was not in the interests of the US or European powers to allow the new republics to form a strong union.[50] The USA made this very clear in 1857 when it exerted pressure on the Peruvian government to stop its diplomacy in favour of ratifying the 1856 Continental Treaty. Concerned with protecting its emerging hegemon status, the USA wished to deter the counter power that could result from such an alliance.[51] The last confederation effort took place in the 1860s. The subsequent Triple Alliance Conflict with Argentina, Brazil and Uruguay against Paraguay (1864–1870), as well as the Pacific War of Bolivia and Peru against Chile (1879–1883), made any further attempt at confederation unrealistic.

However, these treaties offer a legacy. Even if it can be argued that they were mostly addressed to a small Creole elite, they achieved a strong commitment to and consensus on equality. The new republics were determined not to share their territories and bureaucracies, but rather their citizens, who were granted equal treatment, freedom of entry and automatic naturalisation. Among the many principles that these agreements set, they laid the basis for continental citizenship.[52] During the last Congress in 1865, at least four countries made proposals to this effect. Bolivia presented a plan for a community of citizenship whereas Ecuador proposed citizenship and naturalisation for nationals from the signing American States. Colombia suggested allowing dual nationality between these

---

[46] De la Reza, 'La Asamblea Hispanoamericana de 1864–65', on pp. 90–91.
[47] G. de la Reza, '¿Necesidad o Virtud? Razones y Alcances de los Tratados Continentales Hispanoamericanos de 1856', *Historica*, XXXVIII (2014), 61–83.
[48] Anderson, *Imagined Communities*, p. 63.
[49] *Ibid.*, pp. 63–64.
[50] N. Galasso, *Seamos Libres y lo Demás no Importa Nada: Vida de San Martín* (Buenos Aires: Colihue, 2000), p. 483.
[51] De la Reza, '¿Necesidad o Virtud?', p. 80.
[52] J. M. Yepes, *Del Congreso de Panamá a la Conferencia de Caracas 1826–1954* (Caracas: Taller Gráfico Cromotip, 1955, Volume I), p. 208. Other principles of an incipient American International Law include the peaceful solution of controversies, the *uti possidetis juris* or the freedom of navigation of international rivers. *Ibid.*, pp. 205–207.

countries, and Venezuela made a proposal on American citizenship.[53] Even Argentina, which by and large did not participate in the Congresses, decided in 1862 not to ratify the 1856 Continental Treaty since it had already expressly consecrated the principle of legal equality between nationals and foreigners, including Hispano-Americans, in its Constitution.[54]

The Hispano-American as a Bilateral Concern

Bilateral agreements were common currency in nineteenth-century South America. They were much faster to negotiate, sign and ratify than multilateral ones, thus examples are abundant. Colombia signed the first bilateral agreements with other countries in the early 1820s and thereafter, many others followed suit until the end of the century. A domino effect ensued with clauses on equal treatment of regional nationals being adopted in subsequent negotiations. The general rule stood: equal treatment and free mobility were accepted as obvious and natural responses to regulating the status of regional individuals. Just as it is now assumed that those crossing a border should somehow lose certain entitlements, Hispano-American countries generally took the opposite to be true. To emphasise again, the provisions in these agreements were, by and large, much more generous than those signed with non-Hispano-American countries. The following pages identify and describe four different types of agreement that existed during this time period.

Sharing Nationals and Citizens as a Bilateral Practice

The first type of agreements were those granting absolute equality. They included clauses on automatic access to citizenship upon declaration, dual nationality, full equal treatment for those not naturalised and consular protection. The 1822 Colombia–Peru treaty set a paradigm that was then followed by many others. For instance, the 1856 Colombia–Costa Rica agreement mirrors this trend.[55] The treaty provided that citizens in each other's territory would enjoy the same civil rights and guarantees as nationals, including absolute freedom to trade, property protection and access to justice. Most strikingly, however, it facilitated dual citizenship since it did not require renouncing one's

[53] G. Parra-Aranguren, 'La Primera Etapa de los Tratados sobre Derecho Internacional Privado en América (1826–1940)', *Revista de la Facultad de Ciencias Jurídicas y Políticas*, 98 (1996), pp. 60–128, on p. 71.

[54] *Ibid.*, p. 69. The Argentinean government of course had in mind Art. 20 of its 1853 Constitution, which enshrined equal civil rights for foreigners.

[55] Friendship, Commerce, Navigation and Borders Treaty between Nueva Granada and Costa Rica, San José de Costa Rica, 11 June 1856. It was ratified in San José on 18 September 1856: see Arts 2 and 38–40.

previous status, given that the states' friendly relations subsisted. Citizens also enjoyed consular protection, upon request, in territories where their respective consuls were absent.[56]

These accords often followed the 1822 Colombia–Peru model to the letter. For example, the 1841 agreement between Provincia de Corrientes and Paraguay established that the 'sons from both states will be considered as naturals in each other's territory'.[57] Others, such as the 1859 Peru–Venezuela treaty, preferred to specify that citizens or naturals from one party would enjoy the treatment of nationals from the other, as far as their respective constitutions allowed.[58] The 1883 Venezuela–El Salvador accord noted that Venezuelans in El Salvador were to be considered as Salvadorians and vice versa.[59] A similar provision was included in the 1883 Venezuela–Bolivia agreement.[60]

A succinct word regarding the personal scope of these agreements is warranted. The beneficiaries had to be interpreted in line with the respective constitutions. As explained in Chapter 2, after independence the distinction between the national and the citizen was present for many decades, although its exclusionary character slowly became more nuanced. In other words, these agreements certainly did not have the free movement and equal treatment of *everyone* in mind. Some of them, such as the 1859 Peru–Venezuela accord, included both citizens and naturals, thus arguably excluding naturalised nationals, unless they were also citizens. Others, such as the 1841 Provincia de Corrientes–Paraguay Treaty, used the terminology 'sons from both states', thus possibly excluding naturalised individuals. Finally, the 1856 Colombia (Nueva Granada)–Costa Rica agreement referred to citizens. At that time in Colombia, citizens were all males who were married or over twenty-one years old.[61] Although obviously discriminating by gender, overall this was quite a comprehensive and inclusive notion, in which, at least in the letter of the law, race and social status did not play a role. However, in Costa Rica citizens were only males over twenty-one years old who were literate and possessed real estate or received a particular annual rent.[62]

---

[56] *Ibid.*, Arts 32, 38, 40.

[57] Art. 4, Friendship, Commerce and Navigation Treaty between the Government of Provincia de Corrientes and the Republic of Paraguay, Asunción, 31 July 1841. The Provincia de Corrientes later became part of Argentina.

[58] Art. 1, Union Treaty between the Governments of Peru and Venezuela, Caracas, 18 April 1859. This treaty was not ratified. There were also provisions on property protection, mutual recognition of rulings and professional qualifications, as well as on consular protection abroad.

[59] Art. 6, Friendship, Commerce and Navigation Treaty between Venezuela and El Salvador, Caracas, 27 August 1883.

[60] Art. 5, Peace, Friendship, Commerce and Navigation Treaty between Venezuela and Bolivia, Caracas, 14 September 1883.

[61] Art. 3, Nueva Granada Constitution, 20 May 1853.

[62] Art. 9, Costa Rican Constitution, 22 November 1848.

Providing Equal Civil Rights and Other Prerogatives as a Bilateral Practice

A second group of agreements, less far-reaching than the first model, provided for equal civil rights as well as other benefits. This is exemplified in the 1874 Argentina–Peru accord,[63] which provided equal civil rights, including individual protection and that of one's property,[64] exemptions from military service,[65] freedom of trade and navigation, the freedom to reside in any part of the counterpart's territory[66] and reciprocal consular protection abroad, usually upon request and as far as the foreign government would allow.[67] The Calvo Doctrine was also often included: nationals of both parties could use the law and tribunals of the country where they resided, but without any right to establish a diplomatic complaint.[68] Similar provisions were also present in the 1868 Argentina–Bolivia treaty.[69] Here we find the usual clauses on equal rights, exemption from military service, and equal treatment with nationals regarding access to justice, yet with a specific exclusion of political rights; it also included a mechanism of mutual recognition of certain professions.[70] Numerous treaties followed this paradigm of equal civil rights, coupled with other preferences and prerogatives. They include the following accords: 1835 Chile–Peru,[71] 1852 Paraguay–Argentina,[72] 1858 Bolivia–Argentina[73] and 1876 Peru–Chile.[74]

Agreements Developing a Particular Aspect of Citizenship

Agreements that only concentrated on a particular aspect of what we now consider as rights associated with citizenship were rare during the nineteenth century. Some agreements provided for diplomatic protection abroad, such as in the 1854 Nueva Granada–Ecuador and the 1856 Nueva Granada–Chile accords.[75] Besides their innovative character in international law, two aspects

[63] Friendship, Commerce and Navigation Treaty between the Republics of Argentina and Peru. Buenos Aires, 9 March 1874. It was ratified on 15 December 1875.

[64] *Ibid.*, Arts 2 and 31.

[65] *Ibid.*, Art. 3.

[66] *Ibid.*, Art. 6.

[67] *Ibid.*, Art. 31.

[68] *Ibid.*, Art. 4.

[69] Friendship, Commerce and Navigation Treaty between the Republics of Argentina and Bolivia, Buenos Aires, 9 July 1868. It was ratified on 24 September 1869.

[70] *Ibid.*, Arts 3, 6 and 8.

[71] Friendship, Commerce and Navigation Treaty between Chile and Peru, Santiago de Chile, 20 January 1835.

[72] Art. 13, Navigation and Borders Treaty between the Confederation of Argentina and the Republic of Paraguay, Asunción, 15 July 1852. It was ratified on 14 September 1852.

[73] See Arts 5–7, Friendship, Commerce and Navigation Treaty between the Governments of Argentina and Bolivia, Ouro, 7 December 1858. It came into effect on 13 July 1859.

[74] Friendship, Commerce and Navigation Treaty between Chile and Peru, Lima, 22 December 1876. It was ratified on 1 March 1877: see Arts 2–4.

[75] Art. 18, Consular Convention between Nueva Granada and Ecuador, Lima, 10 August 1854. It was ratified in Quito on 3 May 1858. Art. 18, Consular Convention between Nueva Granada and Chile, Santiago, 30 August 1853. It was ratified in Santiago on 9 May 1856.

are especially noteworthy. First, they were the result of multilateral level discussions that had already taken place at the regional Congresses. Rights that did not materialise via unratified multilateral treaties became a reality through bilateral agreements. Second, whereas consular conventions were normal practice between Hispano-American states and countries outside the region, they never included diplomatic protection abroad for nationals but, rather, merely regulated the status of consuls in each other's territory.[76]

Classical Navigation and Commerce Agreements with Further Rights

The fourth and final category of bilateral agreements granted the fewest rights to nationals from the other party. As their name declares, most of the provisions were concerned with navigation and commerce. However, they also incorporated clauses on the treatment of individuals. The most common one established reciprocal freedom of commerce and navigation. For that purpose, citizens of both parties could freely visit the other's coasts and territories in order to trade but also could reside there. They were also allowed to run their own businesses and enjoyed the same security and protection as nationals, including access to tribunals.[77] These agreements regularly incorporated restrictions on mandatory army service. Possibly the first agreement in this category is the one between Nueva Granada and Venezuela, signed in 1842 and ratified in 1844.[78] Several more followed in subsequent decades, including the 1855 Chile–Argentina,[79] 1856 Nueva Granada–Ecuador[80] and 1881 Paraguay–Peru accords.[81]

A notable example of this trend is the 1876 Argentina–Paraguay treaty. Its importance is reflected in the fact that it was signed only six years after the Triple Alliance War ended.[82] The agreement did not include equal civil rights, yet established a wide range of entitlements aligned with those mentioned above.[83] Similarly, the 1895 Bolivia–Chile treaty was signed twelve years after the Pacific War ended and included several provisions on equal treatment.[84]

---

[76] See, for example, the Consular Convention between Nueva Granada and the USA, Washington, 4 May 1850, as well as the Consular Convention between France and Venezuela, 24 October 1856.

[77] See, for example, Art. 15, Friendship, Commerce and Navigation Treaty between Nueva Granada and Ecuador, Bogotá, 9 July 1856. It was ratified in Quito on 26 May 1857.

[78] Art. 5, Friendship, Commerce and Navigation Treaty between Nueva Granada and Venezuela, Caracas, 23 July 1842. It was ratified in Bogotá on 7 November 1844.

[79] Arts 3–4, Peace, Friendship, Commerce and Navigation Treaty between the Republic of Chile and the Argentinean Confederation, Santiago, 30 August 1855. It was ratified on 29 April 1856.

[80] 1856 Treaty between Nueva Granada and Ecuador, Bogotá, 9 July 1856. It was ratified in Quito on 26 May 1857.

[81] Friendship, Commerce and Navigation Treaty between the Republics of Paraguay and Peru, Asunción, 18 June 1881.

[82] Friendship, Commerce and Navigation Treaty between Argentina and Paraguay, Buenos Aires, 3 February 1876. It entered into force on 13 September 1876.

[83] *Ibid.*, see Arts 5, 6, 7, 8, 10 and 11.

[84] Commerce Treaty between the Republics of Chile and Bolivia, Santiago de Chile, 18 May 1895. Arts 1–2 and 4–5 included equal rights regarding the exercise of commerce and industry and

A few features are noteworthy from this last group of agreements. For one thing, during this time period Brazil was not considered part of the common project, even though Brazil signed classic navigation and commerce agreements with various regional countries including Uruguay (1851), Paraguay (1856), Argentina (1856) and Bolivia (1887).[85] Nevertheless, these agreements often only referred to enjoying the same rights, immunities and privileges as those granted to the most favoured nation.[86] In the Brazilian case, the Portuguese national, and not the Hispano-American, represented the intermediate figure between the national and the foreigner.[87]

Additionally, the numerous pacts that South American states ratified with countries outside Hispano-America always fell into this limited fourth category.[88] The first three categories were only used between Hispano-American states. This long practice of bilateral preferential treatment of regional subjects can be explained by understanding that Hispano-Americans, notably Creole elites, were considered to be a step ahead of other foreigners regarding their closeness to the national. National laws and constitutions offer further evidence in favour of this theory.

The Hispano-American as a Constitutional Concern

Analysing the constitutions and citizenship laws in several countries reveals that preferential naturalisation routes and privileged treatment for Hispano-Americans were common practice throughout the region. After independence, various new states swiftly established privileged or even automatic routes to naturalisation for those born in the Hispanic Republics. The importance of this common constitutional culture and experience cannot be understated. It clearly represents the willingness, enshrined in the highest national norms, to readily accept those from Hispano-America as part of the community. This was an approach to membership that does not fit within classical descriptions. People, unlike bureaucracies or territories, could be shared between countries. In other words, the individual – arguably mostly Creole elites – was

acquisition of properties, equal protection of both individuals and property, equal treatment with regard to taxes and exclusion from military service.

[85] Commerce and Navigation Treaty between Uruguay and Brazil, Rio de Janeiro, 12 October 1851. It was ratified in 1852. Friendship, Navigation and Commerce Treaty between the Emperor of Brazil D. Pedro II and the Republic of Paraguay, Rio de Janeiro, 6 April 1856. It was ratified on 9 June 1856. Friendship, Commerce and Navigation Treaty between the Confederation of Argentina and the Emperor of Brazil, Paraná, 7 March 1856. It was ratified on 25 June 1856 in Paraná. Friendship, Commerce and Navigation Treaty between the Empire of Brazil and the Republic of Bolivia, Rio de Janeiro, 18 July 1887.

[86] Art. 6, 1856 Friendship, Commerce and Navigation Treaty between Argentina and the Emperor of Brazil. The term 'most favoured nation' means that the country that receives this treatment must obtain the same privileges as the 'most favoured nation' by the country providing such treatment.

[87] Sacchetta, *Laços de Sangue*.

[88] See Chapter 2, p. 52.

entitled to a common identity in the postcolonial Hispano-American space. The continuity of this regulative choice through several decades of constitutional amendments demonstrates a clear consensus in favour of preferential treatment for Hispano-Americans.[89]

The very first constitutions incorporated automatic naturalisation upon registration. These constitutions came in the shadow of several 'unsuccessful' multilateral treaties – assuming that ratification is the measure of success. These multilateral discussions, far from being failures, were actually fruitful. They planted the seed of a common understanding and approach to free movement, equal treatment, access to citizenship and, later, dual nationality. The continuity is palpable and obvious since despite some countries regularly replacing their constitutions, they nonetheless obstinately maintained these elements.

In Colombia, some form of preferential treatment is distinguishable starting in its first 1821 Constitution.[90] By the 1863 Constitution, those born in the Hispanic Republics were automatically granted citizenship, provided they resided in the territory and expressed their interest to the relevant authority.[91] This preferential treatment continued with the Constitution of 1886[92] and, with some modifications, in the current one of 1991.[93]

In Venezuela, the 1830 Constitution established that those born in Colombia – in either section before partition – and domiciled in the country were to be considered as Venezuelans by naturalisation.[94] Whilst the 1857 Constitution abandoned this route,[95] the 1858 one included all those born in the other Hispano-American Republics as Venezuelans by adoption, as long as they manifested their willingness before the registry.[96] This was expanded in 1864 to those born in the Spanish Antilles, hence incorporating the Spanish Caribbean.[97] All these individuals were to be granted the same rights as Venezuelans, rather than only those of Venezuelans by adoption. With minor modifications, this provision remained in the ensuing seventeen constitutions between 1874 and 1953.[98] Such longevity can only be interpreted as a conscious

---

[89] On the instability of the constitutions in some Latin American states, see: G. L. Negretto, *Making Constitutions: Presidents, Parties, and Institutional Choice in Latin America* (Cambridge University Press, 2013), pp. 20–21. Colombia is a notable exception since its 1886 Constitution lasted until 1991.

[90] To be eligible to become a Senator, those who had been born prior to 1810 in any part of the Americas – which before that time was still dependent on the Spanish Crown – had shorter residence requirements and fewer financial constraints than those born elsewhere outside Colombia. Colombia, Art. 96, 1821 Constitution.

[91] Colombia, Art. 31(4), 1863 Constitution.

[92] Colombia, Art. 8(2), 1886 Constitution. This preferential treatment remained in Law 22-bis 3 February 1936 on the naturalisation of foreigners.

[93] Colombia, Art. 96(2)(b), 1991 Constitution.

[94] Venezuela, Art. 11(4), 1830 Constitution.

[95] Venezuela, Art. 9, 1857 Constitution.

[96] Venezuela, Art. 6(2), 1858 Constitution.

[97] Venezuela, Art. 6(4), 1864 Constitution.

[98] Venezuela, Art. 6(4), 1874 Constitution; Art. 5(4), 1881 Constitution; Art. 5(4), 1891 Constitution; Art. 5(b)(2), 1893 Constitution (this Constitution introduced the term

and unequivocal acceptance of the special status for the other Republics' nationals. With the 1961 Constitution,[99] Venezuela significantly curtailed this preferential treatment: naturalisation was available only to those who obtained a *carta de naturaleza*, although special terms to acquire it were granted for Latin Americans and Spaniards. Reducing preferential treatment was related to Venezuela's particular economic and political situation in the early 1960s: unemployment and an economic recession led actors, such as unions, to pressure the government to restrict migration, notably from Europe.[100] The provisions in the current Constitution of 1999 are discussed below.

In Ecuador, apart from those born in the country, the first 1830 Constitution also recognised those coming from Colombia and residing in the country as Ecuadorians.[101] This continued in the 1835 Supreme norm, which also offered naturalisation to Americans in general after two, rather than the usual five, years of residence.[102] This preferential treatment disappeared in the following constitution[103] but re-emerged in 1845 again using the terminology 'Americans' rather than 'Hispano-Americans'.[104] The four constitutions between 1851 and 1869 did not include any preferential treatment.[105] Nonetheless, an 1867 decree recognised those coming from Chile, Colombia, Peru and Venezuela as citizens.[106] The 1878 Constitution extended this to any Hispano-American residing in the territory and making a declaration for that purpose.[107] After disappearing in the next three constitutions,[108] preferential access was newly enshrined in those of 1929 and 1945.[109] The provision vanished once again

Venezuelans by naturalisation for these nationals); Art. 8(b)(2) 1901 Constitution (here the reference to the Spanish Antilles disappeared and this exclusion has remained in the following constitutions); Art. 8(b)(1), 1904 Constitution; Art. 13(b)(2), 1909 Constitution; Art. 6(b)(2), 1914 Constitution; Art. 10(b)(2), 1922 Constitution; Art. 29(2), 1925 Constitution (the reference is to those born in the Iberoamerican Republics, which has also continued; it seems this was inserted to include Brazil, but also the Caribbean); Art. 29(2), 1928 Constitution; Art. 29(2), 1929 Constitution; Art. 29(2), 1931 Constitution; Art. 29(2), 1936 Constitution (for the first time there is a reference to Spain, which remains in subsequent constitutions); Art. 29(2), 1945 Constitution; Art. 12(3), 1947 Constitution (here the reference is to the Latin-American States; additionally, the possibility to retain dual citizenship is enshrined for the first time); Art. 23(2), 1953 Constitution.

[99] Venezuela, Art. 36, 1961 Constitution.
[100] L. R. Dávila, 'Fronteras Confusas: Impactos Sociales de la Migración' in CEPAL (ed.), *La Migración Internacional y el Desarrollo en las Américas* (Santiago de Chile: CEPAL, 2001), pp. 259–277.
[101] Ecuador, Art. 9(2), 1830 Constitution.
[102] Ecuador, Art. 6(3), 1835 Constitution.
[103] Ecuador, Art. 7, 1843 Constitution.
[104] Ecuador, Art. 6(2), 1845 Constitution.
[105] Ecuador, Art. 6, 1851 Constitution; Art. 6, 1852 Constitution; Art. 5, 1861 Constitution; Art. 6, 1869 Constitution.
[106] Ecuador, Decree 24 October 1867, cited in Ramírez, 'Del Aperturismo Segmentado al Control Migratorio'.
[107] Ecuador, Art. 9(3), 1878 Constitution.
[108] Ecuador, Art. 6, 1884 Constitution; Art. 6, 1897 Constitution; Art. 12, 1906 Constitution.
[109] Ecuador, Art. 9(5), 1929 Constitution; Art. 12, 1945 Constitution; this also included Spanish nationals.

in 1946 but was reintroduced with the condition of reciprocity in 1967 and 1979.[110] The Constitutions of 1998 and 2008 eliminated the privilege.

In Peru as early as 1821, a decree allowed Hispano-Americans to access public employment under the same conditions as Peruvian citizens.[111] The first 1823 Constitution contained a provision facilitating naturalisation for those coming from other independent American territories under conditions of reciprocity.[112] By 1828, Hispano-Americans who had resided in Peru before 1820 were automatically granted citizenship after registration.[113] Following several internal struggles, the 1834 Constitution eliminated the preferential route for Hispano-Americans.[114] In 1839, this was reintroduced so that Hispano-Americans could naturalise upon enrolment in the civic registry.[115] This preferential treatment, removed in the 1856 Constitution,[116] re-emerged in 1860 by recognising both naturals of the Spanish Americas as Peruvians by birth, as well as Spaniards who were in Peru when it proclaimed independence and who continued to reside in the country thereafter.[117] The 1867 Constitution extended this to all foreigners. But since the 1920 Constitution, up to and including the present one from 1993, Hispano-Americans have not been privileged. The only exception is the 1979 text in which Spaniards and Latin Americans – rather than Hispano-Americans – on becoming Peruvians were not required to renounce their previous nationality. This was amended in 1993 amidst concerns regarding the lack of reciprocity Peruvians faced in other Latin American countries.

In Bolivia, the first 1826 Constitution established that citizens from the former Spanish colonies would enjoy citizenship rights in Bolivia based on bilateral treaties. In 1839, rather than the normal ten years of residence, shorter periods of two or four years, depending on whether individuals were married or not, were enshrined for the naturalisation of Hispano-Americans.[118] Later, an 1866 Decree stipulated that South-American – rather than Hispano-American – nationals and Bolivians would have equal exercise of rights, including political ones, except for accession to the Presidency of the executive, legislative or judicial powers.[119] This was later extended to include all Americans, who were not to be considered as foreigners in Bolivia and who could obtain citizenship by simple declaration.[120] However, apart from these two decrees, the constitutions

---

[110] Ecuador, Art. 17, 1967 Constitution; Art. 9, 1979 Constitution.

[111] Peru, Decree 4 October 1821, cited in Vetancourt Aristeguieta, *Nacionalidad, Naturalización y Ciudadanía*, p. 36.

[112] Peru, Art. 21, 1823 Constitution.

[113] Peru, Art. 4, 1828 Constitution.

[114] O. A. Pazo Pineda, 'Report on Citizenship Law: Peru', EUDO Citizenship Observatory, EUI, 2015, p. 4. See Peru, Art. 3, 1834 Constitution.

[115] Peru, Art. 6(6), 1839 Constitution.

[116] Peru, Arts 32–34, 1856 Constitution.

[117] Peru, Art. 34(3), 1860 Constitution.

[118] Bolivia, Art. 11, 1839 Constitution.

[119] Bolivia, Decree on Hispano-American Citizenship, La Paz de Ayacucho, 18 March 1866. On this, see Vetancourt Aristeguieta, *Nacionalidad, Naturalización y Ciudadanía*, pp. 18–24.

[120] Bolivia, Decree 16 July 1868.

following 1839 removed preferential treatment. It only resurfaced in 1967 and 1995 with the ruling that Spaniards and Latin Americans – again rather than Hispano-Americans – could acquire Bolivian nationality without losing their original one, if reciprocity agreements were in place.[121]

In Paraguay, the 1870 and 1940 Constitutions established the government's obligation to encourage not only European but also American immigration.[122] This must be read against the background of the Triple Alliance War, which had decimated Paraguay's population, as well as the need to increase the labour force in the agricultural and livestock sectors.[123]

Finally, in Uruguay, an 1839 Decree adopted a process to recognise high school diplomas and law degrees from other American Republics. American lawyers could practise merely by producing their title rather than passing an exam. According to the decree, this decision was motivated both by the scarcity of local lawyers as well as the convenience brought about by establishing American unity.[124]

A final remark is important regarding provisions in other former Spanish colonies in the Caribbean and Central and North America, rather than only in South America, since this legal construction affected Hispano-Americans. In the case of Central America, the first 1824 Constitution of the Federal Republic[125] included the automatic naturalisation for all those born in the American Republics, after declaring their intention before the local authorities.[126] This provision remained to varying degrees in several subsequent constitutions in Costa Rica,[127] Guatemala,[128] Honduras,[129]

---

[121] Bolivia, Art. 37, 1967 and 1995 Constitutions.

[122] Paraguay, Art. 6, 1870 Constitution; Art. 9, 1940 Constitution.

[123] E. Texidó and G. Baer, 'Las Migraciones en el Cono Sur en el Período 1990–2001' in E. Texidó, G. Baer, N. Pérez Vichich, A. M. Santestevan and C. P. Gomes (eds), *Migraciones Laborales en Sudamérica: El Mercosur Ampliado* (Geneva: ILO, 2003), pp. 4–40, on p. 32.

[124] Uruguay, Decree January 1839, cited in Vetancourt Aristeguieta, *Nacionalidad, Naturalización y Ciudadanía*, pp. 23–24.

[125] The Federal Republic lasted from 1821 until 1841 and was comprised of present-day Costa Rica, El Salvador, Guatemala, Honduras and Nicaragua.

[126] Federal Republic of Central America, Art. 18, 1824 Constitution.

[127] Costa Rica, Arts 58 and 97, 1844 Constitution. This included preferential naturalisation for naturals from other parts of the Americas, including the possibility of being elected as Member of Parliament, something which was not possible for other naturalised foreigners. This was replicated in the 1847 Constitution (Art. 29), but not in the following 1848, 1859, 1869 or 1871 Constitutions. The 1917 norm included preferential provisions for Central Americans (Art. 40) and 'Iberoamericans,' rather than Hispano-Americans, who could naturalise after two rather than five years (Art. 14).

[128] Guatemala's very first 1825 Constitution (Art. 46) included naturals from any of the American Republics who settled there as citizens. With minor modifications, this preferential treatment remained in the Constitutions of 1851, 1879, 1921, 1945, 1956 and 1965. Preferential treatment for Central Americans only came into being with the present constitution of 1985.

[129] In Honduras, the 1848 Constitution (Art. 11) established the automatic naturalisation upon settlement and declaration for that purpose of those who had been born in the American Republics. This was limited to Central Americans in the 1865 and 1873 Constitutions. Again in 1880 (Art. 31), automatic naturalisation was enshrined for Hispano-Americans who renounced their previous nationality and settled in Honduras. With minor modifications, this remained

Nicaragua[130] and El Salvador.[131] In Panama, all constitutions, except the first two of 1904 and 1941, have provided preferential treatment for Hispano-Americans.[132] In the Dominican Republic, preferential naturalisation for those born in the Hispano-American Republics was present in many of its constitutions from the first in 1844 until 1907.[133] Finally, in Mexico the first 1824 Constitution included special provisions for Hispano-Americans,[134] which were then absent from all constitutions after 1836. The present 1917 text incorporates a faster naturalisation route of two, rather than five, years of residence for nationals from any Latin American country, including Belize but excluding Haiti.[135]

Discussion

Now that the multilateral, bilateral and national legal framework has been presented, three questions can be posed. First, what were the reasons for constructing a third legal figure, the Hispano-American, to fit between the national–foreigner binary? Second, were these provisions implemented in practice? Finally, what is the influence, if any, of these provisions today?

in the 1894, 1904, 1924 (which included Spaniards for the first time), 1936, 1957 and 1965 Constitutions.

[130] In Nicaragua, the first 1838 Constitution, in Art. 20, included the automatic naturalisation of naturals from the American Republics who expressed their willingness and were settled there. Although this preferential treatment disappeared in the 1854 and 1858 Constitutions, it was reincorporated in those of 1893, 1898, 1905, 1911 and 1913. The Constitutions of 1939 and 1948 only referred to Central Americans. The 1950 highest norm reintroduced preferential treatment in Art. 19: two rather than ten years of residence were enough to naturalise. It was also required to renounce one's previous nationality. This remained in the 1974 Constitution but not in the present one of 1987, which favours only Central Americans.

[131] El Salvador did not include any preferential treatment other than for Central Americans in its first 1841 Constitution. Beginning with its second 1864 Constitution (Art. 6), though, it established preferential access to all those originating from the other Hispano-American Republics with the simple condition of settlement in El Salvador. With minor modifications, this preferential treatment remained in the 1871, 1872, 1883, 1886, 1939, 1950 and 1962 Constitutions.

[132] In Panama, the Constitution of 1946 (Art. 10) established the naturalisation of nationals by birth in Spain or any independent American nation, provided they fulfilled the same requirements as those for Panamanians to naturalise in that country. This reciprocity clause remained in the 1972 Constitution and is still effective today.

[133] In the Dominican Republic, the 1844 (Art. 7), 1854, 1858 and 1872 (Art. 5) Constitutions included descendants of natives from the former Spanish territories in the Americas as Dominicans, without the need to naturalise, provided they established their residence in the Republic. This preferential treatment disappeared in the 1865, 1866, 1874, 1875, 1877, 1878, 1879 and 1880 Constitutions yet was clearly reincorporated in the 1881, 1887 and 1896 Constitutions for those from Hispano-American Republics as well as from the Spanish Antilles (Art. 7). This was eliminated in the 1907 Constitution and has never been re-established in the following fourteen constitutions, including the present 2015 one.

[134] Arts 21 and 125 of the 1824 Mexican Constitution allowed Hispano-American nationals to be deputies and judges in the Supreme Court, roles prohibited for other foreigners.

[135] H. Hoyo, 'Report on Citizenship Law: Mexico', Florence, EUI, 2015, p. 18.

Explaining the Construction of the Hispano-American

As with the demarcation between the national and the foreigner, the construction of the Hispano-American was an elite project. Indeed, as explained in Chapter 2, only an extremely reduced group of nationals had the chance to become citizens. The ruling Creole elites often mistrusted local populations,[136] and these same elites occupied the government and parliamentary positions in charge of negotiating bilateral and multilateral agreements, as well as drafting national laws and constitutions. Among the upper Creole classes exercising political representation, a strong sense of camaraderie was present. This resulted from the peculiar characteristics of the post-independence process, as well as from cohesion in terms of history, language 'and a shared sense of commonality with (...) groups in neighbouring countries'.[137] The expansion of Catholicism, both 'as an ideology upholding the racial-class-gender status quo, and as an institution' also 'contributed to a region-wide identity especially among the elite'.[138]

The first post-colonial period lasted until the mid-1860s and was marked by ongoing external security threats, including from Spain. It is in this phase that a strong push towards constructing a regional membership, clearly expressed in various multilateral treaties, is most obvious. All the affected countries had widespread concerns regarding possible and actual invasions by both European powers and the USA. Within an international arena reluctant to recognise their sovereignty, the new republics all faced similar challenges in strengthening their viability as states and in constructing nations. They suffered from constant political struggles, were internally weak and had huge domestic gaps based on class and race. Yet security concerns alone cannot explain far-reaching provisions on equal treatment and free movement. Here Max Weber's argument that 'memories of colonization and migration' comprise a crucial aspect in developing a 'subjective belief in a communality of descent' is useful.[139] Idealism, as well as common shared goals, were present until at least 1865.

Reciprocity is important to understand the second post-colonial phase, which was characterised by bilateralism. During this time, numerous covenants were signed, which were mostly related to trade and regulated the reality on the ground. From 1865 onwards, expectations and aspirations were toned down even if bilateralism aimed to go far beyond merely regulating trade. It is against that backdrop that we can understand the addition of numerous provisions

---

[136] E. J. Hobsbawm, 'Nacionalismo y Nacionalidad en América Latina' in P. Sandoval (ed.), *Repensando la Subalternidad. Miradas Críticas desde/sobre América Latina* (Lima: Instituto de Estudios Peruanos, 2010) pp. 311–326.

[137] S. Radcliffe and S. Westwood, *Remaking the Nation. Place, Identity and Politics in Latin America* (London: Routledge, 1996), p. 5.

[138] *Ibid.*, p. 17.

[139] M. Weber, *Wirtschaft und Gesellschaft* (Tübingen: Mohr, 1976) p. 237, quoted in C. Joppke, *Selecting by Origin. Ethnic Migration in the Liberal State* (Cambridge, MA: Harvard University Press, 2005) p. 26.

on equal treatment, mobility and nationality that, as seen in Chapter 2, were absent when dealing with countries outside the region.

Furthermore, domestic constitutional clauses granting preferential treatment show a strong commitment towards the idea of common links binding the region together. As Joppke has explained, one of the ways to justify ethnic preferences is 'to give expression to a historical-cultural community that encompasses more than one state'.[140] This can often overlap with discourse on assimilability.[141] Interestingly, as Herzog has argued, 'the tension between local aspirations and global constructions, and the belief that beyond the municipal realm was a wider community to which one belonged (...) was particularly difficult to manage during the independence period'.[142] The same aspects that tie elites together – language, religion and tradition – were perceived as Hispanic characteristics that many liberal modernisers did not want to celebrate but rather wanted to move beyond.[143] In the end, Creolism, with its different interests and contradictions at the national and regional levels, was as much a unifying force as it was an obstacle in constructing a supranational membership.[144] As Simon has observed, opposition to confederation projects aroused out of provincial Creoles who had seen their capacity to impact policies limited and who thus aimed at destroying such unions and to decentralise federalism 'as means of regaining influence within independent states'.[145]

Implementation in Practice

The introduction of clauses granting equal protections and rights of admission to each other's nationals in bilateral navigation and commerce treaties was not an exclusively Hispano-American endeavour. The most famous examples are the 1858 and 1868 agreements between the USA and China.[146] Their citizens were free to emigrate 'for the purposes of curiosity, of trade, or as permanent residents'.[147] Yet whereas free movement and open borders were central to these agreements, the extension of rights was not comparable to most

---

[140] Joppke, *Selecting by Origin*, p. 24.

[141] *Ibid.*, p. 23.

[142] Herzog, *Defining Nations*, p. 152.

[143] This is evident in the works of Alberdi, who argued in favour of looking to the UK and France as role models: see Alberdi, *Bases y Puntos de Partida para la Organización Política de la República Argentina*.

[144] Herzog, *Defining Nations*, p. 152; Centeno, *Blood and Debt*, pp. 172–173.

[145] Simon, *The Ideology of Creole Revolution*, pp. 188–189.

[146] Treaty of Peace, Amity and Commerce, between the United States of America and China, concluded at Tientsin, 18 June 1858. Additional Articles to the Treaty between the United States of America and the Ta-Tsing Empire of the 18th June 1858, Washington, 28 July 1868, which is also known as the Burlingame Treaty.

[147] See Art. V of the 1868 Treaty. The same clause was enshrined in the Peru–China Treaty on Friendship, Commerce and Navigation, Tientsin (Tianjin), 26 June 1874. Chinese nationals did not have, however, any of the prerogatives in Peru that were granted to Hispano-Americans in other bilateral treaties.

Hispano-American treaties and was limited to those 'enjoyed by the citizens or subjects of the most favoured nation'.[148] Importantly for our purposes, the agreements worked in practice. This can be seen in the number of Chinese nationals that emigrated to the USA, and in the way the adoption of restrictive legislation at the domestic level became more difficult: Presidents in the USA vetoed several initiatives precisely because they breached the treaty.[149]

Even if bilateral agreements were implemented, it is obvious that there might have been divergences between the law on the books and the law in action. These differences are difficult to measure both in the USA and in Hispano-America. The latter has a limited number of academic secondary sources, to which we add the scarcity of court decisions affecting Hispano-American individuals. There were also possible differences between bordering regions, as well as between small villages and large cities. We do not intend to solve this question here. There are, however, several indications that the Hispano-American was recognised as a legal figure who, being closer to the national, was entitled to similar rights both in theory and in practice.

First, the limited cases with available records of administrative practice all point in the direction of implementation. This is the case for bilateral agreements, such as the 1822 Peru–Colombia accord,[150] and also holds true for constitutional provisions, for example, in Venezuela.[151]

Second, many bilateral agreements did not incorporate individual rights. Had these clauses been inapplicable in practice or merely aspirational – as is often the case with constitutional provisions – they would have been included in all bilateral treaties, as well as remained part of national laws and Constitutions when they were amended. By *a contrario* reasoning, it can be argued that, similar to the USA–China example, they were taken seriously when they were enshrined in law.

Third, despite thorough renovations of all other aspects of nationality laws, the fact that the preferential status of Hispano-Americans remained in some cases is a strong indication that these provisions were more than merely theoretical. This is exemplified by the strikingly different 1863 and 1886 Colombian Constitutions. These constitutions are considered antipodal in terms of political vision: the former a model of liberal ideas, the latter a paradigm of the conservative project.[152] In fact, the 1886 text restricted access to citizenship, granted fewer rights to naturalised citizens as well as to foreigners in general and, most crucially, put an end to the absolute *ius soli* tradition in the country.

---

[148] See Art. VI of the 1868 Treaty.

[149] I. Black, 'American Labour and Chinese Immigration', *Past & Present*, 25 (1963), 59–76.

[150] See its application also in Venezuela after its separation from Colombia in the various administrative resolutions mentioned in G. Parra-Aranguren, *La Constitución de 1830 y los Venezolanos por Naturalización* (Caracas: Imp. Universitaria, 1969), on pp. 54–59.

[151] See the references to various resolutions by the Secretary of Interior and Justice in Venezuela, available in *ibid.*, pp. 43–47 and 105–122.

[152] Gargarella, *Latin American Constitutionalism*, p. 40.

However, preferential access to naturalisation for Hispano-American nationals, an innovation introduced by the 1863 Constitution, remained intact.

Fourth, although others who were not Hispano-Americans received preferential treatment in some respects – e.g. freedom of religion in agreements with Great Britain – it was never to the same extent nor was naturalisation included. This exclusion also affected Brazil. It was only much later, in the twentieth century, that Spaniards, and in some cases also Portuguese and Brazilians, were offered a higher preferential status.[153] Had these been cosmetic provisions, countries would have used bilateral covenants to extend them also to other countries with whom they had friendly relationships.

Fifth, whereas the academic legal historical literature is scarce, those who have researched the issue are unanimous in recognising an individual right to access citizenship in these various national provisions.[154]

Finally, it is important to highlight the fact that Hispano-American countries never devoted resources to attract other Hispano-American nationals. This differs from what occurred with European settlers, who were lured through immigration laws granting lands, paying passages or offering tax breaks.[155] Thus, when compared to the number of Europeans landing on the continent, Hispano-Americans benefiting from preferential access to citizenship constituted a small minority, possibly only comprising Creole elites.[156] This aspect probably contributed to the longevity of constitutional preferences in countries such as Colombia or Venezuela that did not receive a large number of immigrants, and certainly not from Hispano-America, during the nineteenth century.

Influence Today

Some countries have kept certain forms of favoured treatment. Today, via their constitution or citizenship laws, three South American states still grant a preferential path towards naturalisation to nationals coming from the region. In Colombia, Latin American and Caribbean nationals – rather than the previously used 'Hispano Americans' – may obtain citizenship after one year

---

[153] See, for example, the 1929 and 1945 Ecuadorian Constitutions, the 1967 Bolivian Constitution and the Venezuelan Constitutions between 1928 and 1953. The only exception is the reference to Spaniards in the 1839 and 1860 Peruvian Constitutions.

[154] On Venezuela, see Vetancourt Aristeguieta, *Nacionalidad, Naturalización y Ciudadanía en Hispano-América*, p. 89 and G. Tell Villegas, *Los Extranjeros. Su Admisión, Su Expulsión* (Caracas: Impr. y Lit. del Gobierno Nacional, 1891), p. 113. On Venezuela and Colombia, see Parra-Aranguren, *La Constitución de 1830 y los Venezolanos por Naturalización* and S. Planas Suárez, *Los Extranjeros en Venezuela: Su Condición ante el Derecho Público y Privado de la República* (Lisboa: Centro Tipográfico Colonial, 1917), p. 212. On Ecuador, see B. Valladares Rueda, *La Nacionalidad y la Naturalización en la Práctica Administrativa* (Quito: Tall. Gráf. Nacionales, 1955), p. 73. On Argentina and Paraguay, see H. Arbo, *Ciudadanía y Naturalización* (Buenos Aires: El Ateneo, 1926), p. 72.

[155] See Chapter 2, p. 47.

[156] See Chapter 1, pp. 10–12.

of residence, rather than five, provided this tallies with the relevant bilateral treaties.[157] In practice, however, reciprocity is not taken into consideration, thus all regional citizens only need to prove a one-year residence period before naturalising.[158] In Venezuela, the residence period is reduced from ten to five years for Latin Americans and nationals from the Caribbean, rather than Hispano-Americans as before.[159] Finally, in Bolivia the constitution provides for the three-year residence period to be reduced on a reciprocal basis via treaties with other countries, primarily again Latin American ones, rather than Hispano-American.[160] Regarding other former Spanish colonies, preferential treatment is still in place for Latin Americans in Costa Rica,[161] Dominican Republic,[162] El Salvador,[163] Honduras,[164] Mexico[165] and Panama.[166] Countries in South America have also given a preference for regional migrants when it comes to regularisation procedures.[167] The influence of this forgotten narrative is also important in a more subtle way. Confirming the common understanding of the regional national, in a legislative rather than discursive framework, may offer momentum to debates on South American citizenship by serving as an additional tool for those moving the process forward at both the national and regional level.[168]

Conclusion

Right from independence, the nascent Hispano-American Republics constructed a new legal figure, the Hispano-American, who was situated in between the dichotomy of the national and the foreigner. This creation was the result of peculiar characteristics stemming from a new group of countries

---

[157] Colombia, Art. 5, Law 43/1993 (1 February) on citizenship.
[158] This is two years in the case of nationals from Spain whereas it is five years for the rest. Escobar, *Report on Citizenship Law: Colombia*, pp. 11–12.
[159] Venezuela, Art. 33, 1999 Constitution. Spaniards, Portuguese and Italians also benefit from this reduced residence period.
[160] Bolivia, Art. 144, 2009 Constitution.
[161] Costa Rica, Art. 14, 1949 Constitution provides for preferential treatment for Central American and 'Iberoamericans', who can naturalise after five rather than seven years.
[162] Dominican Republic, Art. 32 of the 1683/1948 Naturalisation Law establishes that the fees and taxes required to naturalise will be reduced by half for petitioners from Latin America.
[163] El Salvador, Art. 92, 1983 Constitution requires just one year of residence, rather than five, for Spaniards and Hispano-Americans to naturalise.
[164] In Honduras, according to Art. 24 of the 1982 Constitution, Spaniards and Iberoamericans must reside for two, rather than three, years to naturalise.
[165] In Mexico, Art. 20 of the 1998 Nationality Law establishes that Latin Americans must wait two, rather than five, years before naturalising. This provision has been in place since the 1934 Nationality and Naturalisation Law, 20 January. The preferential treatment was already enshrined in Art. 30 of the original text of the 1917 Constitution.
[166] In Panama, the 1972 Constitution establishes in Art. 10 that Spanish and Latin American nationals by birth may naturalise if they fulfil the same requirements requested from Panamanians to naturalise in that particular country.
[167] See Chapter 5, pp. 134–135.
[168] See Chapter 7.

emerging from the same colonial power. We must remember that the 1812 Cádiz Constitution considered all those living in the American continent, with some exceptions, as sharing the same Spanish nationality.[169] The process of creating an intermediate figure was not only discursive, but also legislative, albeit one constructed by and addressed to Creole elites. This chapter has presented numerous multilateral and bilateral agreements, as well as domestic constitutional law, which confirm this. The reference to the Hispano-American continued for several decades until the end of the nineteenth century. Despite all South American states, except for Brazil, utilising the figure, it was stronger in countries such as Colombia and Venezuela than in others such as Argentina and Chile. Thereafter, the Hispano-American legal figure faced a slow decline, partly from two major South American conflicts – the Triple Alliance War and the Pacific War – as well as from the new Pan-American Conferences beginning in 1889, where commercial interests took a leading role. Nonetheless, even when the figure's initial idealism was lost in the twentieth century, the next chapter demonstrates that South American countries continued to consider the Hispano-American as more similar to the national than any other foreigner.

---

[169] See Chapter 2, pp. 34–36.

4

The Legal Construction of the Foreigner as Undesirable in Twentieth-Century South America

[Argentina] has become the promised land for all vagabonds or criminals who do not fit in well in Europe. This is how real criminal associations are being formed primarily in the social underworld of our main population centres.[1]

Introduction

From the 1880s onwards, large numbers of migrants arrived in South America, mostly in Argentina, Brazil and Uruguay. In the 1880s alone, 400,000 disembarked in Brazil and double that in Argentina, tripling the arrivals throughout the previous decade.[2] The Argentinean 'campaign of the desert' in Patagonia in the 1870s had, through displacing and annihilating indigenous populations, opened up enormous lands for cultivation.[3] Faster transatlantic and railway transportation, coupled with increasing European demand for food in a period of industrialisation, positioned Argentina as the breadbasket for Europe. Coinciding with the arrival of more foreigners, the 1880s also manifested the early signs of border closures and migration control. Previous free movement and equal treatment provisions gradually deteriorated in favour of restrictions on various ethnic, racial, ideological, moral, physical and economic grounds, ushering in a new era of control. As if constructing a wall, individual bricks representing despised categories of foreigners were slowly but surely stacked one upon another throughout an entire century of legislative and administrative provisions, up until the 1980s.

---

[1] M. Cané, *Expulsión de Extranjeros (Apuntes)* (Buenos Aires: Imprenta de J. Sarrailh, 1899), p. 11 (author's translation). '[Argentina] se ha transformado en la tierra de promisión para todo vagabundo, ó delincuente que no encuentra ya cabida en Europa. Y así, se van formando, principalmente en los bajos fondos sociales de nuestros primeros centros de población, verdaderas asociaciones de criminales'.

[2] For Brazil see: F. Schulze, 'German-Speaking and Japanese Immigrants in Brazil, 1850–1945' in N. Foote and M. Goebel (eds), *Immigration and National Identities in Latin America* (Gainesville, FL: University Press Florida, 2014), pp. 115–138, on pp. 117–118. For Argentina see: Moya, *Cousins and Strangers*, p. 56.

[3] Rouquié, *The Military and the State in Latin America*, p. 67.

The USA exerted an important influence since its legislation was debated in domestic parliaments in South America.[4] The prohibitions against the entry of convicts and prostitutes, and then Chinese nationals, in 1875 and 1882 respectively, eroded the long-standing tradition of free movement.[5] Later, the assassination of US President McKinley in 1901 by a US-born anarchist of Polish descent instigated further restrictions against those considered to disrupt the established social order and peace.[6]

The relationship between the freedom of movement and a state's sovereignty has been the subject of analysis by classical and present-day scholars alike. Territorial integrity has often been understood as a corollary of sovereignty. Perruchoud has defined the territorial aspect of sovereignty as 'the authority that a State exercises over all persons and things found within its territory'.[7] Entry of foreigners would be based on their own control and admission criteria.[8] Such state authority has been presented as inherently necessary for its own survival and perpetuation.[9] The US Supreme Court was the first to unequivocally affirm this theory:

> It is an accepted maxim of international law, that every sovereign nation has the power, as inherent in sovereignty, and essential to its self-preservation, to forbid the entrance of foreigners within its dominions, or to admit them only in such cases and upon such conditions as it may see fit to prescribe.[10]

This and other rulings adopted between 1889 and 1893[11] immediately influenced Commonwealth jurisdictions[12] and later inspired similar conclusions by South American courts.[13] More recently, this expression

---

[4] For example, Miguel Cané, an Argentinean writer and politician who proposed the first expulsion law adopted in Argentina in 1902, discussed at length and with great detail US migration laws and jurisprudence in his 1899 book: Cané, *Expulsión de Extranjeros*.

[5] USA, Immigration Act of 1875, 18 Stat. 477; Chinese Exclusion Act of 1882, 22 Stat. 58.

[6] USA, Act to Regulate the Immigration of Aliens into the United States (Anarchist Exclusion Act), 3 March 1903.

[7] R. Perruchoud, 'State Sovereignty and Freedom of Movement' in B. Opeskin, R. Perruchoud and J. Redpath-Cross (eds), *Foundations of International Migration Law* (Cambridge University Press, 2012), pp. 123–151, on p. 123.

[8] *Ibid.*, p. 124. V. Chetail, 'The Transnational Movement of Persons Under General International Law: Mapping the Customary Law Foundations of International Migration Law' in V. Chetail and C. Bauloz (eds), *Research Handbook on International Law and Migration* (Cheltenham: Edward Elgar, 2014), pp. 1–74, on p. 1.

[9] J. A. R. Nafziger, 'The General Admission of Aliens under International Law', *American Journal of International Law*, 77 (1983), 804–847, on 804.

[10] USA, *Nishimura Ekiu v. United States* [1892] 142 U.S. 651, Gray J., 659.

[11] Other than *Nishimura Ekiu*, also see: *The Chinese Exclusion Case*, 130 U.S. 581 (1889); *Fong Yue Ting v. United States*, 149 U.S. 698 (1893).

[12] In the UK, see *Musgrove v. Chun Teeong Toy* 1891 A.C. 272. In Canada, see *Attorney-General for Canada v. Cain* [1906] AC 542, 546.

[13] In Argentina, see the 1927 Supreme Court's case *Habeas Corpus de Irene Amor Magaz de González*, 148 Fallos, 410, 414. In Brazil, the Supreme Court referred to *Ekiu* and *Yue* to acknowledge the right to expel and deport aliens in *Habeas Corpus de Vicente Vacirca*, 1908. See

of territorial sovereignty has been reaffirmed in international treaties and jurisprudence.[14]

Various scholars have problematised the historical validity of the state's control claim as an accepted maxim of international law. They argue that free movement, rather than the power to exclude foreigners, was historically the norm. Put differently, the right to exclude individuals would be a recent construction.[15] Specialists such as Nafziger or Martin convincingly maintain that the nineteenth-century US Supreme Court rulings that upheld the exclusion of foreigners were based on a partial and incomplete reading of the works of publicists, such as Vattel.[16] Far from being neutral, these rulings were the expression of exclusionary doctrines upholding 'racial or ideological tests' and were the result of the counsel's failure in developing 'the principle of free movement on behalf of their clients'.[17]

In effect, free movement was protected under international law.[18] In 1892, at the same time the US Supreme Court ruled on *Nishimura Ekiu*, the Institute of International Law confirmed that the free entry of foreigners could not be forbidden in a systematic or permanent fashion; but it could be blocked for reasons of public interest or on extremely serious grounds, such as a dangerous accumulation of people arriving at the same time. Protecting national workers also did not serve as a sufficient reason to deny entry, although certain individuals – such as vagrants, beggars, criminals or suspected offenders, as well as seriously ill individuals – could be banned.[19] Classical publicists also denied 'the state an absolute right to exclude aliens'.[20]

In South America, where free movement and entry provisions were enshrined at the constitutional level,[21] the swerve towards restrictiveness took longer. The possibility of expelling foreigners was not even included in most migration laws in the nineteenth century. The arrival of more immigrants had resulted only in lively debates on the division between nationals and foreigners, as well as the latter's political rights, as exemplified by the great naturalisations

J. Irizarry y Puente, 'Exclusion and Expulsion of Aliens in Latin America', *The American Journal of International Law*, 36 (1942), 252–270.

[14] Art. 79 ICMW; European Court of Human Rights (ECtHR), *Abdulaziz, Cabales and Balkandali v. the United Kingdom* (Judgment) (1985) Series A No. 94, 33–34, para. 67; *European Roma Rights Centre and Others v. Immigration Officer at Prague Airport* [2004] *UKHL* 55. Cited in Chetail, 'The Transnational Movement of Persons Under General International Law', pp. 28–29.

[15] Chetail, 'The Transnational Movement of Persons Under General International Law', p. 29. Nafziger, 'The General Admission of Aliens', 807.

[16] Nafziger, 'The General Admission of Aliens', 823–829; David A. Martin, 'Effects of International Law on Migration Policy and Practice: The Uses of Hypocrisy', *International Migration Review*, XXIII (1989), 547–578, on 547–548.

[17] Nafziger, 'The General Admission of Aliens', 828–829.

[18] For examples, see Chetail, 'The Transnational Movement of Persons Under General International Law', p. 30; Nafziger, 'The General Admission of Aliens', 804–847.

[19] Arts 6, 7 and 12, 'Règles Internationales sur l'Admission et l'Expulsion des Étrangers, session de Genève – 1892', in *Annuaire de l'Institute du droit international*, 12 (1892–1894).

[20] Nafziger, 'The General Admission of Aliens', 810–815.

[21] See Chapter 2, pp. 46–47.

in Brazil and Venezuela.[22] At the same time, Hispano-Americans – or later even Americans to include the whole continent – continued to nurture their privileged treatment. As a scholar eloquently observed in 1928, it is 'one thing to regulate immigration from the Old World; it is another thing to seek to impose restrictions upon immigrants from one American country to another'.[23] This privileged treatment was also adopted by the USA. At the highest peak of restriction, even when the 1921 Quota Act limited the number of immigrants by nationality, the USA never imposed quotas for individuals from any country in the American continent, who were still allowed entry.[24]

Whenever the USA distanced itself from this fraternity spirit, Latin Americans – now including Brazil as a vocal partner – banded together against possible restrictions to their own nationals. These proclamations were often hypocritical since they coexisted with discrimination against foreigners and nationals at home, primarily indigenous populations and Afro-Americans.[25] Yet, with freedom of movement disappearing everywhere by the late 1920s,[26] in comparative terms South America remained a relatively open continent.[27] It was only after the 1929 crash that the region took a more decisive restrictive turn. Decades later, in the 1960s and 70s, with the security doctrine being implemented in full swing, discriminatory laws reached their apex during military regimes. This accumulation of legal exclusions continues to influence legislation and practices today.

This chapter offers a periodisation to explain how South America legally constructed the foreigner as undesirable through a *longue durée* approach. It is divided into two main parts. Sections 2 to 4 cover the first, examining the various exclusions introduced in each of the three periods under analysis (1889–1929, 1930–1959, 1960–1990). Once all countries in South America returned to democracy in the 1980s, the discriminatory character of migration laws was actually the result of a century of exclusions. It did not result – as it is often wrongly assumed – simply from the outcome of military dictatorships' legal architectures in the 1960s and 70s. This finding challenges rosy pictures presenting the region as having unequivocally open arms and offers a much more critical account through a longer historical perspective. Put bluntly, in the 1880s South American laws began to associate the foreigner with criminality,

---

[22] See Chapter 2, p. 53.

[23] J. Brown Scott, 'The Sixth International Conference of American States', *International Conciliation*, 12 (1928–29), 277–349, on 320.

[24] Brazil, Law Decree 3175, 7 April 1941, banning all migration except that of the Portuguese and all American citizens; the USA Emergency Quota Act 1921 restricted the number of immigrants admitted to the USA, based on nationality, but excluding from that number Mexico, Cuba, Central America, South America, Canada and adjacent islands.

[25] FitzGerald and Cook-Martin, *Culling the Masses*, pp. 29–30.

[26] L. Varlez, 'Migration Problems and the Havana Conference of 1928', *International Labour Review*, XIX (1929), 1–19.

[27] H. Fields, 'Closing Immigration throughout the World', *American Journal of International Law*, 26 (1932), 671–699.

political subversiveness, idleness, labour market competition and immorality. Through this process, the foreigner was portrayed as a threat to how elites imagined the nation, either because of individual traits – e.g. political ideas, age, and health – or because of collective national, racial or ethnic constructions – e.g. the exclusion of Asians, Blacks, Roma or Jews.[28]

During the first period (1889–1929), restrictions came from categories based on ethnic, racial, political and moral grounds. Still, comparatively, laws continued to be welcoming and migrants arrived in large numbers, mainly to Argentina, Brazil and Uruguay. The second period (1930–1960) followed the aftermath of the 1929 economic crash, thus incorporating protective measures for national labour markets. Regardless of other considerations and characteristics, the foreigner was excluded since he was viewed as a potential source of labour competition. The number of arrivals dropped spectacularly during these three decades. The third period (1960–1990) witnessed the construction of the foreigner as a threat to military regimes, thus their rights were limited to minimum expression, as were many of natives' rights. National security became the password legitimising both control (of potential future migrants) and expulsion (of current immigrants). During this period, in places such as Chile, the number of foreign residents was the lowest ever experienced in the country's history.

There is overlap between the three periods, with some exclusionary laws lasting for decades. The periodisation is still useful to highlight the moment in which precise restrictions appeared, as well as to offer the reader a more structured analysis of their historical accumulation. In the ten South American countries, we find continued equal consensus, but in two directions: whilst the nineteenth century presented a regional convergence that was open and receptive to Europeans, the twentieth century gradually reversed this tendency.

The second part of this chapter discusses two central aspects of the turn to exclusion. First, we look at how deterring frameworks were diffused and legally transplanted, which was strongly influenced by US practice. This ran in parallel with Hispano-Americans – or, more largely, Latin Americans – exercising solidarity, when risking being the target for discrimination themselves. Second, we examine the reasons behind the continued privileged treatment that, even in periods of extreme restriction, Hispano-Americans continued to enjoy through various international agreements and domestic provisions, at least until the 1960s when military regimes took power. The conclusion to the chapter highlights the influence that the twentieth-century restrictive frameworks continue to play at the political, legislative and administrative levels today. This facilitates the transition towards the second part of the book, in which the present migration and citizenship regime is discussed. A gigantic transatlantic rotating 180 degrees in slow motion in order to shift direction is a suitable metaphor for the obstacles faced in the twenty-first

---

[28] Devoto, *Historia de la Inmigración en la Argentina*, p. 164.

century's movement towards openness and equality which are, in turn, the consequence of the metaphorical wall, which started in the 1880s and which was built throughout an entire century of progressive restrictions.[29]

From the 1889 Pan-American Conference to the 1929 Economic Crash

The Pan-American Conferences became major events at the end of the nineteenth and beginning of the twentieth centuries. The USA took the lead to invite Brazil, Haiti, Mexico, Santo Domingo, and the various Republics of Central and South America to the first International American Conference in Washington in 1889. This represented the incorporation of not only the USA – mostly interested in expanding its commercial interests[30] – but also of Brazil and Haiti into the regional dialogue.[31] These conferences 'became sites where Latin American countries cooperated to limit intervention by the United States and European powers' and in the process 'strengthened Latin American solidarity'.[32] It cannot be forgotten that the USA still publicly defended intervention as a valid policy tool until as late as 1928.[33] Indeed, under the leadership of Latin American states, several agreements and resolutions regarding non-intervention were adopted during the first half of the twentieth century.[34]

Migration and mobility also became part of a Latin American-led agenda, which the USA ignored by not signing agreements that extended rights to migrants. At the same time, domestic laws started denying rights and entry to certain categories of non-nationals. This section presents how exclusions – based on race, ethnicity, political ideology and morals – proliferated in this forty-year period, with many remaining and even extending after the 1929 economic crash.

Exclusion Based on Race and Ethnicity

Although exclusions on racial grounds had existed in the US Southern States since the prohibition of black immigration in 1803,[35] other countries in the Americas remained, at least on paper, isolated from such tendencies.[36] This

---

[29] See Chapters 5–7.
[30] Del Castillo Martínez, *El Congreso de Panamá de 1826*, p. 35.
[31] As discussed in Chapter 3, both Brazil and Haiti had been largely excluded from previous regional discussion among Hispano-American countries. See pp. 60–61.
[32] FitzGerald and Cook-Martin, *Culling the Masses*, p. 54.
[33] J. M. Mathews, 'Roosevelt's Latin-American Policy', *American Political Science Review*, 29 (1935), 805–820, on p. 808.
[34] Art. 8, Montevideo 1933, Convention on the Rights and Duties of States, Seventh International Conference of American States; Buenos Aires Additional Protocol Relative to Non-intervention, Buenos Aires Special Conference for the Maintenance of Peace, 3–26 December 1936.
[35] FitzGerald and Cook-Martin, *Culling the Masses*, p. 40.
[36] Some exceptions include Colombia, where Law 11/1847 excluded immigration for those of 'African race'.

changed in the last two decades of the nineteenth century. In the USA, the 1875 rules prohibiting the entry of convicts and prostitutes, as well as the 1882 exclusion of Chinese nationals, were game changers.[37] This was the first time that, through federal statutes, it became common to restrict the arrival of foreigners, although exclusions had existed at the state level.[38] Its influence soon resonated throughout the Americas.

FitzGerald and Cook-Martin have meticulously analysed the selection and exclusion of migrants in the Americas based on race and ethnicity. They have convincingly argued how Latin American countries adopted restrictions, which had first appeared in the USA, through a process of policy diffusion and emulation. Policy diffusion was also the result of strategic adjustment when countries feared that changes in other states' laws would shift migration flows.[39] However, as McKeown has shown, restrictions were embraced even by countries which did not receive any significant migration flows. In his account, exclusions 'had much to do with a perception of how a civilized country should defined its social and political borders' since this appeared as a requirement 'for international recognition as a modern nation state'.[40]

Introducing restrictions on foreigners ended a period in which migration had often taken place spontaneously, at least for arrivals from Europe. Certainly, the enshrinement of explicit ethnic and racial prohibitions were not surprising in the South American case, where 'purity of blood' had been an obsession since colonial times.[41] Asian arrivals had indeed only been accepted under particular circumstances in the nineteenth century – for example, the Chinese in Peru were meant to occupy positions in the agricultural sector, which Europeans did not fill,[42] as well as in the Venezuelan agriculture and domestic labour markets in the 1850s, immediately following the abolition of slavery.[43] The birth of eugenics in the early twentieth century coincided with a period of development of international organisations, where states discussed selective policies on migrant admission.[44] It was somehow predictable that countries would soon enact legislation mirroring exclusions by race and ethnicity following the US model. This was the case between 1887 and 1916 in all ten countries: Colombia (1887),[45] Ecuador

---

[37] USA, Immigration Act of 1875, 18 Stat. 477. Although the Act referred to convicted criminals and prostitutes in general, its aim was to exclude Chinese women; Chinese Exclusion Act of 1882, 22 Stat. 58. The movement of Chinese indenture servant migrants had already been banned in the USA with the 1862 Coolie Trade Law. See Motomura, *Americans in Waiting*, p. 25.

[38] *Ibid.*, p. 21.

[39] FitzGerald and Cook-Martin, *Culling the Masses*, pp. 22–27.

[40] A. M. McKeown, *Melancholy Order. Asian Migration and the Globalization of Borders* (New York: Columbia University Press, 2008), pp. 320–321.

[41] Loveman, *National Colors*, pp. 61–71.

[42] del Rio, *La Inmigración y Su Desarrollo en el Perú*, pp. 44–51.

[43] FitzGerald and Cook-Martin, *Culling the Masses*, pp. 378–379.

[44] *Ibid.*, pp. 58–64.

[45] Colombia, Law 62/1887 imposed a ban on Chinese nationals, which was lifted in 1892 due to the need for workers for the Panama Canal (then part of Colombia). New restrictions were imposed

(1889),[46] Brazil (1890),[47] Uruguay (1890),[48] Venezuela (1891),[49] Bolivia (1899),[50] Paraguay (1903),[51] Peru (1905),[52] Chile (1915)[53] and Argentina (1916).[54]

Prohibitions mostly affected Chinese, Roma, Jewish and black individuals, but also the Japanese and Middle Easterners. Their *modus operandi* differed from country to country. Occasionally, certain categories contained additional conditions, instead of absolute prohibitions, such as for the Poles (who were mainly Jews) in Colombia.[55] Other countries simply prohibited all non-European, or non-white, immigration.[56] Legislation also shifted between

for Chinese and other nationalities between 1931 and 1948, the year when exclusions ended. *Gitanos* (Roma) were also discriminated against between 1935 and 1943. See FitzGerald and Cook-Martin, *Culling the Masses*, pp. 356–357.

[46] Ecuador, Legislative Decree 12 October 1889. This prohibited the entry of Chinese immigrants. Discrimination against Roma began in 1938 (Art. 17, 1938 Law on Foreigners, Extradition and Naturalisation). They remained in place until 1944 for Chinese nationals and until 1971 for Roma. See FitzGerald and Cook-Martin, *Culling the Masses*, pp. 361–362.

[47] Brazil, Decree 528, 28 June 1890 prohibited the entry of 'blacks and yellows' but remained in force for only two years. Other restrictions included Roma starting in 1934 and Jews before World War II. All restrictions ended on paper in 1980. See FitzGerald and Cook-Martin, *Culling the Masses*, pp. 259–298.

[48] Uruguay, Art. 26, Law 2096, 18 June 1890, prohibited entry to Asians, Africans, Bohemians and 'húngaros' (the last two categories referring to Roma). Restrictions, with various changes, remained until 1938. See FitzGerald and Cook-Martin, *Culling the Masses*, pp. 377–378.

[49] Venezuela prohibited the entry of Asians and individuals coming from the English and Dutch Antilles in Art. 39, Immigration Law, 20 June 1891; also see Art. 3, Immigration Law, 26 August 1894. Exclusions continued until 1966 when a bar on non-white immigration in force since the 1936 Immigration and Colonization Law of 22 July was lifted. See FitzGerald and Cook-Martin, *Culling the Masses*, p. 379.

[50] Bolivia, Supreme Resolution, 5 August 1899 and Supreme Resolution 16 August 1899, excluded Asian immigration; the term Asian referred to Chinese. Exclusion was extended in 1938 to blacks, Jews and Roma. Exclusions remained in place until 1951. See FitzGerald and Cook-Martin, *Culling the Masses*, pp. 351 and 354.

[51] Paraguay, Art. 14, Law 30 September 1903, excluded the entry of citizens of 'yellow race', blacks and Roma. Restrictions remained until 1937. See FitzGerald and Cook-Martin, *Culling the Masses*, pp. 373–374.

[52] In Peru, some limitations were imposed on Chinese migrants in 1905. This increased in the following years. Japanese immigration was restricted from 1936. Restrictions remained until 1954. In the case of Roma, prohibitions were in place from 1937 until 1992. See FitzGerald and Cook-Martin, *Culling the Masses*, pp. 375–376.

[53] In Chile restrictions were introduced for Chinese nationals via the imposition of a special charge, which remained until 1936. See FitzGerald and Cook-Martin, *Culling the Masses*, p. 355.

[54] In Argentina, exclusions largely targeted Roma. Secret consular instructions later targeted Jews. All restrictions ended in 1949. See FitzGerald and Cook-Martin, *Culling the Masses*, pp. 299–332.

[55] For example, Roma (*zíngaros* or *gitanos*) were portrayed as lacking habitual hygiene and thus more easily carrying 'exotic infectious illnesses' and in need of more careful sanitary examination when arriving at the border. See Peru, R.S, Lima 25 November 1910; in Colombia, many nationalities, including Bulgarians, Chinese, Egyptians, Estonians, Greeks, Indians, Latvians, Lebanese, Lithuanians, Moroccans, Palestinians, Polish, Romanians, Russians, Syrians and Turkish, had to fulfil several additional conditions to be allowed entry. Colombia, Art. 1, Decree 397/1937. See L. M. Leal Villamizar, *Colombia Frente al Antisemitismo y la Migración de Judíos Polacos y Alemanes 1933–1948* (Bogotá: Academia Colombiana de Historia, 2015).

[56] See Venezuela, Immigration and Colonisation Law, 8 July 1912 prohibiting all non-European migration; Venezuela, Immigration and Colonisation Law, 22 July 1936 prohibiting the entry of

preferences and exclusions, notably when it came to Asians.[57] Of course, all categories were subject to shifting social constructions, depending on various interests and actors. For instance, the exclusions did not consider the Japanese in Paraguay nor the Syrian-Lebanese in Uruguay as Asians.[58] Restrictions worded in a prima facie non-discriminatory fashion, such as literacy requirements, also affected Europeans but in practice they were imposed with racist objectives.[59] Exclusions were indeed often justified by the need to preserve the ethnic com-position of populations, something that favoured Europeans.[60] Some categories that were in theory not excluded were actually rejected in practice through secret diplomatic circulars: for example, US black nationals in Brazil in the early twentieth century,[61] and Jews later on, whose entry was banned by Argentina,[62] Brazil,[63] Colombia[64] and Uruguay,[65] often via secret consular communications. Nevertheless, even when restrictions were clearly worded, those who were barred occasionally managed to migrate. For example, an estimated 20,000, 25,000 and 45,000 Jews arrived in Bolivia, Brazil and Argentina, respectively, despite prohibitions in place in all three countries.[66] This was the result of a 'paper industry'[67] where various organisations could facilitate forged residence papers, job contracts and other certificates in countries like Argentina and Bolivia. Their respective consulates in Europe were also often involved since

---

non-whites; see Peru, Law 14 October 1893, authorising, protecting and promoting immigration of foreigners of the white race.

[57] This was the case with Asians in Colombia and Peru in the nineteenth century. See FitzGerald and Cook-Martin, *Culling the Masses*, pp. 356 and 374.

[58] FitzGerald and Cook-Martin, *Culling the Masses*, pp. 373 and 377. See in Uruguay, Law 3051/ 1906 exempting Syrians from the 'Lebanon region' from the exclusion.

[59] Sacchetta notes that an important factor in the reduction of Portuguese arrivals in Brazil had to do with the ban on those who were illiterate. Sacchetta, *Laços de Sangue*, p. 212. Brazil, Decree 24.215/1934.

[60] Brazil, Art. 2, Law Decree, 7967, 18 September 1945.

[61] Brazil, Decree 4247, 6 January 1921, regulating the entry of foreigners in Brazil. This decree did not exclude based on race but rather by 'neutral' attributes such as being older than sixty years or blind. However, blacks from the USA were excluded following secret diplomatic circulars. See FitzGerald and Cook-Martin, *Culling the Masses*, pp. 274–276.

[62] Jews were excluded in Argentina before the Second World War through secret diplomatic circulars. See FitzGerald and Cook-Martin, *Culling the Masses*, p. 354.

[63] Brazil, *Circular Reservada* 1522, 6 May 1941. The Ministry of Justice reserved its power to lift the ban in individual cases. However, even those Jews having citizenship from another American nation or Portugal were banned; cited in Sacchetta, *Laços de Sangue*, p. 232.

[64] Various diplomatic cables are cited in Leal Villamizar, *Colombia Frente al Antisemitismo*, p. 57.

[65] S. Facal Santiago, *Movimientos Migratorios en Uruguay. Un Estudio a través del Marco Normativo* (Madrid: Observatorio Iberoamericano sobre Movilidad Humana, Migraciones y Desarrollo, OBIMID, 2017), pp. 14–15.

[66] See FitzGerald and Cook-Martin, *Culling the Masses*, p. 354 for the case of Argentina, pp. 316–318 for Bolivia and p. 288 for Brazil.

[67] Here I borrow the term that David Cook-Martin has used in a more recent context in Argentina. See D. Cook-Martin, *The Scramble for Citizens: Dual Nationality and State Competition for Immigrants* (Stanford University Press, 2013).

they demanded considerable sums of money in return for visas for people escaping Nazi persecution.[68]

Exclusion Based on Political Ideology

A new international order emerged in the 1870s and 80s: England replaced the old 'colonial pact' that South American countries had traditionally held with the Spanish Crown.[69] Economic growth accelerated, mostly through the export of primary goods, ranking some South American countries among the richest in the world in terms of per capita income; that is, until 1929.[70] Such extraordinary development had various ramifications. To begin with, the period 1880–1929 saw the largest number of foreigners arriving in South America, notably in Argentina, Brazil and Uruguay, with Buenos Aires, Rio de Janeiro and Montevideo hosting large migrant populations while being some of the most prosperous cities worldwide.[71] Second, the twentieth century witnessed the rise of 'order and progress' administrations, which resulted from the alliance between liberals and conservatives. These regimes were concerned with speeding up economic growth and imposing control in states affected by rising social unrest and conflict.[72] These governments 'were characterized by their exclusionary legal systems, the concentration of powers in the Executive, limited political rights, and the extreme use of the State's coercive powers'.[73] This state-building process aimed to avoid political upheavals in an attempt to offer credible stability to attract foreign capital.[74] States reacted with an iron fist to workers' uprisings, as exemplified by the massacres in Valparaiso (1903), Buenos Aires (1919) – an event known as the *semana trágica* (tragic week) – and in Guayaquil (1922). Third, socialist and anarchist movements, having first appeared in Europe, strongly influenced the region's labour and union actions, especially in Argentina.[75] Newcomers, mainly Italians, played a crucial role in the organisation of labour movements.[76] It is within this context, with two conflicting forces for and against social rights, that increasing exclusions based on political ideology – notably against those considered as anarchists – made their way into various migration statutes. Anarchism, it must be clarified, was

---

[68] Devoto, *Historia de la Inmigración en la Argentina*, p. 183; M. J. Osterweil, 'The Economic and Social Condition of Jewish and Arab Immigrants in Bolivia, 1890–1980,' in I. Klich and J. Lesser (eds), *Arab and Jewish Immigrants in Latin America. Images and Realities* (Abingdon: Routledge, 1998), pp. 146–166.

[69] Gargarella, *Latin American Constitutionalism*, p. 84.

[70] Bértola and Ocampo, *The Economic Development of Latin America since Independence*, chapter 3.

[71] See Chapter 1, pp. 10–12.

[72] Gargarella, *Latin American Constitutionalism*, p. 84.

[73] *Ibid.*, p. 85.

[74] Rouquié, *The Military and the State in Latin America*, pp. 50–51.

[75] Gargarella, *Latin American Constitutionalism*, pp. 91–95.

[76] A. Angell, 'The Left in Latin America since c. 1920' in L. Bethell (ed.), *Latin America. Politics and Society since 1930* (Cambridge University Press, 1998), pp. 75–144, on p. 79.

a loose umbrella that covered anyone considered to threaten the established social order. Under the label of social protection (*defensa social*), it was easy to put mechanisms of control, classification and expulsion in place for anyone deemed undesirable.

Whereas some provisions permitting the expulsion of foreigners meddling with internal politics had already been present since the late nineteenth century,[77] it was in the first two decades of the twentieth that, beginning in Argentina, they proliferated and were systematised. In 1902, and within the context of a general strike by stevedores, Argentina adopted its Residence Law. This provided for exclusion at the border, or expulsion from the territory, without judicial oversight, of any foreigner whose conduct would compromise national security or public order.[78] The law was put into practice to immediately break the spine of labour movements and profoundly transformed the division between nationals and foreigners.[79] Not only was discrimination against foreigners now possible, but Argentinean laws also incorporated new control mechanisms, such as carrier sanctions, detention, entry bans and incarceration upon return.[80]

Other countries followed suit. The vilification of social and labour demands was widespread.[81] For instance, Brazil adopted an Act of expulsion in 1907, under the framework of protests demanding the adoption of the eight-hour workday.[82] These statutes were broadly worded. It was possible to expel those who 'would provoke manifestations contrary to the established order', 'public order' or who would 'endanger public peace'.[83] Such far-reaching categorisation provided great leeway to administrative authorities. In some cases, foreigners were forbidden from any kind of political expression, participating in political associations and owning newspapers.[84] In others, laws explicitly barred the entry of communists or anarchists.[85] Provisions often became increasingly

---

[77] Colombia, Art. 13, Law 145, 26 November 1888. See examples of expulsions from Venezuela in the late nineteenth century in G. T. Villegas-Pulido, *Los Extranjeros en Venezuela: Su no Admisión – Su Expulsión* (Caracas: Lit. y tip. del Comercio, *1919*), pp. 100 and following.

[78] Argentina, Arts 2–3, Residence Law 4.144/1902.

[79] E. Domenech, 'Inmigración, Anarquismo y Deportación: La Criminalización de los Extranjeros "Indeseables" en Tiempos de las "Grandes Migraciones"', *Revista Interdisciplinar de Mobilidade Humana*, 45 (2015), 169–196, on 175.

[80] Argentina, Residence Law, 4.144, 22 November 1902; Social Defence Law 7.029, 28 June 1910.

[81] Bolivia, Residence Law, 18 January 1911; Brazil, Decree 1641 on expulsion of foreigners from the national territory, Rio de Janeiro, 7 January 1907, and Decree 6486, 23 May 1907; Chile, Law 3446, to impede entry to the country or residence of undesirable elements, 12 December 1918; Colombia, Decree 496 1909 and also see Law 48 on immigration, 3 November 1920; Ecuador, Immigration, Extradition and Naturalisation Law 344, 8 October, 1921; Peru, Law on expulsion of foreigners, 1908; Uruguay, Law 9604, 13 October 1936; Venezuela, Law defining the rights and obligations of foreigners, 16 April 1903, Art. 12.

[82] Sacchetta, *Laços de Sangue*, p. 156.

[83] Bolivia, Art. 2, Residence Law 1911; Chile, Art. 2, Law 3,446/1918.

[84] Brazil, Art. 1, Decree 1641/1907; Ecuador, Art. 19, Law 344/1921; Venezuela, Art. 6, Law 16 April 1903, and Art. 6, Foreigners Law, 30 June 1915.

[85] Colombia, Art. 7, Law 48/1920.

restrictive over time.[86] Their aim was to present the migrant worker as an agitator, subversive to the established order and, therefore, as an enemy of society.

Various regional initiatives proliferated. Within the context of the second Pan-American Conference, several states signed a treaty on extradition and protection against anarchism. Whereas extradition for political offences was excluded, those committing acts classified as pertaining to anarchism could nonetheless be extradited.[87] Argentina took the lead to create a network between police forces, with the objective of forming a South American international police. Whilst such an ambitious goal never came to fruition, two treaties – adopted at the 1905 and 1920 South American Police Conferences – obliged states to exchange information regarding anarchists' acts and on others who had disrupted the social order.[88]

This restraining architecture had an important effect in practice. More than a hundred foreigners were expelled from Brazil in 1907 in just six months.[89] The influence of these provisions expanded for decades and ulterior laws further refined certain exclusions.[90] Prohibitions on owning media companies, participating in political activities, or taking part in unions, took a central position in acts adopted during the military dictatorships in the 1960s and 70s, as will be seen below.[91]

Exclusion Based on Morals and Other 'Inadequacies'

Constraints mushroomed for those deemed non-conforming. These constituted a hodgepodge of categories, including a moral stream banning, for example, prostitutes, beggars and drinkers; banned physical conditions included those

[86] See, for example, Argentina's Law on social defence 7.029, 28 June 1910 introducing further restrictions to the 1902 Law; Brazil, Decree 2741, 8 January 1913, derogating some of the minimum protections against expulsion included in Decree 1641/1907. This was later declared unconstitutional by Brazil's Supreme Court in 1913. On this, see C. Roquette Lopreato, 'O Espírito das Leis: Anarquismo e Repressão Política no Brasil', *Verve*, 3 (2003), 75–91. Also see A. L. Zago de Moraes, 'Crimigração. A Relação entre Política Migratória e Política Criminal no Brasil', unpublished PhD Thesis, Faculdade de Direito da Pontifícia Universidade Católica do Rio Grande do Sul, Porto Alegre, 2015.

[87] Arts 2 and 13, Treaty for the Extradition of Criminals and for Protection against Anarchism, Mexico City, 28 January 1902. Signed by all South American countries except Brazil and Venezuela. It was also signed by the USA.

[88] The methods of identifying criminals in order to facilitate exchange of information between countries had also been the subject of debate at the scientific Latin American congresses in Buenos Aires (1898), Montevideo (1901) and Rio de Janeiro (1905) and of the Pan-American one in Chile 1909 where the USA also participated. D. Galeano, 'Las Conferencias Sudamericanas de Policías y la Problemática de los Delincuentes Viajeros, 1905–1920' in E. Bohoslavsky L. Caimari, C. Schettini (eds), *La Policía en Perspectiva Histórica. Argentina y Brasil (del siglo XIX a la Actualidad)* (Buenos Aires: CD-ROM, 2009), on p. 10.

[89] Sacchetta, *Laços de Sangue*, pp. 157 and 217. This continued between 1930 and 1945 with the expulsion of at least 778 individuals.

[90] Brazil, Decree 4269, 17 January 1921 and *circular reservada* 1522, 6 May 1941.

[91] Brazil, Arts 106 and 107, Law 6815/1980; Chile, Art. 15 Law Decree 1094/1975 still in force.

with disabilities or who were sick, or over sixty years old. Bishops or religious preachers, notably from religions other than Catholicism, such as Jehovah Witnesses or Protestants, were also sometimes excluded.[92]

United States laws, namely the 1917 Immigration Act, were very influential.[93] This Act excluded the entry of 'idiots', epileptics, alcoholics, the poor, criminals, beggars, those with tuberculosis and those with physical disabilities, among others. Brazil was the first to replicate this model, introducing a comprehensive instrument.[94] Its 1921 Act reflected similar wording and prohibited entry for the blind, insane, those suffering from an incurable or grave illness, beggars and those with a physical disability. It also banned those over sixty years old, except when a family member could take care of them and produced a financial deposit.[95] This had important repercussions for families split on both sides of the Atlantic, notably Portuguese nationals.[96] In turn, women travelling alone always had to carry an official document from the country of origin explicitly declaring that the holder was not a prostitute.[97] Argentina quickly followed suit, first in 1919 and then more clearly with its 1923 regulations containing similar exclusionary categories. Both Argentina and Brazil wanted to avoid the arrival of those denied entry into the USA.[98] Argentina also incorporated the concept of 'vicious or useless immigration'.[99] The use of eloquent titles or wording in migration statutes to categorise migrants as dishonest was not solely an Argentinian phenomenon; it was also used by Peru and Uruguay.[100] Other countries – such as Colombia, Ecuador and Peru – that received significantly fewer migrants nonetheless replicated restrictions on physical and moral grounds.[101] This is partly explained by the emerging consensus in the

---

[92] Brazil, *circular reservada* 1522, 6 May 1941; Venezuela, Art. 80(23), 1904 Constitution. In the Venezuelan case, we can find an earlier prohibition of entry to any individuals of the Church of the Society of Jesus in Executive Decree 31 August 1848.

[93] USA, Immigration Act of 1917, 5 February 1917.

[94] Brazil already had some previous experience of prohibiting entry for certain categories. Decree 1566, 13 October 1893 prohibiting entry of beggars and those capable of compromising public health, among others. This was also the case in Venezuela which had, as early as 1854, prohibited the entry of criminal, idle, vicious or infected immigrants. See Venezuela, Art. 8, Law on Immigration, 5 March 1854.

[95] Brazil, Decree 4247, 6 January 1921. See also later decrees in Brazil such as the Law Decree 406, 4 May 1938.

[96] Sacchetta, *Laços de Sangue*, pp. 172–173.

[97] *Ibid.*, p. 173.

[98] FitzGerald and Cook-Martin, *Culling the Masses*, pp. 312–316.

[99] Argentina, Art. 10, Decree 31 December 1923, Regulation to Law on Immigration 817. There had been other restrictions adopted in 1919 on the grounds of health, criminal antecedents and against begging. See Argentina, Decree 31 March 1919.

[100] Peru, Law 4145 on dangerous foreigners; Law 4891 against vagrancy(*sobre la vagancia*), Lima 16 January 1924; Uruguay, Decree on useless immigration (*inmigración inútil*), 10 December 1894, cited in P. Sandonato de León, 'Nacionalidad y Extranjería en el Uruguay. Un Estudio Normo-Político', *Revista de Derecho de la Universidad Católica del Uruguay*, 3, 2008, 175–243, on 196.

[101] Colombia, Law 48, 3 November 1920; Ecuador, Law on Foreigners, Extradition and Naturalisation, 18 October 1921; Peru, Laws 4145/1920 and 4891/1924.

early twentieth century that considered border control 'as a prerequisite to recognition as a self-governing state'.[102]

These laws deepened the division between nationals and foreigners. The latter became associated with all sort of inadequacies that merited control of their entry, residence and expulsion. The foreigner, even the European, was no longer depicted as virtuous, or as a carrier of civilisation and progress. Quite on the contrary, through ongoing fragmentation, the figure of the foreigner became one of suspicion: a source of potential insecurity and instability. This process accelerated as the 1929 economic crash devastated the economies of the New World.

The 1929 Economic Crisis

The 1929 crisis resulted in a further retreat of migration policies on a global scale, including in South America. During its aftermath, military governments took over in Argentina, Brazil, Peru and Uruguay. Their aversion to social rights was paradoxical in a context where, through 'the incorporation of the working class into politics from the 1930s', those same social rights had previously been enshrined in various constitutions.[103]

Within this environment, several laws justified discrimination, by stating that they were in defence of the national worker and in response to growing unemployment.[104] Once again, the USA was the pioneer: President Hoover gave instructions to American consuls in 1930 to limit the number of residence permits available to foreigners.[105] South Americans mimicked these efforts. In Argentina, in order to enter the country, immigrants now needed an already-signed job contract.[106] Deterring mechanisms, such as financial deposits, or the exclusion of third-class passengers (i.e., most migrants) were commonly used.[107] Foreigners were depicted as 'potential competitive labour' and thus subject to discrimination.[108] They were, for example, barred from

---

[102] McKeown, *Melancholy Order*, p. 321.

[103] Gargarella, *Latin American Constitutionalism*, pp. 106–108.

[104] Argentina, Decree 26 November 1932, known as the defence of Argentinean workers, prohibiting embarkation at the port of origin of those without a signed labour contract or support from a family member already established in Argentina. See also Uruguay, Presidential Decree 23 November 1937; Brazil, Art. 2 Law Decree 7967, 18 September 1945.

[105] Fields, 'Closing Immigration Throughout the World', p. 671.

[106] Argentina, Decree 8 November 1932.

[107] Brazil, Arts 1–2 Decree 19.482, 12 December 1930; Colombia, Decree 397/1937; Uruguay, Art. 1 Law 8868, 19 July 1932, and Art. 1 Decree 6 September 1932, and Presidential Decree 24 January 1934; Venezuela, Art. 11 Foreigners Law, 17 July 1937; Argentina, Decree December 1930 imposing a consular fee of 10 pesos for stamping required health, financial solvency and good conduct certificates, cited in D. Cook-Martin, 'Rules, Red Tape and Paperwork: The Archaeology of State Control over Migrants', *Journal of Historical Sociology*, 21 (2008), 82–119, in footnote 18. See also Argentina, Decree 19 January 1934 demanding third-class passengers to produce certificates of good health, conduct and no begging.

[108] Fields, 'Closing Immigration Throughout the World', p. 698. Brazil, Preamble, Decree 19.482, 12 December 1930; Bolivia, Law Decree, 27 March 1938, on norms for the repression of all extremist social tendencies.

unions' management positions.[109] Countries also introduced a maximum percentage of foreign workers allowed in any given company: 15% in both Bolivia and Chile, 10–20% in Colombia, 20% in Peru and 33% in Brazil.[110] Additional restrictions provided that only technicians could be part of the foreign labour force.[111] In Brazil, quotas could only be filled by nationals by birth.[112] The foreigner continued to be considered a foreigner, even after naturalising.

Other aspects of laws affecting migrants became more discretionary. In Argentina, a 1938 Decree transformed landing in the country, even for those fulfilling the requirements, into a completely arbitrary procedure to deny entry to those considered undesirable.[113] In Brazil, provisions on expulsion were enshrined at the constitutional level.[114] Restrictions also made their way into nationality laws. In Colombia, new conditions were imposed to obtain citizenship, namely to prove that the individual naturalisation was beneficial to the country, as attested by five Colombians by birth.[115] In Peru, foreigners needed to re-enrol at the official registry every single year and failure to do so could lead to expulsion.[116]

The combination of restrictive laws and economic uncertainty severely reduced migration flows. In Brazil, the number of arrivals fell from 96,186 in 1929 to 46,027 in 1934.[117] From that year onwards, and following the previous US actions,[118] Brazil introduced nationality quotas.[119] This policy limited annual inflows of each nationality to a maximum of 2 per cent of the total number admitted in the previous fifty years, and had clear ethnic and racial overtones. The nation aimed to conserve its current ethnic composition by avoiding contamination by new elements and the 'degeneration of Brazilian

---

[109] See for example Colombia, Art. 388 Labour Code, Decree 2663, 5 August 1950. This was declared invalid by the Colombian Constitutional Tribunal only in 2000. See Sentence C-385/00, 5 April 2000.

[110] Chile, Art. 15 Labour Code 1931, which, however, included some exceptions; Colombia, Arts 74–75, Labour Code, Decree 2663, 5 August 1950; Bolivia, Art. 3, Supreme Decree 24 May 1939, General Law on Labour, transformed later into Law 8 December 1942; Peru, Law Decree 14.460, 25 April 1963; Brazil, Art. 2, Decree 19.482, 12 December 1930. In Brazil, this was not applied in practice in regions where the foreign labour force was larger. Sacchetta, *Laços de Sangue*, p. 17.

[111] Bolivia, Art. 3, Supreme Decree 24 May 1939; Brazil, Art. 3, Decree 19.482, 12 December 1930.

[112] For example, two thirds of a ship's crew had to be nationals by birth in Brazil, and only this first category, or those who not being Brazilians by birth but who had served in the military, could exercise a liberal profession. Brazil, Arts 132–133, 1934 Constitution.

[113] Argentina, Decree 8972, 1938. Devoto, *Historia de la Inmigración en la Argentina*, p. 182.

[114] Brazil, Art. 113(15), 1934 Constitution.

[115] Colombia, Art. 6, Law 22 bis, 3 February 1936.

[116] Peru, Law Decree 7000, 16 January 1931.

[117] Sacchetta, *Laços de Sangue*, p. 201.

[118] USA, the Emergency Quota Act 1921 restricted the number of immigrants admitted to the USA on a nationality basis to comprise 3 per cent of the total number from that country who were already residing in the USA, according to the 1910 census. This was later further restricted by the Immigration Act of 1924.

[119] Brazil, Art. 121, 1934 Constitution.

society'.[120] The interplay between racial bans and prohibitions on other grounds continued throughout the 1930s and early 1940s in most countries.

Military Dictatorships and the Doctrine of National Security in the 1970s and 80s

By the end of the Second World War, all South America was run by democracies anew. Together with other Latin American and Caribbean states, they played a decisive role in the introduction of human rights and racial equality clauses in the 1945 UN Charter. Latin American countries were in an excellent position to push for this agenda since they constituted a bloc of twenty out of the forty-six states which met at the San Francisco 1945 Conference.[121] By this time, most overarching and explicit racial and ethnic exclusions had largely disappeared from their domestic laws, although other exclusions remained intact.[122] Their draft proposals, coupled with inspiration drawn from clauses in their constitutions as well as from the 1948 Bogotá Declaration, were also instrumental in the final text of the 1948 UN General Assembly Universal Declaration of Human Rights (UDHR).[123]

The Organisation of American States (OAS) was also created in 1948 by the Charter of Bogotá. This treaty must be read together with the 1947 Inter-American Covenant of Reciprocal Assistance signed in Rio de Janeiro. Whereas the Charter emphasises the principle of non-intervention (Article 2), Article 6 of the Rio Covenant provides for measures that can be taken for the common defence of the continent in cases of aggression, including non-armed attacks, which endanger the peace of America. In the 1960s, following the establishment of a communist government in Cuba, the USA favoured military regimes espousing anti-communist ideology in Latin America within the context of the Cold War.[124] Latin America became 'a player in the Cold War – a secondary player it is true, but one that deserved special attention'.[125] Whereas the communist party had been banned in Brazil, Chile, Colombia, Peru and Venezuela in the 1940s,[126] and whilst some military regimes had already been in place in

---

[120] O. Truzzi, 'Reformulações na Política Imigratória de Brasil e Argentina nos Anos 30: um Enfoque Comparativo' in C.E. de Abreu Boucault and T. Malatian (eds), *Políticas Migratórias. Fronteiras dos Direitos Humanos no Século XXI* (Rio de Janeiro: Renovar, 2003), pp. 242–243.

[121] M. A. Glendon, 'The Forgotten Crucible: The Latin American Influence on the Universal Human Rights Idea', *Harvard Human Rights Journal*, 16 (2003), 27–39.

[122] In any case, this did not impede countries such as Chile from adopting, as late as 1953, a law incorporating references to the need to use selective immigration to 'improve the biological conditions of the race'. See Chile, Preamble, Law Decree 69 on Immigration, 27 April 1953.

[123] S. Waltz, 'Universalizing Human Rights: The Role of Small States in the Construction of the Universal Declaration of Human Rights', *Human Rights Quarterly*, 23 (2001), 44–72.

[124] Mirow, *Latin American Constitutions*, p. 243.

[125] Rouquié, *The Military and the State in Latin America*, p. 137.

[126] Gargarella, *Latin American Constitutionalism*, p. 111.

the 1930s after the great depression,[127] the US influence during the 1960s led to a 'struggle against the "internal enemy"' with 'national security' replacing 'national defence'.[128] Already during the 1960s, no less than six military coup d'états took place in South America with the aim of eliminating governments considered too weak or sympathetic towards communism.[129] It was, however, in the 1970s that military administrations became omnipresent, being in eight out of the ten countries: Argentina (1966–1973 and 1976–1983), Bolivia (1964–1970 and 1971–1982), Brazil (1964–1985), Chile (1973–1990), Ecuador (1972–1979), Paraguay (1954–1989), Peru (1968–1980) and Uruguay (1973–1984). Although these military regimes did not have exactly the same characteristics,[130] they were all largely concerned with population control as embedded in the state's security agenda, especially in the Southern Cone, as well as sharing the adoption of restrictive migration regimes and their distrust of the foreigner. These military dictatorships limited population movements as a means of political control, with a complete disregard for migrants' rights.[131] Ukrainian settlers who, under accusations of pro-Soviet tendencies, were imprisoned and tortured in Paraguay in 1955 sadly epitomised this trend.[132]

Migrants' rights were further curtailed everywhere. In Argentina, the 1981 law, popularly named after the country's infamous dictator Videla, denied undocumented immigrants basic social rights, such as health care and education. They could be detained and expelled without judicial oversight and there was no maximum detention period before expulsion took place.[133] Likewise, Brazil's 1980 immigration law was adopted in less than three months under an urgent procedure and placed strong emphasis on national security.[134] Foreigners in Brazil, Paraguay and Uruguay were prohibited from participating in political

---

[127] For example, military regimes were already in Argentina, Brazil, Peru, Uruguay and Venezuela. Military dictatorships had also already occurred during the nineteenth century in countries such as Bolivia, Ecuador and Uruguay; see Rouquié, *The Military and the State in Latin America*, chapter 2.

[128] A. Rouquié and S. Suffern, 'The Military in Latin American Politics since 1930' in L. Bethell (ed.), *Latin America Politics and Society since 1930* (Cambridge University Press, 1998), pp. 145–216, on p. 157.

[129] *Ibid.*, on p. 157.

[130] *Ibid.* For example, in Peru the regime was left-leaning under General Juan Velasco Alvarado, who was in power 1968–1974.

[131] J. Durand and D. S. Massey, 'New World Orders: Continuities and Changes in Latin American Migration', *The ANNALS of the American Academy of Political and Social Science*, 630 (2010), 20–52.

[132] M. Brown, *From Frontiers to Football. An Alternative History of Latin America since 1800* (London: Reaktion Books, 2014), p. 148.

[133] In Argentina, there had already been numerous restrictive measures taken under the military regime in the 1960s such as Decree 4418/65. The 1981 known as *Ley Videla* was the General Law on Migrations and Promotion of Immigration 22.439/81, Buenos Aires 23 March 1981. See Domenech, 'Crónica de una Amenaza Anunciada'; P. Ceriani and D. Morales, *Argentina: Avances y Asignaturas Pendientes en la Consolidación de una Política Migratoria Basada en Los Derechos Humanos* (Buenos Aires: Centro de Estudios Legales y Sociales, 2011).

[134] Brazil, Law 6.815/1980 and Implementing Regulation Decree 86715/81.

activities, including organising demonstrations.[135] In that regard, being the head of a student association was considered sufficient by courts to deny Brazilian citizenship, since the applicant had not proven good behaviour.[136] Beyond limiting rights, migrants had imposed obligations including 'assimilating into the host society' and not 'constituting independent and marginal settlements'.[137] In Argentina, a 1978 citizenship law brought important changes by excluding political rights for the first three years for the newly naturalised.[138] In Ecuador, naturalisation was considered as a governmental discretionary power by 1976 legislation.[139]

Procedures were cumbersome and there were difficulties in obtaining secure residence status, with very few avenues for regular immigration and no mechanisms for regularisation.[140] Consequently, large numbers of migrants remained undocumented, especially in Argentina. There, criminalisation was progressive and took place during both military dictatorships in the 1960s and 1970s. A decree in 1967, eloquently named the 'repression of clandestine migration',[141] signalled the beginning of a period of restrictive measures, also affecting regular migrants, who could be expelled if threatening social peace, national security or public order.[142] True, several decrees were also adopted with a view to regularising migrants from bordering countries in the 1970s but the general trend was consistently exclusionary.[143]

Migration was largely criminalised in other countries too. In Chile, Ecuador and Paraguay, migrants could face prison sentences after using falsified documents, or if they had clandestinely entered the territory.[144] In Argentina,

---

[135] Brazil, Art. 107, Law 6.815/1980; Uruguay, Law Decree 14.878/1979 on foreigners amending Law 9.604 with regard to their entry into the country, Montevideo 5 April 1979; Paraguay, Arts 5–6 Law 470/1974, Asunción, 15 November 1974, impeding the entry of certain foreigners associated with political activities.

[136] P. Jerónimo, 'Report on Citizenship Law: Brazil', EUDO Citizenship, EUI Florence, January 2016, p. 17.

[137] Bolivia, Art. 34, Law Decree 13.344/1976.

[138] Argentina, Nationality and Citizenship Law 21.795/78. This was repealed in 1984 by Law 23.059, which resumed the previous regime established by Law 346, 1 October 1869.

[139] Ecuador, Naturalisation Law. Supreme Decree 276. 2 April 1976; Regulations to the Naturalisation Law, Supreme Decree 277, 14 April 1976.

[140] On the Brazilian case, see, for example: Sbalqueiro Lopes, *Direito de Imigração. O Estatuto do Estrangeiro*. For Ecuador, see: F. Hurtado Caicedo and R. Gallegos Brito, 'Informe Ecuador' (Quito: Programa Andino de Derechos Humanos, 2013).

[141] Argentina, Law Decree 17.294 on repression of clandestine migration, May 1967.

[142] Argentina, Law Decree 18.235/1969. See for a complete enumeration of measures during this period: Mármora *et al.*, 'Políticas Públicas y Programas sobre Migraciones en Argentina', on p. 97.

[143] *Ibid.*

[144] Chile, Arts 68–69 Law Decree 1094/1975 and Executive Decree 597, Santiago, 14 June 1984; Paraguay, Art. 108 Law 978/96; Ecuador, Art. 37 Migration Law adopted by Supreme Decree D. S. 1899, R. O. 382, 30 December 1971, codification 006, R. O. 563, 12 April 2005. On Chile see: C. Stefoni, 'Ley y Política Migratoria en Chile. La Ambivalencia en la Comprensión del Migrante' in B. Feldman-Bianco, L. Rivera Sánchez, C. Stefoni, M. I. Villa Martínez (eds), *La Construcción Social del Sujeto Migrante en América Latina. Prácticas, Representaciones y*

there was a widespread obligation to denounce migrants in an irregular situation. In both Argentina and Paraguay, citizens who helped irregular immigrants for philanthropic reasons were subject to a fine.[145] In Ecuador, the 1971 law favoured deportations and the administrative authorities enjoyed extensive powers during the expulsion procedure, with few possibilities for redress.[146] In Paraguay, its law still provides for imprisonment for up to two years for those using forged documents and the obligation for a number of stakeholders to denounce undocumented migrants.[147] Finally, the actors involved also changed in several countries. Migration and citizenship portfolios, formerly the domain of the Foreign Affairs Ministries, were transferred to those of the Interior in countries such as Chile and Peru.[148]

Immigration rates dramatically fell during this period. In Brazil, only a few dozen migrants entered per year.[149] In Chile, the number of foreign residents reached its historical minimum and represented only 0.7 per cent of its population by 1982.[150] Although the last military dictatorships subsided by the end of that decade, the migration legal architecture continued intact for many more years.[151] If this period represents the building of a mountain to keep migrants out, the descent to the bottom would not be simple. As discussed in the second part of this book, a century of exclusions has left a collection of deeply rooted approaches, discourses and practices that are not easily modifiable.

Discussion

South American leaders have generally been eager to depict their respective countries as both externally and internally inclusive. Externally, the image of an open arms region historically welcoming all migrants has been used as a political rhetorical device. For example, the late Argentinean President Nestor Kirchner repeatedly called on Spain to remember the historic solidarity

Categorías (Quito: FLACSO, Sede Ecuador: Consejo Latinoamericano de Ciencias Sociales, CLACSO: Universidad Alberto Hurtado, 2011), pp. 79–109.

[145] For Paraguay, see Art. 69, Law 470/1974; Argentina, Art. 32, to be read together with Art. 48, Law Decree 22.439/81. See also L. Mármora, 'Las Leyes de Migraciones como Contexto Normativo' in R. Giustiniani (ed.), *Migración: Un Derecho Humano. Comentarios sobre la Ley* (Buenos Aires: Prometeo Libros, 2004), pp. 59–65.

[146] G. Benavides Llerena, S. Sánchez Pinto and G. Chávez. *Informe Alternativo sobre el Cumplimiento de la Convención. Informe Final* (Quito: Coalición Institucional para el Seguimiento y Difusión de la Convención Internacional para la Protección de los Derechos de todos los Trabajadores Migratorios y sus Familiares, 2007), pp. 57–58.

[147] Paraguay, Arts 70 and 108, Law 978/96. This is derogated in the 2016 Proposal Migration Law, Ministry of Interior, General Directorate on Migration.

[148] See Peru, Law Decree 21702 segregating the Ministry of Foreign Affairs from the Directorate General on Migration and incorporating it into the Ministry of Interior starting from 1 January 1977. In Chile, see Arts 91–93, Law Decree 1094/1975.

[149] Sacchetta, *Laços de Sangue*, p. 252.

[150] IOM, *Perfil Migratorio de Chile*, p. 15.

[151] E. Domenech, *Migración y Política: El Estado Interrogado. Procesos Actuales en Argentina y Sudamérica* (Universidad de Córdoba [Argentina], 2009); Ceriani, 'Luces y Sombras'.

Argentina had with thousands of Spanish emigrants at the turn of the twentieth century.[152] At a regional level, when the EU adopted legislation on the expulsion of irregular migrants in 2008, it prompted the governments of all ten countries to demand fair treatment for their nationals in the EU, 'in accordance with the generous reception that hundreds of thousands of European nationals and their descendants enjoyed in South America'.[153] Internally, and particularly since the 1920 and 30s, the 'incorporation of the working class into politics'[154] facilitated the slow inclusion – despite ample contradictions and setbacks – of indigenous and black populations into the political sphere precisely through an emphasis on class rather than race.[155] Ideas about *mestizaje*, 'racial democracies' or 'crucible of races' arose during this period[156] in processes of nation building, which continue to be debated, contested and negotiated in the twenty-first century.[157] Both the internal and the external component have been intrinsically related through racial considerations and celebrating the whitening of populations that Europeans would bring.[158]

This chapter has offered a much more complex account of the alleged historical openness towards migrants. The investigation facilitates an easier understanding of restrictive discourses, laws and practices still ongoing in migration and citizenship law in the region. The last part of this chapter further extends the analysis to include reasoning behind pervasive discriminatory frameworks, the continuous privileged position of the Hispano(Latin)-American national until the 1960s, as well as the impact of restrictions in today's ongoing process of opening up towards an emphasis on human dignity and a rights-based approach.

Explaining Discrimination

The first Pan-American Conference in 1889 marked the beginning of a notably stronger US influence on migration regulation. This coincided with a period beginning in 1875 when the USA started to restrict certain categories, mainly Chinese nationals. US legislation was well known and referred to during parliamentary debates in South America.[159] Intense exchanges took place not only

---

[152] Acosta and Freier, 'Turning the Immigration Policy Paradox Up-side Down?', p. 667.

[153] UNASUR, Declaration by UNASUR on the EU's Returns Directive, Santiago, Chile, 4 July 2008. This declaration was also signed by Guyana and Suriname.

[154] Gargarella, *Latin American Constitutionalism*, p. 106.

[155] G. Reid Andrews, *Afro-Latinoamerica. 1800–2000* (Oxford University Press, 2003), chapter 5.

[156] FitzGerald and Cook-Martin, *Culling the Masses*, pp. 18–19.

[157] See for example: M. Htun, 'Political Inclusion and Social Inequality. Women, Afro-descendants and Indigenous Peoples' in J. I. Domínguez and M. Shifter (eds), *Constructing Democratic Governance in Latin America* (Baltimore, MD: Johns Hopkins University Press, 2008, 3rd edn), pp. 72–96; D. Von Vacano, *The Color of Citizenship. Race, Modernity and Latin American/ Hispanic Political Thought* (Oxford University Press, 2012).

[158] See Chapter 2, p. 59.

[159] See, for example, the discussions for the adoption of the 1890 Uruguayan legislation in: S. Acerenza Prunell, *Los Siriolibaneses y la Ley de 1890: El Racismo como Ordenador de la Política Inmigratoria* (Montevideo: Nordan-Comunidad, 2004–2005).

at the Pan-American Conferences but also in other fora. As FitzGerald and Cook-Martin have exposed, the diffusion of racial selection was facilitated by regional congresses comprised of scientists and demographers, from which such ideas were espoused. However, policy diffusion and its consequential legal transplants were not only the result of emulation but also of strategic adjustment.[160] This was particularly obvious in the relationship between the three largest recipients in the Americas: the USA, Argentina and Brazil. Here, it was common to make parallel changes in order to avoid the arrival of migrants who the other two countries had excluded. For example, the adoption of restrictive frameworks by the USA and Brazil, in 1917 and 1921 respectively, was rapidly mirrored by Argentina in 1923, which had just seen an increase in migrants who had been excluded by US restrictions.[161] Even earlier, in 1894, Uruguay had already legislated against what it considered to be 'useless migration', namely those arriving from Europe via Argentinean or Brazilian ports who travelled on second- or third-class tickets.[162]

Whereas the introduction of restrictions in countries like Argentina, Brazil or Uruguay could have a certain inner logic – in the sense that they had already received a significant number of migrants – it is harder to explain the replication of these clauses in the other seven countries in South America since they had low numbers of arrivals. In line with findings in other areas by Meyer *et al.*, this structural isomorphism, or similarity, results from the 'institutionalization of common world models' that are copied and diffused with little space for alternatives.[163] Policy diffusion is portrayed not 'as a functional response to common economic and structural challenges', but rather as the consequence of the 'spread of institutions and ideologies of population management'. In the early twentieth century, border control transformed into 'an indivisible aspect of sovereignty'.[164] South American countries reaffirmed their status in the international arena by replicating border measures that had achieved status as a 'prerequisite to recognition as a self-governing state'.[165] Regarding this aim, the measures' effectiveness played a minor role and once 'these models were entrenched, it was hard to establish alternatives'.[166]

In any case, South Americans had an ambivalent approach to the foreigner. The arrival of white European migrants was welcomed as a step forward towards 'racial improvement' in national censuses, since 'mestizaje was presumed to reduce the relative influence of Indianness or Africanness on the nation, while

---

[160] FitzGerald and Cook-Martin, *Culling the Masses*, see pp. 22–27.
[161] Devoto, *Historia de la Inmigración en la Argentina*, p. 170; Cook-Martin, 'Rules, Red Tape and Paperwork'.
[162] Uruguay, 1894, implementing regulations to Law 2096, 19 June 1890.
[163] J. W. Meyer, J. Boli, G. M. Thomas and F. O. Ramirez, 'World Society and the Nation-State', *American Journal of Sociology*, 103 (1997), 144–181.
[164] McKeown, *Melancholy Order*, p. 95.
[165] *Ibid.*, p. 321.
[166] *Ibid.*

enhancing the influence of Europeanness or native "whiteness" – never the reverse'.[167] These anxieties about the racial composition of populations meant that elites 'embraced race science as a pillar for their nation-making projects'.[168] Then again, South Americans also found a useful scapegoat in the foreigner, particularly after the 1929 economic crash. The longed-for and idealised migrant of the nineteenth century – the (Northern) white, industrious European with capital – was not necessarily the one who arrived in large numbers from the 1870s and 80s onwards. By the turn of the century, elites became increasingly concerned about the nature of European immigration. These were not 'the yeoman farmers from Protestant Europe' they had hoped to attract but instead uneducated commoners.[169] Immigrants brought not only the needed labour force but also notions about rights and equality that were found to be subversive. Thus, restrictions cannot be simply taken as resulting from an emulation process, nor from the willingness to be perceived as modern states in the international arena. The restrictions were also derived from deeply entrenched domestic concepts of conformity, belonging and exclusion defined by ruling elites. This represented both a continuation of previous nineteenth-century exclusionary traits, such as those based on class to deny citizenship, as well as a reversal in some respects of the former idealisation of European migrants.

The Position of Hispano(Latin)-American Citizens

Many of the exclusions introduced during the twentieth century affected both the foreigner in general, as well as the Hispano-American national, a different legal category identified in Chapter 3. However, even during the decades of increasing restrictiveness, Hispano-Americans continued to have preferential treatment; this category later expanded to Latin Americans, thus also including Brazil. In some countries, and for certain purposes, this was also extended to Spaniards and Portuguese.[170] Most obviously, Hispano-Americans and Brazilians were never subject to any exclusions on grounds of nationality, although a segment of the population fell under broader categories such as blacks, Asians, Roma or Jews. Furthermore, positive preferences continued to be enshrined in domestic laws and international agreements. Whereas idealism – one of the engines behind preferential treatment in the nineteenth century – progressively faded away, the Hispano-American still appeared to be a privileged legal figure, as proven through numerous examples.

---

[167] Loveman, *National Colors*, p. 154.

[168] *Ibid.*

[169] FitzGerald and Cook-Martin, *Culling the Masses*, p. 312. J. Delaney, 'Immigration, Identity, and Nationalism in Argentina, 1850–1950' in N. Foote and M. Goebel (eds), *Immigration and National Identities in Latin America* (Gainesville: University Press Florida, 2014) pp. 91–114, on p. 96.

[170] See, for example, Venezuela 1928 Constitution; Peru 1933 Constitution; Ecuador 1945 Constitution; Bolivia 1967 Constitution.

When it comes to naturalisation, Ecuador,[171] Venezuela[172] and Colombia continued to incorporate preferential access. In Colombia, for instance, the restrictive turn in its 1936 naturalisation law did not affect Hispano-Americans.[173] They still obtained nationality after simple registration, were exempt from any residence period requirement and, unlike other foreigners, they did not need to bring an industry or conduct a useful occupation to be considered, nor did they have to have five Colombians by birth testifying to their good conduct.[174]

Bilateral and multilateral agreements continued to be signed and ratified. They dealt with a large variety of issues, including facilitation of movement to exercise liberal professions,[175] extension of equal civil rights with nationals[176] and consular protection abroad.[177] Other agreements also referred to avoidance

---

[171] In Ecuador, the 1929, 1945, 1967 and 1979 Constitutions included such a route. This disappeared with the 1998 Constitution.

[172] In Venezuela, all fourteen constitutions adopted between 1901 and 1961 included a preferential route for Hispano-Americans. The 1925 Constitution was the first one to use the term Ibero-American Republics to also include Brazil.

[173] Colombia, Art. 6, Naturalisation Law 22 bis, 3 February 1936. This law was in force until 1991. See more on this: Escobar, *Report on Citizenship Law: Colombia*, p. 9.

[174] Colombia, Art. 1, Naturalisation Law 22 bis, 3 February 1936.

[175] There were numerous conventions on the exercise of liberal professions and the recognition of professional titles. See for example: the Convention on the Exercise of Liberal Professions, adopted on 4 February 1889 (ratified by all countries in South America except Chile); Convention for the Exercise of Liberal Professions, Mexico City, 28 January 1902 (signed by the USA as well as all South American States except Brazil and Venezuela); Agreement on Academic Titles, Caracas, 17 July 1911 (ratified by Bolivia, Colombia, Ecuador, Peru and Venezuela); Convention on the Exercise of Liberal Professions, Montevideo, 4 August 1939 (ratified by Argentina, Bolivia, Paraguay, Peru and Uruguay). There were also several bilateral agreements on the same subject, for example: Ecuador–Colombia, Lima, 3 May 1895; Brazil–Chile, Rio de Janeiro, 4 May 1897; Chile–Ecuador, Quito 9 April 1897; Chile–Colombia, Santiago 23 June 1921. The 1923 Resolution on the Unification of Passports (Fifth International American Conference, Santiago, 1923) is also notable. It recommended diminishing or suppressing the requirements to obtain a visa as well as the abolition of passports, to substitute them by national identity certificates to travel between the states in the American continent.

[176] The Convention on private international law, also known as Bustamante Code (Sixth American International Conference), La Habana, 20 February 1928. All South American states signed this convention, as well as Costa Rica, Cuba, El Salvador, Guatemala, Haiti, Honduras, Nicaragua, Panama and the Dominican Republic. However, the Code was only ratified in Brazil, Peru and Venezuela, as well as other Latin American countries outside South America. The USA did not sign the Convention. Also see the 1902 Convention on the Rights of Alienage, which applied to all foreigners and not only to those coming from the signing Republics (Second International American Conference), Mexico City, 29 January 1902. This 1902 instrument was signed by all South American states (except Brazil) as well as by Costa Rica, El Salvador, Guatemala, Honduras, Mexico, Nicaragua and the Dominican Republic. The USA did not sign it. A precedent initiative to codify private law, including provisions on equal civil rights for foreigners, is the 1878 Treaty of Private International Law, Lima 9 November 1878 (ratified by Costa Rica and Peru). On this, see Parra Aranguren, 'La Primera Etapa de los Tratados sobre Derecho Internacional Privado en América'.

[177] Consular Agreement, Caracas, 18 July 1911. It entered into force on 22 August 1915. This was ratified by Bolivia, Colombia, Ecuador, Peru and Venezuela.

of dual citizenship.[178] Softer forms of law were also present, such as the non-binding 1928 Resolution banning obstacles in the emigration and immigration between American states, which originated from a Mexican proposal.[179]

Latin Americans constituted a special category, upon which restrictions were much harder to justify since they were considered to be offensive.[180] Even if the USA was reluctant to sign any treaties regarding mobility, arguing the exclusive competence of national congress on migration control, its quota acts restricting migration by nationality in the 1920s did not apply to those coming from the Americas. Latin Americans strategically banded together to oppose any possible restrictions that the USA may have suggested against their own nationals. With recurrent discrimination at home, FitzGerald and Cook-Martin have argued that '[a]nti-racist statements were in many ways deeply cynical and hypocritical.'[181] Latin American solidarity thus functioned as a mechanism to ensure US exclusions – which had developed based on nationality in the early twentieth century – would not target their own nationals, notably Mexicans. Concerns about emigrants and their rights, rather than universal principled aspirations of equality,[182] were behind Latin America's diplomatic efforts. The need to appear as a respected actor in the international arena, whose nationals could not be discriminated against when abroad, was a central motive. The same countries backing ethnic and racial selection at home could reach consensus, by the time of the eighth Pan-American Conference in 1938, on the need to adopt anti-racist policies at the international level.[183] Importantly, emigration concerns have been key in putting forward liberal declarations, which are not always implemented at home in the early twenty-first century, as will be investigated in the second part of this book.

Special consideration of Latin American nationals lasted for a few decades longer. Even at the highest restriction peak in countries like Brazil, where a 1941 decree completely banned immigration, Americans from the whole

---

[178] The Third International American Conference discussed the condition of naturalised citizens who renew their residence in their country of origin, Rio de Janeiro, 13 August 1906. The Convention was signed by all ten South American states (except Venezuela) as well as by Costa Rica, Cuba, El Salvador, Guatemala, Honduras, Mexico, Nicaragua, Panama and the USA. The 1906 Convention was inspired by the Bancroft Treaties that the USA signed with various countries between 1868 and 1937 to avoid dual nationality. Those who had naturalised in another country but returned to the state of origin were to regain their original citizenship and renounce the more recent one, generally after two years of residence. Three decades later, the 1933 Montevideo Covenant established that those acquiring the nationality of one of the signatories automatically lost their previous one. See the Convention on Nationality (Seventh Pan-American Conference), Montevideo, 26 December 1933. However, this treaty did not derogate the 1906 Convention, which remained in force.

[179] See the Resolution on Emigration and Immigration, La Habana, 15 February 1928, Sixth International Conference of American States.

[180] Brown Scott, 'The Sixth International Conference of American States', p. 320.

[181] FitzGerald and Cook-Martin, *Culling the Masses*, p. 76.

[182] *Ibid.*

[183] *Ibid.*, pp. 25–29.

continent were still allowed entry and largely offered equal treatment.[184] It was only in the 1960s and 70s that the demise of European flows, coupled with draconian measures adopted by military dictatorships to control the populations, put all foreigners under the same deprivation. Both domestic and regional international law shifted in this period. In Paraguay, for example, the constitutional clause to encourage American immigration, which had been present since 1870, disappeared in the 1967 Constitution adopted under a military regime. Proposals on regional mobility at both the bilateral and multilateral level also slowed down in the 1970s. It was only years after the return to democracy, timidly in the 1990s and with stronger momentum following the turn of the century, that positive measures on mobility and migration re-emerged on the agenda.

Conclusion

A century of migratory restrictions has left a profound scar in South America. Racist, unequal and discriminatory choices were not simply an aberration committed by military dictatorships within the context of external pressures in a Cold-War environment, but rather a much more deeply entrenched phenomenon that occurred throughout various decades. After the return to democracy, official immigration discourses continued to remain securitised, restrictive and often openly racist during the 1990s.[185] A century of increasing exclusionary legislative frameworks helps to explain the tortuous journey to adopt more egalitarian laws after redemocratisation. For example, Brazil and Ecuador were only able to approve new, more open migration and citizenship laws in 2017, following a decade of failed proposals and discussion and around forty years after their last bills, adopted under undemocratic regimes, had been passed. Similarly, by mid-2017, and despite numerous proposals for new laws, Chile and Paraguay continued to have their migration frameworks in place, which had originally been adopted in the 1970s under military administrations.[186] The echoes of a century of restrictions still loom large. In Colombia, it was only in 2016 that the Constitutional Court overturned the prohibition of entry for those with disabilities or suffering grave illnesses – exclusions which had been enshrined in a 1920 law.[187] The same country only abolished discriminatory

---

[184] Brazil, Law Decree 3175, 7 April 1941, banning all migration except that of Portuguese and all citizens from the American continent. See also Decree 12 June 1940 exempting Americans from the need to have a visa or passport to enter Uruguay, if their countries of origin did the same in favour of Uruguayans abroad. Cited in Sandonato, 'Nacionalidad y Extranjería en el Uruguay', 198.

[185] Domenech, *Migración y Política: El Estado Interrogado*; Ceriani, 'Luces y Sombras.'

[186] Chile, Law Decree 1904/1975; in Paraguay Migration Law 978/1996 is largely considered to be a copy, almost verbatim, of the Law 470/1974 adopted during the military regime.

[187] Colombia, Constitutional Court, C-258/16 on Art. 7 of Law 48/1920, regarding the exclusion of entry to foreigners with severe, chronic or contagious illnesses (such as tuberculosis) or those who are idle, chronic alcoholics, epileptics or disabled.

compulsory percentages of national workers for companies in 2010, sixty years after they had been adopted.[188] In Brazil, Bolivia and Peru, they still remained in place in 2017.[189]

The way in which exclusion stacked up during a century has also had a resounding impact on daily bureaucratic practices, notably by the police and ministries of the interior. Both institutions have largely opposed a stronger rights-based approach during discussions for new migration laws in several countries. This bureaucratic inertia – under which the foreigner is considered a second-class resident who can be legally discriminated against through various administrative practices and procedures, even when the law does not allow for such discrimination to take place – complicates the shift towards openness heralded in numerous laws and declarations adopted in the twenty-first century and represents a crucial challenge to accessing rights in the region. This will be the subject of the second part of this book.

---

[188] Colombia, abrogated by Art. 65, Law 1429/2010.

[189] Bolivia, 1942 General Labour Law, 8 December 1942; Brazil, Art. 354, Law Decree 5452/1943, 5 January 1943, approving the consolidated version of the labour regulations. Part of the doctrine considers this article to run counter to Brazil's 1988 Constitution, see Sbalqueiro Lopes, *Direito de Imigração*, pp. 590–594; Peru, Legislative Decree 689, 4 November 1991 (this exclusion does not apply to Andean Community workers).

Part II
Consolidation and Transition into the Twenty-first Century

Transitioning into the Twenty-first Century: The New Latin American Constitutionalism

Part I of this book covered the legal construction of the national and the foreigner in South America from the time of independence in the early nineteenth century until the 1980s. Part II will examine how the foreigner has been formulated through legal rules in South America at the end of the twentieth and then in the twenty-first century. Part II is divided into three chapters based on migrants' status: those in an irregular situation, those with residence permits and, finally, regional South American nationals. Taken separately, the chapters relate to the three most important principles enunciated in the South American discourse since the turn of the century: non-criminalisation of irregular migrants; the right to migrate as a fundamental right; and open borders. Each chapter is nonetheless part of the holistic ensemble since the categories of irregular, regular and regional migrant are blurry and undefined in South America. Whilst each chapter prioritises certain relevant elements, they all discuss the three basic stages of any migration trajectory post-departure from the country of origin: entry, residence and, eventually, either expulsion or permanent residence/naturalisation. The key concern is to elucidate whether – and to what extent – path-breaking principles actually exist in the region's discourse, laws or constitutions. By path-breaking, we specifically mean exceptional regulations regarding the foreigner's legal status and the availability of rights that are absent in other jurisdictions.

The following pages introduce Part II in order to offer the reader an account of crucial changes at the constitutional and international level that have taken place in South America since the 1990s. Understanding this legal shift is essential to then correctly locate new forms of migration and citizenship regulation in both domestic and regional law. Chapter 4 concluded by describing how the 1970s and 1980s represent the most restrictive historical point in the treatment of migrants. Discrimination against foreigners was only one element of possibly the darkest period in the history of South America, and more generally, in Latin America. Under the shadow of military regimes, the most egregious crimes against humanity took place with impunity: forced disappearances, extra-judicial executions, torture and arbitrary repression. It is against this background that we evaluate the emergence of a new architecture based on protection at the international, regional and domestic constitutional levels since the 1990s.

Since the return to democracy, and also facilitated by the end of the Cold War, a process known as the new Latin American Constitutionalism or Latin American *Ius Constitutionale Commune* has been taking place.[1] This trend has been labelled as 'transformative constitutionalism'[2] and began with the 1991 Colombian Constitution, followed by others such as in Venezuela (1999), Ecuador (2008) and then Bolivia (2009). Some authors also add the Argentinean text (1994) as well as some traits of the Brazilian one (1988) to the list. The new Latin American Constitutionalism is defined at a procedural level by a more democratic constitution-making method opened to various actors.[3] At a material level, these constitutions incorporate extensive catalogues of rights protecting vulnerable groups – such as afro-descendants and indigenous populations. This approach has been branded as 'original', 'innovative' and as being 'stripped of any fear to invent'.[4]

Of course, not all commentaries have been enthusiastic and ingratiating. The all-encompassing catalogues have prompted debates on an 'inflation of rights' and concerns about 'poetical' texts, rather than real or natural.[5] According to these reviews, the variety of principles they uphold 'sacrifice the instrumental value' of a constitutional text 'in favour of its symbolic dimension'.[6] Article 416(6) in Ecuador's Constitution provides an excellent example since it establishes that Ecuador 'advocates the principle of universal citizenship, the free movement of all inhabitants on the planet, and the progressive extinction of the status of alien or foreigner as an element to transform the unequal relations between countries, especially those between North and South'. The precise meaning of this provision is undeniably elusive.

Considering this, the new constitutions possess a central contradiction since they also continue to concentrate political power in the hands of the executive,

---

[1] A. von Bogdandy, E. Ferrer Mac-Gregor, M. Morales Antoniazzi, F. Piovesan and X. Soley (eds), *Transformative Constitutionalism in Latin America. The Emergence of a New Ius Commune* (Oxford University Press, 2017); A. von Bogdandy, 'Ius Constitutionale Commune en América Latina: una Mirada a un Constitucionalismo Transformador', *Revista de Derecho del Estado*, 34 (2015), 3–50; R. Viciano Pastor (ed.), *Estudios sobre el Nuevo Constitucionalismo Latinoamericano* (Valencia: Tirant lo Blanch, 2012); D. Nolte and A. Schilling-Vacaflor (eds), *New Constitutionalism in Latin America. Promises and Practices* (Farnham: Ashgate, 2012); R. Gargarella and C. Courtis, *El Nuevo Constitucionalismo Latinoamericano: Promesas e Interrogantes* (Santiago de Chile: CEPAL, 2009).

[2] Von Bogdandy, 'Ius Constitutionale Commune', 5.

[3] R. Viciano Pastor and R. Martínez Dalmau, 'Fundamento Teórico del Nuevo Constitucionalismo Lationamericano' in Viciano Pastor (ed.), pp. 11–49, on pp. 25–36.

[4] *Ibid.*, pp. 38–39.

[5] Gargarella and Courtis, *El Nuevo Constitucionalismo Latinoamericano*, pp. 31–32.

[6] P. Salazar Ugarte, 'El Nuevo Constitucionalismo Latinoamericano (Una Perspectiva Crítica)' in L. R. González Pérez and D. Valadés (eds), *El Constitucionalismo Contemporáneo. Homenaje a Jorge Carpizo* (Mexico City: UNAM, 2013), pp. 345–387, on p. 371.

an exacerbated phenomenon known as 'hyper-presidentialism'[7] – a particular feature that is traceable to the first post-independence constitutional texts in the early nineteenth century. Without modifying what Gargarella names 'the engine room' of the constitution, his prediction for the effective materialisation of rights remains bleak and the activation of 'dormant clauses' dependent on judicial action.[8]

National courts, mainly constitutional and supreme courts, emerge as crucial actors facing the challenging task of interpreting the meaning of broadly principled norms.[9] The protective capacity of national courts has been reinforced through international law, particularly the ACHR, and through the IACtHR's jurisprudence.[10] Here we need to distinguish three different interrelated elements. The first is the 'constitutionalization of human rights treaties'.[11] According to von Bogdandy, human rights became the central pillar of the *Ius Constitutionale Commune* through the incorporation of public international law and the IACtHR's jurisprudence into the 'block of constitutionality'.[12] This is not surprising, considering the need to offer reparation after a period of egregious violations of basic rights, and the rampant inequality and exclusion still present in most countries. The hurried ratification of human rights treaties by South American countries during the democratic transition period was thus an 'antidote against authoritarian regressions'.[13] In turn, their accommodation as part of the 'block of constitutionality' resulted from 'the sense that national constitutional law alone was insufficient to resolve the shortcomings in the rule of law and the fulfilment of basic constitutional rights'.[14]

The second element is the Inter-American Court's doctrine on conventionality control. Whereas only cases having exhausted all domestic remedies (in line with the principle of subsidiarity) can reach the inter-American system, the doctrine on conventionality control imposes the obligation on the state – either through national courts or other state authorities – to interpret domestic law, including the constitution, in accordance with the ACHR. This obligation

---

[7] D. Valadés, 'The Presidential System in Latin America: A Hallmark and Challenge to a Latin American *Ius Constitutionale Commune*' in Von Bogdandy *et al.* (eds), *Transformative Constitutionalism in Latin America*, pp. 191–210.

[8] R. Gargarella, 'El "Nuevo Constitucionalismo Latinoamericano"', *Estudios Sociales*, 48 (2015), 169–172; Gargarella and Courtis, *El Nuevo Constitucionalismo Latinoamericano*, p. 33.

[9] Salazar Ugarte, 'El Nuevo Constitucionalismo Latinoamericano', p. 377.

[10] See for example Colombia, Art. 93, 1991 Constitution; Argentina, Art. 75(22), 1994 Constitution; Ecuador, Arts 11(3), 417 and 424, 2008 Constitution; Bolivia, Arts 13(IV) and 256, 2009 Constitution.

[11] M. E. Góngora Mera, *Inter-American Judicial Constitutionalism. On the Constitutional Rank of Human Rights Treaties in Latin America through National and Inter-American Adjudication* (San José: Inter-American Institute of Human Rights, 2011), p. 1.

[12] Von Bogdandy, '*Ius Constitutionale Commune*', pp. 11 and 17.

[13] V. Abramovich, 'Autonomía y Subsidiariedad: El Sistema Interamericano de Derechos Humanos Frente a los Sistemas de Justicia Nacionales' in C. Rodríguez Garavito (ed.), *El Derecho en América Latina. Un Mapa para el Pensamiento Jurídico del Siglo XXI* (Buenos Aires: Siglo Veintiuno, 2011), pp. 211–230, on p. 217.

[14] Góngora Mera, *Inter-American Judicial Constitutionalism*, p. 2.

also extends to consistent interpretation with other inter-American treaties on human rights, as well as with the IACtHR's jurisprudence and its advisory opinions, what has been named as the inter-American *corpus juris* or the real 'block of conventionality'.[15] Thus, national judges are granted 'the role of "courts of first instance" in the enforcement' of the inter-American treaties.[16] As Mera highlights, 'national judges should not be limited to the issue of whether a norm is unconstitutional but in addition they must address (upon the request of the interested party or *ex officio*) whether the norm in question is unconventional, that is, whether the norm restricts or violates the rights recognised in the inter-American treaties ratified by the State'.[17] Should that be the case, state authorities ought to abstain from applying such a law. Today, most South American states recognise the supremacy of international human rights law over domestic provisions, either through a specific reference in their constitutions or through judicial interpretation.[18]

Whereas international law has obtained primacy over domestic law, the same cannot be argued when it comes to constitutional law. Possible clashes are, however, theoretically solved by the third element, namely the *pro homine* principle of interpretation. This establishes that when faced with a particular legal problem, the interpreter 'may give preference to the norm that provides the widest and most extensive protection of human rights, regardless of the source (international/inter-American or national) and its rank in the normative order'.[19] To put it differently, since the American Convention aims at preserving human rights and upholding human dignity, 'its interpretation must be done in favour of the individual'.[20] This principle is now largely accepted by domestic courts and even enshrined in some constitutions.[21]

These three principles (constitutionalisation of human rights, the doctrine on conventionality control and the *pro homine* principle of interpretation) offer national courts a fertile legal soil to develop norm interpretation with a strong focus on a rights-based approach. However, courts face different institutional constraints well plotted by others.[22] In the migration arena, courts face general limitations but we can more specifically add others regarding foreigners' limited access to justice and, for decades, a restrictive legislative panorama

---

[15] E. Ferrer Mac-Gregor coincided with this opinion in 'The Conventionality Control as a Core Mechanism of the *Ius Constitutionale Commune*' in Von Bogdandy *et al.* (eds), *Transformative Constitutionalism*, pp. 321–336, on p. 334.

[16] Góngora Mera, *Inter-American Judicial Constitutionalism*, p. 54.

[17] *Ibid.*, p. 55.

[18] *Ibid.*, p. 58.

[19] *Ibid.*

[20] *Ibid.*, p. 59.

[21] *Ibid.* See Bolivia, Art. 256, 2009 Constitution; Ecuador, Art. 427, 2008 Constitution; Venezuela, Art. 23, 1999 Constitution.

[22] J. F. González-Bertomeu and R. Gargarella (eds), *The Latin American Casebook. Courts, Constitutions, and Rights* (Abingdon: Routledge, 2016).

leaving little space for expansive interpretation. This last obstacle has largely changed with the turn of the century.

The New South American Migration Regime

The regulation of the rights of foreigners constitutes a component – albeit not a central one – of this new Latin American Constitutionalism, or Latin American *Ius Constitutionale Commune*. True, if appreciated in a historical perspective, the extension of rights to foreigners is not a peculiarity of this recent constitutionalism.[23] Moreover, the new constitutional texts are not path-breaking since they merely provide equal treatment on civil rights, mirroring provisions which had been normal during the nineteenth and early twentieth centuries.[24] And yet migrants have entered the legislative and judicial agenda, including that of the IACtHR, both as bearers of fundamental rights and as potentially vulnerable populations, notably irregular migrants, in need of stronger protection.

Ecuador is a paradigmatic case. Its 2008 Constitution incorporates numerous provisions on human mobility, introduces distinctive global-level concepts such as universal citizenship, and grants foreigners political rights at the national level. The reasons for Ecuador's interest in mobility have been presented as an expectation of reciprocity against the backdrop of large numbers of emigrants abroad.[25] Paradoxically, the constitution coexisted for eight years – until the adoption of a new Organic Law on Human Mobility in 2017 – with the restrictive 1971 migration legal framework and more importantly, with discriminatory practices by state administrations.[26] Ecuador's 2017 Law on Human Mobility is an instrument that serves to highlight some of the parallels between new migration laws and the recent Latin American Constitutionalism, as well as its inconsistencies.

The South American rights-based approach to migration, while being chronologically subsequent, draws from the same sources and concerns regarding fundamental rights, and partly results from a strengthened inter-American system of protection. It is now common knowledge that the adoption of the 2004 Argentinean immigration law, the first one of a series of progressive texts in the region, was largely the upshot of a friendly settlement reached before the IACHR in 2003,[27] coupled with the willingness of

---

[23] See Chapter 2, pp. 52–54.

[24] For example, see: Argentina, Art. 20, 1994 Constitution; Bolivia, Art. 14, 2009 Constitution; Brazil, Art. 5, 1988 Constitution; Colombia, Art. 100, 1991 Constitution.

[25] M. Góngora-Mera, G. Herrera and C. Müller, 'The Frontiers of Universal Citizenship. Transnational Social Spaces and the Legal Status of Migrants in Ecuador', *desiguALdades.net Working Paper Series*, 71 (2014), p. 12.

[26] Acosta and Freier, 'Turning the Immigration Policy Paradox Up-side Down?'; Góngora-Mera *et al.*, 'The Frontiers of Universal Citizenship'; J. Ramírez, *La Política Migratoria en Ecuador Rupturas, Tensiones, Continuidades y Desafíos* (Quito: IAEN, 2014, 2nd edn).

[27] IACtHR, Report No. 85/11, Petition 12.306, Friendly Settlement *Juan Carlos de la Torre* (Argentina), 21 July 2011. De la Torre was a Uruguayan national who had been detained and expelled without any judicial oversight after twenty-four years of residence in Argentina.

President Kirchner to repeal a legal framework adopted during the military regime.[28] Argentina's law was then followed by new legislation in Uruguay (2008), Bolivia (2013), Brazil (2017), Ecuador (2017) and Peru (2017), and by proposals not yet adopted at the time of writing in Chile (2017) and Paraguay (2016). While Colombia and Venezuela have adopted new migration laws since the turn of the century, and while they incorporate certain similar principles in some areas, they cannot be included in this enumeration of more progressive laws due to their structure and content.[29] Similar to Argentina, these laws have come about as a means of replacing restrictive frameworks that had often been adopted under the previous authoritarian regimes and that were utilitarian at best and discriminatory and disregarding basic fundamental rights at worst. Whilst each of the new migration laws has peculiarities, it is fair to say that they result from a more extensive debate between civil society groups, academics, government officials and politicians. Materially, the new laws would also be identifiable by extensive catalogues of rights and by a certain boldness and willingness to innovate. The migration sphere has certainly not been immune to the human rights discourse, as epitomised by several of these texts considering the right to migrate as a fundamental one – an innovation at the global level, of which the precise reach has yet to be seen.[30] If South Americans in the twentieth century had followed already-trodden paths, with no space for distinctiveness, in order to appear respectful and *sufficiently sovereign* in the international arena,[31] the present would have an open door for a certain uniqueness in choosing the most suitable answers to particular challenges. These solutions would not necessarily mirror those already imposed by or exercised in Europe and the USA. A different ethos has emerged, which has human dignity as a central component.

Of course, this certain uniqueness cannot be understood in a political vacuum. Any bold statement as to the superiority of a South American approach to migration regulation must be avoided and carefully unpacked. At the turn of the century, coincidently there were various governments with a strong human rights agenda, at least discursively, which found themselves in a particular historical period with immense numbers of co-nationals emigrating to the USA and Europe. Considering the ongoing trends of increasing criminalisation and border closures, often affecting South American nationals abroad, the governments in the region banded together and reacted with enunciations prohibiting such criminalisation and claiming the existence of a right to migrate and the need to open borders. The reader will find similarities here with the approach taken in the 1920s and 1930s when Latin Americans banded together

[28] Ceriani and Morales, *Argentina: Avances y Asignaturas*, on p. 8.
[29] A 2017 law proposal in Colombia for a new comprehensive migration policy has a much stronger focus on the rights of Colombians abroad than on the rights of foreigners in Colombia. See Law Project 148, 19 September 2017.
[30] See Chapter 6.
[31] See Chapter 4, pp. 106–107.

to oppose any possible restrictions in the USA against their own nationals.[32] One could certainly argue that the same concerns about emigrants and their rights – rather than universally principled aspirations of equality – are behind this enunciation of principles today. Yet it cannot be denied that this process has also benefited a more progressive agenda towards immigrants in the region.

South American states, however, also share certain traits affecting the foundations of the rule of law such as 'weak normativity' and a 'lack of institutional capacity' to effectively implement it.[33] These endanger the effective application of rights enunciated in laws, thus once more begging the question as to the rhetorical nature. This same argument has been used to underline the ineffectiveness of the 'progressive' nature of the IACtHR's rulings and advisory opinions, in cases where some countries lack adequate mechanisms to implement the Court's findings.[34] The transition between 'a concept of formal equality' towards one of 'substantive equality' when the problematique of 'structural discrimination' is present, is a central challenge throughout the region.[35] The resulting picture is certainly more balanced and can be better defined, to borrow from Ramírez, as a 'long process of sedimentation', not immune to setbacks, especially when different political agendas are at stake.[36] The adoption in January 2017 of an amending executive decree in Argentina to its migration law by the Macri government, known for its more restrictive approach on migration, clearly illustrates this point.[37]

The next three chapters will bring to light the advances, impediments and contradictions in the legal construction of the foreigner's status in present-day South America. The three principles of non-criminalisation, the right to migrate as a fundamental right and open borders will be assessed by discussing the entry, stay and eventual expulsion or permanent residence/naturalisation of those migrants who are in an irregular situation and those with a residence permit, as well as nationals from regional states.

---

[32] See Chapter 4, p. 109.
[33] Von Bogdandy, 'Ius Constitutionale Commune', pp. 21–22. Abramovich, 'Autonomía y Subsidiariedad', p. 222.
[34] J. L. Cavallaro and S. Erin Brewer, 'Reevaluating Regional Human Rights Litigation in the Twenty-First Century: The Case of the Inter-American Court', American Journal of International Law, 102(2008), 768–827.
[35] Abramovich, 'Autonomía y Subsidiariedad', p. 216.
[36] Ramírez, La Política Migratoria en Ecuador, p. 51.
[37] Decree 70/2017 amending the Immigration Law, Buenos Aires, 27 January 2017.

5

The Construction of the Irregular Immigrant: The Principle of Non-Criminalisation of Undocumented Migration

Firstly, I would like to thank in the name of the Brazilian people all immigrants who helped and continue to help in building our country ... We are truly an immigrant nation ... We are not only a mixed nation but we like being a mixed nation. This forms a large part of our identity, our strength, our happiness, our creativity and our talent ... We consider unfair some of the migration policies recently adopted in some rich countries that have as one of their traits the repatriation of immigrants ... We don't want any privilege for any Brazilian in any part of the globe. We just want you to treat Brazilians abroad like we treat foreigners here in Brazil; like brothers, like partners and like Brazilians.[1]

Introduction

Undocumented migration is the most debated aspect of mobility on a global scale. From calls by the US President to deport 11 million people,[2] to the EU's 'fight against illegal migration',[3] discussions unravel in an incoherent, at times hysterical, fashion. Criminalisation and its rhetoric are on the rise.[4] At the same

---

[1] Former Brazilian President Lula da Silva's speech during the ceremony sanctioning the law on the amnesty for foreigners in an irregular situation in Brazil. Brasilia, 2 July 2009 (author's translation). 'Primeiramente, gostaria de agradecer, em nome do povo brasileiro, a todos os imigrantes que ajudaram e continuam a ajudar a construir o nosso país ... Somos, na verdade, uma nação formada por imigrantes. Não só somos um povo misturado, como gostamos de ser um povo misturado. Daí vem grande parte de nossa identidade, de nossa força, de nossa alegria, de nossa criatividade e do nosso talento ... Consideramos injustas as políticas migratórias adotadas recentemente em alguns países ricos, que têm como um dos pontos a repatriação dos imigrantes. Nos não queremos nenhum privilégio a nenhum brasileiro, em nenhuma parte do mundo. Nós queremos apenas que vocês tratem os brasileiros no exterior como nós tratamos os estrangeiros aqui no Brasil: como irmãos, como parceiros e como brasileiros.' Available at: www.biblioteca. presidencia.gov.br/presidencia/ex-presidentes/luiz-inacio-lula-da-silva/discursos/2o-mandato/ 2009/copy_of_02-07-2009-discurso-do-presidente-da-republica-luiz-inacio-lula-da-silva-durante-cerimonia-de-sancao-da-lei-que-anistia-estrangeiros-em-situacao-irregular

[2] The Guardian, 'Donald Trump Wants to Deport 11 Million Migrants: Is that even Possible?', 27 August 2015. Note that this was written while Trump was still a presidential candidate.

[3] European Commission Communication on a Community Immigration Policy, COM (2000) 757 final, Brussels, 22 November.

[4] B. Anderson, M. J. Gibney and E. Paoletti, 'Citizenship, Deportation and the Boundaries of Belonging', *Citizenship Studies*, 15 (2011), 547–563; J. Huysmans, *The Politics of Insecurity: Fear, Migration and Asylum in the EU* (Abingdon: Routledge, 2006).

time, and in sheer contrast, membership is enhanced when residence is granted through legislative or judicial action. The same government criminalising irregular migrants as criminal offenders today may decide to regularise those same migrants tomorrow.[5] Revolving door mechanisms by which the outsider is, on the one hand, 'granted more opportunities to be included in a national polity while, on the other hand and by the same conditions, is continuously under the threat of expulsion and exclusion',[6] are most obviously found in the paradoxical regulation of irregular migration.

Attempts to classify 'good' regular migrants and 'bad' undocumented ones are ever-present. They are repeatedly misleading because the majority of unauthorised migrants at some point had regular status and lost it through visa-overstay, non-renewal or unauthorised work.[7] Defining migrants as 'irregular' or 'illegal' symbolically functions for states as the last 'bastion of sovereignty'.[8] The undocumented pose a challenge to the 'paradigm of control of population movement'[9] and are portrayed as violating not only the state's 'sovereign exclusionary powers' but also as rupturing 'the social contract which binds the nation'.[10] Criminalisation and rights deprivation are often presented as solutions to drive them out or to deter others from coming.[11]

Irregular migrants are hardly ever presented as residents or transients between the terms of the foreigner and the national. This is even though, as Motomura has highlighted in the US case, 'immigration status is hard to ascertain or is changeable. And even when a violation is clear, its consequences are not.'[12] The passage from irregularity to regularity and citizenship may be facilitated or halted by legislative and administrative measures at various levels, as well as by a myriad of bureaucracies exercising discretion. In the end, defining who exactly is undocumented at any moment is prone to error since the individual's status constantly shifts depending on numerous variables such

---

[5] See the Italian example under the various Berlusconi administrations where criminalisation was always coupled with large regularisation procedures. On this, see: D. Acosta and A. Geddes, 'The Development, Application and Implications of an EU Rule of Law in the Area of Migration Policy', *Journal of Common Market Studies*, 51 (2013), 179–193.

[6] D. Acosta and J. Martire, 'Trapped in the Lobby: Europe's Revolving Doors and the Other as Xenos', *European Law Review*, 39 (2014), 362–379, on 366.

[7] M. Baldwin Edwards and A. Kraler, *REGINE Regularisations in Europe Study on Practices in the Area of Regularisation of Illegally Staying Third-country Nationals in the Member States of the EU* (Vienna: ICMPD, 2009), p. 129.

[8] Dauvergne, *Making People Illegal*, p. 2.

[9] D. Kostakopoulou, 'Irregular Migration and Migration Theory: Making State Authorisation Less Relevant' in B. Bogusz, R. Cholewinski, A. Cygan and E. Szyszczak (eds), *Irregular Migration and Human Rights: Theoretical, European and International Perspectives* (Leiden: Martinus Nijhoff, 2004), pp. 41–57, on pp. 41 and 43.

[10] L. Bosniak, 'Human Rights, State Sovereignty and the Protection of Undocumented Migrants under the International Migrant Workers' Convention' in *ibid.*, pp. 311–344, on p. 331.

[11] A. Aliverti, 'Making People Criminal: The Role of the Criminal Law in Immigration Enforcement', *Theoretical Criminology*, 16 (2012), 417–434; Kostakopoulou, 'Irregular Migration and Migration Theory', p. 55.

[12] Motomura, *Immigration Outside the Law*, p. 21.

as family, length of residence, labour or community involvement, and the dip-lomatic ability of the country of origin in negotiating agreements overnight legalising the status of their nationals abroad.

In South America, the status and rights of migrants in an irregular situation have been a regional concern for decades. Irregular migration first appeared as a concept in the 1930s and 1940s in countries such as Argentina, Brazil and Venezuela, following the demise of open borders, the saliency of excluded cat-egories and the increasing restrictions on access to the labour market. Two elements have historically captured the regulation of irregular migration: expul-sion and regularisation.

This chapter devotes more attention to regularisation since it is a pressing global challenge that everybody is confronting. In South America, pioneering legislative discussions are taking place, challenging global established assumptions on how to control undocumented flows. We can see a clear progress from a general nebulous concern with fundamental rights and migration management as solutions to irregular flows[13] towards a much more emphatic, precise and delineated answer lying in three consecutive aspects: non-criminalisation, rights' protection and regularisation. To various degrees, these three aspirations have become a flagship and been reaffirmed in numerous regional fora.[14] They have also progressed from political statements into legal provisions prohibiting criminalisation and incorporating principles favouring regularisation.[15] Thus, there is a unique aspect to how a group of South American countries are trying to regulate undocumented migration. At a comparative level, it distinguishes them from Europe in certain respects and from the USA in others. It is important to understand those differences. The question arises: what does non-criminalisation entail, how does it affect the interpretation and meaning of the law, and how does it materialise into indi-vidual rights?

This chapter first assesses non-criminalisation, broadly understood as incorp-orating the principles of rights' protection and regularisation. It then asserts two propositions, one descriptive and the other interpretative. The descriptive thesis is that some of the aspects considered as part of the ongoing criminal-isation in Europe and the USA are also present in the South American case, in versions that are sometimes softer and sometimes harsher. The approach is different, however, when it comes to regularisation. As a first reaction when

---

[13] Buenos Aires Declaration, South American Conference on Migration, 19 May 2000.

[14] See XXIII MERCOSUR and Associate States meeting of Ministers of the Interior, Regional Position ahead of the Global Forum on Migration and Development (XXV Specialised Migration Forum) (MERCOSUR/RMI/DI N° 01/08) Buenos Aires, 10 June 2008; 4th meeting of the Andean Community's Migration Forum, Bogotá Declaration, 10 May 2013; the South American Conference on Migration, Asunción Declaration, 5 May 2006.

[15] Argentina, Art. 17, Law 25871/2004; Brazil, Art. 3, Law 13.445/2017; Chile, Arts 7 and 9, 2017 Migration Law Proposal; Ecuador, Art. 2, 2017 Organic Law on Human Mobility; Paraguay, Art. 25, 2016 Migration Law Proposal; Peru, Arts VII and XII, Preliminary Title, Legislative Decree 1350/2017; Uruguay, Art. 52, Law 18.250/2008.

faced with an undocumented migrant, the general rule in Europe and the USA, put in simple terms, is to limit rights and use expulsion. This does not mean that most migrants are expelled or that there are no possibilities to regularise, nor that irregular migrants do not enjoy rights. It simply emphasises the rationale behind the law. South America would reverse this paradigm by prioritising rights protection and regularisation.

As for the interpretative thesis, the chapter has two endeavours. First, it deliberates on the actual legal contours and meaning of rights protection and regularisation by paying close attention to the national, regional and international levels, including the jurisprudence of the Inter-American Court. Second, the chapter concentrates on the political-ideological, legal and social reasons behind this approach to irregularity, as well as its boundaries and flaws, mainly between how regularisation and deportation are juxtaposed.

The chapter is divided into three sections. The first one looks at what is usually associated with criminalisation by distinguishing between measures affecting entry, stay and removal, as well as rights protection at each stage. The key overarching concern is focused on elucidating whether – and if so, to what extent – the principle prohibiting criminalisation materialises in exceptional regulation of the legal status of the undocumented migrant. The second section discusses the prominence of regularisation in South America and analyses its different configurations at the national, bilateral and regional levels. The third part dives into interpreting the reasons behind these patterns of migration regulation and their boundaries. A short conclusion paves the way for Chapter 6, which analyses the right to migrate as a fundamental right, as well as the regulation of non-nationals with a residence permit.

Criminalising Irregular Migration

Over the last thirty years, the criminalisation of irregular migration has expanded in the EU and the USA. This refers to the transformation of migration law from administrative civil law into criminal law. At times, this evolution has coexisted with regularisations, extension of rights and toleration of irregularity. Discourse lies on two opposing poles, with some arguing that granting a secure legal status to those already resident and part of the community is fair, while others highlight the injustice of rewarding those who have breached migration law.[16]

The criminalisation of migration, or *crimmigration*,[17] has attracted attention in the academic fields both in the USA and Europe. For example, Legomsky has investigated the increasing use of criminal law to punish immigration

---

[16] On these debates, see J. Carens, *The Ethics of Immigration* (Oxford University Press, 2013), pp. 129–157.

[17] J. Stumpf, 'The Crimmigration Crisis: Immigrants, Crime, and Sovereign Power', *American University Law Review*, 56 (2006), 367–419.

violations in the USA, coupled with the practice of attaching consequences from immigration law to criminal convictions.[18] In his view, it is problematic that the import of criminal features has not gone hand-in-hand with the bundle of procedural rights relating to adjudication.[19] In the EU's case, Mitsilegas has understood criminalisation as a process comprised of three acts involving measures taken before entry, during the stay and, finally, towards removal.[20]

A note of caution is necessary here. Sometimes the language surrounding criminalisation makes it difficult for lawyers to think carefully about the mechanisms of migration regulation. It is helpful to disaggregate those mechanisms. When we invoke the word criminalisation, we draw a contrast between the use of criminal law as a mode of regulation and the use of civil administrative law. Through that lens, many of the policies included under that umbrella should not be described as criminal law policies. For example, making it a crime to enter a country without authorisation or attaching criminal sanctions to re-entry after deportation are clear examples of the use of criminal sanctions and criminal law to regulate migration policy. This is the criminalisation of migration choices about where to live and the behaviour of people making those decisions. However, visa policies, or even carrier sanctions, are civil regulatory rules, not criminal policies. They have important symbolic implications for the way in which migrants as subjects are construed and their consequences must be taken seriously. That is why they are included here. With this in mind, our attention now shifts to measures taken before entry, during the stay and towards removal.

Criminalisation before Entry into the Territory

Immigration control no longer takes place at the border, but rather beyond it, through strategies that have been labelled as 'extraterritorialisation', namely visa regimes and carrier sanctions.[21] Visa requirements constitute the first obstacle prior to entry. Through requiring a visa, the host state manifests its a priori suspicion towards nationals of countries that may be poor, at war or unstable in other ways.[22] Being on a visa list is often considered as a humiliating experience and seen as an offence to the home state's standing, or worthiness, in the

---

[18] S. H. Legomsky, 'The New Path of Immigration Law: Asymmetric Incorporation of Criminal Justice Norms', *Washington and Lee Law Review*, 64 (2007), 469–528.

[19] *Ibid.*, 472–473.

[20] V. Mitsilegas, *The Criminalisation of Migration in Europe. Challenges for Human Rights and the Rule of Law* (London: Springer, 2015), pp. 2–3.

[21] B. Ryan, 'Extraterritorial Immigration Control: What Role for Legal Guarantees?' in B. Ryan and V. Mitsilegas (eds), *Extraterritorial Immigration Control. Legal Challenges* (Leiden: Martinus Nijhoff, 2010), pp. 3–37, on p. 3.

[22] D. Bigo and E. Guild, 'Policing at a Distance: Schengen Visa Policies' in D. Bigo and E. Guild (eds), *Controlling Frontiers. Free Movement into and within Europe* (Farnham: Ashgate, 2005), pp. 233–263.

international arena. Consequently, newly obtained exemptions are celebrated as historical days of recuperated dignity.

Visa Policy

Except in Ecuador, visa policy in South America does not differ from Europe or other immigration countries such as the USA, Canada or Australia. Generally, nationals from states in Africa, the Caribbean and Asia – apart from Japan and South Korea – need a visa to enter a South American country. The only notable differences are general exemptions for South Africans, Russians and Turks in most countries and for nationals from the Philippines,[23] Thailand and Indonesia in select countries.[24] Nonetheless, nationals from other states throughout the Americas, particularly Cubans, Dominicans and Haitians, require an entry visa for most countries in South America.

Ecuador is partly an exception. On 20 June 2008, it adopted a policy of open borders by withdrawing visa requirements for all countries around the globe. This unprecedented policy, implemented by presidential decree, allowed any foreigner to enter Ecuador's territory without a visa and to stay for up to ninety days. Officially, its main goals ranged from encouraging tourism to implementing the principle of universal citizenship, enshrined in its 2008 Constitution.[25] However, universal visa freedom was short-lived. Only six months after its introduction, visa requirements were reinstated for Chinese nationals, and eighteen months later for Afghanis, Bangladeshis, Eritreans, Ethiopians, Kenyans, Nepalese, Nigerians, Pakistanis and Somalians. The then State Secretary of Migration, Leonardo Carrion, explained how a majority of visitors from these countries had overstayed their visas and thus had become irregular.[26] Whilst immigration from these countries increased only marginally,[27] the police played a powerful role as an institution opposing the visa-free policy.[28] Senegal and Cuba were later added to that list in 2015, a measure presented by the government as preventing violations of human rights in the journey of Senegalese towards Argentina, and Cubans towards the USA. This argument reads poorly with the dozens of Cubans expelled from Ecuador in 2016.[29]

---

[23] For example, Bolivia, Brazil, Colombia, Paraguay and Peru.

[24] Thailand nationals do not need a visa in, e.g., Argentina, Brazil, Chile and Colombia. In turn, Indonesians do not need a visa in, e.g., Chile, Colombia, Paraguay and Peru.

[25] L. F. Freier, 'Open Doors (For Almost All): Visa Policies and Ethnic Selectivity in Ecuador', *CCIS Working Paper* 188, May 2013.

[26] Acosta and Freier, 'Turning the Immigration Policy Paradox Up-side Down?'.

[27] With the noteworthy exception of the net immigration of 2,838 Chinese, the yearly net immigration rates for other African and Asian nationals for which visas were reintroduced averaged at just above 300 per year per country from 2008–2010. *Ibid.*, pp. 683–684.

[28] Góngora-Mera, Herrera and Müller, 'The Frontiers of Universal Citizenship', p. 22.

[29] See critiques by CMW Concluding Observations on the Third Periodic Report by Ecuador, CMW/C/ECU/CO/3.

Carrier Sanctions

Carrier sanctions relate to the privatisation of immigration control. Private actors have been conferred responsibilities which, by their very nature, pertain to public authorities. This makes it harder to hold non-state agents accountable for the breach of individual rights, whilst also introducing more layers of control.[30] This 'criminalization as prevention'[31] has consequences for human rights, notably for the right to seek asylum. Carriers are pushed, when in doubt, 'not to allow the travel of passengers deemed as a risk to immigration control', or else they assume responsibility for the cost of their return.[32] Rather than taking a decision at the border, migration enforcement actually becomes apparent prior to arrival in the territory.[33]

South America follows this general global trend: legislations in all countries have clearly enshrined obligations of both control and return.[34] Whereas some countries establish no sanction in the case of asylum seekers, it is dubious whether a carrier would allow someone who is not adequately documented to embark in the first place.[35] Moreover, carrier sanctions have a lengthy historical tradition in the region since the early twentieth century.[36]

Criminalisation during the Stay

Criminalisation during a migrant's stay has been labelled as 'immigration enforcement through attrition' and has a larger impact in 'creating a hostile context of reception for all migrants, regardless of immigration status'.[37] Two points are notable: first, limiting access to crucial rights, such as health care; second, the attachment of criminal consequences to immigration violations,

---

[30] V. Mitsilegas, 'Extraterritorial Immigration Control in the 21st Century: The Individual and the State Transformed' in B. Ryan and V. Mitsilegas (eds), *Extraterritorial Immigration Control*, pp. 39–65, on p. 58.

[31] Mitsilegas, *The Criminalisation of Migration in Europe*, p. 43.

[32] *Ibid.*

[33] Ryan, 'Extraterritorial Immigration Control', p. 3.

[34] Argentina, Arts 38–50, Law 25.871/2004; Bolivia, Art. 44, Law 370/2013; Brazil, Arts 45–60, Law 13.445/2017; Colombia, Art. 51, Decree 834/2013; Chile, Art. 11, Law Decree 1094/1975; Ecuador, Art. 170, 2017 Human Mobility Law; Paraguay, Art. 99, Law 978/96 and Arts 84–91, 2016 Migration Law proposal, Ministry of the Interior; Peru, Art. 59, Legislative Decree 1350/2017; Uruguay, Arts 60–63, Law 18.250/2008; Venezuela, Art. 26, 2004 Immigration Law. All countries, except for Bolivia and Colombia, have ratified the 1990 UN Migrant Smuggling Protocol, which demands that states oblige 'commercial carriers (...) to ascertain that all passengers are in possession of the travel documents required for entry into the receiving State'. Art. 11(3), Protocol against the smuggling of migrants by land, sea and air, supplementing the United Nations Convention against transnational organised crime, New York, 15 November 2000. United Nations, *Treaty Series*, vol. 2241, p. 507; Doc. A/55/383.

[35] Ryan, 'Extraterritorial Immigration Control', p. 22. See, for example, Brazil, Art. 49, Law 13.445/2017.

[36] See Chapter 4, p. 96.

[37] A. M. Banks, 'The Curious Relationship between Self-Deportation Policies and Naturalization Rates', *Lewis & Clark Law Review*, 16 (2012), 1149–1213, on 1151.

including employer and landlord sanctions, the use of false documents or of marriage for the purpose of obtaining an immigration advantage, as well as unlawful re-entry. It also relates to ascribing immigration consequences to criminal convictions affecting admission, residence or access to citizenship.[38]

Criminalisation during the stay is also present in South America. For example, employer, landlord or hotel sanctions are common tools enshrined in laws.[39] Deportation deriving from criminal convictions is commonplace.[40] In Argentina, the criminal procedural code was amended in 2014 to incorporate immediate expulsion of non-nationals found while committing certain criminal offences and later established a fast-track legal procedure for expulsion.[41]

At the same time, respecting the rights of all migrants, irrespective of legal status, is one of the three basic pillars in the regional discourse on undocumented migration, together with non-criminalisation and regularisation. Considering the aforementioned, this paradigm begs the question as to which rights are included, as well as their sources: the ICMW only recognises education, emergency medical treatment and contractual obligations by employers, but omits many others such as family unity or the right to form trade unions.[42] It is here that the IACtHR, through its comprehensive interpretation of the ACHR, emerges as the principal performer. Two central rights are the bedrock of the Court's approach: due process and the principle of equality and non-discrimination. Notwithstanding their often 'obscure' or 'abstract' application,[43] the Inter-American Court reverses the European Court of Human Rights' (ECtHR) case law where prevalence is given to the state's 'right to control the entry of non-nationals into its territory'.[44] In Europe, Dembour argues that control comes first and human rights only after.[45]

The IACtHR has only endorsed the state's authority to control entry and departure of irregular migrants, after declaring that 'States may not discriminate or tolerate discriminatory situations that prejudice migrants.' In addition, this control must take place 'with strict regard for the guarantees of due process and respect for human dignity'.[46] Due process of law must be guaranteed, independent of their migratory status, so that all individuals can defend their rights in any area, whether civil, criminal, labour, fiscal or of any other nature.[47] Due

---

[38] Legomsky, 'The New Path of Immigration Law', 469–528.

[39] Argentina, Arts 55 and 59, Law 25871/2004; Bolivia, Arts 38, 43 and 46, Decree 1923/2014; Paraguay, Arts 63 and 69, Law 978/96; Uruguay, Art. 46, Decree 394/009; Venezuela, Arts 25, 26 and 36, Law 37.944/2004.

[40] Bolivia, Art. 38, Law 370/2013 imposes a high threshold; Brazil, Art. 54, Law 13.445/2017; Paraguay, Art. 81, Law 978/96; Peru, Art. 58, Legislative Decree 1350/2017; Uruguay, Art. 47, Law 18250/2008; Venezuela, Art. 39, Law 37.944/2004.

[41] Argentina, Art. 35, Law 27063/2014 and Decree 70/2017.

[42] ICMW, Arts 25, 28, 30 and 36–56.

[43] Dembour, *When Humans Become Migrants*, p. 489.

[44] ECtHR, *Abdulaziz, Cabales and Balkandali v. the United Kingdom*.

[45] Dembour, *When Humans Become Migrants*, p. 304.

[46] IACtHR, *Juridical Condition and Rights of the Undocumented Migrants*. Advisory Opinion OC–18/03 of September 17, 2003. Series A, No.18, para. 119.

[47] *Ibid.*, paras 121–126.

process is recognised as essential to human dignity[48] and becomes a central concern under ACHR Articles 8 (fair trial) and 25 (judicial protection). This is most notable in cases involving deprivation of liberty, expulsion or asylum.[49]

Whereas the IACtHR has recognised the state's prerogative to treat irregular migrants differently than nationals or those with legal status, such treatment must be reasonable, objective, proportionate and cannot harm human rights.[50] The state is under an obligation 'to ensure the principle of equality before the law and non-discrimination' regardless of migratory status.[51] This principle particularly affects undocumented migrant workers. In the Court's view in its consultative opinion 18/03, all migrant workers, not only those undocumented, are vulnerable when compared to national workers.[52] Thus, governments may forbid unauthorised migrants from working but, once an employment relationship is established, they enjoy the same labour rights as national workers, regardless of their immigration status.[53] The Court's consultative opinion 18/03 represents the 'most progressive binding international law statement' on the issue of labour rights and is compulsory for all South American countries.[54]

The EU and the USA adopt different approaches. In the former, payment for work already completed constitutes a right in order to avoid employers taking advantage of irregular migrants working for them.[55] This does not extend to all labour rights. In the latter, the Supreme Court, in *Hoffman Plastic*, argued that back payment would encourage irregular migration, whereas the dissent maintained that full implementation would have the opposite result by

---

[48] *Ibid.*, para. 73.
[49] See IACtHR cases: *Vélez Loor v. Panama*. Preliminary Objections, Merits, Reparations and Costs. Judgment of 23 November 2010, Series C No. 218, para. 100; Case of *Nadege Dorzema et al. v. Dominican Republic*. Merits, Reparations and Costs. Judgment of 24 October 2012. Series C, No. 251, para. 154: Case *Pacheco Tineo family v. Bolivia*. Preliminary Objections, Merits, Reparations and Costs. Judgment of 25 November 2013. Series C No. 272, para. 129. The right to information on consular assistance, as deriving from due process, is also considered a fundamental right: *The Right to Information on Consular Assistance in the Framework of the Guarantees of the Due Process of Law*, Advisory Opinion OC–16/99 of 1 October 1999, Series A, No. 16.
[50] *Juridical Condition and Rights of the Undocumented Migrants*, para. 119; *Nadege Dorzema et al. v. Dominican Republic*, para. 233; *Rights and Guarantees of Children in the Context of Migration and/or in Need of International Protection*, Advisory Opinion OC–21/14 of 19 August 2014, Series A, No. 21, footnote 74.
[51] IACtHR, *Juridical Condition and Rights of the Undocumented Migrants*, para. 118; Case of the *Yean and Bosico Children v. Dominican Republic*. Preliminary Objections, Merits, Reparations, and Costs. Judgment of 8 September 2005, Series C No. 155, para. 155; Case *Dominican and Haitian deportees v. Dominican Republic*. Preliminary Objections, Merits, Reparations and Costs. Judgment of 28 August 2014, Series C No. 282, para. 402.
[52] IACtHR, *Juridical Condition and Rights of the Undocumented Migrants*, paras 112, 131 and 160.
[53] *Ibid.*, paras 133–134, 136, 153 and 155–156.
[54] B. Lyon, 'The Inter-American Court of Human Rights defines Unauthorized Migrant Workers' Rights for the Hemisphere: A Comment on Advisory Opinion 18', *NYU Review Law and Social Change*, 28 (2003–2004), 547–596, on 552.
[55] Art. 6, Directive 2009/52 providing for minimum standards on sanctions and measures against employers of illegally staying third-country nationals. See also Case C-311/13 *Tümer* EU: C: 2014: 2337.

discouraging employers from hiring unauthorised workers.[56] Importantly, the IACtHR does not join these policy debates; its argumentation departs from the understanding of non-discrimination as a *jus cogens* norm, which protects all workers, including the undocumented.[57] The Court details the rights which unauthorised workers should enjoy, including, for example, special care for women workers, freedom of association and to organise and join trade unions, collective negotiation, fair wages, social security and a right to rest and compensation.[58] This is coupled with the right to due process of law in order to guarantee that access to justice is genuine.[59] The Court recognises these rights as necessary to ensure the dignity of the worker,[60] going well beyond the rights granted under the ICMW.[61]

Within this strong framework, several countries in South America explicitly provide access to back payments within their legislations,[62] as well as, with different degrees of intensity, to other labour rights for undocumented migrants.[63] Those which do not include such clear clauses are bound by the IACtHR's jurisprudence, including in their national courts.[64] Several laws also establish a right to health care and education under equal conditions compared to nationals.[65] The former goes beyond the ICHR's approach – which has only recognised the obligation to provide emergency treatment[66] – whereas the latter follows the Inter-American Court's view on compulsory access to education.[67] In yet another reversal of the expulsion paradigm, health and education

---

[56] *Hoffman Plastic Compounds, Inc. v. NLRB*, 535 U.S. 137, 140.

[57] IACtHR, *Juridical Condition and Rights of the Undocumented Migrants*, para. 101.

[58] *Ibid.*, para. 157.

[59] *Ibid.*, paras 121–126.

[60] *Ibid.*, paras 157–158.

[61] Lyon, 'The Inter-American Court of Human Rights Defines Unauthorized Migrant Workers' Rights', on 591.

[62] For example: Argentina, Art. 56, Law 25871/2004; Bolivia, Art. 48(2), Law 370/2013; Brazil, Art. 50(4), Law 13.445/2017; Paraguay, Art. 72, Law 978/96; Uruguay, Art. 55, Law 18.250/2008; Venezuela, Art. 49, Law 37.944/2004. See also Paraguay, Art. 39, 2016 Proposal Migration Law, Ministry of the Interior.

[63] Argentina, Arts 16 and 56, Law 25871/2004; Bolivia, Arts 48(2) and 49, Law 370/2013; Brazil, Art. 4, Law 13.445/2017; Uruguay, Art. 17, Law 18.250/2008. See also Paraguay, Art. 4(11), 2016 Proposal Migration Law, Ministry of the Interior.

[64] See Part II, Consolidation, pp. 115–116.

[65] On education see, for example: Argentina, Art. 8, Law 25871/2004; Brazil, Art. 4, Law 13.445/2017; Chile, Art. 14, 2017 Migration Law Proposal; Peru, Art. 9, Legislative Decree 1350/2017; Uruguay, Art. 9, Immigration Law 18.250/2008. On health care see, for example: Argentina Art. 7, Law 25871/2004; Bolivia, Art. 47(3), Law 370/2013; Brazil, Art. 4, Law 13.445/2017; Chile, Art. 13, offering access in cases of emergency, for children or for pregnant women, 2017 Migration Law proposal; Peru, Art. 9, Legislative Decree 1350/2017; Uruguay, Art. 11, Immigration Law 18.250/2008. See also Paraguay, Arts 38–40, 2016 Proposal Migration Law, Ministry of the Interior. Ecuador covers only emergency treatment, Art. 52, 2017 Organic Law on Human Mobility.

[66] Case of *Nadege Dorzema et al. v. Dominican Republic*, para. 108. However, this is the extent of the entitlement in countries such as Ecuador, Art. 52, 2017 Organic Law on Human Mobility.

[67] Case of the *Yean and Bosico Children v. Dominican Republic*, para. 185; Advisory Opinion, *Rights and Guarantees of Children*, para. 164.

service providers are now legally obliged to offer information to individuals on how to regularise their status.[68] Prior to this, the approach mandated that these workers must denounce the migrants' situation to the authorities – an approach still preponderant in many jurisdictions around the globe.[69]

Criminalisation towards Removal

Criminalisation towards removal refers to emphasising deportation of irregular migrants, often coupled with detention and entry bans. These measures have a long history in South America.[70] Nowadays, deportation for those breaching the migration rules continues to be the norm for irregular entry, visa over-stay, use of falsified documents or working without authorisation.[71] Entry bans are also widespread and often imposed for long, or even indefinite, periods.[72] Finally, periods for voluntary departure are sometimes short. For example in Argentina, it is only seventy-two hours.[73]

The IACtHR's jurisprudence also has important consequences in this area.[74] The Court has forbidden punitive deprivation of liberty in order to control migration flows, especially those of an irregular nature.[75] Detention, while not outlawed, is made subject to various requirements: it cannot be automatic, must be individually examined by a judicial authority, and the individual should have access to legal representation and consular assistance.[76] Detention must always be an exceptional measure, for the shortest possible time period and only if suitable alternative measures cannot be taken.[77] Whilst these guarantees

---

[68] Argentina, Arts 7–8, Law 25871/2004; Bolivia, Art. 47(3), Law 370/2013; Uruguay, Arts 36 and 48, Decree 394/2009. See also Paraguay, Art. 41, 2016 Proposal Migration Law, Ministry of the Interior.

[69] By contrast, see, for example, Colombia and Venezuela imposing control obligations on health providers or other authorities to inform on irregular migrants. Colombia, Art. 48, Decree 834/2013; Venezuela, Art. 40, Law 37.944/2004.

[70] See Chapter 4.

[71] Argentina, Arts 29(i), 35, 37, Law 25.871/2004; Bolivia, Arts 22(3), 32, 38, Law 370/2013; Colombia, Arts 16, 19, 27, Decree 834/2013; Ecuador, Arts 137 and 143, 2017 Organic Law on Human Mobility; Paraguay, Art. 81, Law 978/96; Peru, Art. 57, Legislative Decree 1350/2017; Uruguay, Arts 38, 47, 51, Law 18.250/2008; Venezuela, Art. 38, Law 37.944/2004.

[72] In Argentina, it is a minimum of five years, Arts 29(a), 35, 63(b), Law 25.871/2004. In Peru, it can be fifteen years, Art. 54, Legislative Decree 1350/2017. Also see Colombia, Art. 29(6), Decree 834/2013; Ecuador, Art. 140, 2017 Organic Law on Human Mobility; Venezuela, Art. 8, Law 37.944/2004. For indefinite entry bans, see: Bolivia, Arts 39, Law 370/2013 and Art. 37(III), Regulation, DS 1923/2014; Paraguay, Art. 6, Law 978/96.

[73] Argentina, Art. 70, Decree 616/2010.

[74] The Court uses a variety of instruments to reach this conclusion, including UN General Assembly documents. Case of *Vélez Loor v. Panama*, paras 98–99.

[75] *Ibid.*, para. 167; Advisory Opinion, *Rights and Guarantees of Children*, para. 151.

[76] Case of *Vélez Loor v. Panama*, para. 171, and Case *Pacheco Tineo family v. Bolivia*, para. 131.

[77] IACHR, *Human Rights of Migrants, Refugees, Stateless Persons, Victims of Human Trafficking and Internally Displaced Persons: Norms and Standards of the Inter-American Human Rights System*, OEA/Ser.L/V/II. Doc. 46/15 31 December 2015, p. 188. Also see the IACHR, Report on Immigration in the United States: Detention and Due Process, OEA/Ser.L/V/II. Doc. 78/10, 30 December 2010, para. 34.

also largely exist, for example, under EU law, an important distinction is that punitive measures upon re-entry of an undocumented migrant are unlawful in South America.[78]

Detention is indeed scarcely used in South America when compared to other regions. Some countries provide for the possibility of detaining undocumented migrants prior to their expulsion but, by and large, this option is not used regularly.[79] Some of the countries even forbid such an option and incorporate alternative measures by law.[80]

Argentina has turned its policy 180 degrees since 2016. The Decree of Necessity and Emergency No. 70/2017 – which repealed some of the guarantees contained in the Migration Act No. 25871 and introduced a fast-track procedure for the summary expulsion of migrants – has drastically reduced the time frame for appealing against expulsion. Furthermore, detention becomes the norm from as soon as the procedure begins until expulsion is completed, which could be as long as sixty days. In that regard, Argentina opened a detention centre in 2016.[81] Other less coercive measures are not contemplated.[82]

Regularisation of Migrants in South America

Access to documented status is one of the policy options available when dealing with populations in an irregular situation. Two types of regularisation processes are often distinguished. First, there are regularisation procedures defined as one-off processes lasting for a particular period.[83] By contrast, there are also regularisation mechanisms that are permanent, long-term instruments, often

---

[78] Case of *Vélez Loor v. Panama*, paras 166–169. Compare the EU's context in Case C-290/14, *Skerdjan Celaj*, EU: C: 2015: 640.

[79] E. Coria Márquez, G. Bonnici and V. Martínez, *¿Qué Esperamos del Futuro? Detención Migratoria y Alternativas a la Detención en las Américas* (Melbourne: International Detention Coalition, 2017), p. 10. In Argentina, the period is a maximum of fifteen days, which may be prolonged by thirty days, in both cases by a judicial authority; Art. 70, Decree 616/2010. In Argentina, detainees need to be separated from regular prisoners for criminal causes (Art. 72, Decree 616/2010). In Chile, this option is discretionary, Art. 81, Law Decree 1094/75. In Paraguay, the judicial authority may order detention for the minimum indispensable period to ensure removal, Art. 83 Law 978/96.

[80] Ecuador, Art. 145, 2017 Organic Law on Human Mobility; Venezuela, Art. 46, Law 37.944/2004.

[81] Política Argentina, 'El Gobierno creó un centro de detención de migrantes: alarma entre organismos de DDHH', 26 August 2016.

[82] Argentina, Arts 11, 13, 14, 16 and 21, Decree of Necessity and Emergency 70/2017.

[83] A well-known example is the 1986 USA Immigration Reform and Control Act (IRCA) by which permanent residence was granted to different categories of unauthorised migrants. See F. D. Bean, B. Edmonston and J. S. Passel, *Undocumented Migration to the United States. IRCA and the Experience of the 1980s* (Washington, DC: The Urban Institute Press, 1990). The scarcity of permanent mechanisms in the USA had culminated in a stock of around 11 million unauthorised migrants residing in the country by 2015. M. R. Rosenblum and A. G. Ruiz Soto, *An Analysis of Unauthorized Migrants in the US by Country and Region of Birth* (Washington, DC: Migration Policy Institute, 2015).

enshrined in law, whereby the individual has continuous access to apply for secure status.[84]

In South America, access to regular status has long been a policy concern. Regularisation procedures have taken the form of unilateral and bilateral instruments. In turn, a permanent regularisation mechanism is now available for regional migrants through the 2002 MERCOSUR Residence agreement.[85] Crucially, several jurisdictions now provide individuals a right to a time period in which they can attempt to regularise. This turns the tables by prioritising access to legal status rather than deportation and, if implemented correctly, constitutes a far-reaching development and true revolution in a comparative perspective. It also goes beyond the international framework, which does not provide for any right to regularisation.[86]

Regularisation as a Unilateral Concern

Regularisations as a unilateral policy have been part of the legal repertoire since at least 1949, starting in Argentina.[87] Similar measures were taken in the late 1970s and early 1980s in Brazil,[88] Chile[89] and Venezuela.[90] All the remaining countries approved regularisation procedures during the early twenty-first

---

[84] The Spanish *arraigo* procedure is a case in point. Migrants may obtain a residence and work permit after having irregularly resided in Spain if settlement is proven, which may be shown by a labour relationship, after a residence period of two or three years. See D. Acosta, 'The Returns Directive: Possible Limits and Interpretation' in K. Zwaan (ed.), *The Returns Directive: Central Themes, Problem Issues, and Implementation in Selected Member States* (Nijmegen: Wolf Legal Publishers, 2011) pp. 7–24, on p. 22.

[85] See Chapter 7, pp. 180–181.

[86] ICMW, Art. 35; Art. 9, ILO Convention 143 on Migrant Workers, 1975.

[87] Argentina, Decree 15.972, 8 July 1949; this first regularisation procedure was peculiar in that it addressed mostly Jewish residents. It was followed by several others. See: Decree 3.364, 4 August 1958; Decree 49, 3 January 1964; Decree 87, 11 January 1974; Decree 780, 12 January 1984; Decree 1.033, 24 June 1992. Between 1958 and 1992 more than 1,140,000 regional migrants obtained a residence permit in Argentina through these processes. See S. Sassone, 'Migraciones Ilegales y Amnistías en la Argentina', *Estudios Migratorios Latinoamericanos*, 6 (1987), 249–290.

[88] Brazil, Law 6.964, 9 December 1981. This was followed by three other regularisations in 1988 (Law 7.685, 2 December), 1998 (Law 9.675, 29 June) and 2009 (Law 11.961, 2 July). Around 27,000, then 36,990, 40,909 and 45,000 mainly regional citizens were respectively regularised in each procedure.

[89] Chile provided for a regularisation procedure in its 1975 Migration Law, Law Decree 1094, 19 July 1975. A further procedure took place in 1998, regularising around 23,000 individuals (Resolution 2071, 1998). A final procedure took place in 2007 and benefited 47,580 migrants, of which most were Peruvians (35,071), followed by Bolivians (6,145), Colombians (2,003) and Ecuadorians (1,958); see Exempt Resolution granted by the Sub-Secretary of the Interior, RE Nº36339, 22 October 2007.

[90] Venezuela, Decree 616, 22 May 1980, which regularised around 267,000 people, of which 92 per cent were Colombians. See A. Alfonso, *La Experiencia de los Países Suramericanos en Materia de Regularización Migratoria* (Buenos Aires: IOM, 2013), p. 80. Venezuela then launched another controversial regularisation procedure in 2004 since migrants in an irregular situation could also obtain citizenship and the right to vote. Its controversial character relates to the fact that this preceded a revocation referendum against the then President Chavez. Around 358,000 people obtained citizenship with some 127,000 merely regularising and around 312,000 falling under

century.[91] These processes did not have any exceptional features and most beneficiaries were regional migrants. However, the Argentinean *Patria Grande* is
worth mentioning here. This procedure anticipated the MERCOSUR Residence
Agreement, which was put into force in 2009. *Patria Grande* developed in
various steps. Article 23(l) of the 2004 Argentinean Immigration Law provided
that nationals of MERCOSUR, Bolivia and Chile could obtain temporary residency based on citizenship criteria. This was later extended to nationals of
all remaining South American countries who were, or became, MERCOSUR
Associate States.[92] Nationals of MERCOSUR or associate countries who entered
Argentina before 17 April 2006 could regularise their situation, whereas those
who entered after that date could benefit directly from the nationality criteria
to obtain a temporary residence permit.[93]

During the early twenty-first century, regularisations for extra regional
migrants have also taken place. Good examples of this are Dominicans,
Senegalese, Koreans and Haitians in Argentina,[94] Haitians and Cubans in
Ecuador,[95] and, most notably, Haitians in Brazil. Brazil exemplifies how discretion may sometimes facilitate inclusion. Haitians reached South America
via Ecuador, given the possibility of visa-free entry, and then travelled by land
via Peru or Bolivia to Brazil. Faced with the arrival of around 60,000 Haitian
nationals by 2013, Brazil, rather than granting them refugee status or any
other subsidiary protection, offered them permanent residence for humani-
tarian reasons.[96] Around 44,000 Haitians had benefited from such a permit
by 2015.[97] Nationals from other countries – such as Nigerians, Senegalese and

other categories. Decree 2823, 3 February 2004. See Alfonso, *ibid.*, pp. 57–58. Venezuela also
established a regularisation procedure for Peruvians in 2013, Resolution 109/13, 30 April 2013.

[91] Bolivia, Decree 1800, 20 November 2013; Colombia, Decree 3970, 14 October 2008; Ecuador
Executive Decree 248, 9 February 2010, which was applicable to Haitian nationals; Paraguay,
Law 4429, 4 October 2011, implemented by Decree 8373, 3 February 2012; Peru, Law 30103,
8 November 2013 and Supreme Decree No. 002-2017-IN, 2 January 2017, applicable only to
Venezuelans; Uruguay, Art. 6 Decree 394/009 and Immigration Law 18.250/2008, Art. 82.

[92] Argentina, Decree 1169/2004, 13 September 2004 and Disposición Dirección Nacional de
Migraciones 29.929/2004, 17 September 2004.

[93] Argentina, Disposición DNM 53.253/2005, Disposición (DNM) N°14949/2006. It should
be highlighted in any case that, even if circa 225,000 non-nationals regularised their stay,
almost 200,000 were not able to complete the procedure: on this, see Ceriani and Morales,
Argentina: Avances y Asignaturas Pendientes, p. 31.

[94] Argentina, Disposición 001 and 002, Dirección Nacional de Migraciones, 4 January 2013: around
1,700 Senegalese and circa 6,000 Dominican nationals were regularised through this procedure.
For Koreans, a regularisation procedure was established in 2014 by Disposition DNM N° 979/14.
For Haitians, Disposition DNM 1143/2017. On the Senegalese in Argentina and Brazil see J. C.
Tedesco and G. Kleidermacher (eds), *A Imigração Senegalesa no Brasil e na Argentina: Múltiplos
Olhares* (Porto Alegre: EST Edições, 2017).

[95] J. Arcentales Illescas and S. Garbay, *Informe Sobre Movilidad Humana, Ecuador 2011*, Coalición
por las Migraciones y el Refugio, 2012, pp. 47–49.

[96] D. Fernandes, R. Milesi, B. Pimenta, and V. do Carmo, 'Migração dos Haitianos para o Brasil.
A RN n. 97/12: Uma Avaliação Preliminar', *Caderno de Debates*, 8 (2013), 55–70; C. Tinker
and L. Madrid Sartoretto, 'New Trends in Migratory and Refugee Law in Brazil: The Expanded
Refugee Definition', *Panorama of Brazilian Law*, 3 (2015), 1–27.

[97] Portal Brasil, 'Brasil autoriza residência permanente a 43,8 mil haitianos', 11 October 2015.

Bangladeshis – were less fortunate. This was partly solved by regularising some 4,500 failed asylum seekers in 2013 and around 300 Ghanaians in 2016.[98]

Whereas these procedures have provided relief to thousands of residents, discretion is their common feature. They are not innovative, either: European countries regularised more than five million non-EU nationals through similar processes between 1996 and 2007.[99]

Regularisation as a Bilateral Concern

Since the early 1980s, regularisation has become a bilateral concern in the region with all ten countries at some point ratifying bilateral treaties. Around thirty such agreements were adopted in a period extending from at least 1982, when the Quito Act was signed between Colombia and Ecuador, to 2014 when a new permanent migration statute was ratified between the same two countries.

These agreements manifest the acceptance of mobility as a normal state of affairs in the region and, in comparative perspective, feature traits that make them unique. First, there is the common emphasis on fraternity, friendship and historical, cultural and geographical links.[100] Second, regional integration also plays a central role: indeed, it has often been the bilateral solution anticipating multilateral instruments being put into force.[101] Third, these treaties often provide for clear routes towards permanent residence. Fourth, they were unique in that by regularising the household head, on most occasions it implied that residence permits were extended to family members, widely understood to include spouses, children and others.[102] Finally, and most importantly, a historical overview shows a gradual pattern of rights' expansion and the acknowledgement

---

[98] Portal Brasil, 'Brasil regulariza situação de 4.482 trabalhadores estrangeiros', 19 December 2013; Estrangeiros no Brasil, 'Governo concede residência para estrangeiros ganeses', 3 March 2016.

[99] Baldwin Edwards and Kraler, *REGINE Regularisations in Europe*, p. 31.

[100] See, for example, 2005 Argentina–Brazil (Agreement for the Concession of Permanent Residence to Holders of Transitory or Temporal Residency); 2002 Bolivia–Peru (Agreement on Migratory Regularisation); 2012 Colombia–Peru (Framework Agreement on Assistance and Cooperation on Migration); 2006 Bolivia–Paraguay (Agreement on Migratory Regularisation).

[101] For example, Argentina bilaterally anticipated the MERCOSUR Residence Agreement being put into force with Brazil, Uruguay, Bolivia and Peru. See Operative Agreement between the National Migration Directorate of the Republic of Argentina and the Foreigners Department of the Federative Republic of Brazil for the application of the Agreement on Residence for Nationals of the MERCOSUR Member States, signed 29 November 2005 and entered into force on 3 April 2006; Agreement on Exchange of Letters between the Republic of Argentina and the Oriental Republic of Uruguay referring to the Bilateral Application of the Residence Agreement for Nationals of the MERCOSUR Member States, signed in Cordoba on 20 July 2006 and entered into force on the same day; Migratory Agreement between Argentina and Bolivia, signed 21 April 2004, entered into force on 17 October 2006; Agreement on Residence for Nationals of the Republic of Argentina and the Republic of Peru, signed in Buenos Aires on 15 June 2007 and entered into force on 10 December 2009.

[102] See, for example, the 1998 Migration Covenant between Bolivia and Argentina; the 1991 Agreement on the Undocumented between Bolivia and Ecuador; the 1990 Agreement on the Undocumented between Chile and Ecuador; or the 2010 Migration Statute between Ecuador and Venezuela.

that permanent multilateral solutions were needed to address mobility. For example, Argentina signed different covenants with Bolivia and Peru, later renewed several times until a permanent solution facilitating residence was adopted. Similar examples include Brazil and Bolivia as well as Ecuador and Colombia. It is to this multilateralism that we now turn our attention.

Regularisation as a Multilateral Concern

The multilateral agenda has been concerned with regularisation since the 1970s. It was CAN's 1977 Decision that first approached the issue by requesting Member States to regularise migrants who were already working in the host country.[103]

At the MERCOSUR level, the 2002 Residence Agreement's main objective is to deal with the situation of intra-regional migrants in irregular situations. The agreement originated from a Brazilian proposal to adopt a regional amnesty. Instead, the Argentine government presented a permanent mechanism providing legal channels to irregular migrants. In that regard, the MERCOSUR's Agreement permanently confirmed unilateral and bilateral practices that had already existed for years. Nonetheless, the agreement suffers an important drawback: regional migrants who do not obtain a permanent residence permit after two years may fall back into irregularity. This will be the subject of further discussion in Chapter 7.[104]

Regularisation as an Individual Subjective Right

Regulating access to status takes various forms. It ranges from a state's obligation to regularise based on certain family-life cases, to an individual right to obtain residence or to attempt regularisation in other ways. Remarkably, in principle the general rule of expulsion is actually reversed to regularisation. Put differently, it is only when regularisation is not possible that expulsion kicks in. In some cases, regularisation is automatic, in others it is a first option. This is path-breaking and deserves careful analysis.

Family Life

First, regularisation constitutes an individual right in South America when children are involved. This derives from the jurisprudence of the IACtHR, which has clearly established that:

> the rupture of the family unit by the expulsion of one or both parents due to a breach of immigration laws related to entry or permanence is disproportionate in these situations, because the sacrifice inherent in the restriction of the right

---

[103] Arts 27–28, Decision 116: Andean Instrument on Labour Migration. Lima, 14–17 February 1977. See Chapter 7, p. 176.

[104] See Chapter 7, pp. 194–196.

to family life, which may have repercussions on the life and development of the child, appears unreasonable or excessive in relation to the advantages obtained by forcing the parent to leave the territory because of an administrative offence.[105]

This deserves several comments. To begin with, an individual right to regularisation exists for the family member concerned when children possess the nationality of the host state (i.e. were born there, since all countries except Colombia implement *ius soli*) or when they have permanent residence.[106] Expulsion is illegal since it would breach the best interests of the child. A subjective right to regularisation is contrary to practices in the USA and Europe. In the former, around half a million parents of US nationals were deported between 2009 and 2013.[107] In the latter, children who are EU nationals (a minority since *ius sanguinis* is the norm) have a right, in so far as they are EU citizens, to not have their parents deported, but only when that would entail the need to leave the entire EU territory and provided the children are dependent on the parents.[108] In turn, in the ECtHR's view, family life does not entail the right to live in a particular country. For example, in *Omoregie* the ECtHR established that a Norwegian wife of a Nigerian national and their child, also Norwegian, should not have had an expectation that the husband and father, who was in an irregular situation, would have been allowed to remain in Norway, even though no criminal offence had been committed. The Court considered that there were no obstacles for conducting family life either in Nigeria or at a distance. The rights of the child did not deserve any particular discussion.[109]

Second, the IACtHR understands the right to family life in a broad sense since there is 'no single model for a family'. Other relatives, or even individuals who are not actually family members, may be interpreted to fall under the definition of family. The state is obliged to conduct a case-by-case analysis of the configuration of the child's family unit.[110]

Third, the Court does not discuss the situation of migrants who may have committed a criminal offence.[111] This means that countries have more leeway in such cases, although they still need to weigh the interests in conflict, namely family life and 'the authority of the States to implement their own immigration policies in keeping with human rights'.[112] In such cases, the state has to

---

[105] IACtHR, Advisory Opinion, *Rights and Guarantees of Children*, para. 280.

[106] *Ibid.*, para. 277.

[107] R. Capps *et al.*, 'Implications of Immigration Enforcement Activities for the Well-Being of Children in Immigrant Families. A Review of the Literature', Migration Policy Institute and Urban Institute, 2015.

[108] This would be the case when both parents are to be deported but not necessarily when it is only one who is expelled. See CJEU, Cases C-34/09, *Ruiz Zambrano*, 8 March 2011; C-256/11, *Dereci*, 15 November 2011, para. 68.

[109] ECtHR, *Darren Omoregie and Others v. Norway*, No. 265/07, 31 July 2008. Also see the European Commission of Human Rights, *Sorabjee v. the United Kingdom* (dec.), No. 23938/94, 23 October 1995 and *Jaramillo v. the United Kingdom* (dec.), No. 24865/94, 23 October 1995.

[110] IACtHR, Advisory Opinion, *Rights and Guarantees of Children*, para. 272.

[111] *Ibid.*, para. 271.

[112] *Ibid.*, para. 274.

consider the suitability, necessity and proportionality of the measure.[113] In some countries, serious offences – such as crimes against humanity, genocide or terrorism – close the door to this option,[114] although others prohibit expulsion, even under these circumstances.[115]

A number of countries in South America have legislation that provides this individual right when family life and the best interest of the child are at stake.[116] The remaining countries would need to adapt domestic laws to such cases[117] but, meanwhile, national tribunals and administrations are obliged to follow the Inter-American Court's jurisprudence in order to avoid international responsibility.[118] South American countries may of course further extend the subjective right to regularisation in cases of family life to spouses, partners and descendants.[119]

An Individual Right to Attempt Regularisation

Beyond family life, attempting regularisation has materialised as an individual right, parallel to an obligation for the corresponding state. Argentina exemplifies this individual–state dynamic: Article 17 establishes that the government shall provide the adoption and implementation of measures aiming at regularising the status of non-nationals. Once the irregular situation of a migrant is established, the National Migration Directorate is obliged to request him to regularise and to provide a period of between thirty and sixty days for this purpose.[120] During that period, migrants may invoke one of the categories under Article 23 of the law, for example having a binding job offer. With its 2004 immigration law, Argentina opted for a new strategy, moving from the logic of criminalisation and expulsion to that of legalisation and inclusion. Still, the law has a central flaw: Article 29 sets out that those who clandestinely entered Argentina do not have the right to stay. The burden of proof falls onto the migrant, who has to certify his regular entry, for example as a tourist, before regularising his status. This obviously affects only those needing a visa, mainly migrants from Africa, Asia and the Caribbean.

---

[113] *Ibid.*, para. 275.
[114] Bolivia, Art. 38, Law 370/2013.
[115] Brazil, Art. 55, Law 13.445/2017.
[116] Argentina, Arts 22 and 61, Law 25.871/2004; Bolivia Art. 38, Law 370/2013; Brazil Art. 55, Law 13.445/2017; Paraguay, Art. 35, Law 978/96; Uruguay, Art. 48, Law 18.250/2008. In Peru this has been framed as a temporary limited right to regularise during a certain period in 2017. See Peru, Supreme Decree, No. 001-2017-IN, 2 January 2017.
[117] Art. 2, ACHR, Pact of San José.
[118] IACtHR, Advisory Opinion, *Rights and Guarantees of Children*, para. 31. See ruling by Colombian Constitutional Tribunal (Sentencia T-956/13, 19 December 2013, para. 27) where the Court obliges the authorities to regularise an undocumented migrant with a daughter in the country due to the best interests of the child.
[119] See for example: Argentina, Arts 22 and 61, Law 25.871/2004; Bolivia, Art. 38, Law 370/2013; Brazil Art. 55, Law 13.445/2017; Paraguay, Arts 35 and 82, Law 978/96.
[120] Argentina, Art. 61, Law 25.871/2004 and Decree 616/2010.

A similar mechanism, clearly representing a legal transplant, may be found in the Brazilian case, with the difference being that the period to regularise is longer and clandestine entry does not per se impede regularisation.[121] Other countries provide the right to attempt regularisation as a first option.[122] Expulsion becomes possible, as in Argentina, when such an effort is unsuccessful. In others, no true right exists but rather allows mere discretionary governmental power for reasons of convenience,[123] or as an option for the authorities concerned,[124] or it is simply not mentioned.[125] Finally, in some states, those who were smuggled or trafficked in may also obtain a residence permit.[126]

Discussion

For decades, South America's approach to irregular migration was largely restrictive. This reached its peak during the 1970s and 1980s, when various laws criminalised the foreigner within the context of dictatorial regimes.[127] Criminalisation also permeated – and still does in some respects – through many administrative practices. By contrast, the new century has brought a more complex picture with a much stronger accent on the rights of undocumented migrants and on regularisation, albeit with a continued, apparent contradictory emphasis on deportation. This sparks some inquiries, such as: how unique is South America in a comparative perspective? What are the factors behind a shift in discourse and policies in the twenty-first century? I will offer some tentative answers under three umbrellas: legal explanations via the international legal framework and discretion, political reasons under the politics of humiliation and reciprocity, as well as social factors on the ground.

Legal Explanations
The International Legal Framework
The jurisprudence of the Inter-American Court has played an important role. The Court has indeed established a solid regulatory framework on the

---

[121] Brazil, Art. 50, Law 13.445/2017: here it is sixty days, which may be extended by another sixty.
[122] Bolivia, Art. 33, Law 370/2013; Chile, Art. 68, 2017 Migration Law Proposal; Ecuador, Art. 15, 2017 Implementing Regulations Organic Law on Human Mobility. In Ecuador those who have seen their visa revoked cannot attempt regularisation according to the same article and the initial steps to implement this article in 2017 are far from satisfactory due to, for example, the fines imposed on those who are undocumented; Peru, Art. 36, Legislative Decree 1350/2017; Uruguay, Art. 52, Law 18.250/2008.
[123] Colombia, Art. 62, Decree 834/2013; Paraguay, Art. 61, Law 978/96. However, in Paraguay the right is enshrined in Art. 25 of its 2016 Proposal Migration Law, Ministry of the Interior.
[124] Paraguay, Arts 35 and 60, Law 978/96.
[125] The 2004 Migration Law in Venezuela does not discuss regularisation.
[126] Bolivia, Art. 26(III), Law 370/2013. Brazil, Art. 30, Law 13.445/2017.
[127] See Chapter 4, pp. 101–104.

status and rights of undocumented migrants, which is more protective than the ICMW.[128] The *pro-homine* principle of interpretation has helped to position migrants at the centre of the Court's reasoning, with a primary consideration of them as human beings rather than as foreigners.[129] Both the Commission and the Court have referred to the particular situation of vulnerability in which undocumented migrants find themselves.[130] The Court has also emphasised that any immigration status breach shall not be punished as a crime since it 'harms no fundamental legal interests that warrant the protection of the State's punitive authority'.[131] The constitutionalisation of human rights by incorporating public international law and the ICtHR's jurisprudence into the 'block of constitutionality' at the domestic level has allowed domestic courts to reference and apply the Inter-American Court's jurisprudence, as contained in both advisory opinions and rulings.[132]

The Court's momentous approach has been criticised as being out of touch with reality. For example, Mexico – the same country that requested Advisory Opinion 18/03 – did not have an adequate legal regime in place that was capable of implementing the Court's findings.[133] The response by other countries has been mixed. For instance, the Dominican Republic has plainly rejected the Court's interpretation, whilst Panama immediately amended its migration framework to adapt to some of the Court's findings in *Velez Loor*.[134]

A narrow focus on compliance leads to an insufficient account of the ways in which both the Inter-American Court's jurisprudence, and to a lesser extent the ICMW, affect domestic law and practices. A growing body of literature suggests the need to move beyond compliance in order to understand the normative effects of international law.[135] Simmons, for example, has argued that international law influences the policy agenda, legal decisions and the propensity

---

[128] Advisory Opinions have binding character. IACtHR, Advisory Opinion, *Rights and Guarantees of Children*, para. 31. Also see Ferrer Mac-Gregor coinciding with this opinion in 'The Conventionality Control as a Core Mechanism of the *Ius Constitutionale*', p. 329.

[129] Dembour, *When Humans Become Migrants*, p. 302.

[130] IACtHR, *Juridical Condition and Rights of the Undocumented Migrants*; IACHR, Second Progress Report of the Special Rapporteurship on Migrant Workers and their Families in the Hemisphere, para. 64.

[131] IACHR, *Human Rights of Migrants, Refugees, Stateless Persons, Victims of Human Trafficking and Internally Displaced Persons: Norms and Standards of the Inter-American Human Rights System*, OEA/Ser.L/V/II. Doc. 46/15, 31 December 2015, p. 191.

[132] See, for example, the use by the Colombian Constitutional Tribunal of the IACtHR's Advisory Opinion OC-18/03 in Ruling T-956/13, 19 December 2013, para. 18.

[133] Cavallaro and Brewer, 'Reevaluating Regional Human Rights Litigation'.

[134] OAS, Press Release, 'IACHR Condemns Judgment of the Constitutional Court of the Dominican Republic', 6 November 2014. The Panamanian Government adopted Decree 3/2008, which eliminated imprisonment after irregular entry following an entry ban, something that had been imposed since 1960 by Law Decree 16/1960.

[135] R. Howse and R. Teitel, 'Beyond Compliance: Rethinking Why International Law Really Matters', *Global Policy Volume*, 1 (2010), 127–136; B. Kingsbury, 'The Concept of Compliance as a Function of Competing Conceptions of International Law', *Michigan Journal of International Law*, 19 (1998), 345–372.

of groups to mobilise at the national level.[136] Other authors have referred to the importance of acculturation, understood as a 'general process by which actors adopt the beliefs and behavioral patterns of the surrounding culture'.[137] There are examples of both aspects present here. First, compliance in the region relates to a 'complex set of behaviors in a longer time frame'[138] and not to the immediate adoption to the letter of international instruments. Rather, these instruments, including non-legally binding declarations by the SACM, are now considered part of a legal repertoire restricting legislative choices at the domestic level. Indeed, the mere existence of a soft norm increases 'the political costs of acting contrary to the norm' and 'foreclose much of the political space' for introducing exceptions.[139] Second, this opens an avenue for a variety of actors to refer to the international arena in order to enhance mobilisation in favour of change. For example, the 2015 CMW's report on Peru, with its rather critical conclusions and suggestions, influenced certain articles in the final law Peru adopted in 2015.[140] It remains to be seen whether the 2017 CMW's critical report with certain aspects of Ecuador's Organic Law on Human Mobility will have the same effect.[141] The regional epistemic community, including government officials, international organisations, NGOs and academics,[142] uses acculturation as a vehicle of peer pressure. Discussions of legislative projects in Brazil, Chile, Ecuador, Paraguay and Peru have experienced active participation of regional actors. For example, when Chile presented a restrictive proposal for a new migration law in 2013,[143] efforts from various regional actors contributed to its non-adoption. Of course, the international legal framework is insufficient to explain legislative change. The adoption of several restrictive measures by the Argentinean government in late 2016 and early 2017, despite the outcry against them by the IACHR and the UN Committee against Torture, are the best examples of these limits.[144]

---

[136] B. A. Simmons, *Mobilizing for Human Rights International Law in Domestic Politics* (Cambridge University Press, 2009), p. 114. Also see Martin, 'Effects of International Law on Migration Policy and Practice', 554.

[137] R. Goodman and D. Jinks, 'Incomplete Internationalization and Compliance with Human Rights Law', *The European Journal of International Law*, 19 (2008), 725–748, on 726.

[138] Howse and Teitel, 'Beyond Compliance', 131.

[139] Martin, 'Effects of International Law on Migration Policy and Practice', 555.

[140] Concluding observations on the initial report of Peru, CMW/C/PER/CO/1, 13 May 2015, p. 9; Izaguirre *et al.*, 'La nueva Ley de Migraciones en Perú'. This was 2015 Legislative Decree 1236 on Migration which was then replaced in 2017 by Legislative Decree 1350.

[141] CMW Concluding Observations on the Third Periodic Report by Ecuador, CMW/C/ECU/CO/3.

[142] Margheritis, 'Piecemeal Regional Integration'; A. Margheritis, 'Mercosur's Post-Neoliberal Approach to Migration: From Workers' Mobility to Regional Citizenship' in Cantor, Freier and Gauci (eds), *A Liberal Tide?*, pp. 57–80.

[143] Chile, Draft Immigration Law, 20 May 2013.

[144] Committee Against Torture, CAT/C/ARG/CO/5-6, 24 May 2017; Buenos Aires Herald, 'IACHR criticises government's "regressive" immigration policy'.

Discretion

Stable rules that are laid down in advance, publicly promulgated and applied to everyone through formal procedures contribute to both legal certainty and the rule of law. Discretion, by contrast, leads to unpredictable, unequal and often unjust outcomes. Whereas challenges to the rule of law for regional citizens are ever-present,[145] discretion is much more widespread where non-regional migrants are concerned. This partly results from historical processes – as discussed in Chapter 4 – whereby security bureaucracies continue to play a less enthusiastic role in their openness towards the foreigner. Discretion also relates to much deeper challenges to the rule of law in the region, such as the absence of detailed laws, flaws in their general application and in the relations between individuals and state agencies.[146] Extensive executive discretion is by no means unique in South America[147] and, when combined with judicial deference, ensures 'that migration decision-making is closely associated with the exercise of sovereign power'.[148]

When it comes to undocumented migration, discretion has led to unpredictable, yet not always negative, outcomes in the region. The example of Haitians obtaining permanent residence in Brazil is a paradigmatic case. Another example of discretion leading to a benefit for the individual was the Argentinean decision to regularise Dominicans and Senegalese in 2013, as well as Koreans in 2014, which they did through reinterpreting some of the provisions present in its law. However, discretion has also had dramatic negative consequences. In 2004, ahead of a revocation referendum against the then President Hugo Chavez, Venezuela regularised and granted citizenship to around 450,000 undocumented migrants[149] (although the number is highly contested) in a process of dubious legality.[150] In 2015, however, thousands of Colombian nationals were expelled from Venezuela.[151] This wounded not only

---

[145] See Chapter 7, pp. 183–190.

[146] G. O'Donnell, 'Why the Rule of Law Matters', *Journal of Democracy*, 15 (2004), 32–46.

[147] Dauvergne, for example, discusses the expansion of discretion in Canada, the UK, Australia and the USA. Dauvergne, *The New Politics of Immigration*.

[148] C. Dauvergne, 'Sovereignty, Migration and the Rule of Law in Global Times', *Modern Law Review*, 67 (2004), 588–615, on 592.

[149] The exact numbers have never been released. This estimation is based on the then president's own analysis and provided by Tobias Schwarz, who also mentions that around 85 per cent were Colombian nationals: see T. Schwarz, 'Regímenes de Pertenencia Nacional en Venezuela y la República Dominicana Contemporáneas', *Tabula Rasa*, 20 (2014), 227–46, on 234.

[150] A. R. Brewer-Carías, *Régimen Legal de Nacionalidad, Ciudadanía y Extranjería* (Caracas: Editorial Jurídica Venezolana, 2005).

[151] This mass expulsion followed an attack on two Venezuelan soldiers in the border region by members of illegal paramilitary groups in Colombia. According to interviews conducted in Bogotá in 2015 with Colombian authorities, international organisations and different NGOs, the number of people deported or who left out of fear was estimated at around 20,000, including some naturalised Venezuelans and thousands of regular residents. Also see M. Esthimer, 'Protecting the Forcibly Displaced: Latin America's Evolving Refugee and Asylum Framework', Migration Policy Network, 14 January 2016.

procedural rules established in Venezuela's migration and constitutional law, which were utterly disregarded, but also the construction of a regional citizenship. The crucial question is whether the outcome would have been different if Venezuela had already ratified the 1990 UN Convention, as well as the MERCOSUR Residence Agreement, or if it would have still been under the jurisdiction of the IACtHR.[152]

Political Explanations

The Politics of Humiliation

The politics of humiliation have been compellingly laid out by FitzGerald and Cook-Martin. In their view, '[w]hen individuals are banned from immigrating based on their ascriptive categorization, the collective reputation of others sharing that category suffers'.[153] As analysed in Chapter 4, Latin American governments used anti-racism and anti-discrimination as a foreign policy tool in the 1940s, due to concerns that the USA could also apply exclusionary policies against their nationals.[154] A similar situation is vividly represented by the reactions to the EU's Returns Directive, which is the piece of law establishing the procedure for expelling undocumented migrants in Europe. As if having been stabbed in the back, South American states were quick to strongly accentuate their compatriot's positive contribution to Europe, demand fair treatment and underline the historical hospitality with which they had welcomed Europeans in the past.[155] The increasing number of South Americans in Europe meant that governments were paying close attention to their needs, not only as fellow countrymen, but also as potential voters.[156] Local media in South America also turned its coverage to expulsions and mistreatment of their nationals abroad.[157] It is within this context that former President Lula da Silva criticised Europe and the USA when adopting Brazil's regularisation procedure in 2009.[158] This can be interpreted not only as a legitimate complaint but also as a cry out for reciprocity.[159] Thus, states have used more open legislation to voice external demands more credibly, as well as a strategy to internationally appear as being

---

[152] Venezuela's denunciation of the ACHR became effective on 10 September 2013.

[153] D. Cook-Martin and D. FitzGerald, *Culling the Masses*, p. 27.

[154] *Ibid.*, pp. 29–30. See also Chapter 4, pp. 109–110.

[155] MERCOSUR, Declaration of the MERCOSUR States faced with the European Union's Returns Directive, Tucumán 1 July 2008; UNASUR Declaration on the European Union's Returns Directive, Santiago de Chile, 4 July 2008; Acosta, *Latin American Reactions to the Adoption of the Returns Directive*.

[156] A. Margheritis, *Migration Governance across Regions*.

[157] A. C. Braga Martes and O. Goncalves, 'Gestão Multicultural dos Deslocamentos Populacionais', *Politica Externa*, 17 (2008), 105–120.

[158] Acosta and Freier, 'Turning the Immigration Policy Paradox Up-side Down?', 668–669.

[159] This was officially recognised by Romeu Tima Junior, Brazil's National Secretary of Justice at the time. See Alfonso, *La Experiencia de los Países Suramericanos*, pp. 43–44.

respectful of fundamental rights and as part of morally superior, avant-garde migration policy making.[160]

Banding together has sometimes been partly successful. For example, Spain and Portugal – but not other countries, such as Italy – opted for a less stringent implementation of the Returns Directive, and for the parallel approval of certain rights-based approach measures in order to appease concerns by Latin American states.[161]

The Politics of Reciprocity

Reciprocity is another major force. It can be considered as a basic principle of international law and a major 'aspect of bilateralism'.[162] On some occasions, certain 'legal norms have reciprocity as their fundamental normative and/or functional premise'.[163] Bilateral reciprocity has contributed to a broadening of membership for regional nationals in a process that demonstrates the failure of previous restrictive policies.[164] Reciprocity facilitates the acceptance of the neighbouring national and her family as being part of the community. Acceptance and reciprocity thus go hand in hand. Yet, it may be argued that acceptance often comes first and reciprocity only after. This is clear in the passage from bilateralism to multilateralism. For example, in 2004 Argentina accepted the entry, residence and work of South American nationals, well before such right was reciprocally extended to Argentines. Similarly, Uruguay granted immediate permanent residence to all South American nationals in 2014,[165] regardless of the fact the Uruguayans only enjoyed such a benefit in Brazil.[166] Brazil extended the MERCOSUR Residence Agreement – albeit temporarily – to Venezuelans in 2017 before Brazilians benefited from such privileged treatment in Venezuela.[167] Notably, with the exception of the 2003

---

[160] See Final Declaration IX SCM, Quito, 21–22 September 2009, paragraph five: 'We declare our goodwill to guarantee migrants from our region the enjoyment of the same rights we aim for our citizens in transit and destination countries for the sake of the principles of coherence, equality and non-discrimination.' Also see Acosta and Freier, 'Turning the Immigration Policy Paradox Up-side Down?'.

[161] D. Acosta, 'Migration and Borders in the European Union: The Implementation of the Returns Directive on Irregular Migrants in Spain and Italy' in R. Zapata (ed.), *Shaping the Normative Contours of the European Union: A Migration-Border Framework* (Barcelona: Cidob Foundation Edition, 2010), pp. 81–95.

[162] F. Parisit and N. Ghei, 'The Role of Reciprocity in International Law', *Cornell International Law Journal*, 36 (2003), 93–123, on 120.

[163] R. Howse and R. Teitel, 'Beyond Compliance', 129.

[164] See Chapter 3.

[165] Argentina, Art. 23, Law 25.871/2004; Uruguay, Law 19.254, 4 September 2014. The procedure is established in Decree 312 of 2015.

[166] Agreement between the Federal Republic of Brazil and the Oriental Republic of Uruguay on Permanent Residence with the objective to achieve the Free Movement of People, Brasilia, 9 July 2013.

[167] Brazil, National Immigration Council, Normative Resolution 126, 2 March 2017. This also extends the MERCOSUR Residence Agreement to not only Venezuelan nationals, but also those from Suriname and Guyana for a period of one year – which is renewable – starting 2 March 2017.

agreement between Brazil and Portugal, reciprocity has only been successful among countries in the region.[168]

The MERCOSUR Residence Agreement shifts from the bilateral to the multilateral level. Irregularity takes centre stage to facilitate a long-term mechanism offering legal certainty which is often absent in unilateral endeavours. Reciprocity also relates to long-standing historical practices regarding free movement and equal treatment throughout the nineteenth and twentieth centuries.[169]

Domestic Politics

The executive branches in various countries have played a crucial role in the new approach towards irregularity. The concentration of power in this branch of government has acted as a deterrent to a larger, more important role for parliaments.[170] Many of the measures that further extend rights to undocumented migrants have been the result of executive action rather than of legislation adopted by congress. With varying levels of emphasis and commitment, there has been a prominent willingness to position human rights, including migrants' rights, at the centre of the agenda. In Argentina, for example, this must be understood against the backdrop of increased cooperation between historically strong civil society organisations, for whom migration reform had long been a priority issue, and the first Kirchner administration.[171] As discussed in Chapter 1, these liberal discourses developed within the context of emigration and diaspora polices in strong counter-positions to the restrictive immigration rhetoric in the USA and the EU. Although the specific political context of liberalised immigration discourses has been South American *emigration* to Western liberal democracies, their proclaimed values of the universality of migrants' rights and the necessity for regularisation measures fed back into the country's *immigration* discourses, based on the logic of coherence and political reciprocity.[172]

Social Factors on the Ground

A further major aspect relates to flows composed mainly of regional migrants. Flows that are bilateral present more options for cooperation and coordination because it is easier to imagine the kind of bidirectional incentives for both parties. This affects both politics and the legal arrangements. Most regularisation programmes have largely affected regional migrants. For example

[168] Agreement between the Federal Republic of Brazil and the Portuguese Republic on the reciprocal hiring of nationals, 11 July 2003.
[169] See Chapters 3 and 4.
[170] See Part II, pp. 114–115.
[171] Acosta and Freier, 'Turning the Immigration Policy Paradox Up-side Down?', 667–669. Ceriani and Morales, *Argentina: Avances y Asignaturas Pendientes*.
[172] See Chapter 1, pp. 23–24.

in Argentina, 225,000 South American nationals had regularised their stay by 2010 through the *Patria Grande* program, whereas only 11,000 profited from a 2004 procedure for extra-regional migrants.[173] In its 2008 procedure, Chile regularised 50,000 residents of which 90 per cent originated from four countries in South America (Peru, Ecuador, Colombia and Bolivia).[174] Even in Brazil, which continues to be the country with the fewest regional migrants in the population as a percentage of the total number of foreigners,[175] its 2009 regularisation procedure granted status to around 42,000 residents, of which circa 65 per cent were regional citizens.[176] When countries have adopted programmes addressed to extra-regional migrants, the number of recipients has been very small – except in the case of Haitians in Brazil – and thus easier to conduct and legitimise.[177]

Conclusion

In some respects, South American countries share a distinctive approach towards the regulation of irregular migration. An ongoing regional dialogue has assisted in reinforcing this approach and has led to numerous examples of legal transplants. Access to certain rights, such as health care, or the limited role that detention plays, are notable examples of a more liberal trend. By far the most important aspect emerging is regularisation.

There is a conceptual distinction prevalent in the European and US context that often goes unnoticed. When we assess regularisation we can think about it in two ways. First, it can be seen as a procedural right. Under this understanding, the individual who is physically present in the country and apprehended must, prior to deportation, be given an opportunity under the existing substantive migration rules to regularise his status. This is frequently available in various countries. Asylum policies are a common example of this. The individual enters without authorisation but then acquires a procedural right to regularise in the USA or the EU if he can prove his fear to return. The government is not permitted under the law to remove the person before the claim is processed.[178] As Dauvergne observes, 'the *non-refoulement* provision translates into an effective right to remain in a host state'.[179]

The new policies in some South American states generally reflect this idea: anyone the immigration authorities apprehend must be permitted a

---

[173] Acosta and Freier, 'Turning the Immigration Policy Paradox Up-side Down?'.
[174] Martínez Pizarro *et al.*, 'Políticas Públicas sobre Migraciones', p. 183.
[175] In Brazil, only around 29 per cent of all migrants come from the region. See OECD and OAS, *International Migration in the Americas. Third Report*.
[176] Centro de Direitos Humanos e Cidadania do Imigrante (CDHIC), *Brasil Informe sobre a Legislação Migratória e a Realidade dos Imigrantes* (São Paulo: CDHIC, 2011).
[177] For example, 400 Haitians and 650 Cubans in 2010 in Ecuador, around 1,500 Senegalese and 6,000 Dominicans in Argentina in 2014, and 300 Ghanaians in Brazil in 2016.
[178] See, for example, in the EU context: Case C-534/11, *Arslan*, 30 May 2013.
[179] Dauvergne, 'Sovereignty, Migration and the Rule of Law', p. 596.

procedural right to pursue regularisation under the substantive laws prior to his removal. In the USA and the EU, whether the individual has a procedural right tends to largely depend on the form in which enforcement takes place. For example, if the person finds himself before a court, the court may – but is not obliged to – suspend his proceeding if he is married to a national.[180] The problem here is that, *de facto*, the outcome of this procedure is highly contingent on the enforcement context. Indeed, non-nationals are often deported without any proceeding. Thus what the new polices do in some South American states is to extend a practice that crops up in a *de facto* fashion across the board and which appears in a *de iure* manner in the refugee context.

The second way to conceptualise regularisation is to see it as a substantive right. This would entail modifying the present migration categories by adding new ones. This goes beyond a procedural right. The MERCOSUR Residence Agreement may be categorised as an intermediate case between a substantive and a procedural right. Under the procedural approach, the state does not make any changes to the substantive criteria to reside in the country. Any individual within any category is granted an opportunity to apply for regularisation at any given moment, regardless of his irregular status. By contrast, under the substantive approach, the state takes a group of people who do not fit into any category and regularises them anyway. These criteria did not exist before in the law but are introduced precisely for the purpose of regularisation.

However, the best example of the contradictions still present in the South American context is the fact that under the MERCOSUR agreement, regional migrants can fall back into irregularity.[181] Furthermore, restrictive practices and implementation coexist with path-breaking approaches.[182] The liberal discourse has not yet made its way into the legislation of all countries, which has led some authors to discuss 'crimmigration' in particular contexts.[183] In 2016, both Colombia and Ecuador expelled Cubans without any discussion of possible regularisation. In the former, according to some data, the number of deported unauthorised migrants was 34,000 in 2016 alone.[184] Finally, changes in government may also lead towards more restrictive interpretation and implementation of the same law or to modify some of its aspects, as has occurred in Argentina since 2016.

Regularisation procedures are reminiscent of debates that took place during the nineteenth and twentieth centuries. The regional citizen is clearly favoured

---

[180] This is not guaranteed in the European context, where the ECHR has on various occasions ruled that family life in the case of marriage can also be conducted in the country of origin of the non-national. See, for instance: Case *Antwi v. Norway*, application no. 26940/10, 14 February 2012.

[181] See Chapter 7, pp. 194–196.

[182] See, for example, the problems in implementing the *Patria Grande* programme in Argentina in Ceriani and Morales, *Argentina: Avances y Asignaturas Pendientes*.

[183] Zago de Moraes, 'Crimigração'.

[184] D. Carvajal, 'As Colombia Emerges from Decades of War, Migration Challenges Mount', Migration Policy Institute, 13 April 2017.

through reciprocity mechanisms based on commonalities and shared historical experiences, but also on expectations of increased control of who resides in the territory.[185] At the same time, just as it was during the nineteenth and twentieth centuries, a segmented openness approach applies to only some extra-continental migrants.[186] Those coming from wealthy Western countries – i.e. those who do not need a visa – are clearly privileged. On the other hand, African, Asian and Caribbean nationals, whilst having benefited from general or *ad hoc* regularisation procedures, continue to be considered second-class foreigners. Selective restrictive responses to recent extra-continental south–south immigration can be partly explained by schizophrenic public opinion, which welcomes immigration policy liberalisation in theory but rejects those considered to be poor and ethnically 'unwelcome' immigrants. South America's approach upsets assumptions on undocumented migration by prioritising regularisation at the expense of expulsion. Yet, in order to be truly revolutionary, a procedural and substantive right to regularisation would need to apply on a non-discriminatory basis, without distinguishing between those who always enter regularly due to visa-free travel, and those who require visas.[187] It will also need to solve the implementation problems that continue to exist in the application of a procedural right to regularisation in those countries that offer it in their legislations.[188]

[185] See Chapter 7. See for example the arguments provided by the 2016 Uruguayan Framework Document on a Migration Policy, in particular at p. 27, where it is argued that regularisation is preferable so as to order migration flows, improve state control and security and due to the vulnerability and limited access to rights in which migrants in an irregular situation might find themselves. This type of reasoning has proven useful in convincing Interior Ministries across South America as to the suitability to conduct regularisation procedures.

[186] Organisation of American States, *Irregular Migration Flows to the Americas from Africa, Asia, and the Caribbean* (Washington, DC: OAS, 2017). I borrow the expression 'segmented openness approach' from Ramírez, 'Del Aperturismo Segmentado al Control Migratorio'.

[187] Pending implementing the regulations, Brazil adopted a procedure that does not impede regularisation due to irregular entry, and thus does not discriminate between those who need a visa and who are exempt from visas: see Brazil, Art. 50, Law 13.445/2017.

[188] See for example the challenges to regularise for Haitian migrants in Argentina and other countries: IOM and IPPDH, *Diagnóstico regional sobre Migración Haitiana* (Buenos Aires: IOM and IPPDH, 2017), p. 119.

6

The Right to Migrate as a Fundamental Right? The Construction of the Foreigner through Equal Treatment

Free circulation and residence is a basic human right, and has been a principle that the countries in the region have traditionally assumed through their policies of openness and promotion of migration. This principle, historically constitutive in the formation of nations in the region, has remained and increased in the present day, despite tendencies towards the restriction of human mobility that have augmented during the last few years in other regions of the world.[1]

Introduction

Enunciating the right to migrate, often elevated to the category of a human right – and at times coupled with the concept of universal citizenship – has been one of the central pillars of the South American discourse in the twenty-first century. The right to migration relates to the principles of non-criminalisation and open borders, as discussed in Chapters 5 and 7, and anticipates a strong equality framework. If not only nationals, but also foreigners have an inalienable right of entry into, and residence in, the territory of a particular state – as well as a number of rights while residing there – it would signify a radical departure from the traditional understandings of territorial sovereignty that have been generally favoured and considered valid since the late nineteenth century.[2]

In effect, beginning with the UDHR, only two rights relating to human mobility have been acknowledged: the freedom of movement and residence within the borders of a particular state, as well as the right to leave any country, including one's own, and to return to the country in which the individual holds

[1] South American Plan of Human Development of Migrations, Context and Perspectives. Document approved during the tenth South American Conference on Migration by all twelve countries in the region, Cochabamba, Bolivia, 25–26 October, 2010, pp. 16–17 (author's translation). 'La libre circulación y residencia es un derecho humano básico, y ha sido un principio tradicionalmente asumido por los países de la región a través de sus políticas de apertura y promoción de las migraciones. Este principio, históricamente constitutivo de la formación de las naciones de la región, se ha mantenido e incrementado en la actualidad, a pesar de las tendencias a la restricción a los movimientos humanos que han aumentado en los últimos años en otras regiones del mundo.'

[2] Chapter 4, pp. 87–88.

his or her nationality.[3] Found in most international covenants,[4] including the ACHR,[5] these typically exclude the third aspect of mobility: the right to enter the territory of another state. In fact, the opposite is regarded as a well-established principle of international law. For example, the UN Human Rights Committee (HR Committee) indicated that the ICCPR did not recognise the right of foreigners 'to enter or reside in the territory of a State party'.[6] The ECtHR has also clearly espoused this doctrine, and considers that 'as a matter of well-established international law and subject to its treaty obligations, a State has the right to control the entry of non-nationals into its territory'.[7] We face 'a normative disjuncture between departure and admission' in international law.[8]

Historically, domestic constitutional law provided the right of foreigners to enter and reside in individual South American states.[9] Since the early twenty-first century, various policy documents have acknowledged the right to migrate – inclusive of its two elements, immigration and emigration – and have been signed by all governments in the region.[10] Most importantly, it is now also enshrined in some domestic laws. Argentina was the first country to incorporate the right to migrate and considers it 'essential and inalienable to all persons and the Republic of Argentina shall guarantee it based on the principles of equality and universality'.[11] Uruguay recognises it as 'an inalienable right of migrants and their families, regardless of their migratory status'.[12] Bolivia's approach is more cautious. The state shall guarantee all migrant foreigners the right 'to migrate based on the principles of equality, universality and reciprocity'.[13] The word 'foreigners' leaves no doubt as to whom the provision addresses. Yet, the qualification of reciprocity creates an almost insurmountable obstacle and points in the direction of using it merely at the regional level. Paraguay's 2016 draft proposal lays down the right of any foreigner to freely enter the territory in accordance with law.[14] In turn, Chile refers more cautiously in its 2017 law proposal to the freedom of transit and migration by which the state recognises any individual's freedom to enter, remain in and leave the country provided the legal

[3] Art. 13, UDHR.

[4] Art. 12, ICCPR; Art. 8, ICMW; Art. 2, Protocol IV, ECHR; Art. 12, African Charter on Human and People's Rights (ACHPR).

[5] Art. 22, ACHR.

[6] HR Committee, General Comment 15. The position of aliens under the Covenant (Twenty-seventh session, 1986).

[7] ECtHR, *Abdulaziz, Cabales and Balkandali v. the United Kingdom*, para. 67.

[8] Chetail, 'The Transnational Movement of Persons under General International Law', p. 11.

[9] Chapter 2, pp. 46–47.

[10] Declaration on Migration Principles and General Guidelines of the South American Conference on Migration, X SACM, Cochabamba 25–26 October 2010; Montevideo Declaration on Migration, Development and Human Rights of Migrants, VIII SACM, Montevideo 17–19 September 2008.

[11] Argentina, Art. 4, Law 25.871/2004.

[12] Uruguay, Art. 1, Law 18.250/2008.

[13] Bolivia, Art. 12(II)(1), Law 370/2013.

[14] Paraguay, Art. 7 2016, Migration Law proposal, Ministry of the Interior.

regime is respected.[15] Finally, a 2017 law proposal for a new migration policy for Colombia mentions the right to migrate, without defining it, as well as the right to not return – a provision clearly addressed to Colombian emigrants.[16]

Similar provisions are present at the constitutional level. In Ecuador 'the right to migrate is recognised for individuals' and 'no human being will be considered or identified as illegal because of his migratory condition'. Regarding its international relations, the constitution requires that Ecuador 'advocates the principle of universal citizenship, the free mobility of all inhabitants of the planet and the progressive end of the condition of foreigner'.[17] Paradoxically, Ecuador's Constitution also provides a long list of obligations in favour of Ecuadorians abroad and neglects any discussion of what the right to migrate entails for immigrants in the country.[18] As one of the guiding principles, the 2017 Human Mobility Law includes universal citizenship, understood as the individual's right to freely move around the planet while bringing his human rights, regardless of his migratory status, something which should lead to the progressive elimination of the status of 'foreigner'. Also enshrined as a guiding principle, free human mobility entails that the state protects the mobility of all individuals who have the intention to permanently or temporarily move to and reside in a destination.[19] In Uruguay, free access to entering the Republic's territory, as well as stay and exit, are recognised for all individuals. This holds only when the laws and rights of third parties are observed and there are no physical, mental or moral deficiencies that could be detrimental to society, in addition to other requirements imposed by its migration law.[20] Finally, the Argentinean Constitution mandates that 'the government will promote European immigration, and will not be able to restrict, limit or tax the entry into the Argentinean territory of any foreigners whose objective is to cultivate the land, improve industries and introduce and teach sciences and arts'.[21]

Both scholars and international organisations alike have celebrated this incorporation of the right to migrate.[22] Regarded as inalienable, essential and universal in Argentina, Bolivia and Uruguay, it is assumed to be a human right.

---

[15] Chile, Art. 12, 2017 Migration Law Proposal. A previous 2015 draft proposal was more far reaching in its wording. There, the right to migrate was presented as the ability of any individual to 'request residence in the country, harmoniously integrate into Chilean society and be able to leave the Republic's territory, provided the norms established in the national legal order are respected'. This was immediately qualified by the state's parallel ability, in so far as it is sovereign, 'to establish limits to the exercise of such right as necessary in a democratic society, to protect national security, public order, health or public morals and the rights and liberties of any individual'. See Art. 13, Migration Law Draft Bill, Ministry of the Interior and Public Security, 7 October 2015.

[16] Colombia, Art. 5, 2017 Law Proposal for a Comprehensive Migration Policy.

[17] Ecuador, Art. 416, 2008 Constitution.

[18] Ecuador, Art. 40, 2008 Constitution.

[19] Ecuador, Art. 2, 2017 Organic Law and Human Mobility.

[20] Uruguay, Art. 37, 1967 Constitution.

[21] Argentina, Art. 25, 1994 Constitution.

[22] R. Giustiniani (ed.), *Migración: Un Derecho Humano* (Buenos Aires: Prometeo Libros, 2004). See Concluding Observations on the Initial Report by Uruguay, CMW/C/URY/CO/1, 2 May 2014; Concluding Observations on the Initial Report by Argentina, CMW/C/ARG/CO/1, 2 November

Nonetheless, no serious discussion has taken place as to its precise contours and meaning.[23] The main exception would be Uruguay's 2013 report to the CMW where it expressed that: 'The "right to migrate" reflects the independence in conceptual terms of a foreigner's migratory status and his or her status as a human being, which is vastly superior to any other status: it means that the dignity of the human person, upheld by the indisputably guaranteed freedom to exercise his or her basic rights, should not and cannot be impeded by the irregularity of the person's entry into or stay in Uruguayan territory.'[24] Even this attempt at clarification leaves numerous open questions. Does the right to migrate challenge the alleged state right to control entry, residence and expulsion of non-nationals? Or, by contrast, is it a purely ornamental or aspirational provision with few legal implications? Migrants are interested in three particular aspects of migration law: conditions of entry, rights during their stay and the security of their residence to avoid expulsion. If intended to be meaningful, a number of rights during residence – as well as transparent procedures to renewing permits – must be coupled with any right of entry. Clear paths to naturalisation for those interested in settling permanently are also critical.

This chapter discusses how South American migration law constructs the legal status of foreigners with a residence permit. It also analyses the transition between foreigner and national through naturalisation. It contains three sections, divided into entry, stay and expulsion. The following pages do not offer a detailed analysis of all provisions for each category in all ten countries. The scope here is more modest, intended to elucidate some common trends in the region regarding the regulation of the status of non-nationals with a residence permit, as well as their potential access to citizenship.

When compared with the previous migration frameworks – characterised by a restrictive and utilitarian approach – the new laws in South America represent a notable advancement towards a rights-based approach. Their structure and content offer a central emphasis on equal treatment, the universality of certain rights and a concern for human dignity. Whilst the new laws clearly expand the rights foreigners enjoy, it is harder to clarify whether the right to migrate makes any substantial innovation in the legal construction of the foreigner, or whether it represents more of a 'poetical' addition aligned with concerns of an 'inflation of rights' debated earlier in this book.[25] The final section discusses how the resurgence of debates on the right to migrate in South America is more connected to emigration first and regional free movement of people second, to which Chapter 7 is devoted.

2011; Concluding Observations on the Second Report by Ecuador, CMW/C/ECU/CO/2, 15 December 2010.

[23] B. Hines, 'The Right to Migrate as a Human Right: The Current Argentine Immigration Law', *Cornell International Law Journal*, 43 (2010), 471–511; García, *Nueva Política Migratoria Argentina a través de las Acciones ante el Poder Judicial (2004–2010)*.

[24] Initial Report by Uruguay, 30 January 2013, CMW/C/URY/1.

[25] See Part II, pp. 114–115.

A Right of Entry in South America?

With the end of the Second World War, the then prevalent discretion over admission and expulsion was 'fissured and eroded'.[26] A 'qualified duty to admit some aliens in some circumstances' started to take root.[27] Two drivers were pivotal in this expansion. First, the mobility of people was liberalised at both the bilateral and regional level. The EU constitutes the paradigmatic example since EU citizens have a fundamental right to move and reside freely within the territory of all Member States.[28] Second, the expansion of human rights law through general principles and international agreements is of paramount importance.[29] For example, countries can no longer enforce restrictions 'exclusively based on grounds of race, colour, descent or national or ethnic origin'.[30] Openly racist provisions, such as had been legally enshrined in many countries in the region in the twentieth century, are no longer possible.[31] This expansion of international law has also affected the right to family life.

Finally, in addition to the two just mentioned, another parallel development is also relevant. The increasing global recognition of dual citizenship has made it possible for many individuals to enjoy exit and entry rights in more than one state.[32] This tendency has been particularly strong in South America, partly due to the continuous lobbying efforts of diaspora organisations claiming rights abroad.[33]

In this section, we look at the phenomenon of dual citizenship, as well as how the interpretation of family life affects entry and stay for a particular category of foreigners. The possible expansion of the right of entry through multilateral treaties, namely the MERCOSUR Residence Agreement and CAN's Decision 545, is discussed later in Chapter 7. As explained in Chapter 1, refugees and asylum seekers lie outside the scope of this research, thus are not included here.[34]

Family Reunification

Family life has been acknowledged as a crucial aspect enhancing social inclusion in the host state.[35] The right to family life 'includes both a positive

26 Martin, 'Effects of International Law on Migration Policy and Practice', 548.
27 Nafziger, 'The General Admission of Aliens', 805.
28 Arts 20–21, Treaty on the Functioning of the European Union (TFEU); Art. 45, European Union Charter of Fundamental Rights.
29 Martin, 'Effects of International Law on Migration Policy and Practice', 548–550; Perruchoud, 'State Sovereignty and Freedom of Movement', p. 125.
30 Legal Consequences for States of the Continued Presence of South Africa in Namibia (South West Africa) notwithstanding Security Council Resolution 276 (1970) (Advisory Opinion) [1971] ICJ Rep 16, [131]. Cited in Perruchoud, *ibid.*, p. 126.
31 See Chapter 4, pp. 91–95.
32 Spiro, *At Home in Two Countries*.
33 Margheritis, *Migration Governance across Regions*.
34 Chapter 1, pp. 8–9.
35 For example, Council of Europe, Parliamentary Assembly, Recommendation Human Mobility and the Right to Family Reunion, 1686 (2004).

obligation to protect the family and a negative obligation prohibiting any unlawful or arbitrary interference with the exercise of the right to family life'.[36] Family life is intrinsically related to family reunification. In this regard, migrants have three questions in mind: does an individual right to family reunification exist? Which family members may join the sponsor? What are the conditions of residence and rights of family members? A fundamental right to migrate would anticipate positive and wide-reaching responses to these questions.[37]

Despite its importance, no international instrument provides an indisputable right to family reunification and the consequent right of entry for family members. The ICMW merely lays down the states' obligation to 'take measures *that they deem appropriate* and that fall within their competence *to facilitate* the reunification of migrant workers' (emphasis added) with certain family members.[38] The CMW has interpreted such provisions as imposing an obligation on states to incorporate norms regulating family reunification into domestic law and to take practical measures in order to facilitate it.[39] Other Human Rights Treaty bodies have referred to the possible duty of permitting family reunification within a wider concept of family life, derived from the ICCPR or CRC.[40] According to part of the doctrine, facilitating reunification in the case of children is a customary international law norm.[41] In cases involving children in which family life is not possible in any other place, the ECtHR has generally recognised a right to family reunification and entry.[42] In turn, EU migration law is more generous in establishing an individual right to family reunification not only for EU citizens, but also for non-EU nationals with certain family members.[43] The Court of Justice of the European Union (CJEU) has clearly upheld this right in various rulings.[44]

At a regional level, Article 17 of the ACHR affirms that the family is the basic element of society and must be safeguarded. Under such article, the state is under an obligation 'to promote, as extensively as possible, the development

---

[36] Chetail, 'The Transnational Movement of Persons under General International Law', pp. 41–42.

[37] On family life and migrants in an irregular situation see Chapter 5, pp. 135–137.

[38] Namely spouses, partners with an equivalent status to that of marriage, and minor dependent unmarried children, Art. 44, ICMW.

[39] See Concluding Observations on the Second Report by Bolivia, CMW/C/BOL/CO/2, 15 May 2013; Concluding Observations on the Initial Report by Chile, CMW/C/CHL/CO/1, 19 October 2011.

[40] Chetail, 'The Transnational Movement of Persons under General International Law', pp. 42 and 45–6.

[41] *Ibid.*, pp. 43–48.

[42] *Sen v. the Netherlands* (Judgment) (1996) Appl. No. 31465/96, para. 40. Also see the peculiar case of *Hasanbasic v. Switzerland*, Appl. No 52166/09, 7 October 2013.

[43] Directive 2004/38 on the Right of Citizens of the Union and their Family Members to Move and Reside Freely within the Territory of the Member States; Directive 2003/86 on the Right to Family Reunification.

[44] Case C-540/03, *Parliament v. Council*, 27 June 2006, EU:C:2006:429; Case C-578/08, *Chakroun*, 4 March 2010, EU:C:2010:117.

and enhancement of the family unit'.[45] Article 11(2) lays down that everyone has the right to receive protection against arbitrary or abusive interference with his family life. Yet, the IACtHR has interpreted the right to family life as not transcending '*per se* the sovereign authority of the States Parties to implement their own immigration policies in conformity with human rights';[46] rather, both sovereignty and human rights must be weighed against each other.

The IACtHR has established important standards. For example, provisions include the state's obligation to provide for family reunification when it has wrongly expelled a family member on procedural grounds.[47] Moreover, in cases involving children, the concept of 'family' is widely interpreted to include not only the nuclear family but also other relatives such as aunts, uncles, cousins and grandparents or even those 'who are not necessarily family members in a legal sense'. Thus, in cases involving children, 'the State has the obligation to determine, in each case, the composition of the child's family unit'.[48]

South American countries have moved in the direction of recognising an individual's subjective right to family reunification.[49] The concept of family is widely understood to include not only spouses and children, but also parents, grandchildren, siblings or other possible categories.[50] Family members often enjoy equal treatment with nationals in regards to accessing social services, health, education, employment and social security.[51] This approach is notable in at least three respects. First, rights that were originally granted only to

---

[45] IACtHR, Case *Pacheco Tineo family v. Bolivia*, para. 226.

[46] IACtHR, Case *Dominican and Haitian deportees*, para. 417.

[47] *Ibid.*, para. 418.

[48] IACtHR, *Rights and Guarantees of Children*, para. 272.

[49] Argentina, Arts 3(d) and 10, Law 25.871/2004; Bolivia, Art. 12(II)(8), Law 370/2013; Brazil, Art. 4(III), Law 13.445/2017; Chile, Art. 18, 2017 Migration Law Proposal. The 1975 legislation, still in force in Chile, does not incorporate a subjective right to family reunification (Law Decree 1094/75); Peru, Art. V, Legislative Decree 1350, 6 January 2017; Uruguay, Art. 8, Law 18.250/2008. In Ecuador, the right is only available to foreigners who have obtained permanent residence. Ecuador, Art. 63, 2017 Organic Law on Human Mobility. In Paraguay, the right is not regulated in its present law but it is recognised as a right in Art. 42 of its 2016 Migration Law proposal, Ministry of the Interior. In Colombia, family reunification is worded as a state's prerogative: Colombia, Art. 9, Decree 834/2013. A 2017 law proposal for a new migration policy in Colombia establishes that the state shall safeguard the integral protection of families of migrants with the view to facilitate and promote family reunification both abroad and in Colombia. However, it does not establish a subjective right to family reunion. See Art. 6, 2017 Law Proposal for a Comprehensive Migration Policy. In Venezuela, the issue is not discussed in its 2004 Migration law.

[50] Argentina, Art. 10, Law 25.871/2004; Bolivia, Art. 12(II)(8), Law 370/2013; Brazil, Arts 4(III) and 37, Law 13.445/2017; Chile, Art. 18, 2017 Migration Law Proposal; Colombia, Art. 9, Decree 834/2013; Ecuador, Art. 63, 2017 Organic Law on Human Mobility recognises family reunification up to the second level of consanguinity of affinity, although only for permanent residents; Peru, Art. 38, Legislative Decree 1350/2017; Paraguay, Art. 4(9), 2016 Migration Law proposal, Ministry of the Interior; Uruguay, Art. 10, Law 18.250/2008.

[51] Argentina, Art. 6, Law 25.871/2004; Bolivia, Art. 12, Law 370/2013; Brazil, Arts 3–4, Law 13.445/2017; Peru, Arts 37–38, Legislative Decree 1350/2017; Uruguay, Art. 8, Law 18.250/2008.

regional citizens through the 2002 MERCOSUR Residence agreement,[52] were then extended to all non-nationals. Second, the SACM has played an important role in setting the agenda and being the first organisation to verbalise and recognise the right to family reunification for all migrants in South America, not only regional ones.[53] Third, family life acts as a shield against expulsion, notably when the individual is undocumented, but also offers some protection in cases where a criminal offence has been committed.[54] In the case of marriage, and in line with well-established historical practices,[55] this makes it possible to naturalise faster.[56] Finally, in some countries it is possible for family members, often spouses, to directly access permanent residence, without any further requirements.[57]

Dual Citizens

Individuals with two or more nationalities hold an unequivocal right to free movement and immigration at the international level. In effect, their right to leave their own state is permanently paralleled with their right to enter at least one other state's territory, of which they are also a national.[58] This has led to heated academic and policy debates on whether those who naturalise should be allowed to keep their previous citizenship, thus becoming dual nationals, or not.[59]

---

[52] Previous Andean Community Decisions had referred to families of migrant workers but without clearly incorporating a subjective recognition of the right to family reunification. See, for example, Andean Instrument of Labour Migration, Decision 116.

[53] The SACM recognised a subjective right to family reunification for the first time in 2004: Final Declaration, La Paz, Bolivia, 26 November 2004.

[54] See Chapter 5, pp. 135–137 for discussion on irregular migration. Regarding criminal offences, see, for example: Brazil, Art. 55, Law 13.445/2017 and Paraguay, Art. 29, 2016 Migration Law Proposal, Ministry of the Interior.

[55] See Chapter 2, pp. 48–49.

[56] In Argentina, the period is reduced from two years to any time of residence; in Bolivia from three to two years; in Brazil from four to one; in Colombia from five to two; in Venezuela from ten to five. Peru does not reduce the residence needed, maintaining it at two years, but waives some of the other requirements for ordinary naturalisation. Finally, Ecuador discriminates between foreign women who marry an Ecuadorian male, who see their ordinary three years' residence requirement waived, and foreign men who marry an Ecuadorian female citizen, who have their residence requirement reduced from three to two years. See D. Acosta, *Regional Report on Citizenship. The South American and Mexican Cases*, EUI, EUDO Citizenship, Florence, p. 8.

[57] See, for example, Argentina, Art. 22, Law 25871/2004; Ecuador, Art. 63, 2017 Organic Law on Human Mobility; Paraguay, Art. 52, 2016, Migration Law Proposal; Peru, Art. 93, Supreme Decree 007/2017; Uruguay, Art. 33, Law 18.250/2008.

[58] R. Bauböck, 'Temporary Migrants, Partial Citizenship and Hypermigration', *Critical Review of International Social and Political Philosophy*, 14 (2011), 665–693, on 679.

[59] On this, see, among others: P. Spiro, *At Home in Two Countries*; R. Hansen and P. Weil (eds), *Dual Nationality, Social Rights, and Federal Citizenship in the US and Europe. The Reinvention of Citizenship* (New York: Berghahn Books, 2002); T. A. Aleinikoff and D. Klusmeyer (eds), *Citizenship Policies for an Age of Migration* (Washington, DC: Carnegie Endowment for International Peace, 2002).

The number of potential dual nationals has grown in the last few decades. Easier communications mean more people can lead transnational lives. An increased focus on individual rights, introducing gender equality – such as mothers being able to pass on citizenship through birth via *ius sanguinis* – in legal instruments, many countries abolishing conscription, as well as the growing rates of intermarriage, have all contributed to this boom. Within the context of a post-Cold War era, several countries now allow individuals to hold multiple nationalities.[60] This is creating 'new patterns of belonging'[61] and 'breaks with the segmentary logic of the classic nation-state, according to which one could belong to only one state at a time'.[62] Whilst the trend is clear, many states still strip the previous nationality of those who naturalise in a new country.[63]

South America has embraced dual citizenship as a univocal choice since the 1990s. Earlier, South Americans had lost their nationality upon acquiring a different one. Foreigners in South America also had to renounce their nationality before naturalising. This general rule was only broken on a few occasions. For example, Venezuela admitted dual citizenship for its own nationals abroad as early as 1864, retaining this regime until 1947.[64] In the mid-twentieth century, by signing specific bilateral agreements, countries in the region allowed dual citizenship only for other Latin American nationals, as well as for those from Portugal and Spain.[65]

Nowadays, all ten countries except Paraguay[66] accept dual nationality as a general policy. This general shift can be traced back to Colombia's 1991 Constitution. The main reason was pressure from emigrants, who mostly resided in the USA and sought to keep their Colombian nationality upon naturalising abroad.[67] According to Escobar, the anti-immigrant wave in

---

[60] M. M. Howard, 'Variation in Dual Citizenship Policies in the Countries of the EU', *International Migration Review*, 39 (2005), 697–720; T. A. Aleinikoff and D. Klusmeyer, 'Plural Nationality: Facing the Future in a Migratory World' in T. A. Aleinikoff and D. Klusmeyer (eds), *Citizenship Policies*, pp. 63–88.

[61] T. Brøndsted Sejersen, '"I Vow to Thee My Countries" – The Expansion of Dual Citizenship in the 21st Century', *International Migration Review*, 42 (2008), 523–549, on 524.

[62] C. Joppke, 'Citizenship between De- and Re-Ethnicization', *European Journal of Sociology*, 44 (2003), 429–458, on 441.

[63] T. Faist, and J. Gerdes, 'Dual Citizenship in an Age of Mobility', Washington, DC: Migration Policy Institute, 2008.

[64] Venezuela, Art. 7, 1864 Constitution.

[65] See, for example, Bilateral Treaty on Double Nationality between Chile and Spain, 15 November 1958; Bilateral Treaty on Double Nationality between Paraguay and Spain, 25 June 1959; Bilateral Treaty on Double Nationality between Ecuador and Spain, subscribed on 4 March 1964, published in the Official Registry No. 463, 23 March 1965.

[66] Paraguay, Art. 149, 1992 Constitution. Nevertheless, Paraguayan citizens who naturalise abroad often retain their Paraguayan citizenship due to the lack of governmental mechanisms for control and identification. E. Brey, *Report on Citizenship Law: Paraguay*, EUDO Citizenship Observatory, March 2016, p. 11.

[67] C. Escobar, 'Extraterritorial Political Rights and Dual Citizenship in Latin America', *Latin American Research Review*, 42 (2007), pp. 43–75.

the 1990s alerted governments that their emigrants would benefit from naturalising as US citizens.[68] However, many emigrants were only willing to take this step if they could also retain their original nationality. Not only emigrants but also immigrants benefited since the 1991 Constitution removed the requirement to renounce foreign citizenship when becoming Colombian.[69] Afterwards, most South American countries adopted dual citizenship: Brazil (1994), Bolivia (2004),[70] Chile (2005),[71] Ecuador (1996),[72] Peru (1993)[73] and Venezuela (1999).[74]

Four countries merit specific attention. First, Paraguay is the only South American state that does not allow dual citizenship. Nonetheless, the constitution permits the signing of bilateral agreements, something so far only pursued with Spain.[75] Second, Uruguay has accepted since its 1934 Constitution that foreigners can obtain legal citizenship,[76] as well as vote in national elections. This was part of a movement to incorporate foreign workers who were already residing in the country but also coincided with introducing several restrictions for new arrivals.[77] With regard to the right to vote in national elections for foreigners in Uruguay, this has to do with the fact that at the time of this provision, in the 1930s, a number of European states removed the nationality of anyone obtaining a foreign citizenship. Considering that under the Uruguayan Constitution foreigners can never naturalise, in the sense of becoming nationals – an oddity in comparative perspective – but only obtain legal citizenship, these individuals ran the risk of becoming stateless. This constitutional amendment allowed foreigners, who were part of society for all purposes except political ones, to obtain the right to vote, in all elections, except for constitutional plebiscites.[78] Third, Argentina's legislation does not explicitly provide for dual citizenship, nor for any renunciation requirement. The Supreme Court has confirmed dual citizenship through judicial interpretation.[79] Finally, Brazil introduced dual

---

[68] *Ibid.*, on 50.

[69] Colombia, Art. 96, 1991 Constitution. This only entered into force in 1995. See Colombia, Art. 14, Nationality Law 43/1993, as amended by Art. 81, Decree 2150/1995.

[70] Bolivia, Art. 39, Law 2650 amending the Constitution, 13 April 2004; Bolivia, Art. 11, Supreme Decree 27.698/2004.

[71] Chile, Law 20.050, 6 August 2005, amending the Constitution.

[72] Ecuador, Art. 9, Law No. 000. RO/ 2, 13 February 1997, Political Constitution of 1978 codified in 1997.

[73] Peru, 1993 Constitution; and Nationality Law 26.574, 21 December 1995.

[74] Venezuela, 1999 Constitution.

[75] Paraguay, Art. 149, 1992 Constitution. See Agreement on Dual Nationality between Spain and Paraguay (25 June 1959).

[76] Uruguay, Arts 66 and 71, 1934 Constitution.

[77] See Chapter 4 pp. 99–101.

[78] H. Cassinelli Muñoz, *Derecho Público* (Montevideo: Fundación de Cultura Universitaria, 2009), p. 203.

[79] C. Courtis and A. P. Penchaszadeh, 'El (Im)posible Ciudadano Extranjero. Ciudadanía y Nacionalidad en Argentina', *Revista SAAP*, 9 (2015), 375–394, on 385.

citizenship in 1994 but only for natural-born Brazilians.[80] It took Brazil until 2016 to abolish the requirement for foreigners to renounce their previous citizenship when naturalising.[81]

Dual citizenship has become a normal feature of the South American land-scape since the 1990s. This was motivated by concerns about emigrants abroad in a period characterised by large numbers leaving the region.[82] Against that background, multiple citizenship has been a strategy that South American dual nationals use in order to overcome restrictive migration policies in destination countries, as well as a migration tool for South American countries to retain links and protect their diaspora.[83]

The Right to Migrate: Equal Treatment while Resident?

Which rights should admitted migrants have? This fundamental theoretical and practical question can be approached in several ways. For example, the classic division between civil, political and social rights often comes to the fore-front.[84] While there is general agreement that all residents will enjoy civil rights, discrepancies are more common regarding political and social rights.[85] An add-itional difficulty in regulating foreign residents' rights relates to the plethora of categories, fragmented by variables such as skills, length of residence, family links and nationality. It is not uncommon in some jurisdictions to grant highly skilled workers more rights than seasonal migrants enjoy.[86]

For it to be meaningful, countries that publicly defend the right to migra-tion should also have few restrictions on any migrant with a residence permit to enjoy civil, social and, possibly, political rights, regardless of their visa cat-egory. In other words, a right to migration should be intrinsically related to equal treatment. Any other scenario would be counterproductive since it would deprive the right of any *effet utile*: a true right to migrate goes hand in hand with a true right to reside. The following pages look at migrants' access to the labour market, economic and social rights and the franchise. Together with family reunification, these are all elements that the literature considers as facili-tating the legal inclusion of the newcomer.[87]

---

[80] Jerónimo, *Report on Citizenship Law: Brazil*, p. 19.

[81] Brazil, Decree 8.757, 10 May 2016.

[82] See Chapter 1, pp. 13–15.

[83] P. Mateos, 'Introducción' in P. Mateos (ed.), *Ciudadanía Múltiple y Migración. Perspectivas Latinoamericanas* (México D.F.: CIDE, 2015), pp. 9–22, on pp. 11–12.

[84] T. H. Marshall, *Citizenship and Social Class and Other Essays* (Cambridge University Press, 1950).

[85] Carens, *The Ethics of Immigration*, Ch 5.

[86] IOM, *Migración Calificada y Desarrollo: Desafíos para América del Sur*, Cuadernos Migratorios 7, August 2016.

[87] See H. Waldrauch and C. Hofinger, 'An Index to Measure the Legal Obstacles to the Integration of Migrants', *Journal of Ethnic and Migration Studies*, 23 (1997), 271–85; T. Huddleston, O. Bilgili, A. L. Joki and Z. Vankova, *Migrant Integration Policy Index* 2015.

Access to the Labour Market and Quotas

Access to the labour market includes not only the right to work under the direction of others but also the right to self-employment and entrepreneurship. States often restrict both through various methods such as tying residence permits to one job, labour sector or certain region in the national territory. Other restrictions comprise impeding self-employment activities, requiring companies to employ a minimum percentage of national workers, or simply prohibiting labour market access to select categories such as students, family members or investors, or allowing it only after a waiting period. Limitations often diminish with length of residence.[88] Nevertheless, several statutes stipulate that unlawful labour that breaches the conditions of a residence permit may lead to expulsion.[89]

The international framework provides states with some leeway. According to the ICMW, states may 'restrict access to limited categories of employment, functions, services or activities'. They also have 'free choice of remunerated activity in accordance with its legislation concerning recognition of occupational qualifications acquired outside its territory' but they shall provide mechanisms for recognising such qualifications. Additionally, they may limit a migrant's right to freely choose employment during the first two years of residence. Finally, States may grant priority to nationals during the first five years of residence.[90] Once the individual gains employment, however, equal treatment is robust and includes working conditions, terms of employment, unemployment benefits and protection against dismissal.[91]

In South America, laws often incorporate a broad conception of 'the right to work'. For example, in Argentina, Bolivia, Brazil, Ecuador, Peru and Uruguay, migrants enjoy equal treatment with nationals in regards to accessing work and employment.[92] In Argentina, migrants may perform any remunerated activity, being either employed or self-employed, regardless of whether they are permanent residents or not.[93] Other countries also hold similar provisions.[94] In general, employment possibilities are not limited to certain labour sectors.[95]

---

[88] See, for example, Art. 11 of the EU's 2003/109 Directive providing for equal treatment with nationals in a number of areas to third-country nationals who obtain long-term residence after having resided for five years. See D. Acosta, *The Long Term-Residence Status as a Subsidiary Form of EU Citizenship. An Analysis of Directive 2003/109* (Leiden: Martinus Nijhoff, 2011).

[89] Art. 20, ICMW.

[90] Art. 52, ICMW.

[91] Arts 25 and 54, ICMW. Also see Chapter 5, pp. 127–130.

[92] Argentina, Art. 6, Law 25.871/2004; Bolivia, Art. 48, Law 370/2013; Brazil, Art. 3(XI), Law 13.445/2017; Ecuador, Art. 51, 2017 Organic Law on Human Mobility; Peru, Art. 9, Legislative Decree 1350/2017; Uruguay, Art. 16, Law 18.250/2008.

[93] Argentina, Art. 51, Law 25.871/2004.

[94] Bolivia, Arts 12(II)(4) and 48, Law 370/2013; Uruguay, Art. 19 Law 18.250/2008.

[95] Argentina, Art. 6, Law 25.871/2004; Bolivia, Art. 48, Law 370/2013; Brazil, Art. 3(XI), Law 13.445/2017; Colombia, Art. 7, Decree 0834/2013. In Uruguay, the state may limit this possibility to certain labour sectors: Uruguay, Art. 23, Law 18.250/2008.

The shift to a new, more open, paradigm is apparent. Previous legislation – including laws still in force in countries such as Paraguay – was much more restrictive, allowing states to revoke residence permits when the holder was residing outside a particular zone of the country or was conducting an activity different from that allowed upon admission.[96] Similarly, in Venezuela, those working in jobs for which they were not originally hired, or in a different jurisdiction from that authorised, can be deported.[97] Finally, some countries such as Chile continue to apply quotas, a remnant from the aftermath of the 1929 crisis; others have eliminated them, such as Colombia, which did so in 2010.[98]

Economic and Social Rights

Numerous international and regional instruments recognise economic and social rights, also referred to as socio-economic human rights, as entitlements allowing individuals to meet their fundamental needs. All ten countries under analysis have ratified the most relevant international instrument, the ICESCR. Similarly, all countries except Chile and Venezuela have ratified the additional Protocol to the ACHR in the area of economic, social and cultural rights – often referred to as the Protocol of San Salvador.[99] Social and economic rights include not only the right to work but also the right to health care, education, social security and housing. Rampant inequality in the region makes it a challenge to realise such rights in practice, not only for foreigners but also for nationals.[100] Thus, the IACHR has expressed concerns for migrant vulnerability, notably those undocumented, due to frequent discrimination throughout the region while accessing social services to which they are entitled by law.[101]

The new migration laws clearly expand equal treatment between nationals and foreigners, at least as far as written law is concerned. Mostly, they incorporate numerous rights such as access to education and health care, including for the undocumented in some cases, as discussed in Chapter 5,[102] but also social security and housing.[103] In Venezuela, the law simply establishes equal treatment with nationals, with the only limitations being those already

---

[96] Paraguay, Arts 34 and 35, Law 978/96. See also Ecuador, Art. 68.3, Organic Law on Human Mobility.

[97] Venezuela, Art. 38, Law 37.944/2004.

[98] However, the legislation increased the requirements for employers as well as their responsibility to inform the authorities when hiring a non-national. See B. Sánchez Mojica, 'In Transit: Migration Policy in Colombia' in Cantor et al., pp. 81–104, on p. 97.

[99] Additional Protocol to the ACHR in the area of economic, social and cultural rights, Protocol of San Salvador, adopted on 17 November 1988 and entered into force on 16 November 1999. OAS, Treaty Series, No. 69.

[100] A. Ely Yamin (ed.), Derechos Económicos, Sociales y Culturales en América Latina. Del Invento a la Herramienta (México D.F.: Plaza y Valdés, 2006).

[101] IACHR, Second Progress Report of the Special Rapporteurship on Migrant Workers and their Families in the Hemisphere, para. 64.

[102] See Chapter 5, pp. 129–130.

[103] Bolivia, Art. 12, Law 370/2013; Uruguay, Art. 8, Law 18.250/2008.

enshrined in the Constitution.[104] For example, the relevant laws in Argentina and Brazil go as far as recognising absolute equal treatment when it comes to social services and public goods.[105] Peru and Ecuador are more cautious in their approach and do not mention certain entitlements such as housing.[106] Finally, in other countries such as Colombia, Paraguay and certainly Chile (where the Pinochet regime framework is still in place), social rights are absent from the legal frameworks regulating migration.[107]

While these advances are central, difficulties persist in foreigners' effective access to different rights and entitlements. Without any intention of offering an in-depth analysis, which is beyond the scope of this chapter, it suffices to say here that the CMW has identified numerous problems, including demanding long periods of continuous residence before accessing social security benefits,[108] or simply excluding foreigners from them.[109] Tribunals have played a certain role. In Argentina, for example, a 2007 Supreme Court ruling declared as unconstitutional the imposition of a twenty-year residence as a condition to obtain disability benefits.[110] Various reports of independent experts in several countries have also highlighted similar difficulties.[111]

Political Rights

Political rights have historically been related to citizenship. With minor exceptions,[112] the right to vote and to be elected had only been granted to

---

[104] Venezuela, Art. 13, Law 37.944/2004.

[105] Argentina, Art. 6, Law 25.871/2004; Brazil, Arts 3–4, Law 13.445/2017.

[106] Peru, Art. 9, Legislative Decree 1350/2017; Ecuador, Arts 42–52, 2017 Organic Law on Human Mobility.

[107] Colombia, Decree 834/2013; Paraguay, Migration Law 978/96. However, the 2016 Migration Law Proposal in Paraguay incorporates a long catalogue of migrant rights to be enjoyed along with nationals under conditions of equal treatment. See Paraguay, Arts 37–46, 2016 Proposal Migration Law, Ministry of the Interior, General Directorate on Migration. Chile, Law Decree 1094/1975. As in Paraguay, however, new law proposals incorporate an extensive catalogue of rights. See Chile, Arts 11–18, 2017 Migration Law Proposal.

[108] Uruguay, CMW/C/URY/CO/1, 2 May 2014, para. 32.

[109] Argentina, CMW/C/ARG/CO/1, 2 November 2011, paras 29–30.

[110] Argentina, Supreme Court, R. 350. XLI. Recurso de Hecho, R. A., D. c/ Estado Nacional, 4 September 2007.

[111] See, for example, P. Ceriani and D. Morales, *Argentina: Avances y Asignaturas*, pp. 19–23; C. Blouin and A. Enrico, 'Informe Alternativo al Comité de Protección de los Derechos de todos los Trabajadores Migratorios y de sus Familiares Perú', Instituto de Democracia y Derechos Humanos de la Pontificia Universidad Católica del Perú (IDEHPUCP), la Escuela de Derecho de la Universidad Ruiz de Montoya y Encuentros Servicio Jesuita de la Solidaridad, 2017; Coalición por las Migraciones y el Refugio, 'Informe Alternativo sobre el Cumplimiento de la Convención de Naciones Unidas de los Derechos de Todos los Trabajadores Migratorios y sus Familiares', Ecuador 2017.

[112] For example, in Ecuador, an 1895 Decree from 3 December established that foreigners could be elected as Municipal Ministers. See Ramírez, 'Del Aperturismo Segmentado al Control Migratorio'. The Argentinean city of Buenos Aires as well as Chile allowed foreigners to vote in local elections as early as 1917 and 1925, respectively. C. Escobar, 'Migration and Franchise Expansion in Latin America', European University Institute, EUDO Citizenship, Florence, 2017, p. 7.

nationals who also fulfilled age, property, literacy and gender requirements.[113] It is now commonly accepted that all nationals, regardless of their gender, literacy or wealth, have the right to vote in elections at all levels once they reach the majority age. Whilst restrictions on foreigners remain, there is a clear trend, both in Europe and in the Americas, of progressively extending the franchise to non-nationals, at least at the municipal level.[114] Political rights at the national level have also been extended to South Americans residing abroad.[115]

South America is at the forefront of these debates. Three countries extend the franchise to foreigners in national elections without discriminating by citizenship: Chile, Ecuador and Uruguay.[116] In Ecuador – the last country to join the list – foreigners can vote in all elections after five years of legal residence.[117] This period is also five years in Chile,[118] whereas it is fifteen in Uruguay,[119] but neither grant immigrants candidacy rights at the national level. In 2012, Argentina proposed an analogous idea to extend the franchise after two years of residence but it was unsuccessful.[120]

At the municipal level, all countries in South America have extended the franchise to foreigners. A foreigner can obtain the right to vote after two years in Peru, but only after ten or fifteen in Venezuela and Uruguay, respectively. Bolivia imposes a reciprocity condition.[121] Brazil is the only exception since only Portuguese foreign nationals may vote there. A proposal to allow voting at the municipal level for all foreigners entered the Brazilian Senate in 2012 but has not been approved as of the writing of this book in 2017.[122]

Security of Residence, Access to Citizenship and Expulsion

When migrating to another state, the last element of interest for non-nationals is a secured residence status. Jurisdictions will often enable the state to expel those who have entered or are residing without a residence permit,[123] those who have been absent from the territory for a certain period of time, or those

---

[113] See Chapter 2, pp. 41–42.

[114] J.-T. Arrighi and R. Bauböck, 'A Multilevel Puzzle: Migrants' Voting Rights in National and Local Elections', *European Journal of Political Research*, 56 (2017), 619–639.

[115] Escobar, 'Migration and Franchise Expansion in Latin America'.

[116] The only other two countries in the world to do this are Malawi and New Zealand.

[117] Ecuador, Art. 63, 2008 Constitution. Regarding candidacy rights, the individual needs both five years of regular residence as well as two years in the particular jurisdiction where he or she is running as a candidate. Ecuador, Art. 95, Electoral Organic Law, 27 April 2009.

[118] Chile, Art. 14, 1980 Constitution. Also see Chile, 1988 Organic Constitutional Law No. 18700 on Voting and Scrutiny.

[119] Uruguay, Art. 78, 1967 Constitution. Its 1934 Constitution introduced this provision.

[120] See Argentina, Proposal Aníbal Fernández 2012, Project of Law S-2696/12.

[121] For individual country information, see the database EUDO Citizenship, Conditions for Electoral Rights 2017, available at: http://globalcit.eu/conditions-for-electoral-rights/; for individual country profiles and studies, also see: http://eudo-citizenship.eu/country-profiles

[122] Brazil, Proposal to amend Arts 5, 12 and 14 of the Constitution to extend political rights to foreigners, number 25, 2012.

[123] See Chapter 5, pp. 130–131.

who commit a particular type of criminal offence. Regarding expulsion, there are numerous aspects to assess how restrictive a given legal framework is. For instance, they include accessing justice at a procedural and substantive level, decisions about when expulsion is compulsory after a criminal offence and interpreting individual situations, for example evaluating any circumstances such as family life that prevent expulsion.

Access to citizenship is also included in this section for two reasons. To begin with, those naturalising attain the most secure status, one that, in theory, thwarts expulsion for life. Furthermore, naturalisation is the final stage in the transformation process from foreigner to national. In South America, new nationals do not enjoy equal treatment with nationals by birth. This deserves explanation since it is profoundly telling of how the national and foreigner have been constructed in the region, as well as how history still has an impact on it.

Expulsion and Deportation

Foreigners may generally have their residence permits withdrawn if the reason that motivated their entry has ended or if they commit a criminal offence. Under the first category, states often terminate permits when labour contracts end, in the case of divorce or separation for spouses, or when studies conclude. The new South American migration laws often incorporate the possibility of changing legal status while residing in the country.[124] This is available not only for those who entered with a residence permit but also for tourists. Similar to the case of irregular migrants,[125] this establishes the possibility that at any given time during residence under one permit, a migrant may fulfil the substantive criteria required for another visa category and thus has the opportunity to shift to a new status. This procedural right potentially acts as a 'job seeker permit', one that is more readily available to nationals from countries exempt from visa requirements. In principle, the mechanism is open to anyone fulfilling the requirements of a different migration status, thus includes low-skilled workers. This is important for comparative reasons since some states often admit low-skilled workers for limited periods of time, or bar them altogether from entry.[126] Moreover, even in countries offering the possibility of shifting

---

[124] Argentina, Art. 20, Decree 616/2010; Bolivia, Art. 19, Supreme Decree 1923/2014; Brazil, Art. 36, Law 13.445/2017; Ecuador, Art. 69, 2017 Organic Law on Human Mobility; Peru, Art. 30, Legislative Decree 1350/2017 and Art. 65, Supreme Decree 007/2017-IN; Uruguay, Art. 39, Law 18.250/2008. In Colombia, this does not represent an individual procedural right but rather a state's administrative prerogative – except for Andean Community nationals, for whom it is a right. Colombia, Art. 25, Decree 834/2013 and Art. 6(2)(k), Decree 46/2013. Such right is limited to certain categories in Paraguay and does not exist in Venezuela. Paraguay, Art. 48, Law 978/96.

[125] See Chapter 5, pp. 137–138.

[126] T. A. Aleinikoff, 'International Legal Norms on Migration: Substance without Architecture' in R. Cholewinski, R. Perruchoud and E. MacDonald (eds), *International Migration Law: Developing Paradigms and Key Challenges* (The Hague: TMC Asser Press, 2007), pp. 467–479, on 468.

the migrant status, it is often required to abandon the host country territory in order to request such visa at a consulate abroad. In various countries, the procedure simply does not exist.[127]

Under the second category – specifically in the case of criminal offences or administrative breaches – there are two crucial aspects: the threshold under which expulsion is triggered and the grounds limiting expulsion after criminal offences.[128] States often distinguish between temporary residents and permanent ones, who enjoy stronger protection from expulsion. However, this is typically not the case in South America. Compared to other states, the new laws are overall not very innovative, nor offer a particularly enhanced protection against expulsion. They often distinguish between deportation – under which administrative breaches related to irregular migration are incorporated – and expulsion, reserved for criminal offences.[129] Deportation or expulsion is compulsory in a number of cases, including many related to a failure to regularise[130] or entering the territory clandestinely.[131] In some cases, the state can also impose fines.[132] The thresholds leading to expulsion after a criminal offence vary substantially between countries, ranging from automatic compulsory exit after serving any kind of sentence[133] to expulsion after serving a sentence of five years' imprisonment.[134] Moreover, bans on re-entry can last as long as fifteen years.[135] Here the tension between a rights-based approach versus securitisation is more apparent, and certain bureaucracies, such as ministries of the interior and police forces, have left a stronger mark while passing new laws. In the case of Ecuador, for example, those who are considered to be a threat or risk to the internal security of the country based on the information available to the state can see their applications for residence or naturalisation denied.[136] Such wide-ranging and discretionary provisions do not offer the necessary legal certainty needed in administrative procedures.

There are two major possible exceptions to the expulsion of the individual: the aforementioned family life, as well as the right to not undergo

---

[127] R. Cholewinski, 'The Rights of Migrant Workers' in R. Cholewinski, R. Perruchoud and E. MacDonald (eds), *International Migration Law*, pp. 255–274, on 261.

[128] The administrative procedure to challenge an expulsion order is intrinsically related to the fundamental right of access to justice, which is another key issue that goes beyond this chapter's scope, thus is not further discussed here. It suffices to say that in the Argentinean case, Decree 70/2017 raises numerous concerns of infringement of the right to access to justice.

[129] Venezuela, Arts 38–39, Law 37.944/2004.

[130] Peru, Arts 57–58, Legislative Decree 1350/2017; Venezuela, Arts 38–39, Law 37.944/2004.

[131] Ecuador, Art. 143, 2017 Organic Law on Human Mobility; Paraguay, Art. 27, 2016 Migration Law Proposal, Ministry of the Interior.

[132] Venezuela, Arts 36–37, Law 37.944/2004.

[133] Peru, Art. 58, Legislative Decree 1350/2017.

[134] Ecuador, Art. 68, 2017 Organic Law on Human Mobility.

[135] Peru, Art. 54, Legislative Decree 1350/2017. In Ecuador, it varies between two, three, or ten years, depending on the reason behind the deportation or expulsion measure. Arts 140–147, 2017 Organic Law on Human Mobility.

[136] Ecuador, Arts 61.4, 64.4, 79.3 and 85.3, 2017 Organic Law on Human Mobility.

torture or cruel, inhuman, or degrading punishment or treatment (Art. 5, ACHR). The IACtHR has interpreted this non-refoulement obligation in the case of *Wong*, which revolved around the extradition of a Chinese national from Peru, when the death penalty in China could have been a possible outcome.[137] The Court referenced the Inter-American Convention to Prevent and Punish Torture prohibiting states from expelling any person who could face torture or cruel, inhuman or degrading treatment upon return.[138] Moreover, the *Mortlock* case had a similar result: a Jamaican national suffering from HIV/AIDS faced deportation due to a criminal offence in the USA. The IACHR declared that the applicant would receive inadequate treatment in the country of origin, amounting to 'a *de facto* sentence to protracted suffering and unnecessarily premature death', thus violating Article XXVI of the American Declaration of the Rights and Duties of Man.[139]

Access to Citizenship

In theory, naturalisation results in foreigners obtaining complete equal treatment with nationals, including absolute protection from expulsion. When compared to other states, access to citizenship in South America and the status of new nationals are peculiar, and are also still largely influenced by choices made two hundred years ago.[140]

To begin with, automatic *ius soli* for individuals born in the territory is the general rule.[141] *Ius soli* is automatic in the sense that, subject to two minor exceptions, there are no other requirements other than birth in the territory.[142] First, four countries (Argentina, Bolivia, Brazil and Chile) do not grant nationality to those born to parents who are foreign diplomats. Second, Chile does not apply *ius soli* if the parents are in transit.[143] Colombia is the only country

---

[137] IACtHR, *Case of Wong Ho Wing*. Merits, Reparations and Costs. Judgment, 26 June 2012, Series C. No. 297.

[138] *Ibid.*, para. 135.

[139] In the same case, the Commission laid down guarantees to be respected in expulsion procedures, namely: the need to respect due process and to provide an individual decision, prohibiting collective expulsion, respect of the right to family life, as well as life and physical and mental integrity, the right for special protection of children and, finally, prohibiting discrimination on grounds of race, colour, religion or sex, and prohibiting expulsions leading to cruel, degrading and inhumane treatment. IACHR, Admissibility and Merits, No. 63/08, Case 12.534, *Andrea Mortlock* (United States), 25 July 2008, paras 78, 94 and 102. See the approach by the ECtHR in: C. Costello, *The Human Rights of Migrants and Refugees in European Law* (Oxford University Press, 2016), pp. 180–195.

[140] See Chapter 2.

[141] This is also the case in the USA. However, no EU Member State follows automatic *ius soli*.

[142] This certainly does not indicate that there are no problems when it comes to registering births; some populations indeed face numerous obstacles for obtaining nationality. See J. Vengoechea Barrios, *Born in the Americas. The Promise and Practice of Nationality Laws in Brazil, Chile, and Colombia* (New York: Open Society Justice Initiative, 2017).

[143] The previous administrative practice denied nationality to those born to parents in irregular situation. However, in numerous cases the Supreme Court in Chile has confirmed that parents residing in the country without a regular permit cannot be considered as being in transit,

where *ius soli* is not automatic. Persons born in the country to foreign nationals can only become Colombians if their parents are domiciled – being interpreted as legally residing – in the country at the time of birth. This has its historical origins in the circumstances surrounding the 1886 Constitution, which first incorporated the restriction.[144] Apart from this exception, automatic *ius soli* has not historically been discussed and we can observe a very strong continuity in its regulation.[145] In this respect, the IACtHR has interpreted Art. 20 ACHR on the right to a nationality as impeding deprivation of nationality due to immigration status. In fact, individuals do not transmit their immigration status to their children.[146]

Peculiarities do not end with *ius soli*. Residence periods for those willing to naturalise are relatively short, ranging from two years in Argentina and Peru, three in Bolivia, Ecuador and Paraguay, four in Brazil and five in Chile, Colombia and Uruguay (in this last case to access legal citizenship rather than nationality);[147] the only exception is Venezuela, which requires ten years.[148] The historical origins of this trend can be traced back to the years following independence, when waiting periods before naturalisation were considerably shortened as a way to attract settlers.[149] In Argentina, the 1869 law continues to regulate naturalisation. Its Supreme Court had clearly established that residency did not refer to any particular legal category, thus migrants in irregular situations could also apply for nationality after proving two years of dwelling in the territory, something that Argentina amended in 2017.[150] Other countries in the region also require a regular residence permit in order to accumulate the necessary number of years.[151]

thus their offspring is entitled to Chilean nationality. See C. Fuentes Maureira, V. Hugo Lagos, D. Lawson and M. Rodríguez, '3.000 Niños Esperando su Nacionalidad. La Necesidad de Contar con Remedios Colectivos para Resolver Vulneraciones Individuales de Derechos' in Universidad Diego Portales, *Anuario de Derecho Público 2016* (Santiago de Chile: Universidad Diego Portales, 2016), pp. 549–571.

[144] See Chapter 2, p. 58.

[145] Notable exceptions include the 1947 Venezuelan Constitution, which stated that foreign parents had to be domiciled or resident for *ius soli* to apply, a requirement that only lasted six years until the 1953 Constitution. In Chile, there were also some unsuccessful attempts under the first Piñera administration (2010–2014) to impose a similar prerequisite.

[146] IACtHR, *Juridical Condition and Rights of the Undocumented Migrants*, para. 134. Also see IACtHR, Case of the *Yean and Bosico Children*.

[147] Argentina, Art. 2, Law 346 on Citizenship, as amended by Law 26.774, 31 October 2012; Bolivia, Art. 41, Law 370/2013; Brazil, Art. 65, Law 13.445/2017; Chile, Art. 2, Supreme Decree 5142/1960 (and subsequent modifications, the last of which was in January 2016); Colombia, Art. 5, Law 43/1993 on Nationality, as amended; Ecuador, Art. 71, 2017 Organic Law on Human Mobility; Paraguay, Art. 148, 1992 Constitution; Peru, Art. 3, Law on Nationality 26574/1995, as amended; Uruguay, Art. 75, 1967 Constitution, as amended.

[148] Venezuela, Art. 33, 1999 Constitution.

[149] See Chapter 2, pp. 52–53.

[150] Argentina, Law 346 on citizenship, 1 October 1869; Argentina, Supreme Court of the Nation, Ni, I Hsing s/carta de ciudadanía, 23 June 2009. However, Decree of Necessity and Emergency No. 70/2017 has established that such residence must be regular.

[151] See, for example, Art. 142, 2009 Bolivian Constitution.

During the nineteenth century, naturalisation eligibility required property, capital, performing an industry, science or art, or having carried out outstanding services in favour of the state.[152] Whilst most countries now simply demand proof of a source of income or occupation, the old wording is still relevant.[153] For example, in Argentina, those who introduce a new industry or a useful invention, or who come to the country to teach in any field of education can see their residence requirement waived before applying for naturalisation.[154] Also, all the countries except for Colombia have routes to naturalise for those who perform exceptional services in favour of the state.[155]

However, one should not rush into concluding that naturalisation is regulated in a completely liberal fashion. Indeed, several obstacles exist that may account for the strikingly low numbers of individuals who obtain citizenship in each country. In Colombia, for example, the statistics show 108 and 109 naturalisations in 2010 and 2011 respectively. In Peru, the number increased from 589 in 2001 to 1,118 in 2012. In Chile, successful applicants in the period 2005–2014 oscillated between a maximum of 1,225 in 2012 and a minimum of 502 in 2006, a very small percentage of the more than 450,000 foreigners estimated to reside in the country by 2015. In Paraguay, only 777 foreign nationals obtained citizenship between 1996 and 2013.[156]

Some reasons might be suggested for these low numbers, which in any case continue a historical trend.[157] In some cases, such as Paraguay, the need to renounce current nationality except in certain cases (e.g. when holding Spanish citizenship) may act as a powerful deterrent. Other explanations point towards regional flows and the fact that the MERCOSUR Residence Agreement, as seen in Chapter 7, provides regional migrants with rights comparable in certain aspects to nationals, thus limiting incentives to naturalise. A lack of information or government campaigns, and procedures full of administrative obstacles and requirements, also account for this trend.[158] Furthermore, naturalisation does not constitute an entitlement, except in two countries: Argentina and Chile. In Uruguay it is also an entitlement, but there foreigners cannot naturalise and can only obtain legal citizenship as opposed to full nationality. In all the rest, it represents a discretionary power exercised by different authorities, including the executive (e.g. Bolivia, Ecuador, Peru) or the Ministry of Foreign Affairs

---

[152] See Chapter 2, pp. 48–49.

[153] In Paraguay, Art. 148 of the 1992 Constitution still mentions that those willing to naturalise must practise a science, art or industry, but also adds profession, within the country. Uruguay uses the same wording, Art. 75, 1967 Constitution.

[154] Argentina, Art. 2, Law 346 on Citizenship.

[155] Acosta, *Regional Report on Citizenship*, p. 9.

[156] *Ibid.*

[157] See Chapter 2, p. 53.

[158] On Argentina, see Courtis and Penchaszadeh, 'El (Im)posible Ciudadano Extranjero'; on Brazil, see T. G. Blanchette, '"Almost a Brazilian." Gringos, Immigration, and Irregularity in Brazil' in D. Acosta and A. Wiesbrock (eds), *Global Migration. Old Assumptions, New Dynamics* (Santa Barbara, CA: Praeger, 2015), pp. 167–194.

(e.g. Colombia). Moreover, these laws often include requirements which are also common in other jurisdictions, such as a lack of criminal convictions (e.g. in Argentina, Bolivia, Brazil, Chile, Ecuador, Peru), an oath of loyalty (e.g. in Argentina, Colombia), civic knowledge including history, geography or constitutional law (e.g. in Bolivia, Colombia, Ecuador, Paraguay); language proficiency (e.g. in Brazil, Colombia, Ecuador, Paraguay), good behaviour or morals (e.g. in Brazil, Chile, Ecuador, Paraguay, Peru, Uruguay), not posing a danger to public interests or security (e.g. in Chile, Ecuador), as well as good health (e.g. in Brazil and Ecuador).[159]

Finally, as discussed in Chapter 2, naturalised citizens have historically been discriminated against when compared to nationals by birth. Constitutional law has denied naturalised individuals access to the highest positions – mainly in the executive, legislative and judiciary branches.[160] This regional peculiarity continues today in all ten countries.[161] Several types of discrimination can be highlighted. States most often impose limitations on executive power and the position of president, but they usually also apply to the judiciary and legislative branches. Venezuela represents the most extreme example of this historical continuity since naturalised citizens are plainly excluded from several of the highest positions in all three powers or, on other occasions, require fifteen years of residence.[162] All the remaining countries, except Bolivia,[163] also exclude access to the presidency.[164] Access to parliamentary representation and to judge or magistrate positions in the highest tribunals (in the Supreme or Constitutional Courts) is also restricted to citizens by birth in five countries,[165] while three others require a number of years post-naturalisation before they can be elected,[166] or even

---

[159] Acosta, *Regional Report on Citizenship*.

[160] See Chapter 2, pp. 49–50.

[161] In Europe, the European Convention on Nationality, in Art. 5, provides that 'Each State Party shall be guided by the principle of non-discrimination between its nationals, whether they are nationals by birth or have acquired its nationality subsequently.' Council of Europe, ETS 166 – European Convention on Nationality, 6.XI.1997.

[162] Venezuela, Art. 41, 1999 Constitution. It completely excludes taking up office as President, Vice-President, President of the National Assembly, Magistrate at the Supreme Tribunal, General Prosecutor, Ombudsman, posts in certain ministries, among others. It requires fifteen years of naturalised citizenship for all Ministers, Parliamentary Members, Governors and Mayors.

[163] For the first time in history, the 2009 Bolivian Constitution removed the requirement to be citizen by birth for the Presidency. However, to perform several important positions in the police force, the army or to be Vice Minister of Defence, it is necessary to be Bolivian by birth. See Arts 247 and 253, 2009 Bolivian Constitution.

[164] Argentina, Art. 89, 1994 Constitution; Colombia, Art. 191, 1991 Constitution; Chile, Art. 25, 1980 Constitution; Ecuador, Art. 142, 2008 Constitution; Paraguay, Art. 228, 1992 Constitution; Uruguay, Art. 151, 1967 Constitution; Brazil, Art. 12, 1988 Constitution; Peru, Art. 110, 1993 Constitution.

[165] In Brazil, Art. 12, 1988 Constitution; in Colombia, Arts 172 and 232, 1991 Constitution; in Paraguay, Arts 162, 221, 223 and 258, 1992 Constitution; in Peru, Arts 90, 124 and 147, 1993 Constitution.

[166] Six years for Senator and eight for Judge in the Supreme Court in Argentina, Arts 55 and 110, 1994 Constitution; in Chile, naturalised citizens have the option to run for public office or as a

vote.[167] Finally, unlike nationals by birth, states may sometimes deprive newly naturalised citizens of the nationality, for instance if they reside abroad for a certain period (e.g. three years for Ecuador and Paraguay) or by a Court order in Brazil and Venezuela.[168] They are also ineligible – at least for the first five years – for free residence rights throughout South America under the MERCOSUR Residence Agreement and, in some cases, from transmitting citizenship to their offspring if residing abroad.[169]

Discussion

Since the turn of the century, a robust language around human dignity and equal treatment has re-emerged in South America.[170] This pervasive language of rights has become epitomised by the enunciation of a right to migrate, often elevated to the category of a human right. Whilst the legal frameworks adopted by the late twentieth century were restrictive or utilitarian at best, the new laws shift their focus towards a rights-based approach. What are the reasons behind this change and, more importantly, how significant is such a shift?

Rights are often divided between those that are fundamental and those that are not; the first category is more selective, with human rights at its core. Since constitutional bills of rights often enshrine fundamental rights, they are generally better protected and take precedence over other domestic laws. An important part of the literature refers to the increasing confusion as to which rights pertain to each category. It is argued that a 'human rights industry' has stimulated the expansion of the human rights category to be ever more inclusive and specific, resulting in risking 'rights inflation' or 'human rights perfectionism'.[171] Arguably, the proclamation of a right to migrate falls under this category.

When it comes to constructing the legal figure of the foreigner and her rights, two of the aspects mentioned in Chapter 5 come to the forefront: the international legal framework and the yearning for reciprocity. The ICMW, ratified by most states, provides an initial answer regarding which sources states should use for their new migration laws' bills of rights. In turn, the *pro-homine* principle of interpretation allows the IACtHR to conceive the migrant as 'a human being in need of protection' rather than an 'alien subject to the control

---

candidate in popular election only after five years (Art. 10(4), 1980 Constitution); seven years are required to become a Senator and ten for a Judge in the Supreme Court in Uruguay, Arts 98 and 235, 1967 Constitution.

[167] Uruguay requires three years to exercise citizenship rights (Art. 75, 1967 Constitution). In Paraguay, it is two years to become a citizen and thus obtain political rights (Art. 152, 1992 Constitution).

[168] Acosta, *Regional Report on Citizenship*, p. 15.

[169] Ecuador, Peru and Venezuela impose limitations: see *ibid.*, p. 15.

[170] As concerns equal treatment, such language was already present in the nineteenth century: see Chapter 2.

[171] S. Greer, 'Being "Realistic" about Human Rights', *Northern Ireland Legal Quarterly*, 60 (2009), 147–161.

of the sovereign state'.[172] Indeed, Latin America's concern with migrant rights is long-standing – as seen in the first part of this book – first as a destination and, later, as origin countries. As already argued in Chapter 4, Latin American proposals were central to incorporating certain fundamental rights related to human mobility – the right to leave any country, to seek and enjoy asylum and to nationality – in the UDHR (Arts 13–15).[173]

Its importance notwithstanding, the international framework cannot explain the whole picture. Many rights are worded more broadly in South America when it comes to accessing, for instance, family reunion, the labour market and socio-economic and political rights. It is here that the desire for reciprocity and the concern for emigrants emerge as key aspects. Scholars in the region have elucidated how introducing rights for foreigners actually stemmed from the concern for expatriates overseas.[174] For example, this was important in extending the franchise to foreigners in Colombia and Ecuador. When Ecuador granted a voting right to foreigners in national elections in its 2008 Constitution, it mainly had Ecuadorians abroad in mind, rather than non-nationals in the country.[175] Similarly, supporters of the new migration frameworks in Brazil and Chile often make use of the need to reciprocate and thus reflect treatment that is desired for co-nationals abroad in their own domestic frameworks.[176] Small immigrant populations at home also make it easier to introduce certain guarantees in the letter of the law.

All this intertwines with the phenomenon of aspirational language, to which we have already referred in the context of constitutional law.[177] In this light, the right to migrate would appear as largely aspirational. The new Latin American Constitutionalism often announces rights without offering the material conditions and institutional support for fulfilling them.[178] Whilst aspirational language is not negative per se – and may indeed denote an active attempt to realise future goals and dreams that cannot yet be achieved[179] – it can damage the law's legitimacy when the legal context is not considered. One can also appreciate aspirational language as 'purely symbolic'.[180] According to this understanding, the state is not primarily regulating a social aspect, but rather portraying itself in the international arena in a particular fashion. Purely

---

[172] Dembour, *When Humans Become Migrants*, p. 8.

[173] P. G. Carozza, 'From Conquest to Constitutions: Retrieving a Latin American Tradition of the Idea of Human Rights', *Human Rights Quarterly*, 25 (2003), 281–313.

[174] On emigration policies, see: L. Pedroza, P. Palop and B. Hoffmann, *Emigrant Policies in Latin America and the Caribbean* (Santiago de Chile: FLASCO Chile, 2016).

[175] Escobar, *Migration and Franchise Expansion in Latin America*, p. 8. Góngora-Mera, Herrera and Müller, 'The Frontiers of Universal Citizenship', p. 3.

[176] Acosta and Freier, 'Turning the Immigration Policy Paradox Up-Side Down?'.

[177] See Part II, Consolidation, pp. 114–115.

[178] Gargarella, *Latin American Constitutionalism*, p. 201.

[179] K. Lane Scheppele, 'Aspirational and Aversive Constitutionalism: The Case for Studying Cross-Constitutional Influence Through Negative Models', *International Journal of Constitutional Law*, 1 (2003), 296–324, on 299.

[180] Mirow, *Latin American Constitutions*, p. 262.

symbolic provisions may also result from domestic legislative processes, which involve actors with a variety of agendas. Faced with a text that clearly regulates visa requirements, denies entry and expels foreigners, some see including the right to migrate as a victory whereas others interpret it as an impossible dream. Of course, through judicial interpretation, aspirational clauses may 'take root' and become 'protective'.[181] From an optimistic perspective, the Supreme and Constitutional Courts in South America have produced notable rulings and judges can use the constitutionalisation of human rights, the doctrine on conventionality control and the *pro homine* principle of interpretation to advance individuals' rights.[182] A more cautious standpoint will immediately raise concerns affecting the rule of law, such as its 'weak normativity' and 'lack of institutional capacity' to effectively implement it.[183] Courts cannot arguably tackle all of these challenges without the adequate cooperation of other institutional actors.[184]

The right to migrate thus appears as an aspirational provision, an important declaration of intentions, as well as a possible aid in judicial interpretations of the legal frameworks' structure and objectives – but not as a genuine fundamental right. An objective of any migration law or policy is also to make countries appear 'more modern and civilized'.[185] From this point of view, introducing the right to migration can be seen as a successful enterprise or, upon further reflection, an exercise in hypocrisy, an entitlement that will only partly apply to South American regional migrants[186] and to those from Europe and the USA, or other countries exempted from visa requirements, but not to those who need a visa to enter. Continuously emphasising expulsion in all new laws for those who clandestinely enter the territory, in countries with thousands of kilometres of porous borders, testifies to the ongoing importance of territorial sovereignty.

In the present construction of the foreigner in South America, history still plays a notable role beyond enunciating the right of entry. *Ius soli*, short periods of residence prior to naturalisation, as well as extending rights to foreigners are all remnants of previous legislative practices that took root throughout decades in the nineteenth century. The twentieth-century restrictiveness is slowly giving way to a resurgence of old approaches, albeit with numerous contradictions and caveats. A critical approach is crucial here to ensure that legal provisions – that in theory rely on a strong framework of human dignity to entitle the foreigner to equal treatment – materialise in effective access to genuine rights that do not remain dead letters.

---

[181] *Ibid.*, p. 162.
[182] See Part II, pp. 115–117.
[183] Von Bogdandy, '*Ius Constitutionale Commune*', pp. 21–22. Abramovich, 'Autonomía y Subsidiariedad', p. 222.
[184] García, *Nueva Política Migratoria Argentina y Derechos de la Movilidad*.
[185] FitzGerald and Cook-Martin, *Culling the Masses*, p. 21.
[186] See Chapter 7.

Conclusion

Thus far in the twenty-first century, the foreigner has been constructed under a new light. New migration laws in South America are strikingly different to those of the twentieth century, in both their structure and the enumeration of rights they include. Yet, a century-long set of restrictions has left a profound scar: many provisions in the legal texts contradict a rights-based approach.

In the case of irregular migrants, concerns about the situation of diasporic communities in the USA and Europe have been central in shifting attitudes towards the legal position of foreigners. Aspects such as dual citizenship, voting rights and access to socio-economic rights such as health care and education are first and foremost related to this anxiety about the status of nationals abroad. The new laws indeed incorporate numerous emigrant provisions and thus are rightly labelled as human mobility and migration, rather than just immigration. Numerous organisations, including the IACHR and the CMW, have identified and denounced the implementation difficulties as well as discrimination in accessing rights.[187]

This chapter has also argued for the need to look at migration and nationality laws together in order to assess the true openness, or not, of the regulation of the status of the foreigner in a given country. Uruguay is paradigmatic of this in having possibly the most open migration law framework in the region in numerous aspects, but at the same time being the only country where naturalisation is not possible and where foreigners can only obtain legal citizenship and never become nationals – regardless of the period they have resided in the country.

Challenges remain in the region, including whether the right to migrate can be considered as genuinely fundamental, or as a strongly qualified one. Nonetheless, South America offers lessons and perspectives in constructing the foreigner's status that are important but that still need to be better detailed and expanded before being considered truly unique, innovative and path-breaking in a comparative perspective.

---

[187] The last example of this would be the 2017 CMW's Report on Ecuador which, despite acknowledging the advance in rights protection that the 2017 Organic Law on Human Mobility has brought, is very critical of some of its provisions, notably on access to health care, regularisation and unequal treatment with nationals on a number of areas. See Concluding Observations on the Third Periodic Report by Ecuador, CMW/C/ECU/CO/3, 14 September 2017.

7

Open Borders and the Construction of a South American Citizen

> *The Union of South American Nations has as specific objectives: ... The Consolidation of a South American identity through the progressive recognition of rights to nationals of one Member State residing in any of the other Member States, with the aim of achieving a South American citizenship.*[1]

Introduction

This chapter is devoted to the region's free residency and movement of people and completes our analysis of South American migration and citizenship law in the twenty-first century. With the adoption of free residency and mobility agreements, nationals of the countries involved obtain a new status that eliminates, in theory, the possibility of being undocumented. At the same time, regional agreements expand individual rights related to access to the labour market, family reunification, socio-economic entitlements and even political participation. The gradual opening of borders at the regional level, coupled with equal treatment, approximates foreigners' status to a privileged category similar to nationals. Through that process, states partially forfeit their capacity to control who is entitled to reside in their territory.

Freedom to move and reside, as well as open borders, are of course neither new nor unique to South America. As previously discussed, an incipient regional subject was already a legal construction during the nineteenth century.[2] Today, the expansion of human rights law, coupled with the explosion of regional processes of integration, are the two most important phenomena that have limited the state's capacity to restrict the entry of foreigners and their rights.[3] Globally, around 120 countries are presently involved in some economic

---

[1] Art. 3 (i) Founding Treaty of the Union of South American Nations (UNASUR), Brasilia, 23 May 2008 (author's translation). 'La Unión de Naciones Suramericanas tiene como objetivos específicos: ... La consolidación de una identidad suramericana a través del reconocimiento progresivo de derechos a los nacionales de un Estado Miembro residentes en cualquiera de los otros Estados Miembros, con el fin de alcanzar una ciudadanía suramericana.'

[2] See Chapter 3.

[3] S. Iglesias Sánchez, 'Free Movement of Persons and Regional International Organisations' in R. Plender (ed.), *Issues in International Migration Law* (Leiden: Brill, 2015), pp. 223–260.

integration scheme facilitating free movement, either at a bilateral or multilateral level,[4] with varying degrees of development, scope and implementation.[5] For example, the North American Free Trade Agreement (NAFTA) – with its limited mobility for a reduced category of individuals – is paradigmatic of a much more restrained arrangement.[6] By contrast, the EU is presented as the most advanced regime, wherein EU citizens enjoy an individual right to move and reside freely throughout the Member States. The EU is indeed referred to at various points during the present chapter. The intention of these references is not at all to frame the EU as a model for what should be done in South America. Rather, the EU's experience can help to anticipate possible challenges in the construction of a regional mobility regime, suited to the particular idiosyncrasies in South America, and reflect on possible answers before they become truly problematic.

Since the turn of the century, regional mobility and the eventual adoption of a common South American citizenship have taken centre stage.[7] The 2002 MERCOSUR Residence Agreement, as well as the 2003 CAN's Decision 545, have positioned South America as a focal actor at the global level. Whilst a true South American citizenship may remain elusive in the short term, the MERCOSUR Residence Agreement has facilitated access to legal residence for thousands of South Americans.[8] At a moment when EU citizenship and its free movement regime is suffering from contestation, South America could emerge as an alternative model demonstrating multilateral and bilateral efforts. Africa, Central America and the Caribbean, as well as the Post-Soviet space face similar challenges, such as a high degree of informality in labour markets, and

---

[4] Chetail, 'The Transnational Movement of Persons under General International Law', p. 35.

[5] A. Pécoud and P. de Guchteneire (eds), *Migration without Borders: Essays on the Free Movement of People* (New York: Berghahn Books, 2007).

[6] NAFTA partly regulates the entry of business visitors, intra-company transferees, traders and investors. R. Alarcón, 'The Free Circulation of Skilled Migrants in North America' in Pécoud and de Guchteneire (eds), *Migration without Borders*, pp. 243–257. On EU citizenship see: D. Kochenov (ed.), *EU Citizenship and Federalism: The Role of Rights* (Cambridge University Press, 2017).

[7] See 2011 Brasilia Declaration entitled 'Towards a South American Citizenship', Brasilia, 19–21 October 2011; Declaration of the Extraordinary Meeting of the Council of Heads of State and Government of the UNASUR, Quito 4–5 December 2014, para. 14.

[8] According to the most important report, between 2004 and 2013, almost two million South Americans obtained a temporary residence permit in one of the nine countries implementing the agreement, with Argentina, Chile and Brazil taking the lead in granting residence permits. This does not necessarily imply, however, that the increase in regional flows is a result of the agreement. For various reasons, more research is needed to make such conclusions. First, the data show temporary permits granted since 2004 when the agreement was not yet in force. Second, a large number of those having obtained permits under the agreement were already residing in the host country before it came into force. Third, the data are incomplete for many countries. IOM, *Estudio sobre Experiencias en la Implementación del Acuerdo de Residencia del MERCOSUR y Asociados*, XIV South American Conference on Migration, Reference Document, Lima, 16–17 October 2014.

thus could learn from this alternative approach. The significance of a coherent South American model cannot be underestimated.

This chapter first describes the present mobility and residence regime, with select inclusion of South American citizenship debates. It pays special attention to historical developments at the CAN and MERCOSUR level, as well as briefly alluding to UNASUR and the Pacific Alliance. The second section concentrates on contradictions and open questions distressing the current regime and the possibility of future common citizenship. Regional migrants have the same concerns as any other migrant regarding entry, rights during stay and the security of their residence – i.e. against expulsion. All three are affected by the incongruity between different legal instruments, their varied implementation, and the lack of adjudication. The absence of a true right of entry under the MERCOSUR Residence Agreement emerges as a crucial omission. The main concern here is to assess the actual extension of mobility and residence rights in South America: they may point in the direction of a real South American citizenship in the making or, on the contrary, these entitlements may be more appropriately labelled as mere discretionary, executive acts of temporary regularisation for certain regional migrants. The chapter wraps up with some thoughts on whether the mobility agreements emerging correspond to an open-borders vision and if they make it possible to imagine a future South American citizenship.

The Free Movement of People in South America

Since the turn of the century, the debate on regional free movement, residence and, eventually, citizenship has accelerated and been replicated in numerous fora. This section describes the free movement and residence of people under the CAN[9] and MERCOSUR, with a brief reference to UNASUR and the Pacific Alliance.

The Free Movement of People and the CAN

In 1948, the Economic Commission for Latin America (ECLA) – or CEPAL in the Spanish acronym – was established by the UN Economic and Social Council.[10] ECLA's work influenced the adoption of the Montevideo Treaty in 1960, which launched the Latin American Free Trade Association (LAFTA, ALALC Treaty in its Spanish acronym).[11] Its aim was to progressively create

---

[9] This chapter does not intend to discuss every single instrument that CAN has adopted; for a detailed analysis of all the initiatives and instruments, see J. Goizueta Vértiz, I. Gómez Fernández, M. I. González Pascual (eds), *La Libre Circulación de Personas en los Sistemas de Integración Económica: Modelos Comparados. Unión Europea, Mercosur y Comunidad Andina* (Pamplona: Aranzadi, 2012).

[10] See UN Economic and Social Council Resolution 106(VI), 25 February 1948.

[11] Montevideo Treaty for the Establishment of a Zone of Free Trade between Countries in Latin America, 18 February 1960. The Treaty was signed in 1960 by Argentina, Brazil, Chile, Paraguay,

a common market for capital, services and goods; people were not included.[12] In 1967, the summit of the Heads of State of the Americas concluded that such a common market was to be functional by 1985 and would result from merging the Latin American Free Trade Association and the Central American Common Market.[13] It was reasoned that improved terrestrial communications would facilitate the circulation of not only goods but also people.

The uneasiness with the prevalent role that Argentina and Brazil had played[14] led Bolivia, Chile, Colombia, Ecuador and Peru to establish the CAN in 1969 by signing the Cartagena Treaty. The agreement, subsidiary to the 1960 Montevideo Treaty, was open for other states to join.[15] Its objective is to promote development and better standards of living, as well as to accelerate growth through economic integration, with the final aim of transforming the Latin American Free Trade Association into a common market. The free movement of people was once again left out of the final text.

It was only in 1973 that workers came onto the agenda. The Simón Rodríguez Socio-labour Integration Covenant facilitated regional mobility and the protection of migrant workers.[16] Later, the 1976 Andean Labour Migration Instrument (Decision 116) devised a procedure to hire regional workers through national labour migration offices.[17] Regional workers and their families were to enjoy equal treatment in labour rights, education, housing, health care and social security.[18] Member States also had to adopt measures to regularise undocumented migrants.[19] Decision 113 complemented this regime by instituting an Andean Instrument for Social Security. For the first time, individual rights and guarantees were directly derived from the Andean Community. However, the timing of adoption was unfortunate: first, Chile – having been under a military dictatorship since 1973 – left the bloc in 1976. Second, the financial crisis of the 1980s, known as the *década perdida* (lost decade), and the ensuing privatisation

---

Peru and Uruguay. Mexico also signed it. The remaining South American countries did so later: Colombia (1961), Ecuador (1962), Venezuela (1966) and Bolivia (1967).

[12] The 1960 Montevideo Treaty and the LAFTA was then substituted by the Latin-American Integration Association (LAIA, ALADI in its Spanish acronym) instituted by the 1980 Montevideo Treaty, 12 August 1980. Thirteen states are involved: all those in South America – except Guyana and Suriname – and Cuba, Mexico and Panama. Any Latin American country may request to join. Its overall purpose is to reduce obstacles to trade and has an end goal of establishing a common Latin American internal market.

[13] Declaration of the Presidents of the Americas. Summit of the Heads of State of the Americas, Punta del Este, Uruguay, 12–14 April 1967.

[14] O. Saldías, 'Libre Circulación de Personas y la Autonomía del Ordenamiento Jurídico de la Comunidad Andina' in J. Goizueta Vértiz, I. Gómez Fernández, M. I. González Pascual (eds), pp. 187–206.

[15] Art. 109, Cartagena Agreement. Venezuela joined in 1973 and announced its withdrawal in 2006. Chile left the bloc in 1976.

[16] Arts 3 and 4, Simón Rodríguez Covenant on Socio-Labour, signed in Caracas on 26 October 1973.

[17] Art. 7, Decision 116, Andean Instrument on Labour Migration.

[18] *Ibid.*, Arts 12–13.

[19] See Chapter 5, p. 135.

and deregulation policies of the 1990s, left little political willingness to implement these instruments in the ensuing years.[20]

In 1999, coinciding with the Community's thirtieth anniversary, the Presidents of the then five Member States adopted the Cartagena Act, which recognised the need to strengthen regional integration, with the free movement of people playing a central role.[21] Against this background, CAN adopted a new Andean Labour Migration Instrument in 2003 (Decision 545), together with various other measures. This *corpus iuris* provides the right of entry for short stays, certain socio-labour rights and also consular protection abroad.[22]

However, Decision 545 falls short of laying down a truly comprehensive mobility regime. In contrast with initial drafts, where the free movement for all workers and the self-employed were enshrined,[23] the final Decision only includes intra-corporate transferees, frontier and seasonal workers, as well as those accepting a job offer in another Member State. These groups enjoy equal treatment and a number of rights, including family reunion.[24] By 2015, all four Member States – Venezuela left the bloc in 2006 – had transposed the Decision into domestic law.[25] Earlier, in 2008, CAN had first referred to the concept of Andean citizenship with the aims of deepening the process of regional mobility, enhancing the sense of belonging to a common community, as well

---

[20] A. di Filippo and R. Franco, *Integración Regional, Desarrollo y Equidad* (México D.F.: Siglo XXI, 2000), p. 78.

[21] Cartagena Act, 27 May 1999.

[22] Decision 545, Andean Instrument on Labour Migration, Recinto Quirama, Departamento de Antioquia, Colombia, 25 June 2003. Other measures include, in chronological order: Decision 502 on Binational Centres of Assistance at the Border, Valencia, Venezuela, 22 June 2001; Decision 503 on Recognition of National Identification Documents, Valencia, Venezuela, 22 June 2001; Decision 504 on an Andean Passport, Valencia, Venezuela, 22 June 2001; Resolution 527 on an Andean Migration Card, Lima, 11 July 2001; Decision 526 on Separate Entry Counters at Airports in Member States for Nationals and Foreign Residents, Lima, 7 July 2002; Decision 548 on Consular Protection, Quirama, Antioquia, Colombia, 25 June 2003. This has been developed by Resolution 1546, Lima, 20 February 2013; Decision 583 on an Andean Instrument on Social Security, Guayaquil, 7 May 2004; Decision 584 on an Andean Instrument on Security and Health in the Workplace, Guayaquil, 7 May 2004. This last decision is regulated by Resolution 957 from the General Secretariat, Lima, 23 September 2005. Also, the non-binding Andean Charter for the Protection and Promotion of Human Rights includes various provisions on the rights of migrants, Guayaquil, 26 July 2002. Earlier, in 1996, Decision 397 had already established an Andean Migration Card (Tarjeta Andina de Migración [TAM]), Lima, 16 September 1996. For a detailed analysis, see: L. E. Aguilar Cardosa, E. Anaya and C. Blouin, *Guía de Exigibilidad Jurídica de los Derechos Reconocidos en las Decisiones de la Comunidad Andina en Materia de Migraciones* (Lima: Comisión Andina de Juristas, 2015).

[23] CAN's General Secretariat, see Amendment Proposal to Decision 116: Andean Instrument on Labour Migration, Working Document, 4 April 2001.

[24] Arts 10–13, Decision 545.

[25] In Bolivia, it can be argued that Decision 545 has been indirectly implemented through Art. 49(9) of its 2013 Migration Law, which explicitly recognises any rights in regional agreements to be granted to migrant workers. In Colombia, Decree 46, Bogotá, 17 January 2013. In Ecuador, Inter-ministerial Agreement 000054, 26 July 2012. In Peru, Ministerial Resolution 318-2010-TR, Lima, 17 December 2010.

as legitimising the role of its own organisation.[26] In addition to the freedom of movement and residence, Andean citizenship would incorporate human rights protection in an integrated territory and allow political rights to be exercised in direct elections to the Andean Parliament.

Given that Andean instruments were very slowly being adopted and implemented, it led to the peculiar scenario in 2012 where all CAN's Member States had ratified the MERCOSUR Residence Agreement.[27] Thus, when the Fourth Andean Migration Forum took place in 2013, Member States proposed to strengthen a South American area of circulation and residence, and consolidate Andean and South American citizenship, via the convergence of CAN and MERCOSUR, within the framework of a new regional organisation: UNASUR. The forum also decided to codify all communitarian acquis, scattered through various Decisions and Regulations, in a single instrument by adopting an Andean Migration Statute.[28] This statute has been under discussion since 2013 at the level of the Secretariat and the Andean Committee of Migration Authorities.

Finally, in 2015, the Andean Parliament approved the Statute on Human Mobility. It is worth remembering that the Parliament, unlike other institutions in the CAN,[29] does not have legislative powers. For that reason, the Parliament exhorted the Council of Foreign Affairs Ministers to adopt the statute through community law.[30] The statute itself is notable. The preamble recognises the deficient implementation of current instruments and the persistent discrimination against regional citizens. With that in mind, the objective is to establish equal treatment and non-discrimination in a number of areas and through that process 'cooperate to the conformation and consolidation of an Andean and South American citizenship'.[31]

The scope of the Statute on Human Mobility is noteworthy. For the first time, regional migrant workers are referred to as Andean citizens. Furthermore, and most notably, foreigners who are regularly residing within the territory of any Member State are also included within the scope. The principles governing the agreement include not only non-discrimination and equal treatment, but

---

[26] Andean Presidential Council, 'Una Comunidad Andina para los Ciudadanos. Un Proyecto para la Integración Integral de Nuestros Pueblos', September 2008.

[27] Third Andean Forum on Migration, Report, Quito 4–5 October 2012, SG/FAM/III/INFORME. Bolivia had already been part of the agreement since 2009. Moreover, by 2012 only Peru had implemented the Andean Community Acquis. IOM and Andean Community Secretariat, *Avances y Recomendaciones para la Implementación de la Normativa de la Comunidad Andina en Materia de Migraciones* (Lima: IOM-SGCAN, 2012).

[28] Bogotá Declaration, IV Andean Forum on Migration, Bogotá, 9–10 May 2013.

[29] The Andean Council of Ministers of Foreign Affairs, as well as CAN's Commission (composed of one plenipotentiary from each Member State), are the two institutions with legislative powers and can adopt decisions. The General Secretariat may also adopt binding legislation under certain circumstances by way of resolutions.

[30] Art. 3, Andean Parliament, 24 April 2015, Decision No. 1343, by which the Andean Statute on Human Mobility was approved, Medellín, 24 April 2015.

[31] Arts 3(a), 5 and 6, and Preamble, Andean Statute on Human Mobility.

also the recognition of a right to migration and human mobility,[32] the non-criminalisation of migration,[33] the pro-persona interpretation of the law, the unity of the family, and the principle of coherence.

The statute recognises a number of rights in a process of codification and expansion of earlier laws, which are still valid and applicable. They comprise the right of entry, exit and free movement within the territory of the bloc, the right to family reunification, the rights to work, to be self-employed and to seek a job, as well as a brief reference to political rights.[34] Andean citizens would first obtain a two-year temporary permit, with a possibility to apply for permanent residence thereafter. Should the Andean citizen not obtain permanent residence, he may fall into irregularity although he would still be entitled to a few rights, with a parallel obligation for Member States to devise permanent actions facilitating regularisation.[35] This opens numerous questions as to the true meaning of Andean (South American) citizenship, to be discussed below.

The Free Movement of People and MERCOSUR

MERCOSUR[36] was born with the 1991 Asunción Treaty.[37] The original Member States (Argentina, Brazil, Paraguay and Uruguay) tasked themselves with an ambitious aim: to constitute a common market by the end of 1994, where the free circulation of goods, services and factors of production would be ensured. The free movement of people was not mentioned, except as being subsumed within the concept of factors of production. The 1994 Ouro Preto Protocol approved the final institutional and legislative procedural framework for the organisation.[38] Economic liberalisation and open market ideas – within the parameters of the Washington consensus – largely influenced the original aims. This needs to be understood against the background of the 'Enterprise for the Americas Initiative,' unveiled by US President George Bush in 1990, with

---

[32] The right to migration and human mobility is understood here as Andean citizens having the freedom to move to another Member State under the conditions set in the agreement and national law.

[33] See Chapter 5.

[34] Arts 7, 12, 13, 25, 27, 29, Andean Statute on Human Mobility.

[35] *Ibid.*, Arts 43–45 and 48–49.

[36] For a detailed analysis of all the initiatives and instruments, the following references may be consulted: S. Novick, G. Mera and V. Modolo (eds), *Migraciones y Mercosur: Una Relación Inconclusa* (Buenos Aires: Catálogos, 2010); L. Brumat, *Políticas Migratorias y Libertad de Circulación en el Mercosur (1991–2012)*, PhD Thesis, FLACSO, Argentina, 2016.

[37] Treaty of Asunción, 26 March 1991. The original four Member States are Argentina, Brazil, Paraguay and Uruguay. Venezuela joined MERCOSUR in 2012, but its membership was suspended in 2017. Bolivia joined on 17 July 2015 and the only requirement left for its full membership was, at the time of writing in 2017, the final approval by Brazil's Parliament. The remaining six countries in South America are Associate States.

[38] The two most important institutions are the Common Market Council and the Group of the Common Market.

a view to transforming the whole American continent into the world's largest free trade area.[39]

It was only at the turn of the century that the MERCOSUR agenda incorporated the free movement of people. The profound economic and political crisis between 1998 and 2003 put prevalent neo-liberal orientations into question, paving the way for new modes of market governance to emerge, as well as to incorporate the free movement of labour into regional debates. The non-binding 1998 Socio-Labour Declaration – containing certain rights for migrants and frontier workers – conceptualised for the first time the free movement of people as a socio-political issue, rather than a purely economic one.[40] At the same time, hundreds of thousands of South Americans emigrated, many remaining undocumented in their destinations, and foreigners in the region were almost exclusively coming from neighbouring countries.[41]

The adoption of the 2002 MERCOSUR Residence Agreement must be understood against this background, although it was actually the result of a particular historical conjunction. Fernando Enrique Cardoso, the Brazilian President at the time, had encouraged extending the social agenda.[42] Brazil held MERCOSUR's presidency (1 July 2002–1 January 2003) and Cardoso wanted to put a personal stamp on the end of his second and last term as Brazil's President by proposing a measure to advance regional integration.[43] Thus, Brazil put forth a project for a migratory amnesty for MERCOSUR nationals on 30 August 2002, which would regularise all undocumented regional migrants in the four countries through a six-month procedure. Based on previous experience conducting numerous regularisation procedures,[44] Argentina counter-proposed to establish a permanent, rather than temporary, mechanism for MERCOSUR nationals to access residency. The timing was propitious in many respects for Argentina. It coincided with the emigration of thousands of Argentineans to Europe and the USA, thus making it easier to draw comparisons between immigrants at home and emigrants abroad. The Argentinean National Migration Directorate – which had made the proposal – was pragmatic in its approach. It pointed out numerous challenges: the difficulty of patrolling a huge border with neighbouring countries, the importance of better knowledge of those who already resided within the territory for security reasons, as well as the need to offer equal treatment to regional migrants to protect indigenous workers against wage dumping and regional migrants against exploitation.[45]

[39] L. Bizzozero Revelez, 'El MERCOSUR y el Proceso Sudamericano ante la Segunda Década del Siglo XXI ¿Hacia una Consolidación del Nuevo Regionalismo Estratégico?', *Si Somos Americanos, Revista de Estudios Transfronterizos*, 12 (2012), pp. 215–237.
[40] MERCOSUR Socio-Labour Declaration, adopted by the Heads of State, Rio de Janeiro, 10 December 1998.
[41] Texidó and Gurrieri, *Panorama Migratorio de América del Sur 2012*, pp. 25–29.
[42] Bizzozero Revelez, 'El MERCOSUR y el Proceso Sudamericano'.
[43] Alfonso, *Integración y Migraciones*, p. 48.
[44] See Chapter 5, pp. 132–133.
[45] Alfonso, *Integración y Migraciones*, p. 50.

In fact, the agreement's main objective, as unmistakably declared in its preamble, is to solve the problem of intra-regional migrants having irregular migrant status.[46] The driving force was undocumented migration rather than establishing an internal market, such as in the EU. This difference is crucial to understanding the structure of the agreement. Indeed, it does not provide for a right of entry – a major drawback explored below. The individual can either regularise in the host state if he already resides there, or, alternatively, request a residence permit in the Consulate of the country to which he would like to move.

The agreement provides that any national from a MERCOSUR or Associate Member State may obtain a two-year temporary residence permit in another Member State by only providing proof of nationality as well as a clean criminal record for the last five years.[47] Permit holders have the right to work and equal treatment regarding working conditions, access to education for children, and other civil, social, cultural and economic rights that nationals enjoy. They are also granted the right to family reunification, but political rights are not mentioned. In contrast to the EU's regime, where either sufficient resources or employment are required to reside longer than three months, they are not a *conditio sine qua non* for residence in South America. Unlike CAN's Decision 545, the relationship between migration and work is unbounded and the individual may reside in another country for other purposes. After two years of residence, the individual may apply to stay permanently, at which point he must provide proof of sufficient resources to sustain himself in the territory of the host state.

Nine out of the twelve countries in South America have ratified the agreement; those that have not are Guyana, Suriname and Venezuela. In order to go forward with the mobility regime, the Common Market Council, MERCOSUR's highest decision-making body, adopted Decision 64/10 on citizenship on 16 December 2010.[48] Its aim was to establish an action plan to progressively form a MERCOSUR citizenship statute, to be adopted by 2021, coinciding with the organisation's thirtieth anniversary. This would finally implement a free circulation policy for people in the region, which is something that has not yet been achieved.

---

[46] Residence Agreement for Nationals of MERCOSUR Member States, Brasilia, 6 December 2002. It entered into force on 28 July 2009. A parallel agreement with the same provisions was signed on the same date between the four original Member States and Chile and Bolivia as Associate Members.

[47] The agreement applies to Argentina, Bolivia, Brazil, Paraguay and Uruguay as full Member States. Venezuela, membership of which was suspended in 2017, still needs to incorporate the Residence Agreement into its legislation before it can enter into force in the country. The Associate States that benefit from the agreement include Chile, Colombia, Peru and Ecuador. Guyana and Suriname became Associate States on 11 July 2013 but they had not adopted the Residence Agreement by 1 October 2017.

[48] Action Plan for a MERCOSUR Citizenship Statute, MERCOSUR/CMC/DEC. N° 64/10, Foz de Iguazú, 16 December 2010.

The Free Movement of People, UNASUR and the Pacific Alliance

Since 2008, two new regional organisations have emerged in South America.[49] One of the Pacific Alliance's objectives is to move progressively towards the free circulation of goods, services, capital and people.[50] Even though its main objective seems to be to facilitate short business visits through visa exemption agreements, it has also worked on certain aspects of reciprocal consular protection and even on establishing common Embassies, such as the one in Ghana. Discussions have also taken place on possibly developing the free movement of labour.[51] In turn, as one of its objectives in its founding treaty, UNASUR introduced the consolidation of a South American identity through the progressive recognition of rights to nationals of one Member State residing in the territory of another, with the aim of achieving a South American citizenship.[52] Several final declarations from the Council of the Heads of State and Government have reinforced the goal of attaining a true South American citizenship as the backbone of an integrated South American space,[53] and have proposed to establish a single passport.[54] Within that framework, a working group on South American citizenship was created and adopted a conceptual report on a common citizenship, which was approved by UNASUR's Council of Foreign Ministers in 2014.[55] The construction of a South American citizenship

[49] A further regional organisation, CELAC (Community of Latin American and Caribbean States), must be briefly mentioned here. Established in December 2011, CELAC has the objective of serving as a mechanism of dialogue and political concertation between the thirty-three countries of Latin America and the Caribbean. The Heads of State and Government 2016 Declaration included some references to the need to not criminalise migration, as well as to adopt a human rights approach: see the Quito Declaration, CELAC IV Summit, 27 January 2016. CELAC has also conducted various summits dealing exclusively with migration in order to establish a dialogue between countries in South America, Central America, the Caribbean and Mexico. Finally, the Caribbean Community could also be added here. It is a regional organisation with fifteen Member States, including Guyana and Suriname in South America. One of its purposes is to remove restrictions on the free movement of skilled labour.

[50] The Pacific Alliance (*Alianza del Pacífico*) is a Latin American trade bloc. It was created by the Declaration of Lima on 28 April 2011. Its current members are Chile, Colombia, Mexico and Peru. Costa Rica and Panama have expressed their interest in joining.

[51] Agencia EFE, 'Analizan Movilidad Laboral en la Alianza del Pacífico', 8 April 2016.

[52] UNASUR, Union of South American Nations, is a regional organisation comprised of all twelve countries in South America. It aims to construct a cultural, economic, social and political space in the region. The founding Treaty entered into force on 11 March 2011. Art. 3(i), UNASUR founding treaty refers to the South American identity. This is also mentioned in the Preamble as the determination to construct an identity and South American citizenship. Art. 3(k) also specifies that this organisation has an objective of cooperating on migration matters under the strict respect for human and labour rights in order to successfully regularise migration and harmonise policies.

[53] Declaration of the 6th ordinary meeting of the Council of Heads of State and Government of the UNASUR, Lima, 30 November 2012. Declaration of the 7th ordinary meeting of the Council, Paramaribo, 2 September 2013.

[54] Declaration of the 8th ordinary meeting of the Council of Heads of State and Government of the UNASUR, Quito, 4–5 December, paragraph 14.

[55] UNASUR Resolution 14/2014, Council of Foreign Ministers, Conceptual Report on South American Citizenship.

has been positioned as one of the top five items in the organisation's agenda and some debates have taken place regarding the possible adoption of a UNASUR Residence Agreement.[56] Such an agreement would be equivalent to an international treaty that would enter into force only once each Member State had incorporated it into their domestic law.[57]

Incongruity, Implementation and Adjudication

The success in establishing, developing and deepening a mobility regime, and eventual common citizenship, might be tainted by incorrectly appraising its three key challenges: incongruity, implementation and adjudication. All three are intrinsically related and part of a continuum. In the best-case scenario, incongruous instruments affect the legal certainty of the individual, leading, in turn, to deficient implementation by the administration and thus limiting access to justice. In the worst case, incongruous instruments annul the enjoyment of supranational rights through bureaucratic implementation of minimum standards and almost non-existent access to courts, or with little chance of recognition. Both scenarios, as well as those in between, affect rights: they are reduced for regional individuals, change from country to country and depend on extensive legal expertise and advice.

Incongruity

Incongruity refers to the incompatibility and inconsistency between instruments adopted at the level of various international organisations, such as MERCOSUR or CAN. These contradictions get to the core of what regional free movement and citizenship mean, as well as the most essential rights attached to them. If we compare CAN's Decision 545, or the non-legally binding Andean Statute on Human Mobility, to the MERCOSUR Residence Agreement, their differences are noteworthy.

To begin with, the *ratione personae*, or scope, of the agreements is different. Whereas MERCOSUR grants mobility to those who have been nationals of a Member State for at least five years – thus discriminating against newly naturalised citizens[58] – Decision 545 and CAN's Statute do not impose such a requirement, although the former only applies to a limited number of migrant workers.[59] Furthermore, in addition to the requirements of nationality and clean criminal record,[60] in order to obtain a temporary residence for up to two years, the Andean Statute demands the accreditation of sufficient resources,

[56] J. Ramírez, *Hacia el Sur. La Construcción de la Ciudadanía Suramericana y la Movilidad Intrarregional* (Quito: CELAG, 2016).
[57] Art. 12, UNASUR founding Treaty.
[58] Art. 2, MERCOSUR Residence Agreement.
[59] Art. 2(a), Andean Statute on Human Mobility; Arts 2 and 4 Decision 545.
[60] Art. 4, MERCOSUR Residence Agreement.

except for workers, investors and spouses.[61] In turn, regional migrants under the MERCOSUR agreement enjoy equal treatment with nationals in terms of civil, social, cultural and economic rights.[62] This is deliberately drafted in an open manner, which raises problems during implementation, as will be seen below. However, the Andean Statute is more restrictively worded when it comes to, for example, access to health care, since equal treatment is granted only for emergency treatment, whilst Decision 545 remains silent.[63] Finally, in order to expel a regional national, MERCOSUR makes a broad reference to the possibility of imposing restrictions on the grounds of public order and public security.[64] However, CAN's Statute is much more precise, stating that only crimes relating to migrant smuggling or trafficking, drug trafficking and child pornography are sufficient grounds for withholding, or withdrawing, an individual's residence permit.[65] Decision 545 remains silent on this subject.

Thus, the three most crucial questions regarding mobility, namely, who is entitled to move and under which conditions, rights during stay and how secure residence is, are addressed divergently in all three instruments. Incongruity is of course surmountable. Two of the instruments offer two interconnected solutions: accepting more favourable clauses at the national level[66] and the *pro-homine* principle of interpretation.[67] At its simplest level, the more favourable provisions allow countries to unilaterally move beyond the regional framework. For example, Uruguay amended its immigration law in August 2014 to directly grant nationals from MERCOSUR and Associate States permanent – rather than temporary – residence, upon presenting a clean criminal record and proof of South American nationality, including those from Guyana, Suriname and Venezuela.[68] At its most complex level, however, legal counselling and administrative authorities face a difficult task in analysing the more favourable provisions. When this involves examining domestic, regional and international sources, the risk of wrongful application multiplies. Here the *pro-homine* principle can serve as an instrument of judicial interpretation that can repair unlawful administrative action. The principle, mostly developed through the jurisprudence of the IACtHR, establishes that in cases of contradiction, 'the rule most favourable to the individual must prevail'.[69] Although at face value this appears as a simple exercise, in reality it entails extremely complex decisions through which judicial action must allocate a state's resources since

---

[61] Arts 41 and 43, Andean Statute on Human Mobility.

[62] Art. 9, MERCOSUR Residence Agreement.

[63] Art. 14, Andean Statute on Human Mobility.

[64] Art. 8, MERCOSUR Residence Agreement.

[65] Arts 35, 41–43, Andean Statute on Human Mobility.

[66] Art. 11, MERCOSUR Residence Agreement and Art. 71, Andean Statute on Human Mobility.

[67] Art. 3(d), Andean Statute on Human Mobility.

[68] Uruguay, Law 19.254, 4 September 2014.

[69] IACtHR, *Compulsory Membership in an Association Prescribed by Law for the Practice of Journalism* (Arts 13 and 29 American Convention on Human Rights) (1985), Advisory Opinion OC-5/85, (Ser A) No 5, para. 52.

states have not detailed the exact contours of rights at the regional level. For example, when a domestic court faces a claim of access to health care, it should put the more restrictive CAN Statute aside and instead apply MERCOSUR's Agreement since it provides equal treatment of social rights. However, the Tribunal would have to interpret the meaning of 'social rights' considering both national and international laws and then decide accordingly.[70]

Implementation

The incorrect implementation of supranational instruments is the second challenge in ensuring a functional mobility regime. Various circumstances can lead to incorrect implementation. For example, certain aspects might be left unregulated by referencing national law. The MERCOSUR Agreement allows domestic authorities to request a fee to grant a residence permit in accordance with national law, something that results in huge discrepancies in implementation.[71] This may lead to a race of raising fees, thus affecting the *effet utile* of the law since particular countries could make it impossible to access the status. In this context, the EU case offers an interesting example of equal treatment since Member States cannot charge EU citizens more than they charge their own nationals for similar identification documents.[72]

Additionally, various interpretations may result from the norm's unclear wording. For example, the MERCOSUR Agreement provides that states can grant a temporary residence permit of up to two years to the petitioner. This could be interpreted as all temporary residencies last for two years, but not longer, or that temporary residence permits can be shorter than two years. All states have adopted the first meaning except for Chile, which grants a one-year renewable residence permit.[73]

Finally, countries sometimes add requirements that are not present in the supranational instrument. For example, in Argentina, in order to obtain temporary residence, the regional national needs to produce a certificate of domicile or a receipt of a public service – such as water, electricity or gas – in his name, something not enshrined in the MERCOSUR Agreement.[74] A simple solution would be to introduce clauses prohibiting the imposition of additional requirements.[75]

---

[70] See Art. 12, ICESCR.
[71] Art. 4(1)(g), MERCOSUR Residence Agreement. As of 2017, Argentina requested US$67, as opposed to US$250 in Ecuador, for instance, to obtain a MERCOSUR temporary residence permit.
[72] For example, Art. 25(2) of EU's Directive 2004/38 reads: 'All documents mentioned in paragraph 1 shall be issued free of charge or for a charge not exceeding that imposed on nationals for the issuing of similar documents.'
[73] See Oficio Circular 26465, Ministry of the Interior, Chile, 4 December 2009.
[74] See www.migraciones.gov.ar/accesible/indexN.php?mercosur_temporaria
[75] This is found in Art. 41, Andean Statute for Human Mobility.

Adjudication

It has often been contended that the strong intergovernmental character of regional integration and the lack of supranational judicial bodies to ensure implementation and impose sanctions for violations halt the South American free movement of people from advancing.[76] In fact, migrants still largely depend on domestic laws and procedures to access their rights. Deciding on which institution has the capacity to adjudicate is perhaps the most central aspect to construing a meaningful free movement and residence regime, as well as eventual common citizenship. Several options are available ranging from the most intergovernmental to the most supranational.

Interpreting through Dialogue between Governments

So far the interpretation of the MERCOSUR Residence Agreement has taken place through a dialogue of government officials at the level of the MERCOSUR Migration Forum.[77] In accordance with their respective domestic migration laws, each state has divergently implemented the aspects left open in the agreement, such as the definition of who falls under the category of family member for the purposes of reunification. The Residence Agreement itself provides that discrepancies on its reach, interpretation and application must be resolved through whichever mechanism is in force at the particular moment when the controversy arises, provided the parties agree upon it.[78]

The 2002 Olivos Protocol, in force since 1 January 2004, is the current system that regulates how to solve controversies. In brief, the Protocol establishes a two-tiered procedure where an *ad hoc* Arbitration Tribunal decides the first instance whereas the Permanent Revision Tribunal handles the second.[79] The latter Tribunal adopts decisions with the characteristic of *res judicata* and the state parties must accept the results. Either states or natural or legal persons whose rights have been infringed may initiate the procedure. However, their chances of reaching the Permanent Revision Tribunal are slim and depend on a complex and cumbersome procedure, as well as a Member State's participation.[80] Moreover, this system only works for full Member States, not the Associate States. This and other factors explain that less than ten decisions had

---

[76] A. M. Santestevan, 'Free Movement Regimes in South America: The Experience of the MERCOSUR and the Andean Community' in R. Cholewinski, R. Perruchoud and E. McDonald (eds), *International Migration Law: Developing Paradigms and Key Challenges* (The Hague: Asser Press, 2007), pp. 363–386, on p. 384.

[77] See, for example, the minutes from the XLVIII Meeting where some concerns were expressed regarding the lack of effective implementation in certain countries. Acta N° 01/13, Montevideo, Uruguay, 19–21 March 2013.

[78] Art. 13, MERCOSUR Residence Agreement.

[79] Olivos Protocol, 18 February 2002; Amendment to the Olivos Protocol, Rio de Janeiro, 19 January 2007.

[80] Arts 39–44 Olivos Protocol.

been adopted by 2017, all of the cases have been initiated by states and none has dealt with migration.

UNASUR adopts a similarly strong intergovernmental approach since the Brazilian proposal to establish a regional tribunal was never adopted. Here, discrepancies on the interpretation and application of provisions in the Founding Treaty must be resolved through direct negotiations between the states involved. In the case that they do not reach an agreement, the Council of Delegates, an institution with one representative from each Member State, will hear the discrepancy and then formulate non-binding recommendations. A final optional step is to raise the matter to the Council of Foreign Ministers for consideration. The Treaty remains silent as to how to interpret the outcome as well as the consequences of such consideration.[81] Natural or legal persons are not entitled to raise legal demands under this system.

Interpreting through an External Committee

The UN Human Rights Treaty Bodies use an external committee of independent experts to interpret supranational law.[82] This includes the CMW overseeing the implementation and correct interpretation of the same Convention. Participant countries have an obligation to submit reports to the CMW one year after acceding to the treaty and then every five years. The Committee proposes recommendations and observations regarding correct national implementation of the Convention, which then feed into national legislative frameworks and lead to their amendment.[83] These concluding observations have, in the words of Evans, 'an "adjudicatory" flavour'.[84]

However, the CMW's reports demonstrate that there is often a considerable gap between the Convention's formal ratification and its implementation at the domestic level. Looking at countries where two reports are already available, we can see how recommendations have led to improvements in Bolivia and Ecuador, but have been less successful in Colombia and Paraguay. In the Peruvian example, Peru was already discussing new legislation when the CMW published its final report in 2015, which played a constructive role in its final adoption.[85]

The suitability of setting up similar committees to oversee the application of regional free movement agreements, including in South America, remains a possibility. Whether or not they adopt this approach, the region should learn from international committees' deficiencies and limitations. Considering these,

---

[81] Art. 21, UNASUR Founding Treaty.
[82] For an assessment, see P. Alston and J. Crawford (eds), *The Future of UN Human Rights Treaty Monitoring* (Cambridge University Press, 2000). Also see M. Evans, 'Adjudicating Human Rights in the Preventive Sphere' in J. A. Green and C. P. M. Waters (eds), *Adjudicating International Human Rights. Essays in Honour of Sandy Ghandhi* (Leiden: Brill, 2015), pp. 212–234.
[83] ICMW, Arts 72–73.
[84] Evans, 'Adjudicating Human Rights in the Preventive Sphere', p. 216.
[85] Peru CMW/C/PER/CO/1, 13 May 2015.

it would arguably be more productive to establish committees based on a constant dialogue with national authorities and other stakeholders to achieve prevention, rather than concentrating on compliance to the letter of the agreement. This could include incorporating a national implementation and monitoring mechanism similar to that found in some international treaties.[86] With respect to the work of the Committee against Torture, Evans has explained that the focus must be 'on practical steps that might be taken to improve the enjoyment of the right … [and] the pursuit of bettering the immediate situation as a stepping stone toward an end which might either be as yet unachievable in full, or is not yet an agreed outcome'.[87] This would favour prevention through innovative approaches rather than replicating the present flaws of international committees. If the objective is to achieve effective regional migration regimes, these less widely used means of oversight and implementation, with the inclusion of national independent mechanisms, may be both more achievable and similarly effective. National independent mechanisms would also allow for a much more comprehensive and holistic understanding of migration regulation since they involve various ministries and bureaucracies in any given country, thus moving beyond the dialogue often occurring between ministries of foreign affairs and the CMW.

Interpreting through National Courts

As discussed in the introduction to Part II of this book, national courts – mainly constitutional and supreme courts – appear primordial in determining the true reach of wide principled norms enshrined in various legal sources.[88] International law, in particular the ACHR, as well as the IACtHR's jurisprudence, have reinforced the protective capacity of domestic courts. The 'constitutionalisation of human rights treaties' has permitted the incorporation of international law and the Inter-American Court's jurisprudence into the block of constitutionality.[89] In turn, the Inter-American Court's doctrine on conventionality control has obliged states' tribunals and administrative bureaucracies to interpret domestic law, including the constitution, in accordance with the ACHR. This obligation also extends to consistent interpretation with other Inter-American treaties on human rights, and with the IACtHR's jurisprudence and advisory opinions – what has been named as the Inter-American *corpus juris*, or the real 'block of conventionality'.[90] Thus, national judges are

---

[86] Art. 33, CRPD.
[87] M. Evans, 'Challenging Conventional Assumptions. The Case for a Preventive Approach to the Protection of the Freedom of Religion or Belief' in M. Evans, P. Petkoff, J. Rivers (eds), *The Changing Nature of Religious Rights under International Law* (Oxford University Press, 2015), pp. 25–50, p. 46.
[88] Part II, pp. 115–117.
[89] *Ibid.*
[90] E. Ferrer Mac-Gregor, 'The Constitutionalization of International Law in Latin America Conventionality Control. The New Doctrine of the Inter-American Court of Human Rights', *American Journal of International Law Unbound*, (2015), 93–99, on 98.

granted 'the role of "courts of first instance" in the enforcement' of the Inter-American treaties.[91] Finally, when faced with a legal problem, the *pro homine* principle of interpretation requires the interpreter to 'give preference to the norm that provides the widest and most extensive protection of human rights, regardless of the source (international/Inter-American or national) and its rank in the normative order'.[92]

These three principles (constitutionalisation of human rights, doctrine on conventionality control and *pro homine* principle of interpretation) offer national courts a fertile legal soil to interpret regional free movement and residence rules with a strong focus on a rights-based approach. The *pro homine* principle is clearly enshrined within the MERCOSUR Residence Agreement.[93] Several rights that the agreement recognises, such as family life, labour rights and socio-economic and civil ones, refer to fundamental rights enshrined in International Human Right treaties. As such, they are to be considered part of the block of constitutionality and subject to conventionality control. It is here that legal actors, particularly lawyers and advocacy groups, could play a role in expanding the process of incorporating international and regional norms into domestic legal interpretations, aligned with constitutional provisions in most countries, and possibly through strategic litigation.

Interpreting through a Supranational Tribunal: The CAN Case

Andean Community law is directly applicable, is capable of direct effect and has supremacy over national law.[94] In other words, CAN's Decisions do not need to be implemented or approved at national level in order to become accessible. On the contrary, individuals can claim rights derived from CAN instruments before administrative authorities and domestic courts, and they would prevail over any conflicting internal norm.[95] All Decisions, even those demanding the need to adopt a Regulation in order to be fully applicable, are capable of direct effect.[96] National judges may, or in the case of courts of last instance must, request a preliminary ruling to the Andean Court of Justice on the interpretation of Andean Community law.[97] All national authorities must comply with the Community acquis. Thus, if an administration breaches an individual's rights, he can bring an action before a domestic court to annul the act in question affecting rights derived from Community law. The national judge is obliged to guarantee the observance of CAN's legislation. However, and crucially, the

[91] Góngora Mera, *Inter-American Judicial Constitutionalism*, p. 54.
[92] *Ibid.*, p. 58.
[93] Art. 11, MERCOSUR Residence Agreement. Also see Art. 3 of the Andean Statute on Human Mobility.
[94] See Andean Court of Justice Case 3-AI-96 and Case 34-AI-2001.
[95] Aguilar, Anaya and Blouin, *Guía de Exigibilidad Jurídica de los Derechos*, p. 15. See Andean Court of Justice, Case 3-AI-96.
[96] Andean Community Court of Justice's ruling in 100-IP-2011, 8 February 2012.
[97] Aguilar, Anaya and Blouin, *Guía de Exigibilidad Jurídica de los Derechos*, pp. 18–20.

administrative procedure must have been exhausted before the individual can demand this before a national court.[98] In this regard, CAN's system is based on the EU's model and, on paper, provides for similar protection.

However, CAN's Court has only decided two cases affecting migrant workers since it first started operating in 1984. A Colombian national demanded his period of work in Venezuela to be taken into consideration while calculating his pension in Colombia. Decision 583, on an Andean Social Security Instrument, guaranteed this right but required an implementing regulation at the community level that, at the time of the facts, had not been adopted. The Court decided that the absence of such regulation, due to the inactivity of the CAN's Secretariat in passing it, could not affect the effectiveness of rights consecrated by Community law.[99]

Consequently, the CAN's architecture offers the strongest level of supranational adjudication. Several reasons for its inactivity in deciding just two cases affecting workers can be mentioned. First, the free movement legislation is relatively recent and has suffered from a lack of development through implementing regulations. Second, the Tribunal has a reputation of being exclusively interested in economic issues, mainly intellectual property, which occupies 90 per cent of its rulings. Third, Andean Community law has not been the subject of much academic research or teaching at the university level and does not represent a compulsory law module in the region. Moreover, only recently has the Andean Parliament and civil society actors such as the Andean Commission of Jurists shifted their attention to free movement and migration.[100] Similarly, CAN's General Secretariat, in its function as overseer of compliance with Community law, adopted the guidelines as late as 2012 on how Member States must implement, interpret and apply the Community acquis.[101]

Discussion

Does South America offer a new coherent model of human regional mobility? Beyond the challenges of incongruity, implementation and adjudication already analysed, the instruments' actual design, as well as the institutional cacophony, signify that a supranational South American citizenship remains a long-term challenge. Indeed, no fewer than three regional organisations are discussing comprehensive accords. This may result in fragmentation through various, not

---

[98] Ibid., p. 88.

[99] Andean Community's Court, Case 100-IP-2011, p. 10.

[100] During its sessions in Bogotá, 26–29 September 2011, the Andean Parliament approved CAN's Adherence to the MERCOSUR Residence Agreement. In turn, the work of the Andean Commission of Jurists has been central in the diffusion and understanding of community law in the region. See L. E. Aguilar Cardoso (ed.), El Derecho a la Libre Circulación de Personas en la Migración Internacional Intracomunitaria (Lima: Comisión Andina de Juristas, 2010).

[101] See, for example, IOM and Andean Community Secretariat, Avances y Recomendaciones para la Implementación de la Normativa de la Comunidad Andina en Materia de Migraciones.

always coherent, bodies of law, thus affecting the rule of law and legal certainty when clearly identifiable rights are absent.

Yet these issues look insignificant. The distinction between the right to move and the right to reside, the position of those not economically active, the status of extra-regional migrants, and the complete inclusion of regional citizens in the host state are the true stumbling blocks. They get to the core of the three main concerns, namely who can enter, their rights during their stay, and the security of their residence. The answers to these open questions will define whether the region will transform mobility into a sweeping regional citizenship for all residents in South America, or whether it will be a modest attempt to tackle certain aspects surrounding regional migration, with important implications for some individuals' rights, but falling short of a truly path-breaking model.

A Right of Entry for South Americans?

The free movement of individuals in a region has two dimensions: the right to enter another state and the right to consequently reside there. In Europe both dimensions are closely linked since EU nationals have the 'right to move and reside freely within the territory of the Member States'.[102] Paradoxically, the MERCOSUR Residence Agreement does not grant the right to enter another territory to all nationals of the state parties, but only to those who already hold permits under the terms of the agreement. These can be obtained in the origin, in the Consulate of the country to which the individual would like to move, or abroad, via the second state's migration authorities where the person already resides. Thus, the right to circulate is decoupled from the right to reside. Simply put, this means that regional migrants need to convince border guards of their suitability as tourists, and only later can transform their tourist entry into a temporary residence permit. This contradiction results from the continuous role of security actors on regional migration debates and from the emphasis on border control.[103] Thus, whereas MERCOSUR law grants regional nationals a right to reside in the host country based on the criterion of nationality, border guards can deny a migrant's entry if they are uncertain as to the proof of sufficient resources for a short ('tourist') stay, hotel accommodation or return ticket.[104] Residence may materialise for those who manage to cross the border but not for those who do not.

This issue has been the centre of attention since 2014.[105] It has been proposed to establish an entry category for regional migrants, even if the

[102] Art. 21, TFEU; Kochenov (ed.), *EU Citizenship and Federalism*.
[103] Brumat, *Políticas Migratorias y Libertad de Circulación en el Mercosur*, p. 397.
[104] *Ibid.*, p. 250.
[105] IOM, *Informe sobre el Estado de Situación de la Facilitación del Tránsito Fronterizo en Suramérica*, XVI South American Conference on Migration, *Reference Document*, Asunción, 3–4 November 2016.

person would need to register at the border.[106] At the domestic level, the 2017 Ecuadorian Law on Human Mobility grants South American nationals the right of entry upon presentation of their national identification document.[107] Still, the continuous suspicion by border control authorities of South American nationals as potential threats risks any meaningful regional citizenship.

Towards a New Market Citizenship in South America?

Market citizenship has been debated across the European context. The concept expresses the idea that individuals are entitled to reside for longer than three months in another Member State only when they are economically active as workers, are self-employed or are service providers. Those who are not economically active can only reside after proving sufficient resources to sustain themselves, as well as possessing sickness insurance.[108] Since the adoption of an EU citizenship in 1993, the debate has centred on whether such citizenship – understood as a fundamental right to move and reside anywhere in the EU – could be decoupled from the free movement of economically active individuals within the framework of an internal market.[109] The matter has been subject to numerous CJEU rulings.[110]

At first sight, South America has created a much stronger framework for the residence of all, whether or not they are economic actors. The individual only needs to offer proof of nationality and a clean criminal record to obtain a two-year temporary permit. Only later does the individual need to prove licit means of living that allows for his or her subsistence and that of the family. This legislative choice results from taking a pragmatic stance, considering the South American labour market's idiosyncrasies. According to the ILO, 47 per cent of all non-agricultural workers are in the informal sector in Latin America and the Caribbean. This had amounted to around 130 million people by 2013, affecting not only low-income sectors but also young individuals with university degrees, as well as those working in small and medium-sized companies.[111] Thus, any requirement to be engaged in a kind of formal (self-)employed activity would make any mobility regime ineffective. However, those who are unable to change their status into a permanent one after two years fall back into

---

[106] IOM, *Estudio sobre Experiencias en la Implementación del Acuerdo de Residencia del MERCOSUR.*

[107] Ecuador, Art. 84, 2017 Organic Law on Human Mobility.

[108] Art. 7, Directive 2004/38 on the Rights of EU Citizens and Members of their Families. Job-seekers also enjoy the right to move to another Member State to look for a job, as long as they can prove a genuine chance of obtaining employment. Art. 14, Directive 2004/38.

[109] D. Kochenov, 'On Tiles and Pillars: EU Citizenship as a Federal Denominator' in Kochenov (ed.), *EU Citizenship and Federalism*, pp. 1–66.

[110] *Ibid.* and other chapters in the same book.

[111] ILO, *Panorama Laboral 2013. América Latina y el Caribe* (Lima: International Labour Organization, 2013).

irregularity. Consequently, the interpretation of the clause 'licit means of living allowing for subsistence' becomes of paramount importance. Yet, this concept is underdeveloped in the MERCOSUR Agreement and in the draft proposals under discussion; moreover, it will change from country to country, leading to different statuses across the region.

Towards a South American Apartheid?

Balibar famously coined the term 'apartheid européen' to refer to the status of third-country nationals (TCNs), who could not access the mobility and associated rights derived from having EU citizenship.[112] The EU's disinterest regarding a large number of residents within its borders impelled many authors to criticise its exclusionary character.[113] In fact, various NGOs, Members of the European Parliament and scholars proposed extending EU citizenship to long-term resident TCNs – an idea which Member States rejected.[114]

South American scholars and policy makers did not shy away from making these reproaches.[115] Yet, the legislative response so far in South America can at best be described as contradictory and, at worst, exercises hypocrisy. Indeed, the MERCOSUR Residence Agreement excludes naturalised citizens from its scope during the first five years after having obtained nationality. Stronger exclusions are present when it comes to voting rights for regional parliaments at both the MERCOSUR and CAN level. In effect, only Colombians, Ecuadorians and Peruvians by birth may vote in the Andean Parliament elections.[116] Similarly for the MERCOSUR Parliament, Paraguay only allows voting by nationals by birth and Argentina requires a minimum of four years as a national. As a corollary of this, most countries do not allow naturalised citizens to stand as candidates, nor allow national congresses to delegate these individuals to serve in regional parliaments.[117]

Following Balibar's terminology, this could be labelled as an 'apartheid sud-américain' reloaded. As analysed in Chapter 2, it is the result of a long historical tradition where elites have usually distrusted newly arrived migrants, even after naturalisation, due to the fear of foreign intervention. As mentioned

---

[112] É. Balibar, *Nous, Citoyens d'Europe? Les Frontières, l'Etat, le Peuple* (Paris: La Découverte, 2001), pp. 190–191.

[113] K. Groenendijk, 'Security of Residence and Access to Free Movement for Settled Third Country Nationals under Community Law' in E. Guild and C. Harlow (eds), *Implementing Amsterdam* (Oxford: Hart, 2001), pp. 225–240.

[114] D. Kostakopoulou, 'European Citizenship and Immigration after Amsterdam: Silences, Openings, Paradoxes', *Journal of Ethnic and Migration Studies*, 4 (1998), 639–656.

[115] P. Ceriani Cernadas, 'Ciudadanía, Migraciones y Libre Circulación en el Mercosur: ¿Hacia un Paradigma Basado en los Derechos Humanos o la Réplica del Modelo Excluyente de la Unión Europea?', *Revista de Derecho Migratorio y de Extranjería*, 30 (2012), 259–287.

[116] Bolivia does not utilise direct elections to choose its members for the Andean Parliament.

[117] This is the case, for example, in Bolivia, Colombia, Ecuador, Peru and Paraguay. In Venezuela, there is a waiting period of fifteen years for naturalised citizens, whereas in Uruguay it is five years: see Art. 188, 1999 Venezuelan Constitution; Uruguay, Art. 90, 1967 Constitution.

in Chapter 6, domestic-level laws and constitutions continue to enshrine this discriminatory status for naturalised individuals. Paradoxically, there are also developments pointing in the direction of enlarging the scope of free movement agreements to include extra-regional residents. Following a mandate by the Ministers of the Interior,[118] the MERCOSUR Migration Forum has been working on the consolidation of all the migration acquis into a single instrument.[119] The various drafts discussed up until 2016 provide an inconsistent picture. To begin with, the five years' exclusion for naturalised citizens remains in place. However, the draft agreement proposes to regulate admission, entry, transit, stay and exit of not only nationals but also extra-regional migrants who regularly reside in the territory of one of the signatory states.[120] In a comparative perspective, this would represent a path-breaking approach since it places non-regional migrants on an equal footing with regional individuals. However, it would open up all sorts of problems related to reverse discrimination for the first five years against those who naturalise. At the CAN level, both the non-legally binding Andean Statute on Human Mobility, as well as the Andean Migration Statute proposal – under discussion at the Secretariat level at the time of writing – include foreigners regularly residing in the territory of a Member State within their scope.[121] Neither of these two last instruments differentiates between natural and naturalised citizens, thus avoiding instances of discrimination.

Irregular Migrants or South American Citizens? Towards a Regional Temporary Mobility Regime?

A final crucial tension is apparent between the overarching approach in which regional nationals become South American citizens and the limited approach that considers them as temporary guests with a two-year expiry date. When the MERCOSUR Residence Agreement was adopted in 2002, a cautious tactic was agreed upon. Being an Argentinean proposal, the final text of the agreement was modelled upon two migration accords that Argentina made in 1998, one with Peru and the other with Bolivia.[122] These agreements offered regularisation to migrants through first a temporary six-month residence permit that then needed renewing on a yearly basis. The MERCOSUR Agreement added permanent residence to this regulation and extended the length of the temporary

---

[118] Ministers of the Interior Council, 'Brasilia Declaration on the Entry into Force of the Migration Norms Deriving from the Meetings of the Ministers of Interior of the MERCOSUR and Associate States', 12 November 2010.

[119] Draft Proposal for a Consolidated MERCOSUR Migration Agreement, Working Document, MERCOSUR Migration Forum, Montevideo, 17 March 2016.

[120] *Ibid.*, Art. 3.

[121] Art. 1, Andean Statute on Human Mobility; Arts 2 and 16 Proposal for an Andean Migration Statute.

[122] Migration Covenant between the Republics of Peru and Argentina, 1998; Migration Covenant between the Republics of Bolivia and Argentina, Buenos Aires, 16 February 1998.

permit. However, those who do not then apply for permanent residency fall back into irregularity, their situation becoming a matter of national law. This already affects an important number of individuals who cannot renew their permits, then become undocumented and are expelled.[123]

Another aspect lies in migrants who cannot obtain the residence permit to begin with. This has to do with deficient information on the part of all relevant actors in the administration, but also includes migrants themselves.[124] However, at times bureaucratic requirements – such as the proof of a clean criminal record for the last five years – make it impossible for some individuals to obtain a residence permit when the Consulates of their countries of origin refuse to provide such documentation.[125] Since all countries' original migration laws stipulated the requirement of a clean criminal record, states concerned about security issues felt that in this case regional citizens should not receive exceptional treatment.[126] Contrarily in the European case, the burden of proving that the individual may constitute a threat actually falls on the host state rather than on the person moving.[127]

Strikingly, the new mobility proposals still insist on either obtaining permanent residence after two years or falling into irregularity.[128] Two possible solutions have surfaced: either allowing the migrant to renew the temporary residency one more time,[129] or directly granting permanent residence by simply proving nationality and a clean criminal record.[130] As mentioned before, Uruguay has already opted for the latter choice. If the individual directly obtains permanent residence, when is expulsion possible? The draft proposal for a recap of the MERCOSUR Residence Agreement more clearly specifies that

---

[123] Data on this matter are hard to come by but we know that close to 5,000 migrants were expelled from Argentina between 2009 and 2015. Melde estimates that around 75 per cent of these individuals had been from MERCOSUR and Associate States: see S. Melde, *Ahead of the Game? The Human Rights Origins and Potential of Argentina's 2004 Migration Policy*, PhD Thesis: University of Sussex, 2017, on p. 43.

[124] IOM, *Estudio sobre Experiencias en la Implementación del Acuerdo de Residencia*, p. 21.

[125] In Ecuador, there have been instances of Venezuelan nationals having difficulties accessing criminal records from their Consulate. See Sistematización Resumida, Jornada de Discusión sobre la Ley Orgánica de Movilidad Humana Gobierno Autónomo Descentralizado de Pichincha y Facultad Latinoamericana de Ciencias Sociales Miércoles, 26 April 2017.

[126] Brumat, *Políticas Migratorias y Libertad de Circulación en el Mercosur*, pp. 383–384.

[127] See Art. 27(3), Directive 2004/38, which reads as follows: 'In order to ascertain whether the person concerned represents a danger for public policy or public security, when issuing the registration certificate or, in the absence of a registration system, not later than three months from the date of arrival of the person concerned on its territory or from the date of reporting his/her presence within the territory, as provided for in Art. 5(5), or when issuing the residence card, the host Member State may, should it consider this essential, request the Member State of origin and, if need be, other Member States to provide information concerning any previous police record the person concerned may have. Such enquiries shall not be made as a matter of routine. The Member State consulted shall give its reply within two months.'

[128] Art. 45, Andean Statute on Human Mobility; Art. 11 Andean Migration Statute Proposal.

[129] This has been discussed for a new possible MERCOSUR agreement. See Draft Proposal for a Consolidated MERCOSUR Migration Agreement.

[130] Ramírez, *Hacia el Sur*, p. 128.

only public order or public security motivations, provided they are enshrined in national law, could call for expulsion. This would rule out removing individuals who Member States consider a burden on their social assistance system, as is the case under the EU framework.[131] Whilst welfare state benefits are arguably less developed in South America, the extent to which a regional citizenship would be a social one requires further discussion. In that regard, the proposal for an Andean Migration Statute includes a clause making it possible for Member States to limit equal treatment for benefits and programmes related to social assistance and poverty alleviation.[132] The question of course arises as to whether this should also hold for individuals residing for a long period in the host state, and also demonstrates the tension between those favouring a social regional citizenship, and those preferring an economic one.

Conclusion

Numerous authors have debated whether South America's free movement regime constitutes an instance of failure or success. Those celebrating its achievements mention that when the MERCOSUR Residence Agreement was adopted, there were serious doubts that it would even be implemented.[133] They also point out that thousands of MERCOSUR residence permits were granted in the first ten years of the Agreement (2002–2012).[134] Furthermore, they refer to the emergent common discourse in numerous regional fora highlighting a certain fatigue with restrictive responses and the need to explore new alternatives, as well as the alignment of governments with similar agendas, at least until 2015.[135] Numerous policy declarations by all three main regional organisations – CAN, MERCOSUR and UNASUR – have argued in favour of further convergence, consolidation and codification.[136]

More critical views could emphasise that, historically,[137] the adoption of numerous rules and pronouncements have led to little true impact on the lives of regional migrants, that compromises have failed to be implemented and that a simple adoption of new administrative rules – e.g. in Argentina under the Macri government – can lead to decisive setbacks. This is coupled

---

[131] See Directive 2004/38.

[132] Art. 15, Andean Migration Statute Proposal.

[133] Alfonso, *Integración y Migraciones*, p. 51.

[134] Data mentioned by Ramírez *et al.* citing information provided by the former High MERCOSUR Commissioner, Florisvaldo Fier, at an event in 2016. J. Ramírez, I. Ceja, S. Coloma and R. Arteaga, *"Ah, Usted Viene por la Visa Mercosur": Integración, Migración y Refugio en Ecuador* (Quito: CELAG, 2017), p. 16. As mentioned earlier, the number of permits that had been granted under the MERCOSUR Residence Agreement is not a settled matter with other studies pointing to up to 2 million.

[135] Margheritis, 'Piecemeal Regional Integration in the Post-Neoliberal Era'.

[136] For example, Bogotá Declaration, IV Andean Forum on Migration, Bogotá 9–10 May 2013; UNASUR, Conceptual Report on South American Citizenship, Working Group on South American Citizenship 2014.

[137] See Chapters 3 and 4.

with limited access to domestic courts, insufficient knowledge by all relevant actors – including lawyers – of these new agreements, and, finally, the slow pace in which domestic courts apply either CAN or MERCOSUR's Community law in their rulings at the national level.[138] Thus, mobility is exclusively for the wealthy whereas two-year temporary regularisation is available for some, but not all, of the less privileged.

Undoubtedly, South America has made decisive advancements in the direction of a right to reside and receive equal treatment in the territory of a second state. However, if we compare the model emerging to an open borders vision, the remaining challenges are enormous and affect all crucial aspects including entry, rights during the stay and security of residence. The right to circulate, to enjoy equal treatment and to not be expelled except under exhaustive limited circumstances are the three central elements to move in the direction of a real right to mobility and non-discrimination, as well as eventual South American citizenship.[139] Some voices in the region argue that this would also be a first step towards a universal citizenship.[140] Decisions need to be made regarding which form a regional citizenship would take. First, states must consider if citizenship would look like a social citizenship, a market one or something else. Second, they need to decide on whether it would resemble national citizenship or be more comparable to a sort of denizenship, hollowed out of benefits and political rights, but offering the right to work and equality before the law.

Some authors have argued that the region's labour mobility regime is simply characteristic of the general international legal landscape in its fragmentation.[141] In other words, one would not need to be anxious for the numerous, often inconsistent, instruments but rather 'see the regime of labour mobility as an essentially pluralist regime, whose main claim to regulation would not be in a single, self-contained regime – e.g., MERCOSUR or the Andean Community – but rather in the interaction between those regimes'.[142] Following this line, the Latin American tradition of solving conflicts through diplomacy and in a concerted form makes it difficult to envisage new supranational courts appearing in South America.[143] Optimistically, the agreements are being implemented at the national level in the new migration legislations. This should

---

[138] See, for example, the Colombian Supreme Court of Justice Case 35097, 6 March 2012, which references Decision 584 of 2004 on an Andean Instrument of Security and Health in the workplace.

[139] IOM, *Estudio sobre Experiencias en la Implementación del Acuerdo de Residencia*, p. 34.

[140] Final Declaration of the World Conference of the Peoples for a World Without Borders Towards Universal Citizenship (*Conferencia Mundial de los Pueblos por un Mundo sin Muros hacia la Ciudadanía Universal*), Tiquipaya, Bolivia, 21 June 2017.

[141] N. Bernal, M. A. Prada and R. Urueña, 'Intra-Regional Mobility in South America: The Andean Community and MERCOSUR' in M. Panizzon, G. Zürcher and E. Fornalé (eds), *The Palgrave Handbook of International Labour Migration* (Basingstoke: Palgrave Macmillan, 2015), pp. 507–534, on p. 522.

[142] *Ibid.*, p. 523.

[143] Saldías, 'Libre Circulación de Personas', on p. 192.

allow easier access to domestic courts to ensure migrants actually enjoy the rights that supranational instruments grant.[144] In order to move forward and exploit the possibilities of a framework with multiple legal sources deriving from the international, regional and domestic levels there needs to be: training of lawyers and judges at the domestic level, the interaction of such legal actors with the Inter-American Commission and Court on Human Rights, as well as the regional instances that already exist at the MERCOSUR and CAN levels. Thousands of South Americans have seen their legal status and access to rights improving as a result of the MERCOSUR Residence Agreement, as well as CAN's Decision 545. The road towards a true South American citizenship is still long and bumpy, these successes notwithstanding.

---

[144] N. Bernal et al., 'Intra-Regional Mobility in South America', p. 524.

8

Conclusion: Constructing and Deconstructing the Foreigner – An Innovative and Exceptional Approach?

Finally, and before I give the floor to others, I would like to make a brief reflection ... since we think that in the present time in our country, with a profound economic, social, political and institutional crisis, I believe we all have co-patriots, brothers, family members, who are in the USA or Spain today, or in any other country of the so-called 'first world' who are suffering discrimination and ill-treatment. And this National Congress in various projects has taken note of this situation, we have taken steps, have made applications, requests, to these countries so that the rights of our migrants are preserved [there]. And we find it contradictory when we ourselves still don't have those rights consecrated in our own legislation.[1]

Introduction

This book has investigated two hundred years of the legal construction of the 'foreigner' and the 'national' in ten countries in South America through a comparative and historical analysis of its legislative migration and citizenship frameworks. On a global level, South America has opted for the most open discourse on migration and citizenship since the turn of the twenty-first century. This is well exemplified by enunciating the principles of non-criminalisation of irregular migration, the right to migrate as a fundamental right, as well as promoting open borders and universal citizenship. At a time when restrictiveness is predominant around the world, South American policy makers and scholars

---

[1] Ruben Giustiniani, Argentinean MP, who proposed the country's new migration law, finally adopted in 2004; Public Audience 'Migration Legislation in the Republic of Argentina', Conference room of the National Congress, 26 September 2002 (author's translation). This quote first came to my attention in Melde, *Ahead of the Game?* p. 145. 'Finalmente y antes de empezar a dar la palabra quería hacer una brevísima reflexión ... pero nos parece que los tiempos que corren en nuestro país, donde la crisis económica, social, política e institucional, una crisis de una gran profundidad, creo que todos nosotros tenemos compatriotas, hermanos, parientes, que hoy en Estados Unidos, o en España, o en algún país del denominado "primer mundo" están padeciendo discriminaciones y maltrato. Y este Congreso de la Nación en distintos proyectos se ha hecho carne de esta situación, hemos hecho gestiones, hemos hecho solicitudes, pedidos, a estos países para que se preserve el derecho de nuestros migrantes. Y nos parece contradictorio esto cuando nosotros mismos todavía no tenemos en nuestra propia legislación esos derechos consagrados.'

alike present this ideological approach as both innovative and exceptional, as well as part of a morally superior, avant-garde path in policy and law making.

Is South America an innovative and exceptional model? Readers will have formed varying, perhaps non-dichotomous, answers having studied the preceding chapters. South American migration and citizenship law is still developing and in several respects wanting and contradictory, but it is also innovative, exceptional and stimulating at times. Its inconsistent character derives from the juxtaposition between visions based on security and control, heir to the accumulation of restrictive measures in the twentieth century, and a more recent human rights perspective.

Beyond claims of innovation or exceptionalism, two points become obvious. First, both historically and recently, South American countries have approached the legal construction of the foreigner in very similar ways. Second, this regional resemblance of the 'foreigner' is distinctive from the often-discussed US and Western European models. This finding alone confirms the need to extend analyses from the usual parochialism of a handful of countries in Europe and the USA – while nonchalantly adding Australia and Canada. Additionally, it serves as a note of caution to those who generalise global models and theories that were formed from a limited case selection.[2]

In the following pages, this chapter offers a broad overview of the themes that have emerged from evaluating the historical and current immigration and citizenship legal regimes in South America. Then it will attempt to suggest some potential avenues for research to break away from the stale dichotomy focusing solely on the USA and Europe as models of global migration management. In fact, one of the main findings of my analysis is that in terms of migration and citizenship, South America demonstrates several features that cannot be satisfactorily understood or explained utilising some of the major theoretical models that are advertised to be global. This, quite obviously, requires a renewed effort to map out some socio-political dynamics from a conceptual point of view that have been overlooked for too long. This prompts an embarrassing question for migration studies, which should be addressed as a problem in its own right: why has this sub-continent – as well as many others – been largely ignored by migration scholars? Furthermore, recognising the importance of South America as a global alternative to American and European approaches to immigration and citizenship is both an intellectual necessity and an opportunity to produce original answers to contemporary challenges of migration regulation.

---

[2] Recognising parochialism in the literature is rare, thus Joppke must be praised for acknowledging that his account of citizenship and immigration is a 'provincial story, limited to the comfort zone of North America, Western Europe, and the British outlets in Oceania'. C. Joppke, *Citizenship and Immigration* (Cambridge: Polity Press, 2010), p. 147.

Migration and Citizenship Law in the Nineteenth and Twentieth Centuries

From the moment of independence in the early nineteenth century, the nascent Latin American states envisaged themselves 'as being both *different from* and *better than*' Europe and the USA.[3] Whilst both influenced numerous political aspects in the development of the region, Latin Americans, including of course all South American states, made different choices that continue to influence their understanding and regulation of nationality and alienage and that distinguish them from Europe and the USA. In defining the composition of embryonic nations, South American Creole elites placed the utmost value on birth in the territory through establishing *ius soli*. This was the most suitable manner to construct nationals 'out of colonial subjects'[4] in societies with strong social and racial divisions between white, black and Indian groups. This was also a way to enlarge the population – a desirable outcome for countries who needed nationals to fulfil obligations such as military duties. *Ius sanguinis* would not have sufficiently boosted the number of nationals required. Whilst an inclusive conception of *ius soli* – in the sense of applying it to all those born in the state – announced, in theory, the end of racial discrimination, Creoles were eager to maintain their privileged position in the social structure and to limit the influence of heterogeneous populations divided by race and class.[5] Distinguishing between the national and citizen, with only the latter having political rights and access to municipal positions, was used as a recurrent device to continue defining the polity core in racialised, but also gendered terms, permitting only a gradual transformation of society. Only men who were capital holders, literate and, often, married, were 'deemed to have "civic virtue"; only they were capable of self-government; and only they accrued equal rights.'[6] Given this environment, Creole elites continued to hold sway over the political voice. This vision of white elites of European origin holding a dominant role greatly influenced immigration and naturalisation policies, which were used as another tool to define nationhood. Indeed, the image of the perfect immigrant mirrored the image of the perfect citizen. From that vantage point, open borders became a civilising project imagined as white, male, Europeans bringing capital, industries, arts and sciences. Whilst populating territories conceived of as uninhabited, they also contributed to the whitening of mixed-race populations. From the very beginning, open borders – coupled with equal treatment clauses and short residence requirements before naturalisation – were used as another device to lure in these agents of civilisation. Even with that caveat in mind, the

---

[3] N. Miller, 'Latin America: State-Building and Nationalism' in Breuilly (ed.), *The Oxford Handbook of the History of Nationalism*, pp. 378–395, on pp. 389–390.

[4] Appelbaum *et al.*, 'Introduction. Racial Nations', p. 4.

[5] Simon, *The Ideology of the Creole Revolution*, p. 32.

[6] Appelbaum *et al.*, 'Introduction. Racial Nations', p. 4.

free movement of people represented a radical split with the previous colonial system and its restrictions.

The relationship with foreigners, even those who were idealised, was always ambivalent. The category of *extranjero naturalizado* – literally a 'naturalised foreigner' – denotes the importance attached to territorial birth. As such, nationality and citizenship have always been stratified. By this, I am not alluding to Holston's 'differentiated citizenship' in Brazil, where citizenship 'manages social differences by legalizing them in ways that legitimate and reproduce inequality', an aspect persistent since colonial times that could be equally applicable to other South American countries.[7] What I am rather referring to here is the legally sanctioned division between those considered 'naturals' (natives) and those who are 'naturalised'. Today, all ten countries continue to use this distinction. The 'sons of Americans' have been native born in the continent.[8] All the rest were foreigners in perpetuity, excluded from the possibility of holding numerous offices, forever expurgating the original sin of their birth in a foreign land; only their offspring would be '*naturales* of the *patria*'.[9]

Birth within the continent carried such weight that a third legal category in between the national and the foreigner emerged: the Hispano-American subject, who was a former Spaniard from the Americas – arguably those who were identifiable as 'Creoles'. Creolism was in fact a small group of elite with a sense of 'American-ness', who did not see themselves as 'separate from their creole neighbours' and indeed 'identified themselves as Americans – as opposed to Spaniards – but not as a specific subnationality'.[10] This partly explains the difficulties in constructing nations in a region where the gap 'between white, black and Indian within countries was always greater than the differences between any of these groups across borders'.[11] Thus, legislation provided Hispano-American Creoles with a more privileged status. The Hispano-American legal figure represented a different form of membership: a level of polity located not at the national level, but rather at the supranational. In other words, in the Hispano-American context, there was never a simple dichotomy between national or citizen and foreigner. The willingness, enshrined in the highest national norms, to readily accept those from Hispano-America as part of the community through automatic naturalisation represents an approach to membership that clashes with classical descriptions. In other words, these individuals – arguably

[7] J. Holston, *Insurgent Citizenship: Disjunctions of Democracy and Modernity in Brazil* (Princeton University Press, 2009), pp. 3–4. Other authors have argued that the principle of equal citizenship remains unfulfilled also in the USA; for example, S. Sassen, 'The Repositioning of Citizenship and Alienage: Emergent Subjects and Spaces for Politics', *Globalizations*, 2 (2005), 79–94, on 84.

[8] T. Herzog, 'Communities Becoming a Nation: Spain and Spanish America in the Wake of Modernity (and Thereafter)', *Citizenship Studies*, 11 (2007), 151–172, on 163.

[9] Brown, *Adventuring through Spanish Colonies*, pp. 195–196.

[10] Centeno, *Blood and Debt*, p. 24.

[11] *Ibid.*, p. 175.

mostly Creole elites – were entitled to a common identity in the postcolonial Hispano-American space.

The ruling Creole elites often mistrusted local populations,[12] not only on racial grounds, but also due to property and class status.[13] Thus it is unsurprising that, coinciding with a large number of foreigners arriving with third-class tickets from the 1880s onwards, mainly to Argentina, Brazil and Uruguay, the region initiated exclusionary border and migration mechanisms. The previous free movement and equal treatment provisions gradually deteriorated in favour of restrictions on various ethnic, racial, ideological, moral, physical and economic grounds. By the turn of the twentieth century, elites became increasingly concerned about the nature of European immigration. The arrival of white Europeans continued to be welcomed as a step forward towards 'racial improvement' in the elites' vision of nation-making projects.[14] Nonetheless, this longed-for and idealised migrant of the nineteenth century – the white, industrious (Northern) European with capital – did not necessarily describe those arriving in large numbers, who were mostly Southern Europeans, perceived to be less civilised than those from the North.[15] Immigrants naturally filled gaps in the labour force but also brought notions about rights and equality that were found to be subversive. Restrictions then derived from deeply entrenched domestic concepts of conformity, belonging and exclusion that the ruling elites defined.

This represented both a continuation of previous nineteenth-century exclusionary traits – such as denying citizenship based on class[16] – as well as a reversal in some respects of the formerly idealised European migrant. Furthermore, by the early twentieth century, border control transformed into 'an indivisible aspect of sovereignty'.[17] Thus, even the South American countries that received few migrants nonetheless replicated border measures as a 'prerequisite to recognition as a self-governing state',[18] believing that this would reaffirm their newly acquired status in the international arena. Restrictions that slowly started to affect certain Europeans took longer to also include Americans. As a scholar eloquently observed in 1928, it is 'one thing to regulate immigration from the Old World; it is another thing to seek to impose restrictions upon immigrants from one American country to another'.[19] As if constructing a wall, individual bricks representing despised categories of foreigners were slowly but surely stacked one upon another throughout an entire century of legislative and administrative provisions.[20] Exclusion peaked in the 1970s under the context of

---

[12] Hobsbawm, 'Nacionalismo y Nacionalidad en América Latina', pp. 311–326.
[13] Simon, *The Ideology of the Creole Revolution*, p. 32.
[14] Loveman, *National Colors*, p. 154.
[15] Alberdi, *Bases*, pp. 15–17.
[16] Chapter 2, pp. 41–42.
[17] McKeown, *Melancholy Order*, p. 95.
[18] *Ibid.*, p. 321.
[19] Brown Scott, 'The Sixth International Conference of American States', p. 320.
[20] FitzGerald and Cook-Martin, *Culling the Masses*.

military dictatorships, when the legal regulation of the foreigner found its most repressive and denigrating version yet.

Migration and Citizenship Law Today

Discrimination against foreigners was only one element of possibly the darkest period in the history of South America, and more generally, in Latin America. Under the shadow of military regimes, the most egregious crimes against humanity took place with impunity: forced disappearances, extra-judicial executions and torture. It is against this background that a new architecture has emerged since the 1990s, one based on human rights protection at the international, regional and domestic constitutional levels. Newly re-established democracies hastily ratified international human rights instruments as an 'antidote against authoritarian regressions'.[21] The process called the new Latin American Constitutionalism has affected most countries and entails granting international and human rights law a much more prevalent position in the domestic constitutional order. At a material level, new constitutions have incorporated extensive catalogues of rights protecting vulnerable groups – such as Afro-descendants and indigenous populations – but also migrants, who are considered to be vulnerable compared to national workers.[22] The Inter-American Court's increasingly important jurisprudence, as well as the Inter-American Commission, have played a notable role through their emphasis on the need to protect migrants and their rights. It is now common knowledge that the 2004 Argentinean immigration law, the first of a series of more progressive texts in the region, was adopted as a result of a friendly settlement reached before the IACHR in 2003.[23]

Yet, the increasing importance of international law after the demise of heinous dictatorships cannot in itself explain a shift towards more humanely regulating the status of foreigners. Rather, we must bear in mind the transform-ation from an entire continent serving as a destination into one of origin. The enormous number of South Americans who have emigrated since the 1970s, and more specifically at the turn of the century, is crucial for our understanding of new discourses, laws and practices that have emerged since the early 2000s. The principles of non-criminalisation of undocumented migration, the right to migrate as a fundamental right and open borders were first and foremost enunciated with emigrants in mind. The ideas of coherence and fairness – as exemplified by the opening quote in this concluding chapter – made their way into new immigration laws at both the domestic and regional level. The fact

---

[21] Abramovich, 'Autonomía y Subsidiariedad', p. 217.
[22] IACtHR, *Juridical Condition and Rights of the Undocumented Migrants*, paras 112, 131 and 160.
[23] IACtHR, Report No. 85/11, Petition 12.306, Friendly Settlement *Juan Carlos de la Torre* (Argentina), 21 July 2011.

that immigration rates have remained rather low in the region also makes it easier to enunciate such principles.

The resulting migration and citizenship regime in South America is distinctive compared to the global level. Citizenship is mostly regulated based on the same choices that were adopted immediately after independence: *ius soli*; short residence periods before naturalisation; and discrimination between 'naturals' and 'naturalised citizens'. Following similar historical patterns, and despite its alleged liberal nature, the number of naturalisations in South America is strikingly low. This could possibly be the result of a combination between administrative discretion and hurdles, coupled with reduced incentives for those regional migrants who can now, in principle, take advantage of free residence regimes. However, this demands further investigation as to why the transformation mechanism between foreigner and national seems to have so little take-up. In turn, migration law becomes juxtaposed between reconfiguring dated nineteenth-century concepts, such as open borders, with a new political reality where emigration is numerically much larger than immigration. In the early twentieth century, South American states followed already-trodden paths, with no space for distinctiveness; they did so to appear *sufficiently sovereign* in the international arena.[24] Contrarily, the situation in our time portrays a certain uniqueness in regards to choosing the most suitable solutions to present challenges, which closely correspond to the region's idiosyncrasy. These proposed answers do not necessarily mirror those previously exercised in Europe or the USA.

A different ethos has emerged, which has human dignity as a core component and which understands regularisation as the most suitable response to migration flows. Membership in South America was never based on lengthy residence but rather on the individual's contribution to bettering the nation, family links and being part of a larger supranational space. These three elements continue to trump any residence requirements when claiming membership, affecting not only regularisation but also access to residence and citizenship. For example, it is unnecessary that undocumented migrants spend several years in an irregular status before accessing a residence permit; rather, they generally just need to be a South American citizen, a family member of a resident or have an employment offer in the destination.[25] Importantly, in South America the categories of irregular, regular and regional migrant are often blurred and undefined, leading to partial or temporary solutions for individuals.

Rather than a clear rupture with the past, what emerges is a 'migration management perspective' where 'human rights would play a central but ambivalent' role.[26] Rights on paper are sometimes hard to access in practice; they coexist with security and control tools such as visas – affecting mainly individuals

[24] See Chapter 4, pp. 106–107.
[25] See Chapter 5, pp. 135–138.
[26] Domenech, 'Crónica de una Amenaza Anunciada', pp. 66–68.

from Africa, Asia and the Caribbean – and rejection at the border, as well as possible expulsion on many grounds. The provisional character of residence permits, even for those covered under the MERCOSUR Residence Agreement, is possibly the best exemplification of the tension between securitisation and a rights-based approach, which Domenech has labelled as a 'policy of control with a human face' in the Argentinean case.[27] At the same time, the emphasis on the rights for South American emigrants has led states to accept dual citizenship, extend the franchise to foreigners, and sign agreements with reciprocal settlement rights throughout the region. These modifications cannot be characterised as a truly open-borders vision but have nonetheless facilitated the access to rights and a legal status for thousands of individuals. This change demonstrates a dramatic shift in the region's approach, as compared to the twentieth century.

Open Questions in the Literature

As explained earlier, scholars working on migration and citizenship have often reached their conclusions after looking at only the USA and a few countries in Europe – namely France, Germany, the Netherlands and the UK, with the eventual addition of Australia and Canada. Such a limited focus has produced theoretical models that do not seem to properly reflect the dynamics of South America as a region nor of its individual countries. This blind spot in the current literature requires careful exploration both empirically and theoretically in order to revise these models. This refinement may allow us to more profoundly understand the South American case – which offers a different perspective for regions elsewhere in the world that have also found that these alleged 'global' models actually have a limited extension. The following subsections will therefore tentatively propose what seems to be some of the most fruitful potential research avenues in this area. In particular, they highlight the challenges that the South American system faces, which may provoke broader contemporary thought on both migration and citizenship.

Nationals and Foreigners

The USA has been presented as the prototypical example of a country where absolute *ius soli* prevails – including for those born to undocumented parents – an aspect constitutionally protected by the fourteenth amendment.[28] This amendment was adopted in 1868 in the particular historical context of the aftermath of the American Civil War in the USA and a year after the Supreme

---

[27] Domenech, '"Las Migraciones son como el Agua"', 2.

[28] The Fourteenth Amendment's Citizenship Clause reads that '[a]ll persons born or naturalized in the United States, and subject to the jurisdiction thereof, are citizens of the United States and of the State wherein they reside'.

Court ruled to deny blacks access to citizenship in *Dred Scott v. Sanford*.[29] In turn, Europe – particularly Germany – has been portrayed as representing the opposite trend. Only those born to German parents could obtain citizenship at birth. As a result, the number of individuals (often referred to as 'second or third generation') excluded from the polity of the state in which they are born has multiplied.[30] Germany partly amended this in 1999 by introducing a limited form of *ius soli*. However, other European countries continue to rely mostly on *ius sanguinis*.[31]

As explained in Chapter 2, South America has opted for absolute *ius soli* since independence, although this decision was taken for different reasons compared to the USA. Place of birth is taken as a proxy of community membership and it separates nationals from foreigners from the cradle to the grave. Historically, South America has not questioned their use of *ius soli*. The exception to the rule is Colombia, which derogated from absolute *ius soli* as early as 1886,[32] and only Chile has had some voices keen on limiting nationality for those born to undocumented parents.[33] Similarly in the USA, beyond certain debates on so-called 'anchor babies', the fact that *ius soli* has not stirred up much dispute has been interpreted by some as evidence of the 'declining importance of citizenship itself'.[34] Others view *ius soli* as unmodifiable since changing it would mean the 'betrayal of a fundamental national ideal'.[35]

Social membership relates to how boundaries of society are construed in a polity, not only at birth but also through naturalisation. The entire body of scholarly literature has worked from the starting assumption that naturalisation completes the rite of passage from foreigner to national citizen. This is true both in Europe[36] and the USA, with the minor exception that the latter bans naturalised citizens from being elected President or Vice-President of the country. This has led to accounts of citizenship being described as 'internally inclusive' and 'externally exclusive', or hard on the outside and soft on the inside.[37] However, South America, with its continuous discrimination towards naturalised foreigners, empirically contradicts this scheme. In fact, other legal systems could consider the term 'naturalised foreigners' to be an oxymoron, but not in South America where those who naturalise are a different legal category

---

[29] For a more extensive description of the historical context, see: R. Rubio-Marín, *Immigration as a Democratic Challenge. Citizenship and Inclusion in Germany and the United States* (Cambridge University Press, 2000), pp. 177–182.

[30] *Ibid.*, pp. 186–234.

[31] C. Dumbrava and R. Bauböck (eds), *Bloodlines and Belonging: Time to Abandon Ius Sanguinis?* Florence: EUI, Working Paper RSCAS 2015/80.

[32] See Chapter 2, p. 58.

[33] Chile, Art. 166, Draft Migration Law, not adopted, Santiago, 20 May 2013.

[34] P. J. Spiro, *Beyond Citizenship: American Identity After Globalization* (Oxford University Press, 2008), p. 30.

[35] Carens, *The Ethics of Immigration*, pp. 37–38.

[36] See Art. 5 of the European Convention on Nationality prohibiting discrimination between nationals by birth and those who naturalise.

[37] Brubaker, *Citizenship and Nationhood in France and Germany*, Ch 1.

of residents with fewer rights. South America has an imperfect naturalisation legal system, or in the case of Uruguay, no naturalisation at all. Regardless, this does not seem to stir debate, even though it appears as a central flaw in the region's citizenship and migration regime since it fundamentally undermines its aspiration for equality between all residents throughout the polity.

Additionally, the extremely low number of naturalisations that South American states grant each year – despite what are in principle easy to fulfil conditions, given the very short residence period requirements – is another aspect in need of further investigation. Imminent findings stemming from these lines of research rather obviously call for a revaluation of citizenship theories and reveal a need to further explore whether or not other regions across the globe that have been affected by colonial western rule also experience similar phenomena.

The Demise of Citizenship

Over the last three decades, scholars have debated the declining role of citizenship. This is unsurprising given the developments around the concept, such as easier access to citizenship, growing toleration of dual nationality, providing more rights to non-nationals residing within a territory and, in the EU context, the creation of a supranational status. Citizenship, according to Bauböck, would no longer be 'a thick bundle of identity, rights, duties and political engagement that connects individuals to one particular nation-state'.[38] Instead, it would be the emergence of what Joppke has labelled 'citizenship light'.[39]

Hammar used the term 'denizens' in the early 1990s to refer to foreigners who enjoy several civil, social and, to a lesser extent, political rights in a territory, notwithstanding their lack of citizenship.[40] Since then, the vocabulary to describe the transformation of citizenship has multiplied: postnational, supranational and transnational are but a few of them. The main interest, for the purposes of this chapter, revolves around how 'the erosion in the distinction between citizen and alien' – through the latter accessing rights originally associated with nationality – would devalue 'the institution of citizenship'.[41] It is useful to briefly distinguish between concepts and theories that examine similar 'empirical phenomena', namely the demise of 'a singular and unique

---

[38] R. Bauböck, 'Genuine Links and Useful Passports', forthcoming 2018, *Journal of Ethnic and Migration Studies*, p. 1.

[39] Joppke, *Citizenship and Immigration*, Ch 5. However, Shachar argues that, especially after September 11, the draconian measures adopted to regulate migration and the status of foreigners means that, if anything, citizenship today is 'back with a vengeance' and has '*persistent* importance'. See: A. Shachar, *The Birthright Lottery: Citizenship and Global Inequality* (Cambridge, MA: Harvard University Press, 2009), p. 2.

[40] Hammar, *Democracy and the Nation State*, p. 13.

[41] Sassen, *Losing Control?* p. 103.

identity relation between citizens and nation-states' through different 'interpretative frames'.[42]

Postnational citizenship articulates 'the idea of citizenship "beyond" rather than "above" the nation, i.e. a transformation through which state-based citizenship becomes dissociated from national identity altogether'.[43] Citizenship would be undermined by both the continuous promotion and diffusion of 'universalistic rules and conceptions regarding the rights of the individual'[44] as well as the increasing role of international human rights norms resulting in new modalities of membership.[45] Some authors are guilty of conceptual stretching while using the terms postnational as well as supranational citizenship.[46] In reality, the latter refers to the rights that individuals obtain due to their nationality of certain states that partake in a supranational organisation. The exemplary is EU citizenship.[47] Distinctively, transnational citizenship emphasises that migrants as individuals are simultaneously immigrants and emigrants, and thus have certain rights in the destination country whilst also receiving rights from their states of origin – what has been labelled as external citizenship.[48] Discussions on the demise of citizenship have largely concentrated on Western Europe and the USA in the period since the Second World War.[49] As Joppke has observed, the right to immunity from being randomly accused, arrested or imprisoned had already covered all individuals in the 1789 French Declaration of the Rights of Man and of the Citizen. In his view, this casts 'doubt on the novelty of some postnational "personhood" rights'.[50]

Against this background, South America again appears as a troublesome conundrum. To begin with, there is the historical development of rights often associated with citizenship. Nineteenth-century South America represented a region where these rights were available to non-nationals – in many respects there was no clear distinction between citizens and foreigners.[51] The latter could reside in the region and even exercise civil rights without being deported since expulsion provisions were largely non-existent. Indeed, European immigrants had many more entitlements than most national populations. In the case of Hispano-Americans, arguably a small Creole elite, the picture became more complex since they had privileged routes to naturalisation as well as more political rights. This contradicts those who argued that since the French revolution,

---

[42] R. Bauböck, 'Introduction', pp. 1–2.

[43] *Ibid.*

[44] Soysal, *Limits of Citizenship*, p. 145.

[45] Benhabib, *The Rights of Others*, pp. 10 and 21.

[46] Soysal, *Limits of Citizenship*, p. 159. For a multi-level perspective of citizenship to avoid conceptualising EU citizenship as postnational see R. Bauböck, 'The Three Levels of Citizenship within the European Union', *German Law Journal*, 15 (2014), 751–764.

[47] Kochenov, *EU Citizenship and Federalism*.

[48] Bauböck, 'Introduction', p. 3.

[49] In regards to the USA, see: Bosniak, *The Citizen and the Alien*.

[50] Joppke, *Citizenship and Immigration*, p. 29.

[51] See Chapter 2, pp. 52–54.

'[t]he rights of man were inextricable from the substance of citizenship'.[52] South America turns this conventional wisdom on its head.

'Alien citizenship'[53] was a normal reality in South America until the 1930s. Thus, following Brubaker's configuration,[54] citizenship's relevance as an 'instrument' and 'object' of social closure was less salient. It was not an instrument because its main function, which was to allow the state to control who enters its territory, was practically non-existent until the twentieth century. It was not an object either because the limitation of access to citizenship through nationality laws played a marginal role. If anything, citizenship was an instrument and an object of social *openness* for the 'right type' of foreigners who were lured in and then offered easy naturalisation – even automatic in the case of Hispano-Americans. To complicate the picture even further, other rights – e.g. consular protection abroad and recognition of qualifications – were extended to Hispano-Americans through supranational instruments via multilateral and bilateral treaties.[55]

This openness towards the arrival of foreigners led to numerous legal configurations under which individuals could rely on rights derived from both the state of residence and from the one of origin, in what was in effect a transnational situation. Foreigners, especially of European origin, had the advantage of being excluded from certain obligations – e.g. military ones and often taxation – but more importantly, they could rely on diplomatic protection if they needed it. Nineteenth-century South America thus enriches debates on postnational, transnational and supranational forms of membership not only geographically and temporally, but it also demonstrates much more complex membership categorisations based on nationality, class and race. In certain aspects, the South American model contrasts with those in the EU and USA, thus prompting urgent questions as to why this southern continent has taken such a different route, and how these divergent experiences relate to or influence each other, for example through legal transplants or bilateral agreements.

When it comes to present-day regulation, South America offers important new empirical material to analyse the interplay between the postnational, transnational and supranational forms of membership that have been inadequately explored. For example, international human rights – mainly the ACHR, as interpreted by the IACtHR, and the ICMW – cannot singlehandedly explain the process of extending rights to foreigners in recent laws. Furthermore, contrary to what some authors have proposed for North America and Europe, domestic tribunals have not been the main drivers for limiting the capacity of states to control immigration.[56]

---

[52] Soysal, *Limits of Citizenship*, p. 164; Brubaker, *Citizenship and Nationhood in France and Germany*, p. 46.

[53] Bosniak, *The Citizen and the Alien*, pp. 2–4.

[54] Brubaker, *Citizenship and Nationhood in France and Germany*, p. 34.

[55] See Chapter 3.

[56] C. Joppke, 'Immigration Challenges the Nation-State' in C. Joppke (ed.), *Challenge to the Nation-State: Immigration in Western Europe and the United States* (Oxford University Press, 1998),

The increasing entitlements for foreigners can be partly understood as a result of extending rights to South American emigrants abroad. Thus, certain rights – such as political ones – that foreigners have obtained in countries within the region do not derive from immigrant demands in South America, but rather from expected reciprocity from the destination states in which South American emigrants reside.[57] Liberal legislation becomes a vehicle through which external demands may be more credibly voiced in favour of emigrants.[58] Indeed, transnational practices of 'external citizenship'[59] are common for South American states, given their role as primarily emigration countries.[60]

When it comes to supranational citizenship, South America deserves further analysis, too. Similar to Europe, the three main components of such a citizenship would entail the free circulation of people throughout the regional space, equal treatment – notably in access to the labour market and working conditions, with further unclear references to social rights – and some less important entitlements such as consular protection abroad.[61] Similarly to what has happened in Europe, South Americans are very cautious in protecting national sensitivities. As such, policy documents limit discussion of political rights – mainly to elect representatives for regional parliaments – and immediately reassure that any supranational status would broaden, not substitute, national citizenship.[62]

It is here that the historical tension between an idealised vision of a regional *patria grande* and well-entrenched nationalism is more obvious. As explained by Sanahuja, 'nationalism was the foundational discourse of the new postcolonial power, forming the new nations from a legitimising narrative of the ruling (Creole) elites' command over Indians and Afro-descendants'.[63] This difficult equilibrium between the national and regional level has affected all integration initiatives and clearly presents challenges to any supranational membership.

---

pp. 5–48. Some authors have more recently argued that human rights are losing traction as a tool to protect migrants; see, e.g., Dauvergne, *The New Politics of Immigration*, p. 120.

[57] Escobar, 'Migration and Franchise Expansion', p. 8.

[58] See the Final Declaration IX SCM, Quito, 21–22 September 2009, para. 5: 'We declare our good-will to guarantee migrants in our region the enjoyment of the same rights we aim for our citizens in transit and destination countries for the sake of the principles of coherence, equality and non-discrimination' (author's translation). Also see Acosta and Freier, 'Turning the Immigration Policy Paradox Up-side Down?'.

[59] Bauböck, 'Introduction', p. 3.

[60] See Chapter 6, pp. 155–158 and 161–162.

[61] Action Plan for a MERCOSUR Citizenship Statute, December 2010, pp. 2 and 5; Bogotá Declaration, IV Andean Forum on Migration, Bogotá, 9–10 May 2013.

[62] UNASUR, Conceptual Report on a South American Citizenship, Working Group on a South American Citizenship, 2014; Bogotá Declaration, IV Andean Forum on Migration, Bogotá, 9–10 May 2013.

[63] J. A. Sanahuja, 'Regionalismo Post-Liberal y Multilateralismo en Sudamérica: El Caso de UNASUR' in A. Serbín, L. Martínez and H. Ramanzini Júnior (eds), *El Regionalismo 'Post-Liberal' en América Latina y el Caribe: Nuevos Actores, Nuevos Temas, Nuevos Desafíos. Anuario de la Integración Regional de América Latina y el Gran Caribe 2012* (Buenos Aires: CRIES, 2012), pp. 19–72, on p. 21.

Amongst South American organisations, UNASUR has displayed the most interest in boosting a regional identity. They have proposed the adoption of a common passport, special queues for regional nationals at the border, student mobility scholarships, and even a regional song[64] – demonstrating an agenda that is advancing very slowly. At the time of writing UNASUR had indeed stalled.[65]

Thus, South America offers fertile ground for scholars looking to reassess and further investigate the historical novelty of membership configurations beyond citizenship – whether it is postnational, transnational or supranational – and the geographical spaces where such configurations take place. Another avenue is analysing the reasoning behind extending certain rights to foreigners, as well as defining how and when concerns about emigrants may advance immigrants' rights or regional integration mobility schemes. These elements may have policy implications and are begging for original new research.

South America as a Global Influential Model?

When I present my work on South America in any corner of the world someone often poses the following question: What influence might the region's approach have on Europe and the USA? Whilst this query is understandable, I find it a replication, often involuntary, of a Western-centric approach to the global topics of migration and mobility. When almost half of the global movement of people takes place South–South, it might perhaps be more interesting to rephrase the inquiry as to how South America may first offer useful alternatives to migration regulation in other parts of the global South, and then afterwards in Europe or the USA.

South America has already proved to be influential: there are lessons to be learned from a model that, in certain aspects, attempts to be more humane, but also has its implementation deficiencies. Most obviously, other Latin American countries that are bound by the ACHR and subject to the Inter-American Court's jurisprudence and the Inter-American Commission's decisions – as well as having ratified the ICMW – are clear first candidates if one expects a common approach to emerge. Indeed, aspects such as the right to migrate or regularisation as a first option to deal with undocumented migrants are already present in Guatemalan, Mexican and Nicaraguan laws, which have been affected by South American debates.[66]

[64] UNASUR, Conceptual Report on a South American Citizenship, pp. 15–16.
[65] Sanahuja recognises the over-reliance on presidential leadership – and thus sensitivity to political cycles – and limited institutional density as central challenges. J. A. Sanahuja, 'Regionalismo e Integración en América Latina: de la Fractura Atlántico-Pacífico a los Retos de una Globalización en Crisis', *Pensamiento Propio*, 21 (2016), 29–76, on 38–39.
[66] Mexico, Arts 132–137 on regularisation, Migration Law, 25 May 2011; Nicaragua, Art. 118, General Migration and Aliens Law, 31 March 2011; Guatemala, Art. 1, Decree 44/2016, Migration Code.

Central America and Mexico – and to a lesser extent Cuba and the Dominican Republic – share many elements with South America in terms of the historic legal construction of the national and the foreigner. Understanding the inner ethos of a region during such construction is crucial for adequately grasping what might be useful for other corners of the world. For instance, the conditions that led the EU to establish a European citizenship and free movement of people – complete with a strong, albeit not always unproblematic, supranational component of enforcement and adjudication – will not necessarily recur in other regions. In Europe, integration was a political project following disastrous domestic nationalism and the annihilation of millions during World War II. In addition, the insistence of Italian negotiators that free movement was enshrined as a key principle in the 1950s – as a strategy to protect their emigrants in other European countries – was crucial.[67] Given differing contexts, each region must develop its own narratives for regional mobility that makes sense for the time and place.

Through a close examination of one southern region, this book has shown that Europe and the USA are not moulds that are replicated around the globe. Nonetheless, equifinality is not ruled out – various journeys may indeed lead to similar outcomes. For example, when discussing free mobility regimes in other regions, including South America, it is natural to consider the EU and compare such regimes to an idealised EU model. However, such exercises have limited explanatory power if the region's particularities and constraints are blurred or misunderstood. By putting South America on the agenda of academic migration, other scholars specialising in other regions might find it a useful reference to conduct similar historical and comparative analyses, whether it be in Africa, Asia, Central America, the Caribbean, the Gulf countries or the Post-Soviet space. Given the fact that half of the migrants in the entire world – more than 100 million individuals – move between countries in the South, it is peremptory to continue academic production exploring these phenomena. Additionally, regions outside Europe and the USA must initiate a dialogue among themselves, since they might face similar challenges when it comes to mobility.

South America can play a pivotal role in such a dialogue. With all its contradictions, drawbacks and implementation challenges, it is stimulating to be the first one to verbalise a new vocabulary of non-criminalisation, migration as a right and universal citizenship, even if not always proven effective. The effort on the part of so many regional actors to place the migrant front and centre, first as a human being – rather than a mere economic input – is laudable. The Inter-American Court's jurisprudence, with its strong focus on family life, guarantees against detention and wide interpretation of the rights migrants enjoy, is of paramount importance. This jurisprudence provides useful tools for legal actors working in the Global South, but also in Europe and the USA.

---

[67] W. Maas, *Creating European Citizens* (Lanham, MD: Rowman & Littlefield, 2007).

If we always look at the same usual suspects, then what Dauvergne argues might be true: namely, that immigration regulation is characterised by a landscape where 'no new ideas are emerging', or where the only ones emerging point in the direction of further control and restriction.[68] In areas such as irregular migration, a global rethinking is urgently needed. South America offers a new approach to regularisation – one where governments assume that granting residence status is the first option for undocumented migrants under certain conditions.[69] Whilst not exempt from implementation problems, the South American model illuminates a different angle for handling a long-term challenge. South America is contributing with proposals to the Global Compact on Migration for strengthening regularisation mechanisms and providing transparent, non-discretional criteria to access regular status.[70] The approach is not necessarily on normative grounds but rather pragmatic, such as increasing the tax base, controlling who resides in the territory as well as reciprocity towards South American nationals.[71]

Migration will continue to be a global pressing issue for decades to come. Law will not offer solutions to every single challenge that human mobility presents. However, vilifying migrants through legal norms harms not only the individual concerned but society at large. South America – with its own idiosyncrasies and peculiarities – has offered distinctive approaches both historically as well as more recently. The region has displayed repeated tensions juxtaposed between a rights-based agenda versus a restrictive one; as of late, it has leaned towards the former. Argentina's newly restrictive turn in 2017 is a stark reminder that both tendencies will continue to coexist in the future. All those expressing a preference for more open migration and citizenship law and policy have a critical role to play: may we continue working on successful legal arguments, without any false hopes of *fait accompli* but also without dismay.

---

[68] Dauvergne, *The New Politics of Immigration*, p. 7

[69] This gets to the core of an interesting exchange between Carens and Bosniak: the former defends regularisation when the individual has resided for a few years in the host state, whilst the latter criticises the proposal as accepting the continued existence of a 'class of people who are territorially present but have not been here long enough to pass into the privileged group … a resident caste of unprotected, uneducated "pariahs"'. L. Bosniak, 'Response' in J. H. Carens, *Immigrants and the Right to Stay* (Cambridge, MA: MIT Press, 2010), pp. 81–92, on p. 89.

[70] Regional Consultation for Latin America of Civil Society Organizations towards the Global Compact for Safe, Orderly and Regular Migration 1, Quito, Ecuador, 6 October 2017, p. 5.

[71] See Chapter 5.

Afterword

Migration law and, to a lesser extent, nationality and citizenship law, are constantly changing and being modified. The law in this book is good as of 1 October 2017 but numerous developments deserving a brief mention have occurred in the immediate five months since.

In Argentina, the action for annulment of the Decree 70/2017 was unsuccessful before a first judicial instance which served its ruling on late October 2017. This was immediately appealed by the Argentinean Centro de Estudios Legales y Sociales, as well as by the Buenos Aires Ombudsman.

In Brazil, the government adopted on 20 November 2017 the implementing regulations to the new migration law from May 2017. Numerous critiques by various scholars and civil society actors considered them regressive and in opposition to the Brazilian Constitution and the new migration law itself. There will be presidential elections in Brazil in 2018, which will affect the direction the administrative implementation of its new law will take.

In Chile, the committee in charge of the new proposal for a migration law in the Congress decided not to continue with the project on 10 January. It is unclear what will happen during 2018 considering that Sebastián Piñera will again become President. There are some voices asking for a new migration law project along the lines of the one his previous government presented in 2013, but it is uncertain whether that could be approved considering the present configuration of Congress.

In Colombia, a new proposal for a migration law was debated in the second permanent constitutional committee of Colombia's congress in November 2017. The fact that there are elections in that country in 2018 raises a question mark as to the future of such a legislative project.

In Ecuador, the implementing regulations to the 2017 Organic Law on Human Mobility where received with mixed feelings. More importantly, on 20 December 2017 a group of individuals including actors from academia and civil society brought an action challenging the constitutionality of the Organic Law on Human Mobility before the Ecuadorian Constitutional Tribunal. Considering the extensive catalogue of rights granted to foreigners by Ecuador's Constitution and its references to international law, namely the American Convention on Human Rights as interpreted by the Inter-American

Court, this ruling could become a landmark on migrants' rights protection in South America and beyond, and represents the first opportunity in which a constitutional court in the region is going to extensively give its legal view on the validity of a new migration law when measured against certain fundamental rights. Finally, thousands of Venezuelans are continuing to leave the country, with some sources estimating that there are now more than half a million Venezuelans in Colombia alone.

In brief, what these developments show is how migration and citizenship law in South America is a vibrant process where numerous actors, governmental or not, play leading roles in carving out a space for their particular interpretation of national, constitutional, regional and international law. All these processes will affect the ongoing legal construction of the foreigner and the national in South America in years to come.

Bibliography

Abramovich, Victor. 'Autonomía y Subsidiariedad: el Sistema Interamericano de Derechos Humanos frente a los Sistemas de Justicia Nacionales' in C. Rodríguez Garavito (ed.), *El Derecho en América Latina. Un Mapa para el Pensamiento Jurídico del Siglo XXI*. Buenos Aires: Siglo Veintiuno, 2011, pp. 211–230.

Acerenza Prunell, Sylvia. *Los Siriolibaneses y la Ley de 1890: El Racismo como Ordenador de la Política Inmigratoria*. Montevideo: Nordan-Comunidad, 2004/05.

Acosta, Diego. *Latin American Reactions to the Adoption of the Returns Directive*. Brussels: CEPS, 2009.

'Migration and Borders in the European Union: The Implementation of the Returns Directive on Irregular Migrants in Spain and Italy' in R. Zapata (ed.), *Shaping the Normative Contours of the European Union: A Migration-Border Framework*. Barcelona: Cidob Foundation Edition, 2010, pp. 81–95.

The Long-Term Residence Status as a Subsidiary Form of EU Citizenship. An Analysis of Directive 2003/109. Leiden: Martinus Nijhoff, 2011.

'The Returns Directive: Possible Limits and Interpretation' in K. Zwaan (ed.), *The Returns Directive: Central Themes, Problem Issues, and Implementation in Selected Member States*. Nijmegen: Wolf Legal Publishers, 2011, pp. 7–24.

Regional Report on Citizenship. The South American and Mexican Cases. EUI, EUDO Citizenship, Florence, 2016.

Acosta, Diego and Freier, Luisa Feline. 'Turning the Immigration Policy Paradox Up-Side Down? Populist Liberalism and Discursive Gaps in South America', *International Migration Review* 49, 2015: 659–697.

Acosta, Diego and Geddes, Andrew. 'The Development, Application and Implications of an EU Rule of Law in the Area of Migration Policy', *Journal of Common Market Studies* 51, 2013: 179–193.

'Transnational Diffusion or Different Models? Regional Approaches to Migration Governance in the European Union and Mercosur', *European Journal of Migration and Law* 16, 2014: 19–44.

Acosta, Diego and Martire, Jacopo. 'Trapped in the lobby: Europe's revolving doors and the Other as Xenos', *European Law Review* 39, 2014: 362–379.

Aguilar Cardoso, Luis Enrique (ed.). *El Derecho a la Libre Circulación de Personas en la Migración Internacional Intracomunitaria*. Lima: Comisión Andina de Juristas, 2010.

Aguilar Cardoso, Luis Enrique, Anaya, Esther and Blouin, Cécile. *Guía de Exigibilidad Jurídica de los Derechos Reconocidos en las Decisiones de la Comunidad Andina en Materia de Migraciones*. Lima: Comisión Andina de Juristas, 2015.

Alarcón, Rafael. 'The Free Circulation of Skilled Migrants in North America' in Pécoud and de Guchteneire (eds), *Migration without Borders*, 2007, pp. 243–257.

Alberdi, Juan Bautista. *Bases y Puntos de Partida para la Organización Política de la República Argentina, derivados de la Ley que Preside al Desarrollo de la Civilización en América del Sud*. Buenos Aires: Imprenta Argentina, 1852.

Aleinikoff, Thomas Alexander. 'International Legal Norms on Migration: Substance without Architecture' in R. Cholewinski, R. Perruchoud and E. MacDonald (eds), *International Migration Law: Developing Paradigms and Key Challenges*. The Hague: TMC Asser Press, 2007, pp. 467–479.

Aleinikoff, Thomas Alexander and Klusmeyer, Douglas (eds). *Citizenship Policies for an Age of Migration*. Washington, DC: Carnegie Endowment for International Peace, 2002.

'Plural Nationality: Facing the Future in a Migratory World' in Aleinikoff and Klusmeyer (eds), *Citizenship Policies for an Age of Migration*, 2002, pp. 63–88.

Alfonso, Adriana. *Integración y Migraciones. El Tratamiento de la Variable Migratoria en el MERCOSUR y su Incidencia en la Política Argentina*. Buenos Aires: IOM, 2012.

La Experiencia de los Países Suramericanos en Materia de Regularización Migratoria. Buenos Aires: IOM, 2013.

Aliverti, Ana. 'Making People Criminal: The Role of the Criminal Law in Immigration Enforcement', *Theoretical Criminology* 16, 2012: 417–434.

Alston, Philip and Crawford, James (eds). *The Future of UN Human Rights Treaty Monitoring*. Cambridge University Press, 2000.

Anderson, Benedict. *Imagined Communities. Reflections on the Origin and Spread of Nationalism*. London: Verso, 1983.

Anderson, Bridget, Gibney, Matthew J. and Paoletti, Emanuela. 'Citizenship, Deportation and the Boundaries of Belonging', *Citizenship Studies* 15, 2011: 547–563.

Angell, Alan. 'The Left in Latin America since c. 1920' in L. Bethell (ed.), *Latin America. Politics and Society since 1930*. Cambridge University Press, 1998, pp. 75–144.

Appelbaum, Nancy P., Macpherson, Anne S. and Rosemblatt, Karin Alejandra. 'Introduction. Racial Nations' in N. P. Appelbaum, A. S. Macpherson and K. A. Rosemblatt (eds), *Race and Nation in Modern Latin America*. Chapel Hill, NC: University of North Carolina Press, 2003, pp. 1–31.

Arbo, Higinio. *Ciudadanía y Naturalización*. Buenos Aires: El Ateneo, 1926.

Arboleda, Eduardo. 'Refugee Definition in Africa and Latin America: The Lessons of Pragmatism', *International Journal of Refugee Law* 3, 1991: 185–207.

Arcentales Illescas, Javier and Garbay, Susy. *Informe Sobre Movilidad Humana, Ecuador 2011*, Coalición por las Migraciones y el Refugio, 2012.

Arrighi, Jean-Thomas and Bauböck, Rainer. 'A Multilevel Puzzle: Migrants' Voting Rights in National and Local Elections', *European Journal of Political Research* 56, 2017: 619–639.

Baldwin Edwards, Martin and Kraler, Albert. *REGINE Regularisations in Europe Study on Practices in the Area of Regularisation of Illegally Staying Third-country Nationals in the Member States of the EU*. Vienna: ICMPD, 2009.

Balibar, Étienne. *Nous, Citoyens d'Europe? Les Frontières, l'Etat, le Peuple*. Paris: La Découverte, 2001.

Banks, Angela M. 'The Curious Relationship Between Self-Deportation Policies and Naturalization Rates', *Lewis & Clark Law Review* 16, 2012: 1149–1213.

Basadre, Jorge. *La Iniciación de la República. Tomo Primero*. Lima: Fondo Editorial de la Universidad Nacional Mayor de San Marcos, 2002.

Bauböck, Rainer. *Transnational Citizenship: Membership and Rights in International Migration*. Cheltenham: Edward Elgar, 1994.

'Recombinant Citizenship' in M. Kohli and A. Woodward (eds), *Inclusions and Exclusions in European Societies*. London: Routledge, 2001, pp. 38–58.

'Temporary Migrants, Partial Citizenship and Hypermigration', *Critical Review of International Social and Political Philosophy* 14, 2011: 665–693.

'The Three Levels of Citizenship within the European Union', *German Law Journal* 15, 2014: 751–764.

'Introduction' in R. Bauböck (ed.), *Transnational Citizenship and Migration*. London and New York: Routledge, 2017, pp. 1–18.

'Genuine Links and Useful Passports', *Journal of Ethnic and Migration Studies*, forthcoming 2018.

Bean, Frank D., Edmonston, Barry and Passel, Jeffrey S. *Undocumented Migration to the United States. IRCA and the Experience of the 1980s*. Washington, DC: The Urban Institute Press, 1990.

Becker Lorca, Arnulf. *Mestizo International Law. A Global Intellectual History 1842–1933*. Cambridge University Press, 2014.

Benavides Llerena, Gina, Sánchez Pinto, Silvana and Chávez, Gardenia. *Informe Alternativo sobre el Cumplimiento de la Convención. Informe Final*. Quito: Coalición Institucional para el Seguimiento y Difusión de la Convención Internacional para la Protección de los Derechos de todos los Trabajadores Migratorios y sus Familiares, 2007.

Benhabib, Seyla. *The Rights of Others. Aliens, Residents and Citizens*. Cambridge University Press, 2004.

Bernal, Natalia, Prada, María Angélica and Urueña, René. 'Intra-Regional Mobility in South America: The Andean Community and MERCOSUR' in M. Panizzon, G. Zürcher and E. Fornalé (eds), *The Palgrave Handbook of International Labour Migration*. Basingstoke: Palgrave Macmillan, 2015, pp. 507–534.

Berruezo, María Teresa. *La Participación Americana en las Cortes de Cádiz. 1810–1814*. Madrid: Centro de Estudios Constitucionales, 1986.

Bértola, Luis and Ocampo, José Antonio. *The Economic Development of Latin America since Independence*. Oxford University Press, 2012.

Bertoli, Simone, Fernández-Huertas, Jesús and Ortega, Francesc. 'Immigration Policies and the Ecuadorian Exodus', *The World Bank Economic Review* 25, 2011: 57–76.

Bertoni, Lilia Ana. 'La Naturalización de los Extranjeros, 1887–1893: ¿Derechos Políticos o Nacionalidad?', *Desarrollo Económico* 32, 1992: 57–77.

Bigo, Didier and Guild, Elspeth. 'Policing at a Distance: Schengen Visa Policies' in D. Bigo and E. Guild (eds), *Controlling Frontiers. Free Movement into and within Europe*. Farnham: Ashgate, 2005, pp. 233–263.

Bizzozero Revelez, Lincoln. 'El MERCOSUR y el Proceso Sudamericano ante la Segunda Década del Siglo XXI ¿Hacia una Consolidación del Nuevo Regionalismo Estratégico?', *Si Somos Americanos, Revista de Estudios Transfronterizos* 12, 2012: 215–237.

Black, Isabella. 'American Labour and Chinese Immigration', *Past & Present* 25, 1963: 59–76.

Blanchette, Thaddeus Gregory. '"Almost a Brazilian". Gringos, Immigration, and Irregularity in Brazil' in D. Acosta and A. Wiesbrock (eds), *Global Migration. Old Assumptions, New Dynamics*. Santa Barbara, CA: Praeger, 2015, pp. 167–194.

Blouin Cécile and Enrico, Alessandra. *Informe Alternativo al Comité de Protección de los Derechos de todos los Trabajadores Migratorios y de sus Familiares Perú*. Lima: Instituto de Democracia y Derechos Humanos de la Pontificia Universidad Católica del Perú (IDEHPUCP), la Escuela de Derecho de la Universidad Ruiz de Montoya y Encuentros Servicio Jesuita de la Solidaridad, 2017.

Bonfiglio, Giovanni. 'Introducción al Estudio de la Inmigración Europea en el Perú', *Apuntes* 18, 1986: 93–127.

Bosniak, Linda. 'Denationalizing Citizenship' in T. A. Aleinikoff and D. Klusmeyer (eds), *Citizenship Today. Global Perspectives and Practices*. Washington, DC: Carnegie Endowment for International Peace, 2001, pp. 237–252.

'Human Rights, State Sovereignty and the Protection of Undocumented Migrants under the International Migrant Workers' Convention' in B. Bogusz, R. Cholewinski, A. Cygan and E. Szyszczak (eds), *Irregular Migration and Human Rights: Theoretical, European and International Pespectives*. Leiden: Martinus Nijhoff, 2004, pp. 311–344.

The Citizen and the Alien. Dilemmas of Contemporary Membership. Princeton University Press, 2006.

'Persons and Citizens in Constitutional Thought', *International Journal of Constitutional Law* 8, 2010: 9–29.

'Response' in J. H. Carens (ed.), *Immigrants and the Right to Stay*. Cambridge, MA: MIT Press, 2010, pp. 81–92.

Braga Martes, Ana Cristina and Goncalves, Oswaldo. 'Gestão Multicultural dos Deslocamentos Populacionais', *Politica Externa* 17, 2008: 105–120.

Breuilly, John (ed.). *The Oxford Handbook of the History of Nationalism*. Oxford University Press, 2013.

Brewer-Carías, Allan R. *Régimen Legal de Nacionalidad, Ciudadanía y Extranjería*. Caracas: Editorial Jurídica Venezolana, 2005.

Brey, Elisa. *Report on Citizenship Law: Paraguay*. Florence: EUDO Citizenship Observatory, 2016.

Brøndsted Sejersen, Tania. '"I Vow to Thee My Countries" – The Expansion of Dual Citizenship in the 21st Century', *International Migration Review* 42, 2008: 523–549.

Brown, Matthew. *Adventuring through Spanish Colonies. Simón Bolivar, Foreign Mercenaries and the Birth of New Nations*. Liverpool University Press, 2006.

'Not Forging Nations but Foraging for Them: Uncertain Collective Identities in Gran Colombia', *Nations and Nationalism* 12, 2006: 223–240.

From Frontiers to Football. An Alternative History of Latin America since 1800. London: Reaktion Books, 2014.

Brown Scott, James. 'The Sixth International Conference of American States', *International Conciliation* 12, 1928–29: 277–349.

Brubaker, Rogers. *Citizenship and Nationhood in France and Germany*. Cambridge, MA: Harvard University Press, 1992.

Brumat, Leiza. *Políticas Migratorias y Libertad de Circulación en el Mercosur (1991–2012)*. PhD Thesis, FLACSO, Argentina, 2016.

Brumat, Leiza and Torres, Rayen Amancay. 'La Ley de Migraciones 25.871: Un Caso de Democracia Participativa en Argentina', *Estudios Políticos* 46, 2015: 55–77.

Burke, William. *South American Independence: or, the Emancipation of South America, the Glory and Interest of England*. London: J. Ridgway, 1807.

Additional Reasons for our Immediately Emancipating Spanish America: Deduced from the New and Extraordinary Circumstances, of the Present Crisis and Containing Valuable Information, Respecting the Late Important Events both at Buenos Ayres and in the Caraccas: as well as with Respect to the Present Disposition and Views of the Spanish Americans: Being Intended as a Supplement to 'South American Independence'. London: J. Ridgway, 1808.

Derechos de la América del Sur y de México. Caracas: Academia Nacional de la Historia, 1959.

Calvo, Carlos. *Derecho Internacional Teórico y Práctico de Europa y América*. Paris: D'Amijot (Caminos de Hierro), 1868.

Cané, Miguel. *Expulsión de Extranjeros (Apuntes)*. Buenos Aires: Imprenta de J. Sarrailh, 1899.

Cantor, David, Freier, Luisa Feline and Gauci, Jean-Pierre (eds), *A Liberal Tide? Immigration and Asylum Law and Policy in Latin America*. London: Institute of Latin American Studies, 2015.

Capps, Randy, Koball, Heather, Campetella, Andrea, Perreira, Krista, Hooker, Sarah and Pedroza, Juan Manuel. *Implications of Immigration Enforcement Activities for the Well-Being of Children in Immigrant Families. A Review of the Literature*. Washington, DC: Migration Policy Institute and Urban Institute, 2015.

Cárdenas, Mauricio and Mejía, Carolina. 'Migraciones Internacionales en Colombia: ¿Qué Sabemos?', Working Paper no. 30, September 2006, CEPAL.

Carens, Joseph. *The Ethics of Immigration*. Oxford University Press, 2013.

Carozza, Paolo G.. 'From Conquest to Constitutions: Retrieving a Latin American Tradition of the Idea of Human Rights', *Human Rights Quarterly* 25, 2003: 281–313.

Carvajal, Dayra. 'As Colombia Emerges from Decades of War, Migration Challenges Mount', Migration Policy Institute, 13 April 2017.

Cassinelli Muñoz, Horacio. *Derecho Público*. Montevideo: Fundación de Cultura Universitaria, 2009.

Castells Oliván, Irene and Fernández García, Elena. 'Las Mujeres y el Primer Constitucionalismo Español (1810–1823)', *Historia Constitucional* 9, 2008: 163–180.

Castles, Stephen and Davidson, Alastair. *Citizenship and Migration: Globalization and the Politics of Belonging*. New York: Routledge, 2000.

Cavallaro, James L. and Brewer, Stephanie Erin. 'Reevaluating Regional Human Rights Litigation in the Twenty-First Century: The Case of the Inter-American Court', *American Journal of International Law* 102, 2008: 768–827.

Centeno, Miguel A. *Blood and Debt. War and the Nation-State in Latin America*. Pennsylvania University Press, 2002.

Centeno, Miguel A. and Ferraro, Agustín E. 'Republics of the Possible: State Building in Latin America and Spain' in M. A. Centeno and A. E. Ferraro (eds), *State and Nation Making in Latin America and Spain. Republics of the Possible*. Cambridge University Press, 2013, pp. 3–24.

Centro de Direitos Humanos e Cidadania do Imigrante (CDHIC). *Brasil Informe sobre a Legislação Migratória e a Realidade dos Imigrantes*. São Paulo: CDHIC, 2011.

CEPAL. *Economic Survey of Latin America and the Caribbean 2009–2010: The Distributive Impact of Public Policies*. Santiago de Chile: United Nations, 2010.

Ceriani, Pablo. 'Luces y Sombras en la Legislación Migratoria Latinoamericana', *Nueva Sociedad* 233, 2011: 68–86.

'Ciudadanía, Migraciones y Libre Circulación en el Mercosur: ¿Hacia un Paradigma basado en los Derechos Humanos o la Réplica del Modelo Excluyente de la Unión Europea?' *Revista de Derecho Migratorio y de Extranjería* 30, 2012: 259–287.

Ceriani, Pablo and Morales, Diego. *Argentina: Avances y Asignaturas Pendientes en la Consolidación de una Política Migratoria basada en Los Derechos Humanos*. Buenos Aires: Centro de Estudios Legales y Sociales, 2011.

Chen, Chi Yi and Picouet, Michel. *Dinámica de la Población: Caso de Venezuela*. Caracas: UCAB-Orston, 1979.

Chetail, Vincent. 'The Transnational Movement of Persons under General International Law – Mapping the Customary Law Foundations of International Migration Law' in V. Chetail and C. Bauloz (eds), 2014, pp. 1–74.

Chetail, Vincent and Bauloz, Céline (eds), *Research Handbook on International Law and Migration*. Cheltenham: Edward Elgar, 2014.

Chiarello, Leonir Mario (ed.). *Las Políticas Públicas sobre Migraciones y la Sociedad Civil en América Latina. Los Casos de Argentina, Brasil, Colombia y México*. New York: Scalabrini International Migration Network, 2011.

Las Políticas Públicas sobre Migraciones y la Sociedad Civil en América Latina. Los Casos de Bolivia, Chile, Paraguay y Perú. New York: Scalabrini International Migration Network, 2013.

Cholewinski, Ryszard. 'The Rights of Migrant Workers' in R. Cholewinski, R. Perruchoud and E. MacDonald (eds), *International Migration Law: Developing Paradigms and Key Challenges*. The Hague: TMC Asser Press, 2007, pp. 255–274.

Coalición por las Migraciones y el Refugio. *Informe Alternativo sobre el Cumplimiento de la Convención de Naciones Unidas de los Derechos de Todos los Trabajadores Migratorios y sus Familiares*. Ecuador, 2017.

Cook-Martin, David. 'Rules, Red Tape and Paperwork: The Archaeology of State Control over Migrants', *Journal of Historical Sociology* 21, 2008: 82–119.

The Scramble for Citizens: Dual Nationality and State Competition for Immigrants. Stanford University Press, 2013.

Cordova Alcaraz, Rodrigo (ed.). *Dinámicas Migratorias en América Latina y el Caribe (ALC) y entre ALC y la Unión Europea*. Geneva: IOM, 2015.

Coria Márquez, Elba, Bonnici, Gisele and Martínez, Vanessa. *¿Qué Esperamos del Futuro? Detención Migratoria y Alternativas a la Detención en las Américas*. Melbourne: International Detention Coalition, 2017.

Costello, Cathryn. *The Human Rights of Migrants and Refugees in European Law*. Oxford University Press, 2016.

Cottrol, Robert J. *The Long, Lingering Shadow: Slavery, Race, and Law in the American Hemisphere*. Athens, GA: University of Georgia Press, 2013.

Courtis, Corina and Penchaszadeh, Ana Paula. 'El (Im)posible Ciudadano Extranjero. Ciudadanía y Nacionalidad en Argentina', *Revista SAAP* 9, 2015: 375–394.

Dauvergne, Catherine. 'Sovereignty, Migration and the Rule of Law in Global Times', *Modern Law Review* 67, 2004: 588–615.

Making People Illegal. What Globalization Means for Migration and Law. Cambridge University Press, 2008.

The New Politics of Immigration and the End of Settler Societies. Cambridge University Press, 2016.

Dávila, Luis Ricardo. 'Fronteras Confusas: Impactos Sociales de la Migración' in CEPAL (ed.), *La Migración Internacional y el Desarrollo en las Américas*. Santiago de Chile: CEPAL, 2001, pp. 259–277.

de Guchteneire, Paul, Pécoud, Antoine and Cholewinski, Ryszard (eds). *Migration and Human Rights: The United Nations Convention on Migrant Workers' Rights*. Cambridge University Press, 2009.

de Haas, Hein, Natter, Katharina and Vezzoli, Siomona. 'Growing Restrictiveness or Changing Selection? The Nature and Evolution of Migration Policies', *International Migration Review*, 2016, online early view version DOI: 10.1111/imre.12288, 1–44.

Delaney, Jeane. 'Immigration, Identity, and Nationalism in Argentina, 1850–1950' in N. Foote and M. Goebel (eds), *Immigration and National Identities in Latin America*. Gainesville, FL: University Press Florida, 2014, pp. 91–114.

de la Reza, Germán. *El Congreso de Panamá de 1826 y Otros Ensayos de Integración Latinoamericana en el Siglo XIX*. México D.F.: Universidad Autónoma Metropolitana, 2006.

'La Asamblea Hispanoamericana de 1864–65, Último Eslabón de la Anficcionía', *Estudios de Historia Moderna y Contemporánea de México* 39, 2010: 71–91.

'The Formative Platform of the Congress of Panama (1810–1826): The Pan-American Conjecture Revisited', *Revista Brasileira de Política Internacional* 56, 2013: 5–21.

'¿Necesidad o Virtud? Razones y Alcances de los Tratados Continentales Hispanoamericanos de 1856', *Historica* XXXVIII, 2014: 61–83.

del Castillo Martínez, Antonio. *El Congreso de Panamá de 1826 Convocado por el Libertador: Iniciación del Panamericanismo (Sus Actas y Tratados)*. Bogotá: Universidad Jorge Tadeo Lozano, 1982.

de Lombaerde, Philippe, Guo, Fei and Póvoa Neto, Helion. 'Introduction to the Special Collection. South–South Migrations: What is (Still) on the Research Agenda?', *International Migration Review* 48, 2014: 103–112.

del Rio, Mario E. *La Inmigración y su Desarrollo en el Perú*. Lima: Sanmarti y Cia, 1929.

Dembour, Marie-Bénédicte. *When Humans Become Migrants: Study of the European Court of Human Rights with an Inter-American Counterpoint*. Oxford University Press, 2015.

de Paulo Barreto, Vicente and Pimentel Pereira, Vítor. '¡Viva la Pepa!: A História não Contada da Constitución Española de 1812 em Terras Brasileiras', *Revista do Instituto Histórico e Geográfico do Brasil* 452, 2011: 201–223.

De Vattel, Emmerich. *The Law of Nations or the Principles of Natural Law*. 1758.

Devoto, Fernando J. *Historia de la Inmigración en la Argentina*. Buenos Aires: Editorial Sudamericana, 2003.

Di Filippo, Armando and Franco, Rolando. *Integración Regional, Desarrollo y Equidad*. México D.F.: Siglo XXI, 2000.

Domenech, Eduardo. *Migración y Política: el Estado Interrogado. Procesos Actuales en Argentina y Sudamérica*. Universidad de Córdoba (Argentina), 2009.

'Crónica de una Amenaza Anunciada. Inmigración e "Ilegalidad": Visiones de Estado en la Argentina Contemporánea' in B. Feldman-Bianco, L. R. Sánchez, C. Stefoni and M. I. Villa Martínez (eds), *La Construcción Social del Sujeto Migrante en América Latina. Prácticas, Representaciones y Categorías*. Quito: FLACSO, Sede Ecuador and

Consejo Latinoamericano de Ciencias Sociales, CLACSO: Universidad Alberto Hurtado, 2011, pp. 31–77.

'"Las Migraciones son como el Agua": Hacia la Instauración de Políticas de "Control con Rostro Humano". La Gobernabilidad Migratoria en Argentina', *Polis Revista Latinoamericana* 35, 2013: 1–20.

'Inmigración, Anarquismo y Deportación: La Criminalización de los Extranjeros "Indeseables" en Tiempos de las "Grandes Migraciones"', *Revista Interdisciplinar de Mobilidade Humana* 45, 2015: 169–196.

Domínguez Ortiz, Antonio. 'La Concesión de "Naturalezas para Comerciar en Indias" durante el Siglo XVII', *Revista de Indias* 19, 1959: 227–239.

Dumbrava, Costica and Bauböck, Rainer (eds). 'Bloodlines and Belonging: Time to Abandon Ius Sanguinis?'. Florence: EUI, Working Paper RSCAS 2015/80, 2015.

Durand, Jorge and Massey, Douglas. 'New World Orders: Continuities and Changes in Latin American Migration', *The ANNALS of the American Academy of Political and Social Science* 630, 2010: 20–52.

Ely Yamin, Alicia (ed.). *Derechos Económicos, Sociales y Culturales en América Latina. Del Invento a la Herramienta.* México D.F.: Plaza y Valdés, 2006.

Escobar, Cristina. 'Extraterritorial Political Rights and Dual Citizenship in Latin America', *Latin American Research Review* 42, 2007: 43–75.

Report on Citizenship Law: Colombia. Florence: European University Institute, EUDO Citizenship, 2015.

Migration and Franchise Expansion in Latin America. Florence: European University Institute, EUDO Citizenship, 2017.

Escudero López, José Antonio (ed.). *Cortes y Constitución de Cádiz. 200 Años.* Madrid: Espasa Calpe, 2011.

Esipova, Nelie, Ray, Julie, Pugliese, Anita, Tsabutashvili, Dato, Laczko, Frank and Rango, Marzia. *How the World Views Migration.* Geneva: IOM, 2015.

Espinoza, Marcia Vera, Brumat, Leiza and Geddes, Andrew. 'Migration Governance in South America: Where is the Region Heading?', blog entry, MIGPROSP, 4 August 2017.

Esthimer, Marissa. *Protecting the Forcibly Displaced: Latin America's Evolving Refugee and Asylum Framework.* Washington, DC: Migration Policy Network, 2016.

European Commission. *Communication on a Community Immigration Policy*, COM 757 final, Brussels, 22 November 2000.

Evans, Malcolm. 'Adjudicating Human Rights in the Preventive Sphere' in J. A. Green and C. P. M. Waters (eds), *Adjudicating International Human Rights. Essays in Honour of Sandy Ghandhi.* Leiden: Brill, 2015, pp. 212–234.

'Challenging Conventional Assumptions. The Case for a Preventive Approach to the Protection of the Freedom of Religion or Belief' in M. Evans, P. Petkoff and J. Rivers (eds), *The Changing Nature of Religious Rights under International Law.* Oxford University Press, 2015, pp. 25–50.

Facal Santiago, Silvia. *Movimientos Migratorios en Uruguay. Un Estudio a través del Marco Normativo.* Madrid: Observatorio Iberoamericano sobre Movilidad Humana, Migraciones y Desarrollo, OBIMID, 2017.

Faist, Thomas and Gerdes, Jürgen. *Dual Citizenship in an Age of Mobility.* Washington DC: Migration Policy Institute, 2008.

Faúndez García, Rocío. 'The Liberal Dilemma and Immigration Policy in Chile' in D. Rivera Salazar (ed.), *Chile: Environmental and Social Issues*. New York: Nova Science Publishers, 2012, pp. 195–234.

Fernandes, Duval, Milesi, Rosita, Pimenta, Bruna and do Carmo, Vanessa. 'Migração dos Haitianos para o Brasil. A RN n. 97/12: Uma Avaliação Preliminar', *Caderno de Debates* 8, 2013: 55–70.

Ferreira Levy, Maria Stella. 'O Papel da Migração Internacional na Evolução da População Brasileira (1872 a 1972)', *Revista Saúde Pública* 8, 1974: 49–90.

Ferrer, Ada. 'Haiti, Free Soil, and Antislavery in the Revolutionary Atlantic', *American Historical Review* 117, 2012: 40–66.

Ferrer Mac-Gregor, Eduardo. 'The Constitutionalization of International Law in Latin America Conventionality Control. The New Doctrine of the Inter-American Court of Human Rights', *American Journal of International Law Unbound* 109, 2015: 93–99.
'The Conventionality Control as a Core Mechanism of the Ius Constitutionale Commune' in von Bogdandy *et al.* (eds), *Transformative Constitutionalism*, 2017, pp. 321–336.

Fields, Harold. 'Closing Immigration throughout the World', *American Journal of International Law* 26, 1932: 671–699.

Finn, Victoria, Doña Reveco, Cristián and Feddersen, Mayra. 'The South American Conference on Migration: A Regional Approach to Migration Governance', unpublished paper, 2017.

Fischer, Sara, Palau, Tomás, Pérez, Noemia. *Inmigración y Emigración en el Paraguay 1870–1960*. Documento de Trabajo no. 90, Base Investigaciones Sociales IPGH, Instituto Panamericano de Geografía e Historia, 1997.

FitzGerald, David Scott and Cook-Martin, David 2014. *Culling the Masses. The Democratic Origins of Racist Immigration Policy in the Americas*. Cambridge, MA: Harvard University Press.

Freier, Luisa Feline. 'Open Doors (for Almost All): Visa Policies and Ethnic Selectivity in Ecuador', CCIS Working Paper 188, 2013.

Freier, Luisa Feline and Acosta, Diego. 'Beyond Smoke and Mirrors? Discursive Gaps in the Liberalisation of South American Immigration Laws' in Cantor, Freier and Gauci (eds), *A Liberal Tide?*, 2015, pp. 33–56.

Fuentes Maureira, Claudio, Hugo Lagos, Víctor, Lawson, Delfina and Rodríguez, Macarena. '3.000 Niños Esperando su Nacionalidad. La Necesidad de Contar con Remedios Colectivos para Resolver Vulneraciones Individuales de Derechos' in *Universidad Diego Portales, Anuario de Derecho Público 2016*. Santiago de Chile: Universidad Diego Portales, 2016, pp. 549–571.

Gaffield, Julia. *Haitian Connections in the Atlantic World: Recognition after Revolution*. Chapel Hill, NC: University of North Carolina Press, 2015.

Galasso, Norberto. *Seamos Libres y lo Demás no Importa Nada: Vida de San Martín*. Buenos Aires: Colihue, 2000.

Galeano, Diego. 'Las Conferencias Sudamericanas de Policías y la Problemática de los Delincuentes Viajeros, 1905–1920' in E. Bohoslavsky L. Caimari and C. Schettini (eds), *La Policía en Perspectiva Histórica. Argentina y Brasil (del siglo XIX a la Actualidad)*. Buenos Aires: CD-ROM, 2009.

García, Beatriz. *The Amazon from an International Law Perspective*. Cambridge University Press, 2011.

García, Lila. *Nueva Política Migratoria Argentina y Derechos de la Movilidad. Implementación y Desafíos de una Política Basada en Derechos Humanos a través de las Acciones ante el Poder Judicial (2004–2010).* PhD Thesis, University of Buenos Aires, 2013.

Gargarella, Roberto. *Latin American Constitutionalism, 1810–2010: The Engine Room of the Constitution.* Oxford University Press, 2013.

'El "Nuevo Constitucionalismo Latinoamericano"', *Estudios Sociales* 48, 2015: 169–172.

Gargarella, Roberto and Courtis, Christian. *El Nuevo Constitucionalismo Latino-americano: Promesas e Interrogantes.* Santiago de Chile: CEPAL, 2009.

Gaune, Rafael and Lara, Martín (eds). *Historias de racismo y discriminación en Chile.* Santiago de Chile: Uqbar, 2009.

Geddes, Andrew and Boswell, Christina. *Migration and Mobility in the European Union.* Basingstoke: Palgrave Macmillan, 2011.

Geddes, Andrew and Espinoza, Marcia Vera. 'Framing Understandings of International Migration: How Governance Actors Make Sense of Migration in Europe and South America' in A. Margheritis (ed.), *Shaping Migration between Europe and Latin America: New Perspectives and Challenges.* London: Institute of Latin American Studies, 2018.

Geronimi, Eduardo. *Acuerdos Bilaterales de Migración de Mano de Obra: Modo de Empleo.* Geneva: ILO, 2004.

Giustiniani, Rubén (ed.). *Migración: Un Derecho Humano.* Buenos Aires: Prometeo Libros, 2004.

Glendon, Mary Ann. 'The Forgotten Crucible: The Latin American Influence on the Universal Human Rights Idea', *Harvard Human Rights Journal* 16, 2003: 27–39.

Goizueta Vértiz, Juana, Gómez Fernández, Itziar and González Pascual, María Isabel (eds). *La Libre Circulación de Personas en los Sistemas de Integración Económica; Modelos Comparados. Unión Europea, Mercosur y Comunidad Andina.* Pamplona: Aranzadi, 2012.

Gómez Arnau, Remedios. *México y la Protección de sus Nacionales en Estados Unidos.* México D.F.: Universidad Nacional Autónoma de México, 1990.

Góngora Mera, Manuel. *Inter-American Judicial Constitutionalism. On the Constitutional Rank of Human Rights Treaties in Latin America through National and Inter-American Adjudication.* San José: Inter-American Institute of Human Rights, 2011.

Góngora Mera, Manuel, Herrera, Gioconda and Müller, Conrad. 'The Frontiers of Universal Citizenship. Transnational Social Spaces and the Legal Status of Migrants in Ecuador', desiguALdades.net Working Paper Series, 71, 2014.

González Beltrán, Jesús Manuel. 'Legislación sobre Extranjeros a finales del Siglo XVIII', *Revista de Historia Moderna y Contemporánea* 8–9, 1997: 103–118.

González-Bertomeu, Juan F. and Gargarella, Roberto (eds). *The Latin American Casebook. Courts, Constitutions, and Rights.* Abingdon: Routledge, 2016.

Goodman, Ryan and Jinks, Derek. 'Incomplete Internationalization and Compliance with Human Rights Law', *European Journal of International Law* 19, 2008: 725–748.

Goodman, Sara Wallace and Howard, Marc Morjé. 'Evaluating and Explaining the Restrictive Backlash in Citizenship Policy in Europe', *Studies in Law, Politics and Society* 60, 2013: 111–139.

Greer, Steven. 'Being "Realistic" about Human Rights', *Northern Ireland Legal Quarterly* 60, 2009: 147–161.

Groenendijk, Kees. 'Security of Residence and Access to Free Movement for Settled Third Country Nationals under Community Law' in E. Guild and C. Harlow (eds), *Implementing Amsterdam*. Oxford: Hart, 2001, pp. 225–240.

Hammar, Tomas (ed.). *European Immigration Policy. A Comparative Study*. Cambridge University Press, 1985.

   Democracy and the Nation State. Aliens, Denizens, and Citizens in a World of International Migration. Aldershot: Avebury, 1990.

Hansen, Randall and Weil, Patrick (eds). *Dual Nationality, Social Rights, and Federal Citizenship in the US and Europe. The Reinvention of Citizenship*. New York: Berghahn Books, 2002.

Harris, Jonathan. 'Bernardino Rivadavia and Benthamite "Discipleship" ', *Latin American Research Review* 33, 1998: 129–149.

Herzog, Tamar. *Defining Nations. Immigrants and Citizens in Early Modern Spain and Spanish America*. New Haven, CT: Yale University Press, 2003.

   'Communities Becoming a Nation: Spain and Spanish America in the Wake of Modernity (and Thereafter)', *Citizenship Studies* 11, 2007: 151–172.

Hines, Barbara. 'The Right to Migrate as a Human Right: The Current Argentine Immigration Law', *Cornell International Law Journal* 43, 2010: 471–511.

Hobsbawm, Eric J. 'Nacionalismo y Nacionalidad en América Latina' in P. Sandoval (ed.), *Repensando la Subalternidad. Miradas Críticas desde/sobre América Latina*. Lima: Instituto de Estudios Peruanos, 2010, pp. 311–326.

Holston, James. *Insurgent Citizenship: Disjunctions of Democracy and Modernity in Brazil*. Princeton University Press, 2009.

Howard, Marc Morjé. 'Variation in Dual Citizenship Policies in the Countries of the EU', *International Migration Review* 39, 2005: 697–720.

Howse, Robert and Teitel, Ruti. 'Beyond Compliance: Rethinking Why International Law Really Matters', *Global Policy Volume* 1, 2010: 127–136.

Hoyo, Henio. *Report on Citizenship Law: Mexico*. Florence: EUI, 2015.

Htun, Mala. 'Political Inclusion and Social Inequality. Women, Afro-descendants and Indigenous Peoples' in J. I. Domínguez and M. Shifter (eds), *Constructing Democratic Governance in Latin America*. Baltimore, MD: Johns Hopkins University Press, 3rd edn, 2008, pp. 72–96.

Huddleston, Thomas, Bilgili, Ozge, Joki, Anne-Linde and Vankova Zvezda. *Migrant Integration Policy Index*. Brussels: Migration Policy Group, 2015.

Human Rights Committee. General Comment 15: The Position of Aliens under the Covenant (Twenty-seventh session, 1986).

Hurtado Caicedo, Francisco and Gallegos Brito, Romina. *Informe Ecuador*. Quito: Programa Andino de Derechos Humanos, 2013.

Huysmans, Jeff. *The Politics of Insecurity: Fear, Migration and Asylum in the EU*. Abingdon: Routledge, 2006.

Iglesias Sánchez, Sara. 'Free Movement of Persons and Regional International Organisations' in R. Plender (ed.), *Issues in International Migration Law*. Leiden: Brill, 2015, pp. 223–260.

ILO. *Panorama Laboral 2013. América Latina y el Caribe*. Lima: ILO, 2013.

La Migración Laboral en América Latina y el Caribe. Diagnóstico, Estrategia y Líneas de Trabajo de la OIT en la Región. Lima: ILO, 2016.

Instituto Nacional de Estadística e Informática. 'Estadísticas de la Migración Internacional en el Perú 1990–2013', December 2014.

IOM. *La Situación Migratoria en América del Sur.* Buenos Aires: IOM, 2001.

Perú: Estadísticas de la Migración Internacional de Peruanos, 1990–2007. Lima: IOM, 2008.

Perfil Migratório do Brasil 2009. Geneva: IOM, 2010.

(report prepared by René Pereira Morató). *Perfil Migratorio de Bolivia.* Buenos Aires: IOM, 2011.

(report prepared by Carolina Stefoni). *Perfil Migratorio de Chile.* Buenos Aires: IOM, 2011.

(report prepared by Hugo Oddone, Claudina Zavattiero, Cynthia González Ríos, Edith Arrúa Sosa, Elizabeth Barrios). *Perfil Migratorio de Paraguay.* Buenos Aires: IOM, 2011.

Perfil Migratorio de Uruguay. Buenos Aires: IOM, 2011.

(written by Alejandro Morlachetti). *El Papel de las Instituciones Nacionales de Derechos Humanos en la Protección de los Derechos de los Migrantes.* Buenos Aires: IOM, 2012.

Perfil Migratorio de Argentina. Buenos Aires: IOM, 2012.

(elaborated by Anibal Sánchez Aguilar). *Perfil Migratorio del Perú 2012.* Lima: IOM, 2012.

Estudio sobre Experiencias en la Implementación del Acuerdo de Residencia del MERCOSUR y Asociados. XIV South American Conference on Migration, Reference Document, Lima, 16–17 October 2014.

Informe sobre el Estado de Situación de la Facilitación del Tránsito Fronterizo en Suramérica. XVI South American Conference on Migration, Reference Document, Asunción, 3–4 November 2016.

Migración Calificada y Desarrollo: Desafíos para América del Sur, Cuadernos Migratorios 7, August 2016.

IOM and Andean Community Secretariat. *Avances y Recomendaciones para la Implementación de la Normativa de la Comunidad Andina en Materia de Migraciones.* Lima: IOM and Andean Community Secretariat, 2012.

IOM and IPPDH. *Diagnóstico Regional sobre Migración Haitiana.* Buenos Aires: IOM and IPPDH, 2017.

Irizarry y Puente, Julius. 'Exclusion and Expulsion of Aliens in Latin America', *The American Journal of International Law* 36, 1942: 252–270.

Izaguirre, Lorena, Busse, Erika and Vásquez, Tania. 'Discursos en Tensión y Oportunidades de Cambio: la Nueva Ley de Migraciones en Perú' in J. Ramírez (ed.), *Migración, Estado y Políticas. Cambios y Continuidades en América del Sur.* La Paz: Vicepresidencia del Estado Plurinacional de Bolivia-CELAG, 2017, pp. 153–178.

James, Cyril Lionel Robert. *The Black Jacobins.* London: Penguin Books, 2001.

Jerónimo, Patrícia. *Report on Citizenship Law: Brazil.* Florence: EUDO Citizenship, 2016.

Joppke, Christian. 'Immigration Challenges the Nation-State' in C. Joppke (ed.), *Challenge to the Nation-State: Immigration in Western Europe and the United States.* Oxford University Press, 1998, pp. 5–48.

'Citizenship between De- and Re-Ethnicization', *European Journal of Sociology* 44, 2003: 429–458.

Selecting by Origin. Ethnic Migration in the Liberal State. Cambridge, MA: Harvard University Press, 2005.

Citizenship and Immigration. Cambridge: Polity Press, 2010.

Katerí Hernández, Tanya. *Racial Subordination in Latin America: The Role of the State, Customary Law, and the New Civil Rights Response*. Cambridge University Press, 2012.

Kingsbury, Benedict. 'The Concept of Compliance as a Function of Competing Conceptions of International Law', *Michigan Journal of International Law* 19, 1998: 345–372.

Klich, Ignacio and Lesser, Jeffrey (eds). *Arab and Jewish Immigrants in Latin America. Images and Realities*. Abingdon: Routledge, 1998.

Kochenov, Dimitry (ed.). *EU Citizenship and Federalism: The Role of Rights*. Cambridge University Press, 2017.

'On Tiles and Pillars: EU Citizenship as a Federal Denominator' in D. Kochenov (ed.), *EU Citizenship*, 2017, pp. 1–66.

Konetzke, Richard. 'Legislación sobre Inmigración de Extranjeros en América durante la Época Colonial', *Revista Internacional de Sociología* 3, 1945: 269–299.

Koolhaas, Martín, Pellegrino, Adella, Diconca, Beatriz and Santestevan, Ana. 'Las Políticas Públicas sobre Migraciones y la Sociedad Civil en América Latina: el Caso de Uruguay', unpublished document, 2016.

Kostakopoulou, Dora. 'European Citizenship and Immigration after Amsterdam: Silences, Openings, Paradoxes', *Journal of Ethnic and Migration Studies* 4, 1998: 639–656.

'Irregular Migration and Migration Theory: Making State Authorisation Less Relevant' in B. Bogusz, R. Cholewinski, A. Cygan and E. Szyszczak (eds), *Irregular Migration and Human Rights: Theoretical, European and International Pespectives*. Leiden: Martinus Nijhoff, 2004, pp. 41–57.

Lagos Valenzuela, Enrique. 'El Arbitraje Internacional de América', *Anales de la Facultad de Derecho* IV 1938.

Lane Scheppele, Kim. 'Aspirational and Aversive Constitutionalism: The Case for Studying Cross-constitutional Influence through Negative Models', *International Journal of Constitutional Law* 1, 2003: 296–324.

Larrain, Jorge. *Identity and Modernity in Latin America*. Cambridge: Polity, 2000.

Leal Villamizar, Lina María. *Colombia frente al Antisemitismo y la Migración de Judíos Polacos y Alemanes 1933–1948*. Bogotá: Academia Colombiana de Historia, 2015.

Legomsky, Stephen. 'The New Path of Immigration Law: Asymmetric Incorporation of Criminal Justice Norms', *Washington and Lee Law Review* 64, 2007: 469–528.

Look Lai, Walton and Chee-Beng, Tan (eds). *The Chinese in Latin America and the Caribbean*. Leiden: Brill, 2010.

López-Alves, Fernando. 'Visions of the National: Natural Endowments, Futures and the Evils of Men' in Centeno and Ferraro (eds), *State and Nation Making in Latin America and Spain*, 2013, pp. 282–306.

Loveman, Mara. *National Colors. Racial Classification and the State in Latin America*. Oxford University Press, 2014.

Lozano Ascencio, Fernando and Martínez Pizarro, Jorge (eds). *Retorno en los Procesos Migratorios de América Latina. Conceptos, Debates, Evidencias*. Rio de Janeiro: ALAP Editor, 2015.

Lütz, Louis. *Essai Historique sur le Droit d'Aubaine en France*. Geneva: Imprimerie Ramboz et Schuchardt, 1866.

Lyon, Beth. 'The Inter-American Court of Human Rights defines Unauthorized Migrant Workers' Rights for the Hemisphere: A Comment on Advisory Opinion 18', *NYU Review Law and Social Change* 28, 2003–04: 547–596.

Maas, Willem. *Creating European Citizens*. Lanham, MD: Rowman & Littlefield, 2007.

'Equality and the Free Movement of People: Citizenship and Internal Migration' in W. Maas (ed.), *Democratic Citizenship and the Free Movement of People*. Leiden: Martinus Nijhoff, 2013, pp. 9–30.

Mahoney, James and Thelen, Kathleen (eds). *Explaining Institutional Change. Ambiguity, Agency, and Power*. Cambridge University Press, 2010.

Margheritis, Ana. 'Piecemeal Regional Integration in the Post-Neoliberal Era: Negotiating Migration Policies within Mercosur', *Review of International Political Economy* 20, 2012: 541–575.

'Mercosur's Post-Neoliberal Approach to Migration: from Workers' Mobility to Regional Citizenship' in Cantor, Freier and Gauci (eds), *A Liberal Tide?* 2015, pp. 57–80.

Report on Citizenship Law: Uruguay. Florence: European University Institute, EUDO Citizenship, 2015.

Migration Governance across Regions: State-diaspora Relations in the Latin American-Southern Europe Corridor. Abingdon: Routledge, 2016.

Mármora, Lelio. 'Las Leyes de Migraciones como Contexto Normativo' in R. Giustiniani (ed.), *Migración: Un Derecho Humano. Comentarios sobre la Ley*. Buenos Aires: Prometeo Libros, 2004, pp. 59–65.

'Modelos de Gobernabilidad Migratoria. La Perspectiva Política en América del Sur', *Revista Interdisciplinar da Mobilidade Humana* 35, 2010: 71–92.

Mármora, Lelio, Altilio, María Gabriela, Gianelli Dublanc, María Laura and Vega, Yamila 'Políticas Públicas y Programas sobre Migraciones en Argentina. La Participación de la Sociedad Civil' in Chiarello (ed.), *Las Políticas Públicas sobre Migraciones*, 2011, pp. 1–150.

Marshall, Thomas Humphrey. *Citizenship and Social Class and Other Essays*. Cambridge University Press, 1950.

Martin, David A. 'Effects of International Law on Migration Policy and Practice: The Uses of Hypocrisy', *International Migration Review* XXIII, 1989: 547–578.

Martínez, José, Gallardo, Viviana and Martínez, Nelson. 'Construyendo Identidades desde el Poder: Los Indios en los Discursos Republicanos de Inicios del Siglo XIX', in G. Boccara (ed.), *Colonización, resistencia y mestizaje en las Américas, siglos XVI-XX*. Quito, ifea/Ediciones Abya Yala, 2002, pp. 27–46.

Martínez, Ricardo A. *El Panamericanismo. Doctrina y Práctica Imperialista. Las Relaciones Interamericanas desde Bolívar hasta Eisenhower*. Buenos Aires: Aluminé, 1957.

Martínez Pizarro, Jorge and Orrego Rivera, Cristián. *Nuevas Tendencias y Dinámicas Migratorias en América Latina y el Caribe*. Santiago de Chile: CEPAL, 2016.

Martínez Pizarro, Jorge, Soffia, Magdalena, Cubides Franco, José Delio and Bortolotto, Idenilso 'Políticas Públicas sobre Migraciones y Participación de la Sociedad

Civil en Chile', in Chiarello (ed.), *Las Políticas Públicas sobre Migraciones*, 2013, pp. 117–242.

Massey, Douglas S., Arango, Joaquín, Hugo, Graeme, Kouaouci, Ali, Pellegrino, Adela and Taylor, J. Edwards. *Worlds in Motion. Understanding International Migration at the End of the Millennium*. Oxford University Press, 1998.

Masterson, Daniel M. with Funada-Classen, Sayaka. *The Japanese in Latin America*. Champaign, IL: University of Illinois Press, 2004.

Mateos, Pablo. 'Introducción' in P. Mateos (ed.), *Ciudadanía Múltiple y Migración. Perspectivas Latinoamericanas*. México D.F.: CIDE, 2015, pp. 9–22.

Mathews, John M. 'Roosevelt's Latin-American Policy', *American Political Science Review* 29, 1935: 805–820.

McKeown, Adam K. *Melancholy Order. Asian Migration and the Globalization of Borders*. New York: Columbia University Press, 2008.

Melde, Sussane. *Ahead of the Game? The Human Rights Origins and Potential of Argentina's 2004 Migration Policy*, PhD Thesis, University of Sussex, 2017.

Meyer, John W., Boli, John, Thomas, George M. and Ramirez, Francisco O. 'World Society and the Nation-State', *American Journal of Sociology* 103, 1997: 144–181.

Mignolo, Walter D. *The Idea of Latin America*. Oxford: Blackwell Publishing, 2005.

Miller, Nicola. 'Latin America: State-Building and Nationalism' in Breuilly (ed.), *The Oxford Handbook of the History of Nationalism*, 2013, pp. 378–395.

Mirow, Matthew C. *Latin American Law. A History of Private Law and Institutions in Spanish America*. Austin, TX: University of Texas Press, 2004.

'Visions of Cádiz: The Constitution of 1812 in Historical and Constitutional Thought', *Law, Politics and Society* 53, 2010: 59–88.

Latin American Constitutions. The Constitution of Cádiz and its Legacy in Spanish America. Cambridge University Press, 2015.

Mitsilegas, Valsamis. 'Extraterritorial Immigration Control in the 21st Century: The Individual and the State Transformed' in B. Ryan and V. Mitsilegas (eds), *Extraterritorial Immigration Control. Legal Challenges*. Leiden: Martinus Nijhoff, 2010, pp. 39–65.

The Criminalisation of Migration in Europe. Challenges for Human Rights and the Rule of Law. London: Springer, 2015.

Motomura, Hiroshi. *Americans in Waiting. The Lost History of Immigration and Citizenship in the United States*. Oxford University Press, 2006.

Immigration Outside the Law. Oxford University Press, 2014.

Moya, José C. *Cousins and Strangers. Spanish Immigrants in Buenos Aires, 1850–1930*. Berkeley, CA: University of California Press, 1998.

Nafziger, James A. R. 'The General Admission of Aliens under International Law', *American Journal of International Law* 77, 1983: 804–847.

Negretto, Gabriel L. *Making Constitutions: Presidents, Parties, and Institutional Choice in Latin America*. Cambridge University Press, 2013.

Nolte, Detlef and Schilling-Vacaflor, Almut (eds). *New Constitutionalism in Latin America. Promises and Practices*. Farnham: Ashgate, 2012.

Novick, Susana, Mera, Gabriela and Modolo, Vanina (eds). *Migraciones y Mercosur: una Relación Inconclusa*. Buenos Aires: Catálogos, 2010.

Oddone, Hugo and Guidini, Jairo. 'Políticas Públicas sobre Migraciones y Participación de la Sociedad Civil en Paraguay' in Chiarello (ed.), *Las Políticas Públicas sobre Migraciones*, 2013, pp. 243–390.

O'Donnell, Guillermo. 'Why the Rule of Law Matters', *Journal of Democracy* 15, 2004: 32–46.

OECD and OAS. *International Migration in the Americas. Third Report of the Continuous Reporting System on International Migration in the Americas (SICREMI)*. Washington, DC: Organization of American States, 2015.

Offut, Milton. *The Protection of Citizens Abroad by the Armed Forces of the United States*. Baltimore, MD: The Johns Hopkins Press, 1928.

Ong, Aihwa. *Flexible Citizenship: The Cultural Logics of Transnationality*. Durham, NC: Duke University Press, 1999.

Opeskin, Brian, Perruchoud, Richard and Redpath-Cross, Jillyanne (eds). *Foundations of International Migration Law*. Cambridge University Press, 2012.

Organisation of American States. 'IACHR Condemns Judgment of the Constitutional Court of the Dominican Republic'. Press Release, 6 November 2014.

International Migration in the Americas. Third Report of the Continuous Reporting System on International Migration in the Americas. Washington, DC: OAS, 2015.

Irregular Migration Flows to the Americas from Africa, Asia, and the Caribbean. Washington, DC: OAS, 2017.

Osterweil, Marc J. 'The Economic and Social Condition of Jewish and Arab Immigrants in Bolivia, 1890–1980' in I. Klich and J. Lesser (eds), *Arab and Jewish Immigrants in Latin America. Images and Realities*. Abingdon: Routledge, 1998, pp. 146–166.

Páez, Tomás. 'Amid Economic Crisis and Political Turmoil, Venezuelans Form a New Exodus'. Migration Policy Institute, 14 June 2017. Available at: www.migrationpolicy.org/article/amid-economic-crisis-and-political-turmoil-venezuelans-form-new-exodus.

Parisit, Francesco and Ghei, Nita. 'The Role of Reciprocity in International Law', *Cornell International Law Journal* 36, 2003: 93–123.

Parodi, Carlos A. *Politics of South American Boundaries*. Westport, CT: Praeger, 2002.

Parra-Aranguren, Gonzalo. *La Constitución de 1830 y los Venezolanos por Naturalización*. Caracas: Imp. Universitaria, 1969.

La Nacionalidad Venezolana de los Inmigrados en el Siglo XIX. Caracas: Editorial Sucre, 1969.

'La Primera Etapa de los Tratados sobre Derecho Internacional Privado en América (1826–1940)', *Revista de la Facultad de Ciencias Jurídicas y Políticas* 98, 1996: 60–128.

Pazo Pineda, Oscar Andrés. *Report on Citizenship Law: Peru*. Florence: EUDO Citizenship Observatory, EUI, 2015.

Pécoud, Antoine and de Guchteneire, Paul (eds). *Migration without Borders: Essays on the Free Movement of People*. New York: Berghahn Books, 2007.

Pedroza, Luicy, Palop, Pau and Hoffmann, Bert. *Emigrant Policies in Latin America and the Caribbean*. Santiago de Chile: FLASCO Chile, 2016.

Pellegrino, Adela. *Historia de la Inmigración en Venezuela Siglos XIX y XX*. Caracas: Academia Nacional de Ciencias Económicas, 1989.

Perruchoud, Richard. 'State Sovereignty and Freedom of Movement' in Opeskin, Perruchoud and Redpath-Cross (eds), *Foundations of International Migration Law*, 2012, pp. 123–151.

Pierson, Paul. *Politics in Time. History, Institutions, and Social Analysis*. Princeton University Press, 2004.

Planas Suárez, Simón. *Los Extranjeros en Venezuela: Su Condición ante el Derecho Público y Privado de la República*. Lisbon: Centro Tipográfico Colonial, 1917.

Racine, Karen. *Francisco de Miranda: A Transatlantic Life in the Age of Revolution.* Lanham, MD: Rowman & Littlefield Publishers, 2002.

'"This England and This Now": British Cultural and Intellectual Influence in the Spanish American Independence Era', *Hispanic American Historical Review* 90, 2010: 423–454.

Radcliffe, Sarah and Westwood, Sallie. *Remaking the Nation. Place, Identity and Politics in Latin America.* London: Routledge, 1996.

Ramírez, Franklyn and Ramírez, Jacques. *La Estampida Migratoria Ecuatoriana. Crisis, Redes Transnacionales y Repertorios de Acción Migratoria.* Quito: Centro de Investigaciones CIUDAD–UNESCO–ABYA YALA-ALISEI, 2005.

Ramírez, Jacques (ed.). *Ciudad-Estado, Inmigrantes y Políticas. Ecuador, 1890–1950.* Quito: IAEN, 2012.

'Del Aperturismo Segmentado al Control Migratorio' in Ramírez (ed.), *Ciudad-Estado, Inmigrantes y Políticas. Ecuador, 1890–1950,* 2012, pp. 15–52.

La Política Migratoria en Ecuador Rupturas, Tensiones, Continuidades y Desafíos. Quito: IAEN, 2nd edn, 2014.

Hacia el Sur. La Construcción de la Ciudadanía Suramericana y la Movilidad Intrarregional. Quito: CELAG, 2016.

'Lo Crudo, lo Cocido y lo Quemado: Etnografía del Proyecto de Ley Orgánica de Movilidad Humana en Ecuador' in J. Ramírez (ed.), *Migración, Estado y Políticas. Cambios y Continuidades en América del Sur.* La Paz: Vicepresidencia del Estado Plurinacional de Bolivia-CELAG, 2017, pp. 93–127.

Ramírez, I. Ceja, S. Coloma and R. Arteaga, *"Ah, Usted Viene por la Visa Mercosur": Integración, Migración y Refugio en Ecuador.* Quito: CELAG, 2017.

Reid Andrews, George. *Afro-Latinoamerica. 1800–2000.* Oxford University Press, 2003.

Rieu-Millan, Marie Laure. *Los Diputados Americanos en las Cortes de Cádiz.* Madrid: Consejo Superior de Investigaciones Científicas, 1990.

Rock, David. 'Porteño Liberals and Imperialist Emissaries in the Rio de la Plata. Rivadavia and the British' in M. Brown and G. Paquette (eds), *Connections after Colonialism. Europe and Latin America in the 1820s.* Tuscaloosa, AL: University of Alabama Press, 2013, pp. 207–222.

Rodríguez, Mario. *William Burke and Francisco de Miranda: The Word and the Deed in Spanish America's Emancipation.* Lanham, MD: University Press of America, 1994.

Román, Ediberto. *Citizenship and its Exclusions. A Classical, Constitutional, and Critical Race Critique.* New York University Press, 2010.

Romero, Vicente. 'Legislación y Políticas en Nueva Granada y Chile para Atraer la Inmigración Extranjera a Mediados del Siglo XIX', *Amérique Latine Histoire et Mémoire. Les Cahiers ALHIM,* online version 24, published online 8 February 2013.

Ronning, Neale. *Diplomatic Asylum. Legal Norms and Political Reality in Latin American Relations.* The Hague: Martinus Nijhoff, 1965.

Roquette Lopreato, Christina. 'O Espírito das Leis: Anarquismo e Repressão Política no Brasil', *Verve* 3, 2003: 75–91.

Rosenblum, Marc R. and Ruiz Soto, Ariel G. *An Analysis of Unauthorized Migrants in the US by Country and Region of Birth.* Washington, DC: Migration Policy Institute, 2015.

Rouquié, Alain. *The Military and the State in Latin America*. Berkeley, CA: University of California Press, 1987.

Rouquié, Alain and Suffern, Stephen. 'The Military in Latin American Politics since 1930' in L. Bethell (ed.) *Latin America Politics and Society since 1930*. Cambridge University Press, 1998, pp. 145–216.

Rubio-Marín, Ruth. *Immigration as a Democratic Challenge. Citizenship and Inclusion in Germany and the United States*. Cambridge University Press, 2000.

    'Human Rights and the Citizen/Non-Citizen Distinction Revisited' in R. Rubio-Marín (ed.), *Human Rights and Immigration*. Oxford University Press, 2014, pp. 1–18.

Ryan, Bernard. 'Extraterritorial Immigration Control: What Role for Legal Guarantees?' in B. Ryan and V. Mitsilegas (eds), *Extraterritorial Immigration Control. Legal Challenges*. Leiden: Martinus Nijhoff, 2010, pp. 3–37.

Sabato, Hilda. 'On Political Citizenship in Nineteenth-Century Latin America', *American Historical Review* 106, 2001: 1290–1315.

Saboia Bezerra, Maria Helga. 'A Constituição de Cádiz de 1812', *Revista de Informação Legislativa* 198, 2013: 89–112.

Sacchetta Ramos Mendes, José Aurivaldo. *Laços de Sangue. Privilégios e Intolerância à Imigração Portuguesa no Brasil (1822/1945)*. São Paulo: EDUSP/FAPESP, 2011.

Sachar, Ayelet. *The Birthright Lottery. Citizenship and Global Inequality*. Cambridge, MA: Harvard University Press, 2009.

Salazar Ugarte, Pedro. 'El Nuevo Constitucionalismo Latinoamericano (Una Perspectiva Crítica)' in L. R. González Pérez and D. Valadés (eds), *El Constitucionalismo Contemporáneo. Homenaje a Jorge Carpizo*. Mexico City: UNAM, 2013, pp. 345–387.

Saldías, Osvaldo. 'Libre Circulación de Personas y la Autonomía del Ordenamiento Jurídico de la Comunidad Andina' in Goizueta Vértiz, Gómez Fernández and González Pascual (eds), *La Libre Circulación de Personas en los Sistemas de Integración Económica*, 2012, pp. 187–206.

Sanahuja, José Antonio. 'Regionalismo Post-Liberal y Multilateralismo en Sudamérica: El Caso de UNASUR' in A. Serbín, L. Martínez and H. Ramanzini Júnior (eds), *El Regionalismo 'Post-Liberal' en América Latina y el Caribe: Nuevos Actores, Nuevos Temas, Nuevos Desafíos. Anuario de la Integración Regional de América Latina y el Gran Caribe 2012*. Buenos Aires: CRIES, 2012, pp. 19–72.

    'Regionalismo e Integración en América Latina: de la Fractura Atlántico-Pacífico a los Retos de una Globalización en Crisis', *Pensamiento Propio* 21, 2016: 29–76.

Sánchez Mojica, Beatriz Eugenia. 'In Transit: Migration Policy in Colombia' in Cantor, Freier and Gauci (eds), *A Liberal Tide?*, 2015, pp. 81–104.

Sandonato de León, Pablo. 'Nacionalidad y Extranjería en el Uruguay. Un Estudio Normo-Político', *Revista de Derecho de la Universidad Católica del Uruguay* 3, 2008: 175–243.

Santestevan, Ana María. 'Free Movement Regimes in South America: The Experience of the MERCOSUR and the Andean Community' in R. Cholewinski, R. Perruchoud and E. McDonald (eds), *International Migration Law: Developing Paradigms and Key Challenges*. The Hague: Asser Press, 2007, pp. 363–386.

Sassen, Saskia. *Losing Control? Sovereignty in an Age of Globalization*. New York: Columbia University Press, 1996.

'The Repositioning of Citizenship and Alienage: Emergent Subjects and Spaces for Politics', *Globalizations* 2, 2005: 79–94.

Sassone, Susana. 'Migraciones Ilegales y Amnistías en la Argentina', *Estudios Migratorios Latinoamericanos* 6, 1987: 249–290.

Sbalqueiro Lopes, Cristiane Maria. *Direito de Imigração. O Estatuto do Estrangeiro em uma Perspectiva de Direitos Humanos*. Porto Alegre: Nuria Fabris, 2009.

Schulze, Frederik. 'German-Speaking and Japanese Immigrants in Brazil, 1850–1945' in N. Foote and M. Goebel (eds), *Immigration and National Identities in Latin America*. Gainesville, FL: University Press Florida, 2014, pp. 115–138.

Schwarz, Tobias. 'Políticas de Inmigración en América Latina: El Extranjero Indeseable en las Normas Nacionales, de la Independencia hasta los Años de 1930', *Procesos Revista Ecuatoriana de Historia* 36, 2012: 39–72.

'Regímenes de Pertenencia Nacional en Venezuela y la República Dominicana Contemporáneas', *Tabula Rasa* 20, 2014: 227–246.

Secretaría de Estado de Inmigración y Emigración, Observatorio Permanente de la Inmigración. *Anuario Estadístico de Inmigración. Año 2005*. Madrid: Ministerio de Trabajo y Asuntos Sociales, 2007.

Shachar, Ayelet. *The Birthright Lottery: Citizenship and Global Inequality*. Cambridge, MA: Harvard University Press, 2009.

Simmons, Beth A. *Mobilizing for Human Rights International Law in Domestic Politics*. Cambridge University Press, 2009.

Simon, Joshua. *The Ideology of Creole Revolution: Imperialism and Independence in American and Latin American Political Thought*. Cambridge University Press, 2017.

Sobrevilla Perea, Natalia. *The Caudillo of the Andes: Andrés de Santa Cruz*. Cambridge University Press, 2011.

Soysal, Yasemin Nuhoğlu. *Limits of Citizenship. Migrants and Postnational Membership in Europe*. University of Chicago Press, 1994.

Spiro, Peter J. *Beyond Citizenship: American Identity After Globalization*. Oxford University Press, 2008.

At Home in Two Countries. The Past and Future of Dual Citizenship. New York University Press, 2016.

Stefoni, Carolina. 'Ley y Política Migratoria en Chile. La Ambivalencia en la Comprensión del Migrante' in B. Feldman-Bianco, L. R. Sánchez, C. Stefoni, M. I. Villa Martínez (eds), *La Construcción Social del Sujeto Migrante en América Latina. Prácticas, Representaciones y Categorías*. Quito: FLACSO, Sede Ecuador: Consejo Latinoamericano de Ciencias Sociales, CLACSO: Universidad Alberto Hurtado, 2011, pp. 79–109.

Stumpf, Juliet. 'The Crimmigration Crisis: Immigrants, Crime, and Sovereign Power', *American University Law Review* 56, 2006: 367–419.

Tedesco, João Carlos and Kleidermacher, Gisele (eds). *A Imigração Senegalesa no Brasil e na Argentina: Múltiplos Olhares*. Porto Alegre: EST Edições, 2017.

Texidó, Ezequiel and Baer, Gladys 'Las Migraciones en el Cono Sur en el Período 1990–2001' in E. Texidó, G. Baer, N. Pérez Vichich, A. M. Santestevan and C. P. Gomes (eds), *Migraciones Laborales en Sudamérica: El Mercosur Ampliado*. Geneva: ILO, 2003, pp. 4–40.

Texidó, Ezequiel and Gurrieri, Jorge. *Panorama Migratorio de América del Sur*. Buenos Aires: IOM, 2012.

Tinker, Catherine and Madrid Sartoretto, Laura. 'New Trends in Migratory and Refugee Law in Brazil: The Expanded Refugee Definition', *Panorama of Brazilian Law* 3, 2015: 1–27.

Torpey, John. *The Invention of the Passport: Surveillance, Citizenship and the State*. Cambridge University Press, 2000.

Truzzi, Oswaldo. 'Reformulações na Política Imigratória de Brasil e Argentina nos Anos 30: um Enfoque Comparativo' in C. E. de Abreu Boucault and T. Malatian (eds), *Políticas Migratórias. Fronteiras dos Direitos Humanos no Século XXI*. Rio de Janeiro: Renovar, 2003, pp. 242–243.

United Nations, Department of Economic and Social Affairs. *Trends in International Migrant Stock: Migrants by Destination and Origin*, 2015 (United Nations database, POP/DB/MIG/Stock/Rev.2015).

Valadés, Diego. 'The Presidential System in Latin America: A Hallmark and Challenge to a Latin American Ius Constitutionale Commune' in von Bogdandy, Ferrer Mac-Gregor, Morales Antoniazzi, Piovesan and Soley, (eds), *Transformative Constitutionalism in Latin America*, 2017, pp. 191–210.

Valladares Rueda, Bolivar. *La Nacionalidad y la Naturalización en la Práctica Administrativa*. Quito: Tall. Gráf. Nacionales, 1955.

Varela Suanzes-Carpegna, Joaquín. 'Propiedad, Ciudadanía y Sufragio en el Constitucionalismo Español (1810–1845)', *Historia Constitucional* 6, 2005: 105–123.

Varlez, Louis. 'Migration Problems and the Havana Conference of 1928', *International Labour Review* XIX, 1929: 1–19.

Vengoechea Barrios, Juliana. *Born in the Americas. The Promise and Practice of Nationality Laws in Brazil, Chile, and Colombia*. New York: Open Society Justice Initiative, 2017.

Vetancourt Aristeguieta, Francisco. *Nacionalidad, Naturalización y Ciudadanía en Hispano-América*. Caracas: El Cojo, 1957.

Viciano Pastor, Roberto (ed.). *Estudios sobre el Nuevo Constitucionalismo Latinoamericano*. Valencia: Tirant lo Blanch, 2012.

Viciano Pastor, Roberto and Martínez Dalmau, Rubén. 'Fundamento Teórico del Nuevo Constitucionalismo Lationamericano' in Viciano Pastor (ed.), *Estudios sobre el Nuevo Constitucionalismo Latinoamericano*, 2012, pp. 11–49.

Vidal, Roberto, Martín, Rosa María, Sánchez, Beatriz Eugenia and Velásquez, Marco. 'Políticas Públicas sobre Migración en Colombia' in Chiarello (ed.), *Las Políticas Públicas sobre Migraciones*, 2013, pp. 277–446.

Villegas-Pulido, Guillermo Tell. *Los Extranjeros. Su Admisión, su Expulsión*. Caracas: Impr. y Lit. del Gobierno Nacional, 1891.

Los Extranjeros en Venezuela: su no Admisión – su Expulsión. Caracas: Lit. y tip. del Comercio, 1919.

Von Bogdandy, Armin. 'Ius Constitutionale Commune en América Latina: Una Mirada a un Constitucionalismo Transformador', *Revista de Derecho del Estado* 34, 2015: 3–50.

Von Bogdandy, Armin, Ferrer Mac-Gregor, Eduardo, Morales Antoniazzi, Mariela, Piovesan, Flávia and Soley, Ximena (eds). *Transformative Constitutionalism in Latin America. The Emergence of a New Ius Commune.* Oxford University Press, 2017.

Vonk, Oliver. *Nationality Law in the Western Hemisphere: A Study of Grounds for Acquisition and Loss of Citizenship in the Americas and the Caribbean.* Leiden: Martinus Nijhoff, 2014.

Von Vacano, Diego. *The Color of Citizenship. Race, Modernity and Latin American/Hispanic Political Thought.* Oxford University Press, 2012.

Waldrauch, Harald and Hofinger, Christoph. 'An Index to Measure the Legal Obstacles to the Integration of Migrants', *Journal of Ethnic and Migration Studies* 23, 1997: 271–285.

Waltz, Susan. 'Universalizing Human Rights: The Role of Small States in the Construction of the Universal Declaration of Human Rights', *Human Rights Quarterly* 23, 2001: 44–72.

Watson, Alan. *The Nature of Law.* Edinburgh University Press, 1977.
    'Comparative Law and Legal Change', *Cambridge Law Journal* 37, 1978: 313–336.
    Legal Transplants. An Approach to Comparative Law. Athens, GA: University of Georgia Press, 2nd edn, 1993.

Weyland, Joseph. 'La Protection Diplomatique et Consulaire des Citoyens de l'Union Européenne' in E. A. Marias (ed.), *European Citizenship.* Maastricht: European Institute of Public Administration, 1994, pp. 63–68.

Wright, Doris Marion. 'The Making of Cosmopolitan California: An Analysis of Immigration, 1848–1870', *California Historical Society Quarterly* 19, 1940: 323–343.

Yepes, José María. *Del Congreso de Panamá a la Conferencia de Caracas 1826–1954.* Caracas: Taller Gráfico Cromotip, 1955.

Zago de Moraes, Ana Luisa. 'Crimigração. A Relação entre Política Migratória e Política Criminal no Brasil'. Unpublished PhD Thesis, Porto Alegre, 2015.

Zahler, Reuben. 'Heretics, Cadavers, and Capitalists. European Foreigners in Venezuela during the 1820s' in M. Brown and G. Paquette (eds), *Connections after Colonialism. Europe and Latin America in the 1820s.* Tuscaloosa, AL: University of Alabama Press, 2013, pp. 191–206.

Zorrilla, Rubén H. *Cambio Social y Población en el Pensamiento de Mayo (1810–1830).* Buenos Aires: Belgrano, 1978.

Newspaper Articles

Agencia EFE. 'Analizan Movilidad Laboral en la Alianza del Pacífico', 8 April 2016.

Buenos Aires Herald. 'IACHR Criticises Government's "Regressive" Immigration Policy', 24 March 2017.

The Economist. 'The New New World: Long an Exporter of Talent, Latin America is now Importing it', 6 April 2013.

Estrangeiros no Brasil. 'Governo Concede Residência para Estrangeiros Ganeses', 3 March 2016.

The Guardian. 'Donald Trump Wants to Deport 11 Million Migrants: Is that even Possible?', 27 August 2015.

Política Argentina. 'El Gobierno Creó un Centro de Detención de Migrantes: Alarma entre Organismos de DDHH', 26 August 2016.

Portal Brasil. 'Brasil Regulariza Situação de 4.482 Trabalhadores Estrangeiros', 19 December 2013.

'Brasil Autoriza Residência Permanente a 43,8 Mil Haitianos', 11 October 2015.

Legislation: South American Countries

Argentina

Disposición Dirección Nacional de Migraciones 1143 sobre Regularización de Haitianos, 15 March 2017 [Regulation National Migration Directorate on the Regularisation of Haitians].[1]

Decreto 70/2017 Modificación Ley Nº 25.871, Buenos Aires, 27 January 2017 [Decree Amending the Migration Law].

Ley 27.063, Código Procesal Penal, 4 December 2014 [Procedural Criminal Code].

Disposición Dirección Nacional de Migraciones 979 sobre Regimen Especial de Regularización de Ciudadanos de Nacionalidad Coreana, 24 April 2014 [Regulation National Migration Directorate on a Special Regime of Regularisation of Nationals of Korean Nationality].

Disposición Dirección Nacional de Migraciones 002 sobre Regularización de Nacionales Senegaleses, 4 January 2013 [Regulation National Migration Directorate on the Regularisation of Senegalese Nationals].

Disposición Dirección Nacional de Migraciones 001 sobre Regularización de Nacionales Dominicanos, 4 January 2013 [Regulation National Migration Directorate on the Regularisation of Dominican Nationals].

Ley 26.774 de Ciudadanía Argentina modificando la Ley 346, 31 October 2012 [Law on Citizenship amending Law 346].

Proyecto de Ley de Aníbal Fernández S-2696/12, 3 October 2012 [Law Proposal].

Decreto 616, Reglamento de la Ley de Migraciones, 3 May 2010 [Decree Implementing Regulations to the Migration Law].

Disposición Dirección Nacional de Migraciones 14949 modificando la Disposición 53.253, 11 April 2006 [Regulation National Migration Directorate amending Regulation 53.253].

Disposición Dirección Nacional de Migraciones 53.253, Programa Nacional de Normalización Documentaria Migratoria Extranjeros Nativos de los Estados Parte del Mercado Común del Sur y sus Estados Asociados, 15 December 2005 [Regulation National Migration Directorate on a National Programme of Documents Normalisation for Foreigners who are Natives from MERCOSUR and Associate States].

---

[1] Items in each section are listed in reverse chronological order.

Decreto 1169/2004, Regularización de la Situación Migratoria de Ciudadanos Nativos de Países fuera de la Órbita del MERCOSUR, que al 30 de Junio de 2004 Residan de Hecho en el Territorio Nacional,13 September 2004 [Decree on Regularisation of Non-MERCOSUR Nationals Residing in Argentina by 30 June 2004].

Ley 25.871 de Migraciones, 21 January 2004 [Law on Migration].

Constitución Nacional de la República de Argentina, Santa Fe, 22 August 1994 [National Constitution of the Republic of Argentina].

Decreto 1.033, 24 June 1992 [Decree].

Ley de Ciudadania y Naturalización 23.059, 22 March1984 [Law on Citizenship and Naturalisation].

Decreto 780, 12 January 1984 [Decree].

Ley General de Migraciones y Fomento de la Inmigración 22.439, Buenos Aires, 23 March 1981 [General Law on Migrations and Promotion of Immigration].

Ley de Nacionalidad y Ciudadanía 21.795, 18 May 1978 [Law on Nationality and Citizenship].

Decreto 87, 11 January 1974 [Decree].

Decreto Ley 18.235, June 1969 [Law Decree].

Decreto Ley 17.294 sobre Represión de Inmigración Clandestina, 23 May 1967 [Law Decree on Repression of Clandestine Migration].

Decreto Reglamentario sobre Inmigración 4418, 14 June 1965 [Implementing Regulations on Immigration].

Decreto 49, 3 January 1964 [Decree].

Decreto 3364, 4 August 1958 [Decree].

Decreto 15.972 sobre Indulto General a los Extranjeros que Ingresaron al País en Violación de las Disposiciones Legales o Reglamentarias, 8 July 1949 [Decree on General Amnesty to Foreigners who Entered the Country Violating Legal Regulations].

Decreto 8972, 1938 [Decree].

Decreto, 19 January 1934 [Decree].

Decreto sobre Restricciones a la Inmigración, 26 November 1932 [Decree on Restrictions to Immigration].

Decreto, 8 November 1932 [Decree].

Decreto sobre Desembarco de Inmigrantes y Pasajeros e Impedimentos de Admisión, 31 December 1923 [Decree on the Disembarkment of Immigrants and Passengers and on Admission Impediments].

Decreto sobre Inmigración, 31 March 1919 [Decree on Immigration].

Ley de Defensa Social 7.029, 28 June 1910 [Law on Social Defence].

Ley de Residencia 4.144, 17 November 1902 [Law on Residence].

Ley 817 de Inmigración y Colonización (Ley Avellaneda), 19 October 1876 [Law on Immigration and Colonisation].

Ley 346 de Ciudadanía, Buenos Aires, 1 October 1869 [Citizenship Law 346].

Ley 145 de Ciudadanía, Buenos Aires, 7 October 1857 [Citizenship Law 145].

Constitución de la Confederación Argentina, Santa Fe, 1 May 1853 [Constitution of the Argentinean Confederation].

Constitución, Buenos Aires 24 December 1826 [Constitution].

Decreto 22 September 1822 [Decree].

Ley 2 August 1821 [Law].

Estatuto Provisional de la Provincia de Santa Fé (Argentina), 26 August 1819 [Provisional Statute of the Santa Fé Province].

Decreto sobre Fomento de la Inmigración y Colonización de la Tierra Pública, 4 September 1812 [Decree on the Promotion of Immigration and Colonisation of Public Land].

Bolivia

Decreto Supremo 1923, Reglamento a la Ley de Migración,13 March 2014 [Supreme Decree Implementing Regulations to the Law on Migration].

Decreto Supremo 1800 sobre Regularización, 20 November 2013 [Supreme Decree on Regularisation].

Ley 370 de Migración, 8 May 2013 [Migration Law].

Constitución Política del Estado de Bolivia, El Alto de la Paz, 7 February 2009 [Political Constitution of the Bolivian State].

Reglamento sobre Doble Nacionalidad y Recuperación de la Nacionalidad Boliviana, Decreto Supremo 27698, 24 August 2004 [Supreme Decree on the Implementing Regulations on Dual Nationality and Recovery of Bolivian Nationality].

Ley 2650, Modificando la Constitución, 13 April 2004 [Law Amending the Constitution].

Constitución Política del Estado de Bolivia, 6 February 1995 [Political Constitution of the Bolivian State].

Decreto Ley 13.344, Ley de Inmigración, 30 January 1976 [Law on Immigration].

Constitución Política del Estado de Bolivia, La Paz, 2 February 1967 [Political Constitution of the Bolivian State].

Ley General del Trabajo, 8 December 1942 [General Labour Law].

Decreto Supremo, Ley General del Trabajo, 24 May 1939 [General Labour Law].

Decreto Ley, 27 March 1938 [Law Decree].

Ley de Residencia, 18 January 1911 [Law on Residence].

Resolución Suprema, 16 August 1899 [Supreme Resolution].

Resolución Suprema, 5 August 1899 [Supreme Resolution].

Decreto, 16 July 1868 [Decree].

Decreto sobre Ciudadanía Hispanoamericana, La Paz de Ayacucho, 18 March 1866 [Decree on Hispano-American Citizenship].

Constitución Política de 1839, 26 October 1839 [Political Constitution].

Constitución Política de 1826, 19 November 1826 [Political Constitution].

Brazil

Resolução Normativa 126, Conselho Nacional de Imigração, Dispõe sobre a Concessão de Residência Temporária a Nacional de País Fronteiriço, 2 March 2017 [Normative Resolution on Temporary Residence for Nationals of a Bordering State].

Lei 13.445, Institui a Lei de Migração, 24 May 2017 [Migration Law].

Decreto 8.757, Altera o Decreto n° 86.715, de 10 de dezembro de 1981, para Dispor sobre a Situação Jurídica do Estrangeiro na República Federativa do Brasil, 10 May 2016 [Decree Amending Decree 86.715 of 1981 on the Legal Situation of Foreigners in Brazil].

Proposta de Emenda à Constituição n° 25, 2012 [Proposal to amend Arts 5, 12 and 14 of the Constitution to Extend Political Rights to Foreigners].

Lei 11.961, Dispõe sobre a Residência Provisória para o Estrangeiro em Situação Irregular no Território Nacional e dá Outras Providências. 2 July 2009 [Law Establishing the Provisional Residence of Foreigners in an Irregular Situation in the National Territory].

Lei 9.675, Amplia, para o Estrangeiro em Situação Ilegal no Território Nacional, o Prazo para Requerer Registro Provisório, 29 June 1998 [Law Extending the Period for Foreigner in an Illegal Situation to Obtain a Provisional Registration].

Lei 7.685, Dispõe sobre o Registro Provisório para o Estrangeiro em Situação Ilegal em Território Nacional, 2 December 1988 [Law on the Provisional Registration of Foreigners in Illegal Situation in the National Territory].

Constituição da República Federativa do Brasil, Brasilia, 5 October 1988 [Constitution of the Federative Republic of Brazil].

Decreto no. 86.715, Regulamenta a Lei nº 6.815, de 19 de agosto de 1980, 10 December 1981 [Decree Regulating the 1980 Foreigner's Statute].

Lei 6.964, Altera Disposições da Lei nº 6.815, de 19 de agosto de 1980, 9 December 1981 [Law Amending the 1980 Foreigner's Statute].

Lei no 6.815, Estatuto do Estrangeiro, 19 August 1980 [Foreigner's Statute].

Decreto no 7.967, Dispõe sôbre a Imigração e Colonização, e dá outras Providências, 18 September 1945 [Decree on Immigration, Colonisation and other Affairs].

Decreto-Lei 5.452, Aprova a Consolidação das Leis do Trabalho, 1 May 1943 [Law Decree Approving the Consolidation of the Labour Laws].

Circular Reservada 1522, 6 May 1941 [Classified Memo].

Decreto-Lei no. 3.175, Restringe a Imigração e dá outras Providências, 7 April 1941 [Law Decree 3175 Restricting Immigration and other Affairs].

Decreto-Lei no. 406, Dispõe sôbre a Entrada de Estrangeiros no Território Nacional, 4 May 1938 [Law Decree on the Entry of Foreigners into National Territory].

Constituição da República dos Estados Unidos do Brasil, Rio de Janeiro, 16 July 1934 [Constitution of the Republic of the United States of Brazil].

Decreto no 24.215, Dispõe sobre a Entrada de Estrangeiros em Territorio Nacional, 9 May 1934 [Decree on Entry of Foreigners into the National Territory].

Decreto no. 19.482, Limita a entrada, no Território Nacional, de Passageiros Estrangeiros de Terceira Classe, Dispõe sobre a Localização e Amparo de Trabalhadores Nacionais, e dá outras Providências, 12 December 1930 [Decree limiting the Entry into National Territory of Foreign Passengers travelling in Third Class, on the Localisation and Support of National Workers, and other Issues].

Decreto no. 4.269, regula a Repressão do Anarchismo, 17 January 1921 [Decree Regulating the Repression of Anarchism].

Decreto no 4.247, Regula a Entrada de Estrangeiros no Territorio Nacional, 6 January 1921 [Decree Regulating the Entry of Foreigners into National Territory].

Decreto 2.741, 8 January 1913 [Decree].

Decreto no. 6.486, Manda observar as instrucções expedidas para a execução do decreto n. 1641, de 7 de janeiro do corrente anno, 23 May 1907 [Decree Instructing to Execute Decree 1.641].

Decreto no. 1.641 (Lei Adolfo Gordo), Providencia sobre a Expulsão de Estrangeiros do Territorio Nacional, 7 January 1907 [Decree on Expulsion of Foreigners from the National Territory].

Decreto no. 1.566, Regula a Entrada de Extrangeiros no Territorio Nacional e sua Expulsão durante o Estado de Sitio, 13 October 1893 [Decree Regulating the entry of Foreigners into the National Territory and their Expulsion during the State of Siege].

Constituição da República dos Estados Unidos do Brasil, Rio de Janeiro, 24 February 1891 [Constitution of the Republic of the United States of Brazil].

Decreto no. 528, Regularisa o Serviço da Introducção e Localisação de Immigrantes na Republica dos Estados Unidos do Brasil, 28 June 1890 [Decree Regulates the Service to Introduce and Locate Immigrants in the Republic of the United States of Brazil].

Decreto no. 58-A, Providencia sobre a Naturalização dos Estrangeiros Residentes na Republica, 14 December 1889 [Decree on the Naturalisation of Foreigners Residing in the Republic].

Lei Imperial n. 3.353, 13 May 1888 (Lei Áurea), Decreto de Extinção da Escravidão no Brasil [Imperial Law Abolishing Slavery].

Decreto 808-A, Contêm varias Disposições sobre a Naturalisação dos Estrangeiros actualmente Estabelecidos como Colonos, nos diversos lugares do Imperio, ainda não reconhecidos Brasileiros, 23 June 1855 [Decree containing various Dispositions on Naturalisation of Foreigners now established as Settlers in various places of the Empire but not yet Recognised as Brazilians].

Lei sobre Naturalisação dos Estrangeiros, Rio de Janeiro, 23 October 1832 [Law on Naturalisation of Foreigners].

Constituição Política do Império do Brasil, 25 March 1824 [Political Constitution of the Empire of Brazil].

Decreto sobre as Condições com que Podem ser Admittidos no Brazil os Subditos de Portugal, 14 January 1823 [Decree on the Conditions under which Portuguese might be Admitted to Brazil].

Chile

Proyecto de Nueva Ley de Migraciones, Santiago, 21 August 2017 [Migration Law Proposal].

Propuesta de Ley de Migraciones, Ministerio del Interior y Segurida Pública, 7 October 2015 [Migration Law Draft Bill, Ministry of the Interior and Public Security].

Proyecto de Ley de Inmigración y Extranjería, 20 May 2013 [Proposal for an Immigration Law].

Oficio Circular 26465 del Subsecretario del Interior. Ministry of the Interior, Chile, 4 December 2009 [Memo by the Subsecretary of Interior].

Resolución Exenta dada por el Subsecretario del Interior, RE N°36339, Dispone Proceso de Regularización en el País de Extranjeros, 22 October 2007 [Resolution Granted by the Under-secretary of the Interior on a Regularisation Procedure for Foreigners].

Ley 20050, Modificación de la Constitución, 20 August 2005 [Law Amending the Constitution].

Resolución Exenta 2071, Amnistía Provisoria 7 August 1998 [Provisional Amnesty Resolution].

Ley Orgánica Constitucional 18700 sobre Votaciones Populares y Escrutinios, 6 May 1988 [Organic Constitutional Law on Voting and Scrutiny].

Decreto Ejecutivo 596, Aprueba Nuevo Reglamento de Extranjería, 14 June 1984 [Executive Decree Approving Implementing Regulations on Immigration].

Decreto Ley 1094, establece Normas sobre Extranjeros en Chile 19 July 1975 [Law Decree establishing Norms on Foreigners in Chile].

Decreto Supremo 5142, Fija el Texto Refundido de las Disposiciones sobre Nacionalización de Extranjeros, 29 October 1960 [Decree on Naturalisation of Foreigners].

Decreto Ley 69, crea el Departamento de Inmigración y Establece Normas sobre la Materia, Santiago, 27 April 1953 [Law Decree Creating the Department of Immigration and Establishes Norms on the Subject].

Código del Trabajo, 13 May 1931 [Labour Code].

Ley 3.446 que Impide la Entrada al País o la Residencia en él de Elementos Indeseables, 12 December 1918 [Law Impeding Entry into the Country or Residence to Undesirable Elements].

Ley de Colonización, 18 November 1845 [Law on Colonisation].

Constitución Política de la República de Chile, 25 May 1833 [Political Constitution of the Republic of Chile].

Constitución Política del Estado de Chile, 30 October 1822 [Political Constitution of the Chilean State].

Colombia

Proyecto de Ley 148 'Por medio del cual Establecen Lineamientos para la Política Integral Migratoria en Colombia y se Dictan otras Disposiciones', 19 September 2017 [Law Proposal for a Comprehensive Migration Policy].

Decreto 834 por el cual se Establecen Disposiciones en Materia Migratoria, 24 April 2013 [Decree Establishing Regulations on Migration].

Decreto 46 por el cual se Adopta la Guía para la Implementación de la Decisión 545 de la Comunidad Andina (CAN) 'Instrumento Andino de Migración Laboral', 17 January 2013 [Decree Implementing CAN's Decision 545, Andean Instrument on Labour Migration].

Ley 1429, por la cual se Expide la Ley de Formalización y Generación de Empleo, 29 December 2010 [Law on the Formalisation and Generation of Employment].

Decreto 3970 por el cual se Dictan Disposiciones sobre Regularización de Extranjeros, 14 October 2008 [Decree on Regularisation of Foreigners].

Decreto 2150, por el cual se Suprimen y Reforman Regulaciones, Procedimientos o Trámites Innecesarios Existentes en la Administración Pública, 5 December 1995 [Decree Amending Law 43 on Nationality].

Ley 43 sobre Nacionalidad, 1 February 1993 [Law 43 on Nationality].

Ley 6 de 1991 por la cual se Reglamenta la Especialidad Médica de Anestesiología, 16 January 1991 [Law on the Medical Anaesthesiology Specialisation].

Constitución Política de Colombia, Bogotá, 4 July 1991 [Political Constitution of Colombia].

Decreto 2363, sobre Código Sustantivo del Trabajo, 5 August 1950 [Decree on a Sustantive Labour Code].

Decreto 397, por el cual se Establecen Requisitos para la Entrada al País de Extranjeros Pertenecientes a Determinadas Nacionalidades, 17 February 1937 [Decree Establishing the Requirements for the Entry into the Country of Foreigners of certain Nationalities].

Ley 22bis, por la cual se Reforman y Adicionan las Disposiciones Relativas a la Naturalización de Extranjeros, 3 February 1936 [Law Reforming Certain Rules on the Naturalisation of Foreigners].

Ley 48 sobre Inmigración y Extranjería, 3 November 1920 [Law on Immigration and Foreigners].

Decreto 496, por el cual se Reglamentan las Leyes sobre Inmigración y se deroga el Decreto 1218 de 1908 (17 de noviembre), 19 November 1909 [Decree Regulating the Laws on Immigration].

Ley 145 sobre Extranjería y Naturalización, 26 November 1888 [Law on Foreigners and Naturalisation].

Ley 62, por la cual se Hacen Varias Prohibiciones, Bogotá, 24 April 1887 [Law through which Various Prohibitions are Made].

Constitución Política de la República de Colombia, Bogotá, 5 August 1886 [Political Constitution of the Republic of Colombia].

Constitución Política de los Estados Unidos de Colombia, Rionegro, 8 May 1863 [Political Constitution of the United States of Colombia].

Constitución Política de la República de la Nueva Granada, Bogotá, 21 May 1853 [Political Constitution of the Republic of Nueva Granada].

Decreto, 10 September 1847 [Decree].

Ley 11, 1847 [Law].

Ley sobre Inmigración de Extranjeros, 2 June 1847 [Law on Immigration].

Decreto, 5 June 1843 [Decree].

Ley 14 sobre Naturalización de Extranjeros, 11 April 1843 [Law on Naturalisation of Foreigners].

Constitución Política del Estado de la Nueva Granada, 29 February 1832 [Political Constitution of the State of Nueva Granada].

Constitución de la República de Colombia, Bogotá, 29 April 1830 [Constitution of the Colombian Republic].

Decreto para Promover la Inmigración de Extranjeros y la Colonización de Tierras de la Gran Colombia, Bogotá, 7 June 1823 [Decree to Promote the Immigration of Foreigners and the Colonisation of Land].

Constitución de la Gran Colombia, 30 August 1821 [Constitution of Gran Colombia].

Plan de Reforma o Revisión de la Constitución de la Provincia de Cundinamarca (Colombia) de 1812, 13 July 1815 [Reform Plan or Revision of the 1812 Constitution of the Province of Cundinamarca (Colombia)].

Constitución de Cartagena de Indias, 14 June 1812 [Constitution of Cartagena de Indias].

Constitución de la Barcelona Colombiana, 12 January 1812 [Constitution of Barcelona Colombiana].

Acta de Federación de las Provincias Unidas de la Nueva Granada, 27 November 1811 [Act on the Federation of the United Provinces of Nueva Granada].

Ecuador

Reglamento a la Ley Orgánica de Movilidad Humana, 3 August 2017 [Implementing Regulations to the Organic Law on Human Mobility].

Ley Orgánica de Movilidad Humana, Quito, 9 January 2017 [Organic Law on Human Mobility].

Acuerdo Interministerial 000054, Implementación del Instrumento Andino de Migración Laboral, 26 July 2012 [Inter-ministerial Agreement Implementing the Andean Instrument of Labour Migration].

Decreto Ejecutivo 248 sobre Regularización de Nacionales Haitianos, 9 February 2010 [Executive Decree on Regularisation of Haitian nationals].

Ley Orgánica Electoral, 27 April 2009 [Electoral Organic Law].

Constitución Política de la República de Ecuador, 20 October 2008 [Political Constitution of the Republic of Ecuador].

Constitución Política de la República de Ecuador, Riobamba, 5 June 1998 [Political Constitution of the Republic of Ecuador].

Constitución Política del año 1978 codificada en 1997, Ley No. 000. RO/ 2, 13 February 1997 [Political Constitution of 1978 codified in 1997].

Constitución Política de la República de Ecuador, Quito, 27 March 1979 [Political Constitution of the Republic of Ecuador].

Decreto Supremo 277, Reglamento a la Ley de Naturalización 14 April 1976 [Supreme Decree, Implementing Regulations Law on Naturalisation].

Decreto Supremo 276, Ley de Naturalización, 2 April 1976 [Supreme Decree Law on Naturalisation].

Ley de Migración adoptada por Decreto Supremo D.S, 1899 R. O. 382, 30 December 1971 [Migration Law adopted by Supreme Decree].

Constitución Política de la República de Ecuador, Quito, 25 May 1967 [Political Constitution of the Republic of Ecuador].

Constitución Política de la República de Ecuador, Quito, 5 March 1945 [Political Constitution of the Republic of Ecuador].

Ley de Extranjería, Extradición y Naturalización, 16 February 1938 [Law on Foreigners, Extradition and Naturalisation].

Constitución Política de la República de Ecuador, Quito, 26 March 1929 [Political Constitution of the Republic of Ecuador].

Ley 344 de Inmigración, Extradición y Naturalización, 8 October 1921 [Law on Immigration, Extradition and Naturalisation].

Constitución Política de la República de Ecuador, Quito, 23 December 1906 [Political Constitution of the Republic of Ecuador].

Constitución Política de la República de Ecuador, Quito, 12 January 1897 [Political Constitution of the Republic of Ecuador].

Decreto, 3 December 1895 [Decree].

Decreto Legislativo, 12 October 1889 [Legislative Decree].

Constitución de la República de Ecuador, Quito, 4 February 1884 [Constitution of the Republic of Ecuador].

Constitución de la República de Ecuador, Ambato, 31 March 1878 [Constitution of the Republic of Ecuador].

Constitución de la República de Ecuador, Quito, 9 June 1869 [Constitution of the Republic of Ecuador].

Decreto, 24 October 1867 [Decree].

Ley 47, Quito, 17 July 1861 [Law 47].

Constitución de la República de Ecuador, Quito, 10 April 1861 [Constitution of the Republic of Ecuador].

Constitución de la República de Ecuador, Guayaquil, 30 August 1852 [Constitution of the Republic of Ecuador].

Decreto del 25 de julio de 1851 por el que se Abole la Esclavitud [Decree of 25 July 1851 Abolishing Slavery].

Constitución de la República de Ecuador, Quito, 25 February 1851 [Constitution of the Republic of Ecuador].

Constitución de la República de Ecuador, Cuenca, 3 December 1845 [Constitution of the Republic of Ecuador].

Constitución Política de la República de Ecuador, Quito, 31 March 1843 [Political Constitution of the Republic of Ecuador].

Constitución Política de la República de Ecuador, 13 August 1835 [Political Constitution of the Republic of Ecuador].

Constitución Política de la República de Ecuador, 11 September 1830 [Political Constitution of the Republic of Ecuador].

Paraguay

Propuesta Ley de Migraciones, Ministerio del Interior, Dirección General de Migraciones, 2016 [Proposal Migration Law, Interior Ministry, General Directorate on Migration].

Decreto 8373 por el cual se Reglamenta la Ley 4429, 3 February 2012 [Decree Implementing Regulations Law 4429].

Ley 4429 que Regulariza la Residencia de Extranjeros en Situación Migratoria Irregular, 4 October 2011 [Law Regularising the Residence of Foreigners in Irregular Situation].

Ley 978 sobre Migraciones, 8 November 1996 [Law on Migration].

Constitución Nacional del Paraguay, 20 June 1992 [National Constitution of Paraguay].

Ley 470 sobre Migraciones, 15 November 1974 [Law on Migrations].

Constitución Nacional del Paraguay, 10 July 1940 [National Constitution of Paraguay].

Ley, 30 September 1903 [Law].

Constitución de la República del Paraguay, 18 November 1870 [Constitution of the Republic of Paraguay].

Ley que Establece la Administración Política, Asunción, 16 March 1844 [Law Establishing the Political Administration].

Peru

Decreto Legislativo 1350 de Migraciones, Lima, 6 January 2017 [Legislative Decree on Migration].

Decreto Supremo, No. 001-2017-IN, Aprueban Lineamientos para el Otorgamiento del Permiso Temporal de Permanencia para las Personas Extranjeras Madres o Padres de Hijos/as Peruanos/as Menores de Edad e Hijos/as Mayores de Edad con Discapacidad Permanente, 2 January 2017 [Supreme Decree on Conditions to Grant Temporary Residence Permits to Foreign Parents of Peruvian Minors or Adults with a Permanent Disability].

Decreto Supremo No. 002-2017-IN, Aprueban Lineamientos para el Otorgamiento del Permiso Temporal de Permanencia para las Personas de Nacionalidad Venezolana, 2 January 2017 [Supreme Decree on the Conditions to Grant Temporary Residence Permits to Venezuelan Nationals].

Decreto Legislativo 1236 de Migraciones, 25 September 2015 [Legislative Decree on Migration].

Ley 30103 que Establece el Procedimiento que Regulariza la Residencia de Extranjeros en Situación Migratoria Irregular, 8 November 2013 [Law Establishing the Procedure to Regularise the Residence of Foreigners in an Irregular Situation].

Resolución Ministerial 318-2010-TR, Implementando el Instrumento Andino de Migración Laboral, Lima, 17 December 2010 [Ministerial Resolution Implementing the Andean Instrument of Labour Migration].

Ley de Nacionalidad 26.574, 21 December 1995 [Nationality Law].

Constitución Política de Perú, 29 December 1993 [Political Constitution of Peru].

Decreto Legislativo 689, Dictan la Ley para la Contratación de Trabajadores Extranjeros, 5 November 1991 [Law on the Hiring of Foreign Workers].

Constitución Política de Perú, 12 July 1979 [Political Constitution of Peru].

Decreto Ley 21702, Incorporán al Ministerio del Interior Dirección de Migraciones, 23 November 1976 [Law Decree Incorporating into the Interior Ministry the National Migration Directorate].

Decreto-Ley 14.460, Obligando a los Empleadores a Ocupar Personal Peruano en una Proporción no Menor al 80%, 25 April 1963 [Law Decree Requiring Employers to Hire a Proportion of Peruvians of at least 80% of the Total Staff].

Decreto Ley 7000, sobre Reinscripción de Extranjeros,16 January 1931 [Law Decree on the Reenrolment of Foreigners].

Ley 4891 sobre la Vagancia, Lima, 16 January 1924 [Law on Vagrancy].

Ley 4045 sobre Extranjeros Peligrosos, Lima, 21 September 1920 [Law on Dangerous Foreigners].

Constitución para la República de Perú de 1920, Lima, 27 December 1919 [Constitution for the Republic of Peru of 1920].

R.S., Lima, 25 November 1910.

Ley sobre Expulsión de Extranjeros, 1908 [Law on Expulsion of Foreigners].

Ley, 14 October 1893 [Law].

Constitución Política de la República Peruana, Lima, 13 November 1860 [Political Constitution of the Peruvian Republic].

Constitución Política de la República Peruana, Lima, 19 October 1856 [Political Constitution of the Peruvian Republic].

Decreto, 25 January 1845 [Decree].

Constitución Política del Perú de 1839, Huancayo, 10 November 1839 [Political Constitution of Peru].

Decreto del General Salaverry, Declarando Ciudadanos del Perú a todos los Extranjeros que Quieran Inscribirse en el Registro Cívico, Lima, 14 March 1835 [Decree of General Salaverry, Declaring as Peruvian Citizens all those Foreigners willing to Register as such].

Constitución Política de la República Peruana, 18 April 1828 [Political Constitution of the Peruvian Republic].

Constitución Política de la República Peruana Sancionada por el Primer Congreso Constituyente, 12 November 1823 [Political Constitution of the Peruvian Republic sanctioned by the First Constitutional Congress].

Decreto, Lima, 19 April 1822 [Decree].

Decreto, 4 October 1821 [Decree].

Decreto del General José de San Martín, Lima, 27 August 1821 [Decree of General José de San Martín].

Uruguay

Documento Marco sobre Política Migratoria en Uruguay, 29 August 2016 [Uruguayan Framework Document on a Migration Policy].

Decreto 312 Reglamentación de los Artículos 27 Literal B) y 33 de la Ley 18.250 Relativos al Trámite de Residencia Permanente de Familiares de Uruguayos y Nacionales de los Estados Parte y Asociados del MERCOSUR, 30 November 2015 [Decree Regulating Access to Permanent Residence for Family Members of Uruguayans and Nationals of MERCOSUR and Associate States].

Ley 19.254, Modificaciones a la Ley de Migraciones 18.250. Obtención de Residencia Permanente a Familiares de Uruguayos y de Nacionales de los Estados Parte y Asociados del MERCOSUR, 4 September 2014 [Law Amending 18.250 Migration Law. Obtaining Permanent Residence for Family Members of Uruguayans and of Nationals of MERCOSUR Member and Associate States].

Decreto 394, Reglamentación de la Ley de Migraciones, 24 August 2009 [Decree Implementing Regulations Migration Law].

Ley de Migraciones 18.250, 6 January 2008 [Migration Law].

Decreto Ley 14.878 sobre Migraciones, 5 April 1979 [Law Decree on Migrations].

Constitución de la República Oriental del Uruguay, 15 February 1967 [Constitution of the Oriental Republic of Uruguay].

Decreto, 12 June 1940 [Decree].

Decreto Presidential, 27 November 1937 [Presidential Decree].

Ley 9604 de Inmigración (Modificación), Montevideo, 13 October 1936 [Law on Immigration (Amendment)].

Decreto Presidencial, 24 January 1934 [Presidential Decree].

Decreto, 6 September 1932 [Decree].

Ley 8868 de Inmigración, 19 July 1932 [Law on Immigration].

Ley 3051 de Inmigración y Exclusión, 23 June 1906 [Law on Immigration and Exclusion].

Decreto sobre la Inmigración Inútil, 10 December 1894 [Decree on Useless Immigration].

Ley 2096 de Inmigración, Montevideo, 10 June 1890 [Law on Immigration].

Ley 320 sobre Colonización, Montevideo, 4 June 1853 [Law on Colonisation].

Constitución de la República, 28 June 1830 [Constitution of the Republic].

Venezuela

Resolución 109/13, Normas para Facilitar la Regularización de los Ciudadanos de Nacionalidad Peruana, 30 April 2013 [Norms to Facilitate the Regularisation of Citizens of Peruvian Nationality].

Ley de Extranjería y Migración Venezolana 37.944, 24 March 2004 [Law on Migration].

Decreto 2823, Reglamento para la Regularización y Naturalización de los Extranjeros y las Extranjeras que se encuentran en el Territorio Nacional, 3 February 2004 [Decree Regulations to Regularise and Naturalise Foreigners who are in the National Territory].

Constitución de la República Bolivariana de Venezuela, Caracas, 30 December 1999 [Constitution of the Bolivarian Republic of Venezuela].

Decreto 616, Matrícula General de Extranjeros, 22 May 1980 [Decree on General Enrolment of Foreigners].

Constitución de la República de Venezuela, Caracas, 23 January 1961 [Constitution of the Republic of Venezuela].

Constitución de la República de Venezuela, Caracas, 11 April 1953 [Constitution of the Republic of Venezuela].

Constitución de los Estados Unidos de Venezuela, Caracas, 5 July 1947 [Constitution of the United States of Venezuela].

Constitución de los Estados Unidos de Venezuela, Caracas, 23 April 1945 [Constitution of the United States of Venezuela].

Ley de Extranjeros, 17 July 1937 [Law on Foreigners].

Ley de Inmigración y Colonización, 22 July 1936 [Immigration and Colonisation Law].

Constitución de los Estados Unidos de Venezuela, Caracas, 16 July 1936 [Constitution of the United States of Venezuela].

Constitución de los Estados Unidos de Venezuela, Caracas, 7 July 1931 [Constitution of the United States of Venezuela].

Constitución de los Estados Unidos de Venezuela, Caracas, 29 May 1929 [Constitution of the United States of Venezuela].

Constitución de los Estados Unidos de Venezuela, Caracas, 22 May 1928 [Constitution of the United States of Venezuela].

Constitución de los Estados Unidos de Venezuela, Caracas, 24 June 1925 [Constitution of the United States of Venezuela].

Constitución de los Estados Unidos de Venezuela, Caracas, 19 June 1922 [Constitution of the United States of Venezuela].

Ley de Extranjeros, 30 June 1915 [Law on Foreigners].

Constitución de los Estados Unidos de Venezuela, Caracas, 13 June 1914 [Constitution of the United States of Venezuela].

Ley de Inmigración y Colonización, 8 June 1912 [Immigration and Colonisation Law].

Constitución de los Estados Unidos de Venezuela, Caracas, 5 August 1909 [Constitution of the United States of Venezuela].

Constitución de los Estados Unidos de Venezuela, Caracas, 27 April 1904 [Constitution of the United States of Venezuela].

Ley que define los Derechos y Obligaciones de los Extranjeros, 16 April 1903 [Law defining the Rights and Obligations of Foreigners].

Constitución de los Estados Unidos de Venezuela, Caracas, 13 April 1901 [Constitution of the United States of Venezuela].

Ley sobre Inmigración, 26 August 1894 [Immigration Law].

Constitución de los Estados Unidos de Venezuela, Caracas, 12 June 1893 [Constitution of the United States of Venezuela].

Ley sobre Inmigración, 20 June 1891 [Immigration Law].

Constitución de los Estados Unidos de Venezuela, Caracas, 9 April 1891 [Constitution of the United States of Venezuela].

Constitución de los Estados Unidos de Venezuela, Caracas, 4 April 1881 [Constitution of the United States of Venezuela].

Constitución de los Estados Unidos de Venezuela, Caracas, 23 May 1874 [Constitution of the United States of Venezuela].

Resolución,1 December 1865 [Resolution].

Constitución de los Estados Unidos de Venezuela, Caracas, 28 March 1864 [Constitution of the United States of Venezuela].

Constitución de Venezuela, Valencia, 24 December 1858 [Constitution of Venezuela].

Constitución de Venezuela, 16 April 1857 [Constitution of Venezuela].

Decreto Ejecutivo, 2 July 1855 [Executive Decree].

Decreto de 24 de marzo de 1854 por el que se Abole la Esclavitud [Decree of 24 March 1854 Abolishing Slavery].

Ley de Inmigración, 5 March 1854 [Immigration Law].

Decreto Ejecutivo, 31 August 1848 [Executive Decree].

Ley, 24 May 1845 [Law on the Provision of Land to Immigrants].

Decreto, 13 June 1831 [Decree to Promote Immigration by the Inhabitants of the Canary Islands].

Constitución de Venezuela, Valencia, 22 September 1830 [Venezuelan Constitution].

Constitución de Venezuela, Angostura, 15 August 1819 [Venezuelan Constitution].

Constitución de la Provincia de Caracas, 31 January 1812 [Constitution of the Province of Caracas].

Constitución de Venezuela, Valencia 21 December 1811 [Venezuelan Constitution].

Constitución de la Provincia de Mérida, 31 July 1811 [Constitution of the Merida Province].

Ley de 1 de julio sobre los Derechos del Pueblo, 1 Julio 1811 [Law of 1 July on the Rights of the People].

Legislation: Countries in Latin America outside South America

Costa Rica

Constitución Política de Costa Rica, San José, 7 November 1949 [Political Constitution of Costa Rica].

Constitución Política de Costa Rica, San José, 8 June 1917 [Political Constitution of Costa Rica].

Constitución Política de Costa Rica, San José, 7 December 1871 [Political Constitution of Costa Rica].

Constitución Política de Costa Rica, San José, 18 February 1869 [Political Constitution of Costa Rica].

Constitución Política de Costa Rica, San José, 27 December 1859 [Political Constitution of Costa Rica].

Constitución Política Reformada de Costa Rica, San José, 30 November 1848 [Political Reformed Constitution of Costa Rica].

Constitución Política de Costa Rica, San José, 10 February 1847 [Political Constitution of the State of Costa Rica].

Constitución Política del Estado de Costa Rica, San José, 9 April 1844 [Political Constitution of the State of Costa Rica].

Dominican Republic

Constitución Política de la República Dominicana, Santo Domingo de Guzmán, 13 June 2015 [Political Constitution of the Dominican Republic].

Ley no. 1683 sobre Naturalización, 16 April 1948 [Naturalisation Law].

Constitución Política de la República Dominicana, Santo Domingo, 11 September 1907 [Political Constitution of the Dominican Republic].

Constitución Política de la República Dominicana, Santo Domingo, 12 June 1896 [Political Constitution of the Dominican Republic].

Constitución Política de la República Dominicana, Santo Domingo, 15 November 1887 [Political Constitution of the Dominican Republic].

Constitución Política de la República Dominicana, Santo Domingo, 23 November 1881 [Political Constitution of the Dominican Republic].

Constitución Política de la República Dominicana, Santo Domingo, 18 May 1880 [Political Constitution of the Dominican Republic].

Constitución Política de la República Dominicana, Santo Domingo, 11 February 1879 [Political Constitution of the Dominican Republic].

Constitución Política de la República Dominicana, Santo Domingo, 1 June 1878 [Political Constitution of the Dominican Republic].

Constitución Política de la República Dominicana, Santo Domingo, 10 May 1877 [Political Constitution of the Dominican Republic].

Constitución Política de la República Dominicana, Santo Domingo, 9 March 1875 [Political Constitution of the Dominican Republic].

Constitución Política de la República Dominicana, Santo Domingo, 4 April 1874 [Political Constitution of the Dominican Republic].

Constitución Política de la República Dominicana, Santo Domingo, 14 September 1872 [Political Constitution of the Dominican Republic].

Constitución Política de la República Dominicana, Santo Domingo, 26 September 1866 [Political Constitution of the Dominican Republic].

Constitución Política de la República Dominicana, Santo Domingo, 14 November 1865 [Political Constitution of the Dominican Republic].

Constitución Política de la República Dominicana, Moca, 19 February 1858 [Political Constitution of the Dominican Republic].

Constitución Política de la República Dominicana, Santo Domingo, 23 December 1854 [Political Constitution of the Dominican Republic].

Constitución Política de la República Dominicana, San Cristobal, 6 November 1844 [Political Constitution of the Dominican Republic].

El Salvador

Constitución de la República de El Salvador, 16 December 1983 [Constitution of the Republic of El Salvador].

Constitución de la República de El Salvador, San Salvador, 8 January 1962 [Constitution of the Republic of El Salvador].

Constitución de la República de El Salvador, San Salvador, 7 September 1950 [Constitution of the Republic of El Salvador].

Constitución de la República de El Salvador, San Salvador, 20 January 1939 [Constitution of the Republic of El Salvador].

Constitución de la República de El Salvador, San Salvador, 13 August 1886 [Constitution of the Republic of El Salvador].

Constitución de la República de El Salvador, San Salvador, 6 December 1883 [Constitution of the Republic of El Salvador].

Constitución de la República de El Salvador, San Salvador, 9 November 1872 [Constitution of the Republic of El Salvador].

Constitución de la República de El Salvador, San Salvador, 16 October 1871 [Constitution of the Republic of El Salvador].

Constitución de la República de El Salvador, San Salvador, 19 March 1864 [Constitution of the Republic of El Salvador].

Constitución de la República de El Salvador, San Salvador, 18 February 1841 [Constitution of the Republic of El Salvador].

Guatemala

Decreto 44, Código de Migración, 18 October 2016 [Migration Code].

Constitución de la República de Guatemala, 31 May 1985 [Constitution of the Republic of Guatemala].

Constitución de la República de Guatemala, 15 September 1965 [Constitution of the Republic of Guatemala].

Constitución de la República de Guatemala, 6 February 1956 [Constitution of the Republic of Guatemala].

Constitución de la República de Guatemala, 11 March 1945 [Constitution of the Republic of Guatemala].

Constitución Política de la República Federal Centroamericana (including Guatemala, Salvador and Honduras), Tegucigalpa, 9 September 1921 [Political Constitution of the Federal Republic of Central-America].

Constitución de la República de Guatemala, 11 December 1879 [Constitution of the Republic of Guatemala].

Acta Constitutiva de la República de Guatemala, 19 October 1851 [Constitutive Act of the Republic of Guatemala].

Constitución Política del Estado de Guatemala, Guatemala, 11 October 1825 [Political Constitution of the State of Guatemala].

Honduras

Constitución de la República de Honduras, 11 January 1982 [Constitution of the Republic of Honduras].

Constitución de Honduras, Tegucigalpa, 3 June 1965 [Constitution of Honduras].

Constitución de Honduras, Tegucigalpa, 19 December 1957 [Constitution of Honduras].

Constitución de Honduras, Tegucigalpa, 28 March 1936 [Constitution of Honduras].

Constitución de Honduras, Tegucigalpa, 19 September 1924 [Constitution of Honduras].

Constitución de Honduras, Tegucigalpa, 2 September 1904 [Constitution of Honduras].

Constitución de Honduras, Tegucigalpa, 14 October 1894 [Constitution of Honduras].

Constitución de Honduras, Tegucigalpa, 1 November 1880 [Constitution of Honduras].

Constitución de Honduras, Comayagua, 23 December 1873 [Constitution of Honduras].

Constitución de Honduras, Comayagua, 28 September 1865 [Constitution of Honduras].

Constitución de Honduras, Comayagua, 5 February 1848 [Constitution of Honduras].

Mexico

Ley de Migración, 25 May 2011 [Migration Law].

Ley de Nacionalidad, 23 January 1998 [Nationality Law].

Ley de Nacionalidad y Naturalización, 20 January 1934 [Nationality and Naturalisation Law].

Constitución Política de los Estados Unidos Mexicanos, 5 February 1917 [Political Constitution of the United States of Mexico].

Constitución Federal de los Estados Unidos Mexicanos, 31 January 1824 [Federal Constitution of the United States of Mexico].

Nicaragua

Ley General de Migración y Extranjería, 31 March 2011 [General Migration and Aliens Law].

Constitución Política de la República Nicaragua, Managua, 9 January 1987 [Political Constitution of the Republic of Nicaragua].

Constitución Política de la República Nicaragua, Managua, 14 March 1974 [Political Constitution of the Republic of Nicaragua].

Constitución Política de la República Nicaragua, Managua, 1 November 1950 [Political Constitution of the Republic of Nicaragua].

Constitución Política de la República Nicaragua, Managua, 21 January 1948 [Political Constitution of the Republic of Nicaragua].

Constitución Política de la República Nicaragua, Managua, 22 March 1939 [Political Constitution of the Republic of Nicaragua].

Constitución Política de la República Nicaragua, Managua, 3 April 1913 [Political Constitution of the Republic of Nicaragua].

Constitución Política de la República Nicaragua, Managua, 10 November 1911 [Political Constitution of the Republic of Nicaragua].

Constitución Política de Nicaragua, Managua, 30 March 1905 [Political Constitution of of Nicaragua].

Constitución Política para los Estados Unidos de Centro América (Nicaragua, Honduras y el Salvador), Managua, 27 August 1898 [Political Constitution for the United States of Central America].

Constitución Política de la República Nicaragua, Managua, 10 December 1893 [Political Constitution of the Republic of Nicaragua].

Constitución Política de la República Nicaragua, Managua, 19 August 1858 [Political Constitution of the Republic of Nicaragua].

Constitución Política de Nicaragua, Managua, 30 April 1854 [Political Constitution of Nicaragua].

Constitución Política del Estado Libre de Nicaragua, Leon, 12 November 1838 [Political Constitution of the Free State of Nicaragua].

Panama

Decreto Ley 3 que Crea el Servicio Nacional de Migración, la Carrera Migratoria y Dicta Otras Disposiciones, 22 February 2008 [Law Decree Creating the National Migration Service and other Regulations].

Constitución Política de la República de Panamá, 11 October 1972 [Political Constitution of the Republic of Panama].

Constitución Política de la República de Panamá, 1 March 1946 [Political Constitution of the Republic of Panama].

Decreto Ley 16 sobre Migración, 30 June 1960 [Law Decree on Migration].

Republic of Central America

Constitución de la República Federal de Centroamérica, 22 November 1824 [Constitution of the Federal Republic of Central America].

Legislation: Countries outside Latin America

France

Loi du 14 juillet 1819 relative à l'abolition du droit d'aubaine et de détraction [Law Abolishing the *droit d'aubaine* and the *droit de détraction*].

The 1804 French Civil Code, also known as Napoleonic Code or *Code civil des Français*.

The Constitution of the 1791 National Assembly, 3 September 1791.

Portugal

Constituição Política da Monarquia Portuguesa, Lisboa, 23 September 1822 [Political Constitution of the Portuguese Monarchy].

Spain

Constitución Española de 1869, Madrid, 6 June 1869 [Spanish Constitution of 1869].

Constitución de Cádiz de 1812, 19 March 1812 [Cádiz Constitution].

Decreto sobre Igualdad de Derechos entre Españoles Europeos y Ultramarinos, 15 October 1810 [Decree of 15 October 1810 on the equality of rights between Europeans and overseas Spaniards].

USA

Immigration Reform and Control Act (IRCA), Pub.L. 99–603, 100 Stat. 3445, enacted 6 November 1986.

Immigration Act of 1924, 24 May 1924.

Emergency Quota Act 1921, ch. 8, 42 Stat. 5, 19 May 1921.

Immigration Act of 1917, 5 February 1917.

An Act to Regulate the Immigration of Aliens into the United States (Anarchist Exclusion Act), 3 March 1903.

Immigration Act of 1875, 18 Stat. 477.

Chinese Exclusion Act of 1882, 22 Stat. 58.

Bilateral Agreements

Acuerdo entre la República Federal de Brasil y la República Oriental de Uruguay sobre Residencia Permanente con el Objetivo de Alcanzar la Libre Movilidad de Personas, Brasilia, 9 July 2013 [Agreement between the Federal Republic of Brazil and the Oriental Republic of Uruguay on Permanent Residence with the objective to achieve the Free Movement of People].

Acuerdo Marco de Asistencia y Cooperación en Materia Migratoria entre Colombia y Perú, 6 March 2012 [Framework Agreement on Assistance and Cooperation on Migration].

Estatuto Migratorio entre Ecuador y Venezuela, Caracas, 6 July 2010 [Migration Statute between Ecuador and Venezuela].

Acuerdo sobre Residencia para Nacionales de la República de Argentina y la República de Perú, Buenos Aires, 15 June 2007 (entered into force on 10 December 2009) [Agreement on Residence for Nationals of the Republic of Argentina and the Republic of Peru].

Acuerdo sobre Regularización Migratoria entre el Gobierno de la República del Paraguay y el Gobierno de la República de Bolivia, Asunción, 20 October 2006 [Agreement on Migratory Regularisation].

Acuerdo por Canje de Notas entre la República Argentina y la República Oriental del Uruguay relativo a la Aplicación Bilateral del Acuerdo sobre Residencia para Nacionales de los Estados Partes del MERCOSUR, Córdoba, 20 July 2006 [Agreement on Exchange of Letters between the Republic of Argentina and the Oriental Republic of Uruguay referring to the Bilateral Application of the Residence Agreement for Nationals of the MERCOSUR Member States].

Acuerdo entre la República Argentina y la República Federativa del Brasil para la Concesión de Residencia Permanente a Titulares de Residencias Transitorias o Temporarias, Puerto Iguazú, República Argentina, 30 November 2005 [Agreement for the Concession of Permanent Residence to Holders of Transitory or Temporary Residency].

Acuerdo Operativo entre la Dirección Nacional de Migraciones de la República Argentina y el Departamento de Extranjeros de la República Federativa del Brasil para la Aplicación del Acuerdo sobre Residencia para Nacionales de los Estados Partes del MERCOSUR, 29 November 2005 (entered into force 3 April 2006) [Operative Agreement between the National Migration Directorate of the Republic of Argentina and the Foreigners Department of the Federative Republic of Brazil for the application of the Agreement on Residence for Nationals of the MERCOSUR Member States].

Acuerdo Migratorio entre la República Argentina y la República de Bolivia, 21 April 2004 (entered into force on 17 October 2006) [Migratory Agreement between Argentina and Bolivia].

Acordo entre a República Portuguesa e a República Federativa do Brasil sobre a Contratação Recíproca de Nacionais, Lisbon, 11 July 2003 [Agreement between the Federal Republic of Brazil and the Portuguese Republic on the Reciprocal Hiring of Nationals].

Acuerdo de Regularización Migratoria entre la República del Perú y la República de Bolivia, Huatajata, 26 January 2002 [Agreement on Migratory Regularisation between Peru and Bolivia].

Convenio de Migración entre Argentina y Perú, Buenos Aires, 1998 [Migration Covenant between Peru and Argentina].

Convenio de Migración entre Argentina y Bolivia, Buenos Aires, 16 February 1998 [Migration Covenant between Bolivia and Argentina].

Acuerdo sobre Indocumentados, Quito, 17 May 1991 [Agreement on Undocumented Migrants between Bolivia and Ecuador].

Acuerdo sobre Indocumentados, Quito, 26 September 1990 [Agreement on Undocumented Migrants between Chile and Ecuador].

Convenio Ecuador–España sobre Doble Nacionalidad, 4 March 1964 [Bilateral Treaty on Double Nationality between Ecuador and Spain].

Convenio Paraguay–España sobre Doble Nacionalidad, 25 June 1959, modificado por protocolo adicional, Madrid, 30 March 2001 [Bilateral Treaty on Double Nationality between Paraguay and Spain, modified by Additional Protocol].

Convenio Chile–España sobre Doble Nacionalidad, 15 November 1958 [Bilateral Treaty on Double Nationality between Chile and Spain].

Convenio sobre el Ejercicio de Profesiones Liberales entre Chile y Colombia, Santiago 23 June 1921 [Covenant on the Exercise of Liberal Professions between Chile and Colombia].

Convenção que Regula o Exercício das Profissões Liberais entre a República dos Estados Unidos do Brasil e a do Chile, 4 May 1897 [Covenant Regulating the Exercise of Liberal Professions between the Republic of the United States of Brazil and Chile].

Convenio sobre Reconocimiento de Títulos Profesionales entre Chile y el Ecuador, Quito 9 April 1897 [Covenant on the Recognition of Professional Titles between Chile and Ecuador].

Tratado de Comercio entre las Repúblicas de Chile y Bolivia, Santiago de Chile, 18 May 1895 [Trade Treaty between the Republics of Chile and Bolivia].

Convención sobre Libre Ejercicio de Profesiones Liberales entre Ecuador y Colombia, Lima, 3 May 1895 [Covenant on the Free Exercise of Liberal Professions].

Tratado de Amistad, Comercio y Navegación entre el Imperio de Brasil y la República de Bolivia, Rio de Janeiro, 18 July 1887 [Friendship, Commerce and Navigation Treaty between the Empire of Brazil and the Republic of Bolivia].

Tratado de Paz, Amistad, Comercio y Navegación entre Venezuela y Bolivia, Caracas, 14 September 1883 [Peace, Friendship, Commerce and Navigation Treaty between Venezuela and Bolivia].

Tratado de Amistad, Comercio y Navegación entre Venezuela y el Salvador, Caracas, 27 August 1883 [Friendship, Commerce and Navigation Treaty between Venezuela and El Salvador].

Tratado de Amistad, Comercio y Navegación entre las Repúblicas de Paraguay y Perú, Asunción, 18 June 1881 [Friendship, Commerce and Navigation Treaty between the Republics of Paraguay and Peru].

Tratado de Amistad, Comercio y Navegación entre Chile y Perú, Lima, 22 December 1876 [Friendship, Commerce and Navigation Treaty between Chile and Peru].

Tratado de Amistad, Comercio y Navegación entre Argentina y Paraguay, Buenos Aires, 3 February 1876 [Friendship, Commerce and Navigation Treaty between Argentina and Paraguay].

Tratado de Amistad, Comercio y Navegación entre el Perú y la China, Tientsin (Tianjin), 26 June 1874 [Treaty on Friendship, Commerce and Navigation between Peru and China].

Tratado de Amistad, Comercio y Navegación entre las Repúblicas de Argentina y Perú, Buenos Aires, 9 March 1874 [Friendship, Commerce and Navigation Treaty between the Republics of Argentina and Peru].

Additional Articles to the Treaty between the United States of America and the Ta-Tsing Empire of 18 June 1858, Washington, 28 July 1868, also known as the Burlingame Treaty.

Tratado de Amistad, Comercio y Navegación entre las Repúblicas de Argentina y Bolivia, Buenos Aires, 9 July 1868 [Friendship, Commerce and Navigation Treaty between the Republics of Argentina and Bolivia].

Tratado de Amistad, Comercio y Navegación entre Venezuela y Italia, Madrid, 19 June 1861 [Treaty on Friendship, Commerce and Navigation between Venezuela and Italy].

Tratado de Unión entre los Gobiernos de Perú y Venezuela, Caracas, 18 April 1859 [Union Treaty between the Governments of Peru and Venezuela].

Tratado de Amistad, Comercio y Navegación entre los Gobiernos de Argentina y Bolivia, Ouro, 7 December 1858 [Friendship, Commerce and Navigation Treaty between the Governments of Argentina and Bolivia].

Treaty of Peace, Amity and Commerce, between the United States of America and China, concluded at Tientsin, 18 June 1858.

Tratado de Amistad, Comercio y Navegación entre Prusia y demás estados del Zollverein Alemán y la Confederación Argentina, Paraná, 19 September 1857 [Treaty of Friendship, Commerce and Navigation between Prussia and the Argentinean Confederation].

Convención Consular entre Francia y Venezuela, 24 October 1856 [Consular Convention between France and Venezuela].

Tratado de Amistad, Comercio y Navegación entre Nueva Granada y Ecuador, Bogotá, 9 July 1856 [Friendship, Commerce and Navigation Treaty between Nueva Granada and Ecuador].

Tratado de Amistad, Comercio, Navegación y Fronteras entre Nueva Granada y Costa Rica, San José de Costa Rica, 11 June 1856 [Friendship, Commerce, Navigation and Borders Treaty between Nueva Granada and Costa Rica].

Tratado de Amistad, Comercio y Navegación entre el Emperador de Brasil D. Pedro II y la República de Paraguay, Rio de Janeiro, 6 April 1856 [Friendship, Navigation and

Commerce Treaty between the Emperor of Brazil D. Pedro II and the Republic of Paraguay].

Tratado de Amistad, Comercio y Navegación entre la Confederación Argentina y el Emperador de Brasil, Paraná, 7 March 1856 [Friendship, Commerce and Navigation Treaty between the Confederation of Argentina and the Emperor of Brazil].

Tratado de Paz, Amistad, Comercio y Navegación entre la República de Chile y la Confederación Argentina, Santiago, 30 August 1855 [Peace, Friendship, Commerce and Navigation Treaty between the Republic of Chile and the Argentinean Confederation].

Convención Consular entre Nueva Granada y Ecuador, Lima, 10 August 1854 [Consular Convention between Nueva Granada and Ecuador].

Convención Consular entre Nueva Granada y Chile, Santiago, 30 August 1853 [Consular Convention between Nueva Granada and Chile].

Tratado de Navegación y Fronteras entre la Confederación Argentina y la República de Paraguay, Asunción, 15 July 1852 [Navigation and Borders Treaty between the Confederation of Argentina and the Republic of Paraguay].

Tratado de Comercio y Navegación entre Uruguay y Brasil, Rio de Janeiro, 12 October 1851 [Commerce and Navigation Treaty between Uruguay and Brazil].

Tratado de Paz, Amistad, Comercio y Navegación entre Perú y Bélgica, London, 16 May 1850 [Treaty on Peace, Friendship, Commerce and Navigation between Peru and Belgium].

Convención Consular entre Nueva Granada y los Estados Unidos de América, Washington, 4 May 1850 [Consular Convention between Nueva Granada and the USA].

Tratado de Amistad, Comercio y Navegación entre la República de la Nueva Granada y su Majestad el Rey de los Franceses, Bogotá, 28 October 1844 [Treaty on Friendship, Commerce and Navigation between the Republic of Nueva Granada and his Majesty the King of the French].

Tratado de Amistad, Comercio y Navegación entre Nueva Granada y Venezuela, Caracas, 23 July 1842 [Friendship, Commerce and Navigation Treaty between Nueva Granada and Venezuela].

Tratado de Amistad, Comercio y Navegación entre el Gobierno de la Provincia de Corrientes y la República de Paraguay, Asunción, 31 July 1841 [Friendship, Commerce and Navigation Treaty between the Government of Provincia de Corrientes and the Republic of Paraguay].

Tratado de Amistad, Comercio y Navegación entre Chile y Perú, Santiago de Chile, 20 January 1835 [Friendship, Commerce and Navigation Treaty between Chile and Peru].

Convención Provisoria de Amistad, Comercio y Navegación entre el Estado de la Nueva Granada y su Majestad el Rey de los Franceses, Bogotá, 14 November 1832 [Provisional Convention of Friendship, Commerce and Navigation between the State of Nueva Granada and his Majesty the King of the French].

Tratado de Amistad, Navegación y Comercio entre Colombia y los Países Bajos, London, 1 May 1829 [Treaty on Friendship, Navigation and Commerce between Colombia and the Netherlands].

Tratado de Amizade, Navegação e Commercio entre o Senhor D. Pedro I, Imperador do Brasil e Jorge IV, Rei da Grã-Bretanha, Rio de Janeiro 17 August 1827 [Treaty on Friendship, Navigation and Commerce between Brazil and Great Britain].

Tratad de Amistad, Alianza, Comercio y Navegación entre las Repúblicas de Chile y las Provincias Unidas del Río de la Plata, Santiago de Chile, 20 November 1826 [Treaty on Friendship, Alliance, Commerce and Navigation between the Republics of Chile and the United Provinces of the Río de la Plata].

Tratado de Unión, Liga y Confederación Perpetua entre la República de Colombia y las Provincias Unidas de Centroamérica, Bogotá, 15 March 1825 [Union, League and Perpetual Confederation between the Republic of Colombia and the United Provinces of Central America].

Tratado de Amistad, Comercio y Navegación celebrado entre las Provincias Unidas del Río de la Plata y Su Majestad Británica, Buenos Aires, 2 February 1825 [Treaty on Friendship, Commerce and Navigation between the United Provinces of the Río de la Plata and her British Majesty].

Convención General de Paz, Amistad, Navegación y Comercio entre la República de Colombia y los Estados Unidos de América, Bogotá, 3 October 1824 [General Convention on Peace, Friendship, Navigation and Commerce between the Republic of Colombia and the United States of America].

Tratado de Amistad, Unión, Liga y Confederación Perpetua entre Colombia y México, Mexico City, 3 October 1823 [Friendship, Union, League and Perpetual Confederation between Colombia and Mexico].

Tratado de Amistad y Alianza entre Colombia y Buenos Aires, Buenos Aires, 8 March 1823 [Friendship and Alliance Treaty between Colombia and Buenos Aires].

Tratado de Unión, Liga y Confederación Perpetua entre la República de Colombia y Chile, Santiago, 21 October 1822 [Union, League and Perpetual Confederation Treaty between the Republic of Colombia and Chile].

Tratado de Unión, Liga y Confederación Perpetua entre la República de Colombia y el Estado de Perú, Lima, 6 July 1822 [Union, League and Perpetual Confederation Treaty between the Republic of Colombia and the Peruvian State].

Regional Organisations of the Americas

Andean Community (CAN)

Parlamento Andino, Decisión 1343 que Aprueba el Estatuto Andino de Movilidad Humana, Medellín 24 April [Andean Parliament's Decision No. 1343, approving the Andean Statute on Human Mobility].

Foro Andino de Migraciones, Cuarto Foro, Declaración de Bogotá, 9–10 May 2013 [Andean Migration Forum, Bogotá Declaration].

Resolución 1546, Reglamento de la Decisión 548 Mecanismo Andino de Cooperación en materia de Asistencia y Protección Consular y Asuntos Migratorios, Lima 20 February 2013 [Resolution, Implementing Regulations on Decision 548 on Consular Protection].

Foro Andino de Migraciones, Tercer Foro, Informe, SG/FAM/III/INFORME. Quito, 4–5 October 2012 [Andean Migration Forum, Third Report].

Consejo Andino Presidencia, 'Una Comunidad Andina para los Ciudadanos. Un Proyecto para la Integración Integral de Nuestros Pueblos', September 2008 [Andean Presidential Council].

Resolución 957, Reglamento del Instrumento Andino de Seguridad y Salud en el Trabajo, Lima, 23 September 2005 [Resolution, Implementing Regulations to the Andean Instrument on Security and Health in the Labour Place].

Decisión 584, Instrumento Andino de Seguridad y Salud en el Trabajo, Guayaquil, 7 May 2004 [Decision on an Andean Instrument on Security and Health in the Workplace].

Decisión 583, Instrumento Andino de Seguridad Social, Guayaquil, 7 May 2004 [Decision on an Andean Instrument on Social Security].

Decisión 548, Mecanismo Andino de Cooperación en Materia de Asistencia y Protección Consular y Asuntos Migratorios, Quirama, Antioquia, Colombia, 25 June 2003 [Decision on Consular Protection].

Decisión 545, Instrumento Andino de Migración Laboral Recinto Quirama, Departamento de Antioquia, Colombia, 25 June 2003 [Andean Instrument on Labour Migration].

Carta Andina para la Promoción y Protección de los Derechos Humanos, Guayaquil, 26 July 2002 [Andean Charter for the Protection and Promotion of Human Rights].

Decisión 526, Ventanillas de Entrada en Aeropuertos para Nacionales y Extranjeros Residentes en los Países Miembros, Lima, 7 July 2002 [Decision on Separate Entry Counters at Airports in Member States for Nationals and Foreign Residents].

Secretariado General de la CAN, Propuesta de Modificación de la Decisión 116: Instrumento Andino de Migración Laboral, Documento de Trabajo, 4 April 2001 [CAN's General Secretariat, Amendment Proposal to Decision 116: Andean Instrument on Labour Migration, Working Document].

Resolución 527, Modificación del Contenido y Formato de la Tarjeta Andina de Migración [TAM], Lima, 11 July 2001 [Resolution on an Andean Migration Card].

Decisión 502 sobre Centros Binacionales de Atención en Frontera (CEBAF), Valencia, Venezuela, 22 June 2001 [Decision on Binational Centres of Assistance at the Border].

Decisión 503, Reconocimiento de Documentos Nacionales de Identificación), Valencia, Venezuela, 22 June 2001 [Decision on Recognition of National Identification Documents].

Decisión 504, Pasaporte Andino, Valencia, Venezuela, 22 June 2001 [Decision on Andean Passport].

Decisión 397, Tarjeta Andina de Migración [TAM], Lima, 16 September 1996 [Decision on an Andean Migration Card].

Decisión 116, Instrumento Andino de Migración Laboral. Decimoséptimo Periodo Extraordinario de Sesiones de la Comisión. Lima, 14–17 February 1977 [Andean Instrument on Labour Migration].

Convenio Sociolaboral Simón Rodríguez, Caracas, 26 October 1973 [Simón Rodríguez Covenant on Socio-Labour].

Acuerdo de Integración Subregional Andino, 'Acuerdo de Cartagena', Cartagena de Indias (Colombia), 26 May 1969. [Andean Agreement on Sub-regional Integration, Cartagena Agreement].

CELAC

Declaración Política de Quito, IV Cumbre de la CELAC, Quito, 27 January 2016 [Quito Political Declaration, CELAC IV Summit].

Declaración de Caracas estableciendo la CELAC, Caracas, 3 December 2011 [Caracas Declaration establishing CELAC].

MERCOSUR

Foro Migratorio del MERCOSUR, Proyecto de Acuerdo Único Migratorio del MERCOSUR, Documento de Trabajo, Montevideo, 17 March 2016 [MERCOSUR Migration Forum, Draft Proposal for a Consolidated MERCOSUR Migration Agreement, Working Document].

Foro Migratorio del MERCOSUR, Reunión XLVIII, Acta N° 01/13, Montevideo, Uruguay, 19–21 March 2013 [MERCOSUR Migration Forum, Minutes, XLVIII Meeting].

Plan de Acción para el Estatuto de la Ciudadanía MERCOSUR, MERCOSUR/CMC/ DEC. N° 64/10, Foz de Iguazú, 16 December 2010 [Action Plan for a MERCOSUR Citizenship Statute].

Consejo de Ministros de Interior, 'Declaração de Brasília sobre Entrada em Vigência das Normas Migratórias Emanadas das Reuniões de Ministros do Interior do Mercosul e Estados Associados', 12 November 2010 [Ministers of the Interior Council, Brasilia Declaration on the Entry into Force of the Migration Norms Deriving from the Meetings of the Interior Ministers of the MERCOSUR and Associate States].

Declaración de los países del MERCOSUR ante la Directiva de Retorno de la Unión Europea', Tucumán 1 July 2008 [Declaration of the MERCOSUR States faced with the European Union's Returns Directive].

Reunión Ministros del Interior del MERCOSUR y Estados Asociados XXIII, *Postura Regional sobre Política Migratoria con vistas al Foro Mundial de Migraciones y Desarrollo* (XXV Foro Especializado Migratorio del Mercosur y Estados Asociados). (MERCOSUR/RMI/DI Nº 01/08), Buenos Aires, 10 June 2008 [XXIII MERCOSUR and Associate States meeting of Interior Ministers, Regional Position ahead of the Global Forum on Migration and Development (XXV Specialised Migration Forum)].

Declaración de Principios Migratorios del MERCOSUR, Santiago de Chile, 17 May 2004 [MERCOSUR Declaration on Migration Principles].

Acuerdo sobre Residencia para Nacionales de los Estados Miembros del MERCOSUR, Brasilia, 6 December 2002 [Residence Agreement for Nationals of MERCOSUR Member States].

Protocolo de Olivos, 18 February 2002; y su modificación, Rio de Janeiro, 19 January 2007 [Olivos Protocol and its Amendment].

Declaración Socio-Laboral del MERCOSUR adoptada por los Jefes de Estado, Rio de Janeiro, 10 December 1998 [MERCOSUR Socio-Labour Declaration, adopted by the Heads of State].

Protocolo Adicional al Tratado de Asunción sobre la Estructura Institucional del MERCOSUR (Protocolo de Ouro Preto), 17 December 1994 [Additional Protocol on the Institutional Structure of MERCOSUR, Ouro Preto Protocol].

Tratado de Asunción, por el que se dio la creación del Mercado Común del Sur y su estructura institucional básica, Asunción 26 March 1991 [Treaty of Asunción creating MERCOSUR and setting its basic institutional structure].

Organisation of American States

Additional Protocol to the ACHR in the area of Economic, Social and Cultural Rights, Protocol of San Salvador, adopted on 17 November 1988 and entered into force on 16 November 1999. OAS, Treaty Series, No. 69.

American Convention on Human Rights (ACHR), 'Pact of San José', Costa Rica, 22 November 1969. Entry into force on 18 July 1978.

American Declaration of the Rights and Duties of Man (American Declaration), also known as the Bogotá Declaration, Charter of the OAS, 30 April 1948.

Pacific Alliance

Acuerdo Marco de la Alianza del Pacífico, Paranal, Antofagasta (Chile), 6 June 2012 [Framework Agreement on the Pacific Alliance].

Declaración Presidencial por la cual se establece la Alianza del Pacífico, Lima, 28 April 2011 [Presidential Declaration of Lima establishing the Pacific Alliance].

South American Conference on Migration

Declaración de Buenos Aires. Posicionamiento de la Conferencia Suramericana sobre Migraciones ante el II Diálogo de Alto Nivel sobre Migración Internacional y Desarrollo de las Naciones Unidas, 28 August 2013 [Buenos Aires Declaration. Positioning of the South American Conference on Migration before the II UN High Level Dialogue on International Migration and Development].

Declaración sobre Principios Migratorios, X SACM, Cochabamba 25–26 October 2010 [Declaration on Migratory Principles].

Declaración Final, IX CSM, Quito, 21–22 September 2009 [Final Declaration IX SACM].

Declaración de Montevideo sobre Migración, Desarrollo y Derechos Humanos de los Migrantes, VIII SACM, Montevideo 17–19 September 2008 [Declaration on Migration, Development and Human Rights of Migrants].

Declaración Final, VI CSM, Asunción, Paraguay, 5 May 2006 [Final Declaration, VI SCM].

Declaración Final, V CSM, La Paz, Bolivia, 26 November 2004 [Final Declaration, V SCM].

Declaración Final, I CSM, Buenos Aires, 18–19 May 2000 [Final Declaration, I SCM].

UNASUR

Declaración de la Reunión Extraordinaria del Consejo de Jefas y Jefes de Estado y de Gobierno de Unasur, Quito 4–5 December 2014 [Declaration of the Extraordinary Meeting of the Council of UNASUR Heads of State and Government].

Resolución 14/2014, Consejo de Ministros de Relaciones Exteriores, Informe Conceptual sobre Ciudadanía Suramericana, Guayaquil (Ecuador), 4 December 2014, UNASUR/CMRE/RESOLUCIÓN N° 14/2014 [UNASUR Resolution 14/2014, Council of Foreign Ministers, Conceptual Report on South American Citizenship].

Declaración de la Séptima Reunión Ordinaria del Consejo de Jefes de Estado y de Gobierno del UNASUR, Paramaribo, 2 September 2013 [Declaration of the Seventh Ordinary Meeting of the Council].

Declaración de la Sexta Reunión Ordinaria del Consejo de Jefes de Estado y de Gobierno del UNASUR, Lima, 30 November 2012 [Declaration of the Sixth Ordinary Meeting of the Council of Heads of State and Government of the UNASUR].

Declaración de Brasilia, Hacía la Ciudadanía Suramericana, Brasilia, 19–21 October 2011 [Brasilia Declaration entitled 'Towards a South American Citizenship'].

Declaración de UNASUR sobre la Directiva de Retorno de la Unión Europea, Santiago, Chile, 4 July 2008 [Declaration by UNASUR on the EU's Returns Directive].

Tratado Constitutivo de la Unión de Naciones Suramericanas (UNASUR), Brasilia, 23 May 2008, entry into force 11 March 2011 [Treaty Constitutive of the Union of South American Nations].

Agreements, Pan-American Conferences

Protocolo adicional relativo a no intervención (Conferencia Interamericana de Consolidación) de la Paz, Buenos Aires, 3–26 December 1936 [Additional Protocol Relative to Non-intervention, Buenos Aires Special Conference for the Maintenance of Peace].

Convención sobre Nacionalidad (Séptima Conferencia Internacional Americana) Montevideo, 26 December 1933 [Convention on Nationality (Seventh Pan-American Conference)].

Convención sobre Derechos y Deberes de los Estados (Séptima Conferencia Internacional Americana) Montevideo 1933, [Convention on the Rights and Duties of States, Seventh International Conference of American States].

Resolución sobre Emigración e Inmigración (Sexta Conferencia Regional Americana), La Habana, 15 February 1928 [Resolution on Emigration and Immigration (Sixth International Conference of American States)].

Convención sobre Derecho Internacional Privado, Código Bustamante (Sexta Conferencia Internacional Americana), La Habana, 20 February 1928 [Convention on Private International Law, also known as the Bustamante Code (Sixth American International Conference)].

Convención sobre Condiciones de los Extranjeros (Sexta Conferencia Internacional Americana), La Habana, 20 February 1928 [Convention on the Condition of Foreigners (Sixth American International Conference)].

Resolución sobre Unificación de Pasaportes (Quinta Conferencia Internacional Americana), Santiago, 1923 [Resolution on the Unification of Passports (Fifth International American Conference)].

Convención que Fija la Condición de los Ciudadanos Naturalizados que Renuevan su Residencia en el País de su Origen, Rio de Janeiro, 1906 [Convention on Naturalised Citizens who move back to their Country of Origin].

Tratado de Extradición y Protección contra el Anarquismo, Mexico City, 28 January 1902 [Treaty for the Extradition of Criminals and for Protection against Anarchism, Second International American Conference].

Convención sobre el ejercicio de profesiones liberales (Segunda Conferencia Internacional Americana, 1901–1902), Mexico City, 28 January 1902 [Convention on the Exercise of Liberal Professions].

Convención relativa a los Derechos de Extranjería (Segunda Conferencia Internacional Americana, 1901–1902), Mexico City, 29 January 1902 [Convention relative to the Rights of Aliens].

Other Regional Agreements in the Americas

Regional Consultation for Latin America of Civil Society Organizations towards the Global Compact for Safe, Orderly and Regular Migration, Quito, Ecuador, 6 October 2017.

Declaración Final Conferencia Mundial de los Pueblos por un Mundo sin Muros hacia la Ciudadanía Universal, Tiquipaya, Bolivia, 21 June 2017 [Final Declaration of the World Conference of the Peoples For a World Without Borders Towards Universal Citizenship].

Tratado de Montevideo que Instituye la Asociación Latinoamericana de Integración, 12 August 1980 [Montevideo Treaty Establishing the Latin American Association of Integration].

Declaración de los Presidentes de América, Reunión de Jefes de Estado Americanos, Punta del Este (Uruguay), 12–14 April 1967 [Declaration of the Presidents of the Americas. Summit of the Heads of State of the Americas].

Tratado de Montevideo para el Establecimiento de una Zona de Libre Comercio entre Países de América Latina, 18 February 1960 [Montevideo Treaty for the Establishment of a Zone of Free Trade between Countries in Latin America].

Inter-American Covenant of Reciprocal Assistance (Rio Pact), Rio de Janeiro, 2 September 1947.

Convención sobre el Ejercicio de Profesiones Liberales, Montevideo, 4 August 1939 [Convention on the Exercise of Liberal Professions].

Acuerdo Consular, Caracas, 18 July 1911 [Consular Agreement].

Acuerdo sobre Títulos Académicos, Caracas, 17 July 1911 [Agreement on Academic Titles].

Convención sobre el Ejercicio de Profesiones Liberales, Montevideo, 4 February 1889 [Convention on the Exercise of Liberal Professions].

Tratado de Derecho Internacional Privado, Lima 9 November 1878 [Treaty of Private International Law].

Tratado de Comercio y Navegación entre los Gobiernos de Perú, Bolivia, Colombia, Ecuador, Guatemala, El Salvador y Venezuela, Lima, 12 March 1865 [Commerce and Navigation Treaty between the Governments of Peru, Bolivia, Colombia, Ecuador, Guatemala, El Salvador and Venezuela].

Tratado de Confederación y Alianza entre las Repúblicas de Venezuela, Nueva Granada, Gautemala, El Salvador, Costa Rica, México y Perú, Washington, 8 November 1856 [Confederation and Alliance Treaty between the Republics of Venezuela, Nueva Granada, Guatemala, El Salvador, Costa Rica, Mexico and Peru].

Tratado Continental entre Chile, Ecuador y Perú, Santiago de Chile, 15 September 1856. [Continental Treaty between Chile, Ecuador and Peru].

Convención Consular entre Perú, Chile, Ecuador y Nueva Granada, Lima, 8 February 1848 [Consular Convention between Peru, Chile, Ecuador and Nueva Granada].

Tratado de Comercio y Navegación entre Perú, Bolivia, Chile, Ecuador y Nueva Granada, Lima, 8 February 1848 [Commerce and Navigation Treaty between Peru, Bolivia, Chile, Ecuador and Nueva Granada].

Tratado de Unión, Liga y Confederación Perpetua entre las Repúblicas de Colombia, Centroamérica, Perú y los Estados Unidos de México, Panamá, Panama, 15 July 1826 [Union, League and Perpetual Confederation Treaty between the Republics of Colombia, Central America, Peru and the United States of Mexico].

United Nations Instruments

International Convention for the Protection of All Persons from Enforced Disappearance (ICPPED), New York, 20 December 2006, entry into force on 23 December 2010. United Nations, *Treaty Series*, vol. 2716, p. 3.

Convention on the Rights of Persons with Disabilities (CRPD), New York, 13 December 2006, entry into force on 3 May 2008. United Nations, *Treaty Series*, vol. 2515, p. 3.

Protocol against the Smuggling of Migrants by Land, Sea and Air, Supplementing the United Nations Convention against Transnational Organized Crime, New York, 15 November 2000. United Nations, *Treaty Series*, vol. 2241, p. 507; Doc. A/55/383.

International Convention on the Protection of the Rights of All Migrant Workers and Members of their Families (ICMW), New York, 18 December 1990, entry into force 1 July 2003. United Nations, *Treaty Series*, vol. 2220, p. 3.

Convention on the Rights of the Child (CRC), New York, 20 November 1989, entry into force on 2 September 1990. United Nations, *Treaty Series*, vol. 1577, p.3.

Convention against Torture and Other Cruel, Inhuman or Degrading Treatment or Punishment, New York, 10 December 1984, entry into force on 26 June 1987. United Nations, *Treaty Series*, vol. 1465, p. 85.

Convention on the Elimination of all Forms of Discrimination against Women (CEDAW), New York, 18 December 1979, entry into force on 3 September 1981. United Nations, *Treaty Series*, vol. 1249, p. 13.

International Covenant on Civil and Political Rights (ICCPR), New York, 16 December 1966, entry into force on 23 March 1976. United Nations, *Treaty Series*, vol. 999, p. 171 and vol. 1057, p. 407.

International Covenant on Economic, Social and Cultural Rights (ICESCR), New York, 16 December 1966, entry into force on 3 January 1976. United Nations, *Treaty Series*, vol. 993, p. 3.

International Convention on the Elimination of All Forms of Racial Discrimination (ICERD), New York, 21 December 1965, entry into force on 4 January 1969. United Nations, *Treaty Series*, vol. 660, p. 195.

Universal Declaration of Human Rights, General Assembly Resolution 217 A, Paris, 10 December 1948.

UN Economic and Social Council Resolution 106(VI), 25 February 1948.

Other International Instruments

Institut de Droit International, 'Règles Internationales sur l'Admission et l'Expulsion des Étrangers, session de Genève – 1892,' in *Annuaire de l'Institut de droit international*, 12 (1892–1894).

Institut de Droit International, Session de Genève – 1874 Utilité d'un accord commun des règles uniformes de droit international privé [Usefulness of an Agreement on Uniform Rules of Private International Law].

Committee Against Torture (CAT)

Concluding Observations on the Combined Fifth and Sixth Periodic Reports of Argentina, CAT/C/ARG/CO/5–6, 24 May 2017.

Committee on Migrant Workers

Concluding Observations on the Third Periodic Report by Ecuador, CMW/C/ECU/CO/3, 14 September 2017.

Concluding Observations on the Initial Report of Peru, CMW/C/PER/CO/1, 13 May 2015.

Concluding Observations on the Initial Report of Uruguay, CMW/C/URY/CO/1, 2 May 2014.

Concluding Observations on the Second Report by Bolivia,CMW/C/BOL/CO/2, 15 May 2013.

Initial Report by Uruguay, 30 January 2013, CMW/C/URY/1.

Concluding Observations on the Initial Report by Argentina, CMW/C/ARG/CO/1, 2 November 2011.

Concluding Observations on the Initial Report by Chile, CMW/C/CHL/CO/1, 19 October 2011.

Council of Europe

Council of Europe, Parliamentary Assembly, Recommendation Human Mobility and the Right to Family Reunion, 1686 (2004).

Council of Europe, ETS 166 – European Convention on Nationality, 6 November 1997.

European Union Law

Directive 2009/52/EC of the European Parliament and of the Council of 18 June 2009 providing for minimum standards on sanctions and measures against employers of illegally staying third-country nationals, OJ L 168, 30.6.2009, pp. 24–32.

Directive 2008/115/EC of the European Parliament and of the Council of 16 December 2008 on common standards and procedures in Member States for returning illegally staying third-country nationals, OJ L 348, 24.12.2008, pp. 98–107.

Consolidated Version Treaty on the Functioning of the European Union, 2008 OJ C 115/47.

Directive 2004/38/EC of the European Parliament and of the Council of 29 April 2004 on the Right of Citizens of the Union and their Family Members to Move and Reside Freely within the Territory of the Member States OJ L 158, 30.4.2004, pp. 77–123.

Directive 2003/109, Concerning the Status of Third-country Nationals who are Long-term Residents, 25 November 2003, OJ L 16, 23.1.2004, pp. 44–53.

Directive 2003/86 on the Right to Family Reunification OJ L 251, 03/10/2003 P. 0012–0018.

Treaty on European Union (Maastricht text), July 29, 1992, 1992 O.J. C 191/1.

International Labour Organization

Convention on Domestic Workers, 2011 (No. 189). Entry into force on 5 September 2013.

Convention 143 Migrant Workers (Supplementary Provisions), 1975 (No. 143). Entry into force on 9 December 1978.

Migration for Employment Convention (Revised), 1949 (No. 97). Entry into force on 22 January 1952.

Migration for Employment Recommendation (Revised), 1949 (No. 86).

Case Law

International/Regional
Andean Court of Justice

Interpretación prejudicial de oficio de los artículos 8 y 9 y de la Disposición Transitoria Primera de la Decisión 583 de la Comisión de la Comunidad Andina, Case 100-IP-2011, 8 February 2012.

Acción de Incumplimiento interpuesta por la Secretaría General de la Comunidad Andina contra la República del Ecuador, Case 34-AI-2001.

Acción de incumplimiento interpuesta por la Junta del Acuerdo de Cartagena contra la República de Venezuela, Case 3-AI-96.

European Commission of Human Rights

Sorabjee v. the United Kingdom (dec.), No. 23938/94, 23 October 1995.
Jaramillo v. the United Kingdom (dec.), No. 24865/94, 23 October 1995.

European Court of Human Rights

Hasanbasic v. Switzerland, Appl. No 52166/09, 7 October 2013.
Antwi v. Norway, application no. 26940/10, 14 February 2012.
Darren Omoregie and Others v. Norway, application No. 265/07, 31 July 2008.
Sen v. the Netherlands (Judgment) (1996) Appl. No. 31465/96, 21 December 2001.
Abdulaziz, Cabales and Balkandali v. the United Kingdom, applications no. 9214/80; 9473/81; 9474/81, PC Judgment (ECtHR), 28 May 1985.

European Court of Justice

Case C-290/14, *Skerdjan Celaj*, 1 October 2015, EU: C:2015:640.
Case C-311/13, *Tümer*, 5 November 2014. EU:C:2014:2337.
Case C-534/11, *Arslan*, 30 May 2013. EU:C:2013:343.
Case C-256/11, *Dereci*, 15 November 2011, EU:C:2011:734.
Case C-34/09, *Ruiz Zambrano*, 8 March 2011, EU:C:2011:124.
Case C-578/08, *Chakroun*, 4 March 2010, EU:C:2010:117.
Case C-540/03, *Parliament v. Council*, 27 June 2006, EU:C:2006:429.

Inter-American Commission

Human Rights of Migrants, Refugees, Stateless Persons, Victims of Human Trafficking and Internally Displaced Persons: Norms and Standards of the Inter-American Human Rights System, OEA/Ser.L/V/II. Doc. 46/15, 31 December 2015.

Report on Immigration in the United States: Detention and Due Process, OEA/Ser.L/V/II. Doc. 78/10, 30 December 2010.

Admissibility and Merits, No. 63/08, Case 12.534, *Andrea Mortlock* (United States), 25 July 2008.

Second Progress Report of the Special Rapporteurship on Migrant Workers and their families in the hemisphere, OEA/Ser.L/V/II.111, Doc. 20 rev., 16 April 2001.

Inter-American Court of Human Rights

Dominican and Haitian deportees v. Dominican Republic. Preliminary Objections, Merits, Reparations and Costs. Judgment of August 28, 2014. Series C No. 282.

Rights and guarantees of children in the context of migration and/or in need of international protection. Advisory Opinion OC-21/14 of August 19, 2014. Series A No. 21.

Pacheco Tineo family v. Bolivia. Preliminary Objections, Merits, Reparations and Costs. Judgment of November 25, 2013. Series C No. 272.

Nadege Dorzema et al. v. Dominican Republic. Merits, Reparations and Costs. Judgment of October 24, 2012. Series C, No. 251.

Case of Wong Ho Wing. Merits, Reparations and Costs. Judgment, 26 June 2012, Series C. No. 297.

Report No. 85/11, Petition 12.306, Friendly Settlement *Juan Carlos de la Torre* (Argentina), 21 July 2011.

Case of Vélez Loor v. Panama. Preliminary Objections, Merits, Reparations and Costs. Judgment of November 23, 2010. Series C, No. 218.

Yean and Bosico Children v. Dominican Republic. Preliminary Objections, Merits, Reparations, and Costs. Judgment of September 8, 2005. Series C No. 155.

Juridical Condition and Rights of the Undocumented Migrants. Advisory Opinion OC-18/03 of September 17, 2003. Series A No.18.

The Right to Information on Consular Assistance in the Framework of the Guarantees of the Due Process of Law. Advisory Opinion OC-16/99 of October 1, 1999. Series A No. 16.

Compulsory Membership in an Association Prescribed by Law for the Practice of Journalism (Arts 13 and 29, American Convention on Human Rights) (1985), Advisory Opinion OC-5/85, (Ser A) No 5.

International Court of Justice

Legal Consequences for States of the Continued Presence of South Africa in Namibia (South West Africa) notwithstanding Security Council Resolution 276 (1970) (Advisory Opinion) [1971] ICJ Rep 16, [131].

National

Argentina

Supreme Court, Ni, I Hsing s/carta de ciudadanía, 23 June 2009.

Supreme Court, R. 350. XLI. Recurso de Hecho, R. A., D. c/ Estado Nacional, 4 September 2007.

Supreme Court, *Habeas Corpus de Irene Amor Magaz de González*, 148 Fallos, 410, 414. 8 June 1927.

Brazil

Supreme Court, *Habeas Corpus de Vicente Vacirca*, 1908.

Canada

Attorney-General for Canada v. Cain [1906] AC 542, 546.

Colombia

Colombian Constitutional Court, Ruling C-258/16, 18 May 2016.

Colombian Constitutional Court, Ruling T-956/13, 19 December 2013.

Colombian Supreme Court of Justice Case 35097, 6 March 2012.

Colombian Constitutional Court, Ruling C-385/00, 5 April 2000.

United Kingdom

European Roma Rights Centre and Others v. Immigration Officer at Prague Airport [2004] *UKHL* 55.

Musgrove v. Chun Teeong Toy 1891 A.C. 272.

USA

Hoffman Plastic Compounds, Inc. v. NLRB, 535 U.S. 137, 140.

Fong Yue Ting v. United States, 149 U.S. 698 (1893).

Nishimura Ekiu v. United States [1892] 142 U.S. 651, Gray J., 659.

The Chinese Exclusion Case, 130 U.S. 581 (1889).

Index